Overtime

ALSO BY JOHN U. BACON

Blue Ice

America's Corner Store

The Spark

Bo's Lasting Lessons

Three and Out

Fourth and Long

Endzone

Playing Hurt

The Great Halifax Explosion

The Best of Bacon

Overtime

Jim Harbaugh and the Michigan Wolverines at the Crossroads of College Football

John U. Bacon

HARPER LUXE

An Imprint of HarperCollinsPublishers

HarperCollins books may be purchased for educational, business, or sales promotional use. For information, please e-mail the Special Markets Department at SPsales@harpercollins.com.

FIRST HARPERLUXE EDITION

ISBN: 978-0-06-294423-8

HarperLuxe™ is a trademark of HarperCollins Publishers.

Library of Congress Cataloging-in-Publication Data is available upon request.

19 20 21 22 23 LSC 10 9 8 7 6 5 4 3 2 1

To my coaches

Jack Harbaugh told me we need only one coach to believe in us to change our lives. I've had five. Thank you Ross Childs, Mack Mackenzie, Roy Bolles, Bob Cope, and Al Clark. You were great.

Contents

Introduction: Why This Book   1

Prologue: The Crossroads   5

Part I: Preseason

Chapter 1: Looking for "The Guy"   23

Chapter 2: Big Ten Media Days   33

Chapter 3: The Harbaughs   39

Chapter 4: The Risks and Rewards—
Real and Perceived   55

Chapter 5: Countdown to Kickoff   74

Part II: September

Chapter 6: Drowned Out by the Echoes   91

Chapter 7: The Gambler   110

Chapter 8: Growing Up Harbaugh   125

Chapter 9: Friday Nights, No Lights   149

Chapter 10: Stopping a Losing Streak   162

Chapter 11: The Rocket Scientist   169

Chapter 12: Student-Athletes   179

Chapter 13: The Victory After the Game   205

Chapter 14: It Takes a Village   212

Chapter 15: Harbaugh in High School   232

Chapter 16: Emptying the Bench   243

Chapter 17: The Lightning Rod   259

Chapter 18: To the Brink and Back   276

Part III: October

Chapter 19: The Backup   291

Chapter 20: Tragedy at Maryland   300

Chapter 21: Making a Little History   308

Chapter 22: The Eye in the Sky Never Lies   318

Chapter 23: Michigan Man   331

Chapter 24: O-Line U   344

Chapter 25: The Anonymous O-Lineman   353

Chapter 26: The Revenge Tour Commences   363

Chapter 27: The Can't Miss Kid   378

Chapter 28: Bad Blood   386

Chapter 29: "Cavalry's Coming"   401

Part IV: November

Chapter 30: "If Football Was Taken Away"   423

Chapter 31: Captain Comeback   451

Chapter 32: "Hard to Beat the Cheaters"   466

Chapter 33: Turning the Tables   490

Chapter 34: A Modest Proposal   501

Chapter 35: Business Trip   511

Chapter 36: Prodigal Son   519

Chapter 37: The Perfect Trap   532

Chapter 38: Collapse in Columbus   539

Part V: Postseason

Chapter 39: Hard Choices   559

Chapter 40: What Really Matters   570

Chapter 41: Consolations   579

Epilogue: Was It Worth It?   590

Acknowledgments   615

Overtime

Introduction
Why This Book

When I published *Endzone: The Rise, Fall, and Return of Michigan Football* in 2015, I thought it would be my last book on the subject.

I had started a decade earlier by coauthoring a book with Bo Schembechler, *Bo's Lasting Lessons: The Legendary Coach Teaches the Timeless Fundamentals of Leadership*. In it, Schembechler explained what Michigan football stood for, how it should be run—even if doing it the right way didn't guarantee a national title—and the lessons the rest of us could apply to our own lives.

After Schembechler died in 2006 many people attached to Michigan football seemed to forget his principles, the program lost its way, and the sport itself seemed determined to self-destruct. That's what I wrote about in my next three books.

Three and Out: Rich Rodriguez and the Michigan Wolverines in the Crucible of College Football explored what happened when the Michigan football family fractured over a controversial coach. *Fourth and Long: The Fight for the Soul of College Football,* a comparison of four Big Ten programs, warned what could happen if greed overcame passion. *Endzone* showed how quickly even a venerable program like Michigan's could falter when that happened.

In that unhappy epoch Michigan fans sensed that something larger than the Wolverines' win-loss record was at stake. They feared the program's traditional values of honesty, integrity, and a deeply shared sense of purpose were eroding. During that dark decade you could hear a common refrain among the Wolverine faithful: "This is not Michigan."

I was born in University of Michigan Hospital, where my dad served on the pediatric faculty for decades. I've earned two degrees from the school, I occasionally teach there on the side, and I've reported on Michigan athletics for years. Yes, I love the place, without apology.

But I've had a few lover's quarrels with my alma mater, and have never hesitated to call out the university's leaders when things have gone awry. I've exhumed Fielding Yost's racism in the mainstream press; investigated the Michigan basketball players' high-end cars that led to an NCAA investigation; and explored the damaging, shortsighted decisions of a former Michigan athletic director, which cost me my press pass for two seasons.

I can't say any of it was fun, but I can say I would do it all again. That's because I believe a reporter can be loyal to an institution and still tell the truth about it. In fact, it's that very loyalty that requires such honesty, or else we are being loyal to a false idol.

Throughout my research on *Endzone*, I saw thousands of Michigan devotees—students, faculty, lettermen, alumni, and fans—work tirelessly inside and outside the athletic department, often risking their financial well-being, their job security, or both, to right the ship in time to make a plausible pitch for Jim Harbaugh to return to Ann Arbor. And against all odds, he did.

After Harbaugh restored the program's foundation, I thought I was done writing books on Michigan football. But a couple of years after publication of *Endzone*, I saw a new story emerging.

The Harbaugh era raised a question no one was asking: What would happen if Michigan followed Schembechler's bible once again and ran the program the right way, but fell short of a national title? How much would the faithful value what had been regained? Would it be enough for them to feel the program was worth following, supporting, even believing in again?

I decided these questions demanded one more book.

I interviewed more than a hundred coaches, players, staffers, parents, and others connected to the program, some as many as a dozen times, from July 2018 to May 2019, filling more than a thousand pages of single-spaced notes. Unless otherwise noted, the interviews cited in this book are exclusive.

I wanted to find out how the whole machine worked when it was humming properly, from the head coach to the equipment manager.

I wanted to see what the media's two-dimensional caricature of Jim Harbaugh was missing.

I wanted to learn what a pivotal season looked like from the players' perspective, and what it *meant* to them—not just as athletes, but as human beings.

Finally, I wanted to see if the sport's rewards outweighed its risks for those young men who make those decisions, and those sacrifices.

This book is the product of that search.

Prologue
The Crossroads

On Friday night, August 31, 2018, the University of Michigan football team, ranked 14th in both preseason polls, hunkered down for the night at the Blue Chip Casino in Michigan City, Indiana, which offers rooms for as low as $79, often hosts musical acts from Chicago, and presents Bride Blu, "Northwest Indiana's premier bridal fair."

Normally about an hour's drive from South Bend, the next day the trip would take twice that long, even with a police escort, because some 80,795 fans would clog the highways and streets on their way to Notre Dame Stadium to watch the renewal of one of football's greatest rivalries. The last time the two titans played, in 2014, Notre Dame whitewashed the Wolverines 31–0, which marked the beginning of the end for Michigan's previous head coach, Brady Hoke.

Michigan fans were anxiously hoping Hoke's successor, Jim Harbaugh, would not only fulfill the promise of his first two seasons, when the Wolverines went 10-3 both years, but take the next steps by beating Ohio State for the first time in seven years, capturing Michigan's first Big Ten title in 14 years, and maybe even getting to the national title game for the first time since it had been created two decades ago.

Their hopes were matched by their fears: that an opening loss to Notre Dame would lead to another failed season—which is exactly how the 2017 team's 8-5 record was perceived by Michigan's coaches, players, fans, and critics alike. On the eve of the new campaign, Michigan fans were poised to erupt in cheers or collapse in groans.

Their deeper dread, frequently expressed on fan blogs and social media, was simple: if Jim Harbaugh, who had been received as a savior when he defied the NFL experts and returned to his alma mater, could not lead the Wolverines out of the wilderness and back to the promised land, perhaps no one could.

If Michigan fans had grown edgy by the eve of the 2018 Notre Dame game, they had their reasons—more than a decade's worth. Even including Michigan's sterling 2006 squad, which peaked with an 11-0 record and a number two national ranking, in the decade spanning from 2005 to 2014 the Wolverines had won 73 games against 53 losses, cementing a 10-year average of 7-5—the kind of record expected of second-tier programs like Indiana and Minnesota, not mighty Michigan. Meanwhile, Ohio State was racking up 110 wins over the same span, and even Michigan State had 84, with three other Big Ten teams ahead of the Wolverines.

But it wasn't just the uncharacteristically bad records that marked that overcast era. It was a stronger sense that Michigan had lost its way. The very values that had grounded Michigan's gridiron success seemed to disappear with the wins.

The mere fact of Harbaugh's return on December 30, 2014, was all the proof Michigan fans needed that they weren't crazy, after all. Their memories of better days were not mirages, and their belief in a brighter future not delusional.

Harbaugh's arrival not only foretold a return to glory on the gridiron but a promise to burnish the beliefs Michigan fans were convinced separated Michigan from the many programs trying to win at all costs. The Michigan ideal was simple, if not easy: a football program that would outperform others in the classroom and promote exemplary conduct in the community, while avoiding the many temptations to cheat that seemed to beset all but a few of the top teams.

No school's fight song makes a bigger claim than Michigan's. Unlike the others, which invariably urge their teams on to victory, "The Victors" celebrates a contest already won.

"Hail! to the victors valiant.

"Hail! to the conqu'ring heroes."

But if "The Victors" claims a lot, it expects a lot, too—not merely that the Wolverines be crowned "Champions of the West," but that they also be "Leaders and Best." Michigan students, faculty, and alumni have taken this to mean Michigan's records and titles alone don't tell the whole story. The Wolverines will not only beat you; they'll do it the right way—with real students, actual amateurs, playing by the rules.

As 2014 was ending Michigan fans could imagine only one man who could achieve all this: James Joseph Harbaugh.

His father, Jack, coached for Bo Schembechler from 1973 to 1980. Jack's second son, Jim, was the Wolverines' starting quarterback from 1984 to 1986, winning a Big Ten title and earning league MVP honors before embarking on a 14-year NFL career, followed by a great run as the head coach at the University of San

Diego, Stanford, and the San Francisco 49ers. When Harbaugh left the bright lights and big cities of the NFL for Ann Arbor and trips to South Bend, Indiana, East Lansing, Michigan, and Columbus, Ohio, he stunned the pundits and thrilled the fans, who received him not simply as a great coach, but as Michigan's messiah.

Harbaugh delivered immediately, pushing the 2015 Wolverines from five wins to ten his first year, then leading the 2016 squad to a nine-game winning streak before losing at Iowa by a point. Two weeks later against second-ranked Ohio State, the Wolverines lost by three points in double overtime, and finally by one point to Florida State in the Orange Bowl. A total of five points produced three road losses—but in college football, no one receives partial credit.

Still, the storyline was straightforward: Harbaugh had brought Michigan back to the edge of the sport's top echelon, and the only question remaining was not if but when he would finish the job.

But in Harbaugh's third season, 2017, his Wolverines suffered demoralizing defeats to Big Ten foes Michigan State, Penn State, Wisconsin, and Ohio State before dropping to South Carolina in the Outback Bowl. Worse, the team's weakest links were its offensive line, which had been Michigan's strongest position group for decades, and its quarterback, where Harbaugh's famed ability to get the most out of his signal callers seemed to elude him.

The disappointing 8-5 season cost the Wolverines in the recruiting wars, too, leaving Harbaugh with a 22nd-ranked class, by far his worst since the transition class of 2015, and Michigan's worst "non-transition" class in nearly a decade. What seemed so close 12 months earlier suddenly seemed to be falling out of reach.

This naturally brought the critics out in full force. They frequently pointed out that in Harbaugh's first three years he had gone a collective 2-7 against Michigan State, Ohio State, and Michigan's bowl opponents; 5-7 against ranked teams; and had stretched Michigan's ignoble streak of road losses to ranked teams to a very un-Michigan-like 16—fifth longest such streak in the nation, on a short list with Purdue, Kansas, and Vanderbilt, hardly Michigan's football peers.

Perhaps no coach in America had received more criticism than Harbaugh, whose every tweet, comment, and expression was scrutinized endlessly on sports pages, blogs, Twitter, and radio shows. He has more Twitter followers than any coach in America, college or pro, and might be the nation's most recognizable sideline general, too. His critics constantly claim he is an over-paid, over-rated bust, while at the same time reporting every NFL team looking for a coach is about to back up a Brinks truck to secure Harbaugh's services.

Contrary to popular opinion, it was patently false that Harbaugh was on the "hot seat" heading into the 2018 season. At Michigan only one man gets to vote on that: athletic director Warde Manuel, who remained squarely in Harbaugh's corner.

But it was true that if Harbaugh suffered another 8-5 season, or worse, rival coaches would be only too eager to tell Harbaugh's recruits that his job was in danger, as they had the previous year. If the recruits believed it, Michigan would have two subpar recruiting classes in a row, and fans would soon see the difference on the field. If Michigan dropped a few more games to Notre Dame, Michigan State, and Ohio State, the whirlpool would generate a power of its own that would be very hard to reverse, no matter who was in charge. After a year or two, the NFL—which is free of recruiting, alumni, and lettermen—could become much harder to resist.

Harbaugh's job wasn't riding on the coming season. But his happiness, and the future of the program, might have been.

There weren't many tangible reasons to think Michigan would be better in 2018, either. The coaches' poll ranked five Big Ten teams in the nation's top 14, four from the Big Ten East Division alone: #3 Ohio State, #9 Penn State, #12 Michigan State, and #14 Michigan, plus #7 Wisconsin, which happened to be one of three West Division teams on Michigan's 2018 schedule.

Worse, due to a couple of odd scheduling changes left over from former athletic director Dave Brandon's administration, Michigan would have to play all three rivals—Notre Dame, Michigan State, and Ohio State—on the road. If that wasn't tough enough, during the middle of the season the Wolverines would have to run "the gauntlet," as Michigan's players were already calling it that summer, a brutal stretch consisting of Wisconsin, Michigan State, and Penn State, three top-twelve teams that had all beaten Michigan the previous year. Winning two of three felt like a reach, while getting swept again seemed entirely possible.

Just for kicks, Michigan would also have to play Indiana and Northwestern, two midlevel teams that always seemed to push the Wolverines to the edge of an upset before falling just short, often in overtime.

If the Wolverines wanted to prove they belonged with the big boys, this would be the season to do it.

For all these reasons 28 Big Ten media members picked Michigan to finish fourth in the seven-team East Division. The Big Ten East was rightly considered one of the toughest divisions in college football, if not *the* toughest, but the idea of Michigan keeping company with Indiana, Maryland, and Rutgers in the bottom half of the division did not sit well with the Wolverines.

Beating the 11th-ranked Fighting Irish on the season's opening day with the nation watching would give the Wolverines a sizeable boost, and take a lot of heat off head coach Jim Harbaugh.

Harbaugh would be the first to tell you he was hardly the only person in Schembechler Hall who had pushed all his chips in.

Of the 8,760 hours in a year, fans watch their favorite players perform for a mere 60 of them. How do we weigh the remaining 8,700 hours, which Michigan's players spend working in the weight room, the classroom, and the community, where they have achieved uncommon levels of success?

The media generally ignores their dual status as student-athletes, and assumes most college athletes do, too. But for the players on Michigan's team, at least, there is no duality. Monday starts at 6 a.m. with two hours of weightlifting, followed by three classes, then meetings, practice, physical therapy, dinner, and a few hours of studying. Then comes Tuesday. If they failed to compete against some of the best students in the country, or crossed a line in the dorms or the bars, they would lose football, and so much of what they were working for.

The coaches would spend those 8,700 hours away from the stadium recruiting, drafting practice and game plans, watching ungodly amounts of video—of practice, games, opponents, and recruits—and yes, actually coaching, the dessert in the middle of their 16-plus hour days.

"They hold two-hour meetings to prepare two hours of practice," recruiting director Matt Dudek told me. "Then they spend eight hours for game prep *every day,* then two hours of recruiting calls and texts in the evening, plus practice, which can run two-to-four hours. That's fourteen to sixteen hours a day, every day, from August through December, and some days more. And somewhere in there, they've got to sleep and eat and see their families."

It's not much easier in the offseason, when the coaches painstakingly script 15 spring ball practices, install new plays, watch endless film, and spend still more time on recruiting. They might leave Schembechler Hall at seven, instead of 10 or 11, to make an 11-hour day during the quietest part of the year.

Dudek forgot to mention staffers like him. Schembechler Hall is home to 67 full-time employees who

work 100-hour weeks from the end of July to the beginning of January, with more staff working in the
Weidenbach athletic administration building across the
parking lot. At Schembechler Hall the strength and
conditioning coaches arrive at 4 a.m. The athletic trainers arrive 90 minutes later, and don't leave until 9 p.m.,
while the video and communications teams are lucky to
get a few hours of sleep on the weekends. The staff does
everything from feeding 200 people three meals a day
to tutoring Michigan's 137 players in every imaginable
subject.

Ask a Michigan football coach, staffer, player, or
parent what outsiders don't understand, and invariably
the first thing they say is: "No one has any idea how
much work goes into this."

When I asked star linebacker Devin Bush Jr. about
this, he laughed and imitated a classmate's voice, "'You're
playing a game! You get a free education! You don't have
to pay for food and housing!'

"Let me tell you: We pay for all that stuff every time
we wake up at five-thirty in the morning. When you
go home for holidays, we're practicing. When you go
home for the summer, we're in class, and the weight
room. When you're at the beach, we're doing two-a-
days. We pay for it all."

They all, in their own way, had to answer a central question: Was big-time college football worth the countless sacrifices it demanded? And how would they measure the value of what they gained—a Big Ten title, an NFL contract, a college degree, or something else?

Whatever the fans had riding on the Notre Dame game, the coaches, players, and staffers had much more.

For Harbaugh the stakes were even higher than the outcome of the Notre Dame game. The quintessential Michigan Man had always seen himself as fighting for more than Michigan, or even the prestige of the nation's oldest conference. He often said his priorities were Faith, Family, and Football—in that order, though the three probably ranked closer than he let on. Every chance he had—on TV or radio, at football camps across the country, or any podium that would have him—he defended the sport of football itself, which had been under assault from doctors, reporters, principals, and parents.

But outside of Harbaugh's faith, perhaps, there was virtually no aspect of Harbaugh's life that would not be enhanced by beating Notre Dame—or made tougher with a loss. When they say, "Winning solves a lot of problems," it's correctly implied that losing creates at least as many, from the postgame press conference to the ride home to the agony of watching the tape again and again, while the media and fans pound you, your staff, and your players on every platform. On top of all that, it would be pretty hard to save a sport without first succeeding at it.

Losers don't get to be reformers.

After a big team dinner of steak, chicken piccata, baked potatoes, and a pasta bar with a chef cooking made-to-order dishes with steak strips, shrimp, and chicken, and before the team watched that week's film, *Waterboy,* Harbaugh walked to the front of the room, wearing his trademark navy blue hat with the thin Bo Schembechler–style *M* in the center (which required special permission from the University to use); his old-school glasses, which reminded Harbaugh of both Malcolm X and Ohio State's Woody Hayes; a long-sleeve navy blue T-shirt with the Schembechler-style *M* in the center; and Lululemon khaki pants, perhaps more closely identified with Harbaugh than any of the other millions of men who wear them.

When he got to the front, he went over the game plan one more time, then got to his message. Although Harbaugh's speeches don't make the paint peel off the walls like Schembechler's—Harbaugh has self-effacingly said from the podium, "I'm not a great talker"—when he's inspired he's as good as any on the stump. And on this night he was inspired—hammering home how hard they'd worked, how much they'd sacrificed, and how much the next day's game meant—and so were his players.

"This is the most excited I've been to start a season since my senior year in high school," said Zach Gentry, who had made the move from New Mexico to Ann Arbor, and from quarterback to tight end. "For me, opening at Notre Dame, that's going to be an unbelievable experience. I was hoping I'd get to play there at some point, one of the greatest environments in college football. We've all been wanting to play Notre Dame since we got here, and no one on our team has played in that game. The renewal of the rivalry is special—and we're extremely excited and confident.

"But it's like coach told us: This is our first game, so we're going to mess up the most, make the most mistakes. It's going to come down to who can recover fastest and eliminate the mistakes by the fourth quarter."

Outspoken defensive end Chase Winovich publicly delivered the capstone quote: "We'll know where we stand after this one."

Even before the opening kickoff started the 2018 season, everyone in the Blue Chip Casino meeting room knew they would be judged almost solely on their record, especially against Notre Dame, Michigan State, and Ohio State.

But how would they judge themselves?

PART I

Preseason

Chapter 1
Looking for "The Guy"

Spring 2018

In 2017, for only the second time in Jim Harbaugh's 14-year coaching career, his team took a significant step backward, mainly due to a porous offensive line and inconsistent quarterback play. The Wolverines were undefeated and ranked eighth going into their fourth game against Purdue, when a late and dangerous hit knocked Wilton Speight out for the year. They won that game but lost five of their next nine, which is what can happen when you have to use your backup quarterback, then your backup's backup.

Michigan's 1971 team could put Tom Slade at quarterback to run the option and block for the tailbacks behind him, while completing just 27 of 63 passes for the entire season, and still finish the regular season undefeated. Today's quarterbacks can complete that many passes in a single game—and often have to, if their teams are going to be successful. The position has become too important for a team to get very far without an elite passer.

"The great thing about having a great defense is most games you'll keep it close," Winovich told me. "Four of our [five] losses last year were down to the wire, one-score games decided in the fourth quarter. But to win those close games, you need a quarterback you can rely on. Against Rutgers [Brandon] Peters was playing really, really well, but that was the only time all season I felt like we had *the guy*. It's tough on defense when you know if you let them have one touchdown it could cost you the game, especially when you have a defense that likes to take risks and blitz."

The answer appeared from an unlikely source: the University of Mississippi, whose star quarterback Shea Patterson decided to visit Michigan in early January 2018, with an eye to transferring. At the same time Winovich was considering coming back for his fifth year, and ran into Patterson at Scorekeepers, a popular college bar.

"If you come here," Winovich told him, "I'll come back."

"If you come back," Patterson countered, "I'll come here."

Both proved good on their word, but the NCAA rules require transfer players to sit out a season. Could Patterson get an exception? Despite the NCAA's notorious capriciousness, Patterson was willing to take that chance.

Because Patterson's new teammates were in the middle of their 12-month leases he stayed in West Quad, which was a novelty for him. At Ole Miss, like many football-centric schools, the players are not required to stay in student dorms, while Michigan requires them to stay in the dorms for two years. Although they usually room with teammates, the rest of the building is filled with "normal" students, which provides a more authentic college experience.

"It was a little strange at first," Patterson told me. "You don't have a fridge, the bathroom is down the hall, and the laundry is in the basement. But classes are so close you can walk there, and the experience was actually really, really cool, because I got to be a regular college student, and meet other students."

The new surroundings helped keep Patterson's

mind off the all-important question: would the NCAA rule he was eligible to play in 2018? If you think that sounds simple—college students transfer all the time, after all—you need to understand a few counterintuitive things about college athletics. If you're a college athlete, you can transfer—but only with the permission of your previous coach, for some reason, and you can't compete at your new school until you've sat out one season. Otherwise, the NCAA reasons, student-athletes would transfer from school to school whenever they thought they might find a better fit. In other words, they could do exactly what other students—and their coaches, for that matter—do every year.

It looked like Patterson would have to sit out a season before he could play for Michigan, but he had a wildcard, which he hoped to parlay into an exception to the rule. The NCAA had just slapped Ole Miss with three years' probation, scholarship reductions, and no postseason play in 2018 for a variety of egregious recruiting violations. If Patterson stayed he'd be in for a rough ride. Worse, Patterson claimed his coaches had lied to him when they told him they weren't going to be in big trouble, when they knew otherwise. On that basis, Patterson appealed to the NCAA to waive the transfer rule and allow him to play for Michigan right away.

This put the NCAA's leaders in a tough spot, thanks to their contradictory rules. If they let Patterson play immediately they feared it would establish a precedent for other players whose coaches lied to them—not exactly a small club. But if they refused Patterson's appeal they would once again be accused of punishing a student-athlete to defend a thoroughly corrupt coach— because that's exactly what they'd be doing.

Common sense and decency would seem to dictate that Patterson be allowed to play that fall, but common sense and decency don't always matter. Ole Miss's leaders fought Patterson's appeal because they didn't want to admit he was right.

"I tried to remain optimistic," Patterson told me, "but some days I couldn't stand waking up. Not even knowing if I could play—that was that depressing. Man, am I really not going to be able to play next year—and watch everybody else play? Football is kind of my getaway, something I can do and forget about everything else in the world for a while and have fun in the moment. I can't tell you how much fun it is.

"But you only get so many games in a season, you're only playing games three months out of the year, and the rest is preparing for those moments. It means a little bit more when you and your teammates are working so hard for it, and you've gotten close, which we had."

Patterson was born and raised in Toledo, Ohio, and grew up going to Michigan games until his family moved to Hidalgo, Texas, near the Mexican border. Despite being an outsider in almost every way, he won over his teammates and became their starting quarterback as a ninth grader, earning an offer from Arizona by season's end.

The Pattersons moved the next year to Shreveport, Louisiana, where Shea once again had to prove himself to a new coaching staff and team, who had already settled on their starter. But once again, Patterson proved he was better, while managing to turn the very teammate he was beating out into a lifelong friend.

After leading his team to two state titles Patterson played one year at IMG Academy in Florida, where all four major scouting services ranked him the top pro-style prospect in the nation. He turned down offers from just about every major program to play at Ole Miss. When he transferred to Michigan he would have to beat out the quarterbacks already there, while winning over his teammates. Nothing new for him.

By the end of spring ball Patterson was well on his way to accomplishing both. His new teammates couldn't help imagining the season they might have with him at the helm.

"You could tell pretty quickly that Shea could be the

guy we'd been missing," Winovich told me in the summer of 2018. "You have to respect him. If I'm going against him in a drill, I might shade off an extra foot or two to make sure he doesn't burn me. His confidence level is definitely not a question. You want to play quarterback at Michigan, you better think you're the best, because that's a pressure cooker like no other. Shea's got that, and he's got the team."

Patterson was Michigan's presumptive starting quarterback, but because the coaches couldn't be sure he'd be eligible, during the fifteen spring practices Brandon Peters and Dylan McCaffrey took snaps with the first team, while Patterson and true freshman Joe Milton took snaps with the second team. The longer the NCAA's decision was delayed the more it hampered everyone.

To win this case Patterson's parents retained a big-name lawyer, Tom Mars, Wal-Mart's former general counsel. He happened to be very familiar with Ole Miss, having spent 900 hours representing Ole Miss's previous coach, Houston Nutt, in a lawsuit against the school. They settled out of court, which included a public apology from Ole Miss to Nutt.

Mars volunteered his expertise and stacks of files to Michigan's compliance officer, Elizabeth Heinrich, hoping together they could convince the NCAA's leaders to declare Patterson eligible. The two have very different styles—not surprising given their disparate occupations—but they needed each other if Patterson was going to win his case. The NCAA is always reluctant to make exceptions to its rules, but also feared exhuming the many skeletons in Ole Miss's closet, delivering one more blow to college athletics when the NCAA could least afford it. With Mars and Michigan working together, Patterson had a fighting chance.

But Patterson still didn't have an answer when the annual blue-white scrimmage, scheduled for April 14, marked the end of spring ball. The spring had been at least partially wasted.

After Patterson finished his final exams in late April 2018, he packed and headed to the team buses in front of Schembechler Hall that would send them to Detroit Metro Airport, then to Paris for the team trip. (More on that later.) The prospect of trying to enjoy himself with his teammates overseas while his eligibility was still up in the air was not one he savored. But as Patterson walked to Schembechler Hall his father texted him to call Heinrich in compliance.

"She's got some news for you," he wrote.

Like most top quarterbacks Patterson is unusually adept at staying cool under pressure in front of thousands of fans and millions of viewers. But this process wasn't played on his turf, and he had no control over the outcome. It got to him.

"I couldn't tell if it was good news or bad news," Patterson recalled. "As I was walking across the parking lot to her office, I was trying to stay cool, but I couldn't keep calm. My head was spinning. I was a little emotional."

While Patterson made his way across the parking lot to Heinrich's office, a call from Mars spoiled the surprise: the NCAA had granted his immediate eligibility. He would be able to play in September. After Mars delivered the good news, he was surprised by the silence on the other end.

"I couldn't express what I was feeling," Patterson said. "I was getting emotional, and literally couldn't speak."

When Patterson told me this months later, the feeling was still so strong he closed his eyes and tilted his head back to compose himself. By the time he could spit out a proper thank you to Mars he had arrived at Heinrich's office, and gave her a hug.

"Here are your papers," she said.

"Look, I know there are much bigger things going on in the world than this," Patterson said later, "but it just felt so good to get that over with. I was free! *I was free!* Now I could just focus on my teammates, and winning games."

In a pivotal season for the Wolverines, they would be led by the most important transfer the program had ever seen.

"Right now we feel like we've got the guy, and we haven't felt that in a while," Winovich said days before the Notre Dame game. "And if someone on defense tries to hit him in practice, I might take that guy out. Shea's worth his weight in gold."

Winovich knew Patterson would have to be, because Michigan's 2018 schedule "is brutal—just brutal. We all knew that coming into this year, and we all came back. But we know it's not going to be easy.

"But this is what you sign up for."

.

Chapter 2
Big Ten Media Days

July 23–24, 2018

Just like the swallows returning to Capistrano, every summer Big Ten football coaches, players, and reporters swarm to Chicago for Big Ten Media Days. But the swallows are more quotable.

Every summer we learn all fourteen teams had a great offseason. They worked really hard in the weight room, the classroom, and yes, the community, and have tremendous senior leadership. If someone struck a gong every time a coach used the word "excited," you wouldn't be able to talk to the person sitting next to you.

Not so Harbaugh. After taking the podium he skipped the usual five-minute pep talk about the state of his team and his coaching philosophy to say, "Good afternoon. Glad to be here. I'll take any questions."

And that was it, breaking the record for the shortest preamble.

Someone started a question with a long setup about Michigan having more experienced players coming back this season, contrasted that with last year's Michigan team, the youngest in the country, and closed with the reporter asking how Harbaugh felt about all that.

Harbaugh replied, "I feel great about it, Ed. Yeah."

Then Harbaugh stared out at the crowd of reporters, waiting for the next question. Another reporter prefaced his question by saying Harbaugh was the "most hyped coach in college football," yet had not finished higher than third in his division, and had beaten Michigan State and Ohio State only once in six tries. So how will he meet expectations?

Harbaugh didn't take the bait. Despite fielding a dozen questions like that, usually preceded by a long list of criticisms, Harbaugh's blood pressure didn't seem to rise one tick the entire press conference. He replied to this particular question by saying, "We need to improve. That will lead to success. That will lead to championships." Next question.

When another reporter asked Harbaugh how he would "prove to the Michigan community" that he can beat Michigan's rivals, Harbaugh replied, completely stripped of emotion or irony, "Improvement will lead to success and that will lead to championships."

Reporters groused on Twitter about Harbaugh's short, flat answers, but they probably didn't see him in the breakout interviews that followed. There, when reporters asked him about his players or his coaches, he went off on long soliloquys about tailback Karan Higdon or defensive coordinator Don Brown, complete with anecdotes, humor, and passion, clearly enjoying himself. And that's the simple answer to the riddle that is Coach Harbaugh: If you ask him about himself—or his record, his reputation, or anything else that reflects directly on him—you'll get five words. But if you ask him about the people in his building, you'll get five minutes.

Yet about the only news that seemed to come out of those two days of interviews was Harbaugh's short, staccato answers to often silly, obvious, or annoying questions—for which Harbaugh received a pile of criticism nationwide.

We didn't realize the big story had already been planted under our noses: the first night of the conference Ohio

State's Urban Meyer had fired assistant coach Zach Smith.

Five years earlier Meyer had handled another crisis that broke right before the Big Ten Media Days with great aplomb. When four of his players were facing separate legal issues, he simply released them from the team. When he took the podium he explained what happened and what they were doing about it, then answered a few questions. And just like that, it was over.

In my interviews with Meyer he had always been admirably direct and forthright, following the strategy Michigan athletic director Don Canham had told me years ago: "Never turn a one-day story into a two-day story."

But Meyer seemed to forget that lesson at the 2018 Big Ten Media Days, where the room was buzzing with Brett McMurphy's story on Zach Smith, his ex-wife accusing him of physical abuse, and what Urban Meyer's role in the mess might be. When a reporter asked Meyer if he knew about Smith's 2015 domestic violence incident, Meyer could have said, "Those are private legal issues we're working on."

Instead he claimed he was never told anything about it—no how, and no way—then challenged the credibility of Brett McMurphy, who happened to have the time, the ability, and the motivation to dig deeper. We soon learned that Meyer's denial simply wasn't true, then Smith's ex-wife contradicted more of Meyer's claims.

Ohio State felt it had no choice but to put Meyer on paid administrative leave while an internal committee investigated the situation. In the meantime journalists who cover the team, including columnist Ramzy Nasrallah of the leading Buckeye blog, *Eleven Warriors*, told me that while Zach Smith had mastered the playbook as well as any assistant during Meyer's tenure, his coaching effectiveness had been openly questioned for years, particularly when his blue-chip players routinely underachieved at OSU. Nasrallah once observed Smith "bouncing around a closed practice prior to the 2017 season shouting along to the music being pumped out through the speakers as two coaches did his job, while he paid little to no attention to his unit."

Urban Meyer paid Smith $340,000 a year. One reason: he was the grandson of esteemed Ohio State coach Earle Bruce, Meyer's lifelong mentor. Another reason could be a threat from Smith, who told his wife if he was punished, "I'll take everyone at Ohio State down with me." How he planned to do that remains an open question.

When Meyer recognized his job was in jeopardy, he

released a carefully worded statement that said, in part, "My words must be clear [and] completely accurate . . . Unfortunately I failed." That was a smart restart.

While most pundits were predicting Meyer could never survive this scandal, especially in the era of #MeToo, it seemed very unlikely Ohio State would fire him, simply because he was too good a coach. In Meyer's six years at Ohio State he'd already won six division titles, two Big Ten titles, and a national title—plus two prior national titles at Florida. Not least, he also had a perfect 6-0 record against That Team Up North. (If you don't think that matters, ask former Ohio State coach John Cooper.)

Instead, as wiser folks predicted, on August 22, 2018, Ohio State gave Meyer a formal rebuke and suspended him for three games, only one of which, against Texas Christian, did the Buckeyes have any real chance of losing. Meyer would be on the sidelines in September against Penn State, the second-biggest game on the Buckeyes' schedule, which meant he would certainly be there on November 24, against Michigan.

Chapter 3
The Harbaughs

I n the NFL every franchise is pretty much the same. The coaches, the players, the staffers, and even the plays are all interchangeable parts that circulate around the league in a fast-paced game of musical chairs, creating an amazingly high level of uniformity. Most games boil down to a few plays.

Thus NFL teams, with no students, alumni, faculty, or traditions to satisfy, don't have the kind of cultures college teams can boast. When Bill Parcells leaves the New England Patriots to coach the archrival New York Jets, nobody seems to care. NFL personnel function like toasters: you can plug people in just about anywhere, and they'll work the same way they did for their last team.

But in the college game, culture is everything—

and strikingly different not just from the Big Ten to the SEC, but even from Michigan to Michigan State to Ohio State. (Ask anyone associated with any of those schools—and prepare to listen at length to what makes their culture superior.) A pro sports fans can also claim their team is superior, but for proof they can point only to victories, not values.

One big reason: professional teams draft their players, while college recruits get to choose their teams. During recruiting season the top *players* have the power, not the coaches, and pick their schools largely on "fit." The most common phrase: "When I visited, this school just felt right."

Discounting for now the coaches who pay recruits, every player who lines up for Michigan, Ohio State, or Alabama has chosen to be part of those teams—and it makes a difference. Rare is the NFL veteran who does not feel a greater loyalty to the college team where he played four years than the pro team where he played ten.

That's why, when a big-name college coach moves from one major program to another, there is no guarantee of success. It's not simply a matter of plugging the same toaster into a new socket and waiting for the toast to pop up. It's more akin to a heart transplant. For it to succeed you must make sure your new leader has the same blood type as the school, the right-sized heart, and everyone does everything they can on both sides of the process to ensure the new organ is not rejected as a foreign body.

This explains why so many Big Ten schools have hired native sons to turn their programs around. In 1989 Wisconsin hired three-sport star Pat Richter to restore their deflated department, which hadn't done much in football or basketball since Richter's senior year, 1961–62. In 2006 Northwestern named arguably its best football player, Pat Fitzgerald, to lead the Wildcats. In 2012 Ohio State brought back former assistant coach Urban Meyer; two years later Michigan lured Harbaugh back to Ann Arbor; and in 2018 Nebraska convinced its last national title quarterback, Scott Frost, to resurrect the Cornhuskers.

When these tradition-steeped programs find their match, it's a thing of beauty. But when coaches don't click, things can turn ugly, and fast.

You could see it during Michigan's Rich Rodriguez years. He had been highly successful at every stop of his career, and turned down Alabama the year before accepting Michigan's offer at the end of 2007. Three years after Michigan's Dave Brandon fired him in 2011, Rodriguez would win the 2014 Pac-12 Coach of the Year honors, before being fired in 2017 after two subpar seasons and headlines over an extramarital affair.

But at Michigan, Rodriguez could not win over enough Michigan Men to buy himself enough time to make the change work. As he told his staff minutes after Brandon fired him, "It was a bad fit from the start."

A similar dynamic unfolded from 2010 to 2014 in Michigan's athletic director's office. This was far more surprising because the AD in question, Dave Brandon, had been a former Michigan football player, a highly respected regent, and the CEO of Domino's Pizza—all the credentials you'd think would add up to a very successful run. But his tenure went awry almost from the start—first privately, and then publicly. The phrase I heard repeatedly from discontented stakeholders: "This is not Michigan."

So what *is* Michigan? Perhaps it's easier to show than tell—but if you wanted an example, Jim Harbaugh's life story would not be a bad place to start.

His father, Jack, was born in 1939 in the tiny hamlet of Crestline, Ohio, just an hour north of Columbus. His mother raised Jack and his four siblings while his father worked as an engineer for the Penn-Central Railroad.

Jack received daily helpings of the state's rich football culture, which produced Paul Brown, Woody Hayes, and Bo Schembechler, just to name a few, and their timeless values: honesty, integrity, and hard work; say what you mean, and do what you say. Many Ohioans believed these bedrock values were expressed most clearly on a competitive football team.

Jack played two years on his high school's varsity basketball team, and four each in football and baseball. In 1957, after being named an all-state quarterback and shortstop his senior year, he enrolled at Bowling Green University, just ninety minutes away. There he played football for future Hall of Famer Doyt Perry (a Bo Schembechler mentor), for whom BGSU has since named the stadium, and alongside Dave McClain and Larry Smith, who would later coach Wisconsin and USC, respectively.

Jack worked just as hard to impress a cheerleader in his freshman biology class, which happened to be taught by the father of Olympic figure skating champion Scott Hamilton.

"English!" the former Jackie Cipiti corrected her husband. "It was *English* class!"

"Well, I'm going to talk about biology," he said. "I do remember this: the moment I saw her I thought, 'My god she's the most beautiful thing I've ever seen in my life.' Took me four weeks to muster the confidence to ask her out for coffee. After we dated a couple times, she told me, 'Well, you're a little too full of yourself.' I didn't know what that meant! But I knew it wasn't good."

"No," she corrected him. "I said you had a chip on your shoulder!"

"Same thing! Can't make that into a compliment!"

After Jackie broke up with Jack's roommate, Jack got another chance. Judy Perry, the coach's daughter, was dating Dave McClain, the future Wisconsin head coach. One day they were driving Jack back to Crestline when Judy Perry asked him, "Have you ever thought about asking Jackie Cipiti out?"

"Pretty much all the time!" he confessed.

"I think it would be a good idea if you did."

Jack did as instructed, re-took the test, and passed with flying colors. Years later he explained, "Hey, I'm coachable!"

In the era of freshman ineligibility, Jack could play only three seasons of varsity football. During Jack's three years, however, Doyt Perry's teams went 24-3, winning the small college national title in 1959, Jack's junior year.

Before both Jack and Jackie graduated in 1961, the Buffalo Bills of the American Football League, in its second year, used their 25th pick to select Jack Harbaugh. Just three days into camp the Bills cut him, so Jack returned to Ohio to coach the Canton-McKinley junior high school team that season. The next year he assisted the high school team in Perrysburg, Ohio. Just down the road at Toledo Memorial, Jackie gave birth to John on September 23, 1962, and Jim 15 months later—seven months before Urban Meyer would be born in the same hospital.

When Jack became the head coach at Eaton High School in the southwest corner of Ohio, he quickly earned a reputation as a turn-around specialist, emphasizing the fundamentals Doyt Perry had taught him.

Jack didn't do it with money. Longtime Michigan equipment manager Jon Falk recalls when he was a student equipment manager at Talawanda High School in Oxford, Ohio (home of Miami University), he forgot to bring the footballs for their game against Jack's Eaton squad. When he asked Jack if he could borrow some of their footballs to warm up, Jack said, "Sure," and handed Falk a football.

"Just one?" Falk asked.

"We only have two," Jack explained.

After two seasons in Eaton Jack took over the team at Xenia High School in southwest Ohio. He led them to an 8-1-1 record while winning the league title and coach of the year. His success earned him an invitation to assist at Morehead State in Kentucky, his first college post.

Their oldest son, John, was about to turn five years old that fall, with a late birthday for school. Jack's proposal to hold John back was quickly vetoed by his mother-in-law.

"She was a very strong individual," Jack recalled. "'That's ridiculous! This little guy is so bright, he already knows the alphabet and can count to a hundred! He needs to be in school!' Well, I folded up like an accordion in the wind."

The decision made John one of the youngest kids in his grade, while Jim, born December 23, 1963, would always be one of the oldest—a difference that would affect their athletic fortunes.

After one year at Morehead State Jack spent three seasons assisting at his alma mater, Bowling Green, before the Harbaughs moved to the University of Iowa in 1971, where Jack coached the defensive backs.

The Harbaughs had made it to the Big Ten, the nation's dominant conference, but it didn't feel like the big time. The couple, now with three young kids, had to cash in all six years of their state of Ohio retirement accounts, totaling about $6,000, to cover the down payment on a small house previously owned by Wayne

Fontes, the future Detroit Lions head coach. On their first day in their first home Jack was recruiting a player 80 minutes away when an assistant coach called him: "You need to come home now. One of your sons was just hit by a postal worker, and I'm taking him to the hospital."

Jack roared off for Iowa City.

"When Jim was a kid, he never unzipped his coat," Jack explained. "He always pulled it on over his head like a sweater. He was pulling his jacket on while he was running across the street and got hit by a car going over the hill. He fractured his leg so they gave him a plaster cast—and he kept breaking the cast, because he wouldn't sit still.

"That was our first day in Iowa City. And that was Jim."

It might not even have been Jim's most memorable day there.

"My first real competitive experiences happened back in Iowa City," Jim told me. "I was six, maybe seven, trying out for the NFL's Punt, Pass, and Kick competition. That was a big deal. I signed up months in advance. John and I did the one in Iowa City, and I won first place: a trophy of a football player wearing a helmet, standing straight up.

"John didn't win his age group, so two weeks later, when we had the state finals—probably in Des Moines—and my parents couldn't take me, I got a ride in a station wagon with three local kids who qualified.

"My kick spiraled like a top and went way over to the side. It was *sickening* to watch. When they measured how far off center it was, and subtracted that from my distance, I might have had negative yardage. My punt and throw were good, but the kick killed me, and I didn't win.

"But two of the kids in our car did win and got these super cool trophies which had a set of goal posts and a football in the middle. So on the car ride home they're happy and they're celebrating with their super cool trophies, and I'm in the backseat, on the left side," he stood up to demonstrate, leaning against a wall in his office, "with the side of my face against the window, staring outside, just as miserable as can be. And no, I have not forgotten it!"

Although the Hawkeyes went a dismal 4-17-1 during Jack Harbaugh's two years, their defense was surprisingly strong, allowing fewer than 20 points a game in 1972.

"At Iowa," Jack joked, "our secondary was damn good because we couldn't stop the run."

That, and Doyt Perry's strong recommendation,

were enough for Bo Schembechler to hire Jack at Michigan, where the Wolverines had just won their third Big Ten title in four years, with many more to come.

You'd think such a promotion would have made life a little easier for the Harbaughs, but Michigan offered only $16,000 a year, and the cheapest house they could find was a three-bedroom, 1,300-square-foot home at 1814 Anderson Avenue, a block behind Fraser's Pub, for $33,000.

"We didn't think there was any way we could possibly pay for it," Jack said. "I think our property taxes were unbelievable!"

Jackie subsidized their income by working in the Michigan ticket office for Al Renfrew, the former hockey coach, along with assistant coach Jerry Hanlon's wife, Anne. The Harbaughs could afford only one car, a yellow Dodge station wagon.

Many days Jackie would drive Jack to the football building early in the morning, then drop the kids off at St. Francis Elementary, a Catholic school on Stadium Boulevard. When she couldn't take Jack he would stand on the corner, nervously checking his watch, waiting for fellow assistant coach Denny Brown to pick him up.

"I swear he was late every morning," Jack recalled. "So we'd get to the morning meeting three or four minutes late—a complete no-no with Bo. But Denny went to Michigan, and he's smarter than I am, so he would always let me go in first, and take the brunt of Bo's wrath, while I felt Denny breeze right behind me to his seat, unnoticed."

"Nobody in our family had ever been taller than six feet," Jim told me, "and I was determined to be the first. I had my mind set on six-two as the goal and drank as much milk as I could possibly drink—and not that candy-ass two-percent stuff, either! Whole milk!"

Showing his systematic approach to achieving goals at an early age, Jim signed up to deliver his class's milk cartons at lunch, which earned him a free one every day, and allowed him to take the leftover cartons of kids who were absent or didn't want theirs.

"After junior high, Jim caught up to me," John said, "and finally in high school he grew taller than me— six-one, six-two—and topped out at six-three, the tallest of the Harbaughs."

The Harbaughs may have lacked a big house, fancy cars, or fame, but they all remember their years in Ann Arbor as their happiest. When Jack handed the kids their lunches he would tell them, "Attack this day with an enthusiasm unknown to mankind!" While driving the family in their station wagon, Jack would ask them, "Who's got it better than us?" And they would respond, "Nooooo-body!"

At the center of their family life was football.

"As soon as we got to Ann Arbor," Jack recalled, "our boys are badgering me to go out for the little league football team. Even back then, I wasn't for that."

Perhaps to the surprise of contemporary critics, Schembechler and Jack both felt it best to play flag football until seventh grade, then tackle.

"But Jackie's hammering away on me," Jack said. "She's going to the practices, and the boys are all over me. So once again I folded like a house of cards." On the plus side, Jack said, "Football puts you through such highs and lows, that it really teaches you resiliency."

"When we moved to Ann Arbor," Jim told me, "I signed up for Punt, Pass, and Kick again, and now I'm nine years old. And this time my kick was better, and I won the region. And that's what you do: You compete, and when you come up short, you practice harder to make sure you don't feel that way again—because it's a horrible feeling!"

Jack and the boys loved everything about their new hometown, not least their special relationship with Michigan football.

"Bo's pregame speeches are the best I've ever heard,"

Jack said. "Even after four or five years on Bo's staff, hearing his speeches would make the hair on the back of my neck rise."

But working for Schembechler was not easy. Every task was assigned and graded—right down to the "movie coach," who would pick the team film for Friday nights. Jack lasted only one week in that capacity.

"I was happy to be relieved of my duties," he said. "With Bo, you had to watch closely to see if he had the spark in his eye. If he didn't, no matter how angry he was acting, you could push back, or even joke with him. But if he had that spark—watch out! That was your warning for trouble."

Early in Jack's tenure on Schembechler's staff the two men got into a shouting match on the practice field. After Jack finished his point, he turned to walk away— "then I noticed everyone in front of me had stopped to stare, and I knew the old man must've been storming up behind me."

Jack's instincts proved correct. The second Jack turned around, "I saw Bo chasing after me, and in a flash, he was in my face, and letting me have it, finger pounding my chest—full force. The whole show."

Jack knew if he backed down he'd lose all credibility with his players, the rest of the staff, and possibly Bo himself. But if he took Bo on, he might be chased off the field.

"So what'ya do? I just stared back at him, while he pontificated at some length."

After practice that night Jack met with his defensive backs. As soon as he walked in the room, his players stood up to give their position coach a standing ovation. Years later Schembechler told Mitch Albom he knew about it, and admired Jack's players for doing it.

"With Bo," Jack said, "you didn't ask for more!"

In his first year in Ann Arbor, Jack Harbaugh realized the incredible demands of the job would prevent him from doing all he wanted to do as a father. So one day when he came home he told his wife, "Jackie, when it comes to this family, you're the offensive coordinator, you're the defensive coordinator, and you're the head coach. You handle it all. I'll never question your decisions, and whatever you need from me—to stay out of it, or to march up the stairs and bring the boom down—that's what I'll do."

Their system worked pretty well, due partly to Jackie's fearlessness when it came to disciplining her much larger boys.

Despite the incredible hours both parents were

putting in, Jim's fourth grade hockey coach, Dave McGuigan, now a biotech executive in San Diego, remembers them coming to every game. Since those could start as early as 5:45 in the morning, and were occasionally held on outdoor rinks, that represented a significant commitment.

Jack's job had its perks for the boys, too. When Bo's wife, Millie, invited the assistant coaches' wives out for lunch, Jackie mentioned how hard it was for their husbands to see their children.

Millie asked the wives, "Do you bring your kids to practice?"

No, they said, not mentioning that they wouldn't dare.

"Well, you should," Millie said.

Two days later, Bo casually announced to his assistant coaches, "I've given this some thought, and I've decided you can bring your kids down to practice."

Only Jack knew the truth: Bo hadn't decided that. Millie had.

Jack grinned, and wisely kept his mouth shut.

But that decision, whoever made it, would change Jim's life.

Chapter 4
The Risks and Rewards—
Real and Perceived

Grand Rapids, Michigan, August 11, 2018

Football has two big problems: safety, and the perceptions of the game's risks, which many parents believe are far too high, especially when placed against its rewards, which seem far too low. Judged accordingly, many parents are concluding it's just not worth it.

For medical professionals the public's intense interest is a double-edged sword. Concussions have become a hot button topic, for good reason, creating important reforms—and a lot of misunderstanding. How the sport handles the issue will likely determine the fate of football.

The fear of becoming permanently damaged is not irrational, of course. Brain injuries can cause problems ranging from splitting headaches to dementia and just about everything in-between, including diminished "impulse control," causing victims to act on sudden urges they would have easily resisted before their injuries. That, in turn, can generate destructive decisions, and even lead to suicide, which many doctors believe is often an impulsive decision.

Talk to almost any doctor or athletic trainer on the issue, or read just about any book, however, and you quickly find the issues aren't as simple or clear as we would like to believe. For example, acute concussion symptoms typically last two or three days, and concussions tend to resolve themselves in a week to ten days. But smaller, more frequent hits can be damaging, too, and might result in chronic traumatic encephalopathy, or CTE. Yet in the public's mind concussions and CTE are often lumped together. While we'd be foolish to ignore the potential dangers of either, there are surprisingly few controlled studies involving CTE and football.

But parents and players can't afford to wait for the science. They must make their decisions now, which is why participation in football is falling precipitously.

The damage that concussions, CTE, and closed

head injuries can inflict hasn't changed, but our focus on them has, particularly after two former NFL players committed suicide by shooting themselves in the chest to preserve their brains for study. In both cases scientists discovered severe CTE, though neurologists are quick to point out it's impossible to know if that led to their suicides.

As tragic as that is, it doesn't mean a kid playing football today is doomed to a similar fate. For starters, the current generation of former players in their 60s and 70s will likely be the most damaged we'll ever see. They played through two-a-day practices, often on Astroturf, with inadequate equipment and looser rules, in an era when concussions were called "getting your bell rung," and people laughed them off.

Former offensive tackle Dan Dierdorf, who was inducted into the College Football Hall of Fame for his play at Michigan and the NFL Hall of Fame for his career with the St. Louis Cardinals, is still sharp as can be—witness his excellent work on national TV and now Michigan radio broadcasts—but he walks with a cane. When I asked him if he'd just had hip surgery, he said, "No, surgical fatigue." He had already had 20 or more operations—he'd lost count—and he will likely have more.

"What did me in? Astroturf. I'm convinced. In St.

Louis, and most of the league then, we played on concrete."

Because Dierdorf's generation is the one we see aging now it's hard to believe things will be better for the next one. But they will be, because they now play on much safer fields with much better equipment, wiser rules, and improved medical protocols and care. High school, college, and pro teams have dramatically reduced hitting in practice—the Michigan High School Athletic Association just slashed the amount of time allowed for full-contact practice per week from 90 minutes to 30 minutes—and they would be smart to eliminate tackling in grade school football, too, something both Jack Harbaugh and Bo Schembechler were advocating in the seventies.

Dr. Jeffrey Kutcher, an international expert on brain injuries, has worked with the Olympics, the NBA, the player associations of the NFL and NHL, and formerly Michigan football. He understands the dangers as well as anyone, but cautions against jumping to conclusions based on media reports. Contrary to popular belief, for example, the data show that NFL players do *not* die sooner than others, but actually live longer, and the risk of concussions in football is not dramatically greater than it is in soccer, with women's gymnastics and cheerleading not far behind.

"My advice is to first understand clearly why your son or daughter wants to play any particular sport," Dr. Kutcher told me. "What do they get out of it? Make sure they're doing it for the right reasons. Second, you need to have a coaching staff that respects the brain and its importance to a healthy life. What is their approach to hitting? Do they have a medical plan in place?"

But the question is not simply whether football is safe enough to play. It's whether parents *think* it's safe—and whatever the risks, are the rewards worth it? Because even if football becomes safer than checkers, if parents don't believe it's worth it, they won't let their kids play. Parents wisely tend to think long-term. If they conclude playing football has no more lasting value than playing checkers, their kids are definitely out. Once a critical mass of kids decides to play something else, even those who want to play will struggle to find a team to play for.

Football has two problems: the health risks of the game, and the perception of those risks compared to the benefits. The sport is finally doing a much better job on the first problem—but it's still doing a horrible job on the second.

Michigan's athletic trainers spend their careers working on the former. David Granito worked with the

New England Patriots' training staff until Harbaugh hired him to lead Michigan's in 2016. Granito works with veteran Phil Johnson and a staff of eight, including three interns who are also certified clinicians, each qualified to run a high school or small college program. That might sound like a big staff until you realize they treat more than 140 players, twice what the Patriots treat with seven clinicians.

With a 20-to-1 ratio at Michigan, the staff works much longer hours. During winter and summer workouts, the athletic trainers work about 12 to 14 hours a day. That increases during spring ball, "fall camp," and the season, when the staff gets to Schembechler Hall before the 6 a.m. workouts begin, and doesn't leave until 9 p.m.

They start their day by taping 300 ankles. Watching them do it is mesmerizing. They use as many as six different kinds of tape, but usually start with adhesive stretch tape, a soft, gauzy variety, completing ten revolutions around the foot, ankle, and lower leg, then pick up a roll of 1.5-inch athletic tape for 20 more rotations— making it smooth and tight without feeling restrictive, all in less than 60 seconds. They can get a player on and off the table with both ankles taped in under three minutes, with some relaxed barbershop chatter thrown in. They go through 60,000 rolls of tape a year on ankles alone—and still more for elbows, wrists, fingers, feet, and toes—at a cost of about $120,000 per year.

After taping the ankles they treat about 100 players with special injuries or illnesses. On the day I visited, they had already seen six players with the flu, three with dental issues, two with eye problems, and 30 players who needed them to set up and monitor modified workouts—all before 6 a.m.

"We don't discriminate between the All-Americans and the walk-ons," Granito said. "If you need treatment, you get the best we can give, no matter who you are."

Almost three centuries ago German philosopher Immanuel Kant established one of the central precepts of moral philosophy when he made the distinction between treating humans as a means to an end, or as an end in and of themselves. If you take the former view, you focus on players who might win you national titles and ignore those who won't. If you take the latter view, you treat them all equally. Michigan's athletic trainers might not read a lot of Kant, but they clearly follow the view that all the people who walk through their doors are important, and their futures matter beyond football.

Since the average treatment takes about 60 to 90 minutes, and each trainer can keep up to ten treatments going at once, each trainer sees 10 to 15 players a day for treatment or rehab, and triple that for daily interactions, including ankle taping. The staff treats 250 players a week, and they don't go home until they finish their "round up," where they review all their current cases, about 9 p.m.

"I don't think the average person has any idea of the hours we put in," Granito told me. They're amused when people ask them: "What do you do in the offseason?"

Answer: scale back from 100 hours a week to about 50.

"Outsiders think what we do is kind of glamorous," Granito said. "But if you don't like this kind of work, a few hours of TV time aren't going to make it worth it. I tell students, 'If you're in this for the glamour of it, get out now. It won't add up.'"

But for those athletic trainers who care about the quality of work they do, there are real benefits to working for Michigan football.

"I could not work in a standard health care model where you can bill for this, but not for that," Granito said. "So they spend twenty minutes doing this, but not the thing that really helps. Here, we don't care about insurance or HMOs, because none of that applies. So we're free to do whatever's best for the patient.

"To the credit of this institution, when it comes to the health and well-being of the athletes, the answer is almost always, 'Whatever you need,' whether that's a better piece of equipment, another operation, or the second opinion of someone not in our system. That's a very refreshing thing, because sometimes we have to call in a big expense, like a special, high-end $800 knee brace for the linemen—and we need 60 of them— and nobody balks. If I were to go to Warde [Manuel, the athletic director] for something we need but is a bit more expensive, I'll walk in with 30 reasons why, but once I say, 'This is better for our guys,' I don't need the other 29 reasons. He's in."

This includes $300,000 a year, or about $1,000 a day, for "expendables": tape, Band-Aids, gauze, and rubber gloves. They spend some $150,000 a year on X-rays, MRIs, CT scans, and other diagnostic tests. Over Phil Johnson's 20-year career, the university has contributed $50,000 for his continuing education—essential for keeping current.

Granito and Johnson know that all the medical needs of the players combined don't attract the attention a single concussion can—whether diagnosed by color commentators or actual doctors—and that's particularly true at Michigan.

"Given the media coverage we get here, this might as well be an NFL team," said Granito, whose previous employer was the New England Patriots. "The number one thing is to do what's right, then deal with the public perception. But concussions have become such a hot button, there really is no such thing anymore as making a solely scientific decision on it. Even if the science says he's fine and can go back in, once we even examine someone, he's done for the day, and maybe longer. He's out."

When a player came to the sideline during the 2018 season saying, "My head hurts. I think I have a concussion," they gave him the full concussion protocol. Although his helmet hadn't contacted anyone, and his test results were *better* than his baseline test taken before the season, "you can't touch it," Granito told me. "He's out. The coaches didn't push back. Part of that is self-preservation. They know an undiagnosed concussion can kill a coach. Like coach Harbaugh always says, 'You can't mess with the head or the heart.' Once you're dealing with either, that player is out."

Michigan's hyper-cautious approach would generate some interesting results that season. The 2018 football team's three worst injuries wouldn't happen on the field. One player would rupture a pectoral muscle wrestling in his apartment, another would suffer a moped accident, and the third would trip and fall while helping his parents and break his ankle.

"Look, the game has inherent dangers, and I don't think you can sugarcoat that," Granito said. "We work hard to prevent the preventable with the best possible equipment, coaching, and care. But you can still get hurt playing this game, or any game. We just think the risks of the sport, when properly coached, have been greatly exaggerated. Women's soccer has almost the same rates of concussions, and those teams have one athletic trainer, if you're lucky. But no one talks about that."

Addressing football's first problem, making the game safer, immediately gets you to the sport's second problem, assessing whether the risk is worth it—a fact not lost on the athletic trainers.

"I would tell a parent that the fundamentals of life are so apparent in football," Granito said. "Everything you're going to face in the real world, after you're done with school, you'll face here—the ups and downs. To me, football prepares a young man for what they're going to face when the world hits them—and I think the game has never been safer."

The Harbaughs were working on the equation from the other end: extolling the rewards of the game. For them, football has always meant much more than a livelihood—and that's a good thing, because all three Harbaugh men got into the coaching business for peanuts.

In John Harbaugh's 2015 essay, published on the Baltimore Ravens' website and quoted in *USA Today*, he writes, "The game of football is under attack. We see it every day in the headlines and on the news. The medical concerns are pressing. The game has taken its share of criticism. President Barack Obama said that if he had boys, he wouldn't let them play football. Even LeBron James has publicly said no football in his house.

"The question is asked over and over: Why would anyone want to play football? And why would anyone let their kids play?

"Here's my answer: I believe there's practically no other place where a young man is held to a higher standard.

"Football is a metaphor for life," requiring physical courage, sacrifice, accountability, and selflessness, and offers the rewards of mental strength, confidence, and being part of something bigger than yourself.

Because only a small percentage of high school players will play in college, he writes, it's only when "they look back on it several years later, that they realize the difference the sport made in their lives. They are proud of playing the game.

"Have you ever met anybody who accomplished playing four years of high school football, and at the end of that run said, 'Man, I wish I wouldn't have played'? It doesn't get said.

"We know that football players aren't perfect. Nobody is. But millions of former players, one by one, can recount the life-altering principles they learned from football.

"They know the value of football is the *values* in football."

"Millions of young men have learned lessons in football that they could only learn through playing this game.

"That is why football matters."

Football's value had been ingrained in both Harbaugh boys long before they moved out of the house. The speeches their father and mother delivered to a group of football parents in Grand Rapids, Michigan, on August 11, 2018, made manifest where their sons had learned it.

On a hot, sunny Saturday Jack Harbaugh, who had quietly turned down a sizeable speaking fee for the event, ran up to the outdoor stage at a high school football field and immediately got the crowd going with his trademark question, "Who's got it better than us?!"

They knew their line: "Noooooobody!"

With that Jack was off and running, hitting all the major points from John's essay.

"Football is the greatest game, in my judgment, that has ever been invented," Jack said. He then acknowledged safety is a real concern, and all risk can't be eliminated, but with better equipment, rules, and protocols, the game is much safer.

"I want to see our game in a good place," he said, then paraphrased John's line: "I've never met a man who played football who said he wished he hadn't. I've met many who said they wish they had. So I would encourage all parents: if your son wants to play football, don't be the one who stops him."

Because Jackie rarely takes the stage she spent weeks writing and practicing before the event.

"She was writing up a storm," Jack told me. "I said, 'Jackie, you've got way too much stuff.' And I think, 'This is not going to be good.' But when she walked up to the stage she left the stack of pages on the podium and just started talking to the parents—and she had 'em."

Jackie's main point: get out of the way so kids can enjoy the value of competition.

"The kids know what the score is even when adults aren't keeping it," she said, and the moms nodded. "They know who can read better. They know who can sing better. Why pretend? When you know the score, you can start working on your weaknesses. Nothing made me happier as a mother than to see my kids compete. Don't we adults all compete every day? Why would we not want to prepare our kids for that?"

When Jackie Harbaugh left the stage the crowd gave her a standing ovation.

Their second son has given the value of football a lot of thought, too.

"Certainly for me, the competition is the best part," Jim told me. "But it's not the only thing. I've played a lot of sports, and they all have their benefits, but I'm convinced football is uniquely suited to make you a better person.

"To start, it's just so hard. Basketball is usually fun. Baseball is usually fun. But there are plenty of times when football is just not fun. You train a lot, you practice a lot, you have meetings. There is so much work to do just to get to the season. And then you practice five days for each game. No other sport has a ratio like that. The games are fun—when you *win*—but there's always a struggle.

"No one said it better than Fielding Yost," Jim added, citing Michigan's first legendary coach. Harbaugh launched into one of Yost's favorite quotes, verbatim: *"No man can be a football player who does not love the game. Half-heartedness or lack of earnestness will eliminate any man from a football team. The love of the game must be genuine. It is not devotion to a fad that makes men play football; it is because they enjoy their struggle."*

"That's it, right there: It's the struggle. And if you don't like that, you're probably not going to like football, or be any good at it."

Jim addressed another virtue, commonly overlooked: structure.

"That's a beautiful word. With structure, you can have common goals and you can see yourself improving, and you can feel good about yourself. Structure has *never* been a negative—not to me. If you can't deal with structure, you're not gonna like football."

For an example, Harbaugh cited his wife Sarah's family, of which she is the eleventh of eleven kids.

"Just to go on a family vacation with them is a triumph of organizational logistics. These guys want to go to the aquarium, and we want to go see a game, and those guys want to go to the beach. Big group paralysis is never more evident than at a Feuerborn family vacation.

"Well, we've got 200 people here in Schembechler Hall. If we don't have a clear set of goals and a system for achieving them, it's going to be chaos, mayhem. We're not going to get very far."

Jack provided an anecdote: "It must've been 2007 or so, when Jim first got to Stanford. We were going to John's lake house for five days in Tawas [Michigan]. We were all on the beach, but Jim was inside cranking out the entire year's schedule from the first day of camp to the end of the season. And he did that every year."

He still does. By mid-February he already had scripted all 15 practices for spring ball to keep 140 players active and improving every minute, plus every workout, and every meeting.

"We might tweak it as we go," Jim said, "but we're ready."

When Harbaugh played at Michigan Schembechler would quote Fielding Yost in the first team meeting, from memory.

"I ask *no man* to make a *sacrifice*. On the contrary! We ask him to do the *opposite*. To live clean, come clean, think clean. That he stop doing all the things that destroy him physically, mentally and morally, and begin doing all the things that make him *keener, finer,* and *more competent.*"

"It says it all," Schembechler once told me. "You don't *sacrifice* to play football. We're just asking you to do what you should be doing *anyway.*"

"For all the controversy surrounding the sport," Jim concluded, "if it's coached correctly, *it makes you better*—physically and mentally."

He cited Matt Mitchell, a walk-on from nearby Dexter who returned for his fifth year in the hopes of getting into his first game.

"His body's changed, he's stronger, he's in the best condition of his life," Harbaugh said, "and he's always going to remember that. He has a confidence that's *earned.* There's a happiness that goes with it, a deep happiness.

"Football makes you stronger mentally, too. A lot of people will tell you what you can't do, and that can bring you down. But there a lot of ways you can make yourself feel good about yourself: performing an act of kindness for a stranger, finishing a term paper, working out in the weight room. You can do these things every day, and they don't require anyone else's approval. Nothing stopping you. All up to you."

Harbaugh also signed on to Immanuel Kant's precept: people were not to be used as a means to an end; they were the end itself. He believed a well-run football program would make them better—not just for that Saturday, but for decades to come.

However critics would regard Harbaugh's message, there was no question he believed it.

Chapter 5
Countdown to Kickoff

August 2018

On Saturday, August 25, just three days after Ohio State suspended Meyer for three games, the Wolverines put in another sharp, intense practice. Everything seemed to be coming together for their contest against Notre Dame exactly one week later.

Shea Patterson had established himself as the starter, developing good chemistry with a much-improved receiving corps led by Tarik Black, who had missed the previous season with a broken left foot. Hiring former Florida head coach Jim McElwain to work with the wide-outs was already paying off, and Don Brown's stellar defense had the benefit of facing Michigan's improved offense every day to hone their skills. None of this guaranteed victory against Notre Dame, but these players had become the team the coaches wanted to take into battle.

And then on a simple play Tarik Black went down with a broken foot—this time his right. A few plays later defensive end Rashan Gary injured his right shoulder—and he wasn't even sure how he did it. In the Twitter-verse the team lived in, word got out on both injuries by dusk—with plenty of misinformation thrown in.

Losing the team's top receiver for at least a couple of months was a tremendous blow to the offense, and to Patterson in particular. But the possibility of losing Rashan Gary for the Notre Dame game alone hit just as hard. The game was too big, and Gary too important to their odds of winning.

Gary was born in 1997 in Plainfield, New Jersey, about 20 miles west of Staten Island, and raised by his mother, Jennifer Coney-Shepherd. His father, William Gary, was absent far more often than not, but his mom is a force of nature who constantly looked out for her son and pushed him.

Rashan was bigger than his peers, a great athlete from the start, but he struggled academically.

"I'm in sixth grade, but reading at the fourth-grade level," he told me. "And I'm working hard. I'm paying attention. Why am I not keeping up with these guys? Am I stupid? Why does he see an 'E' and I don't?"

In addition to Rashan's sluggish progress, his mom was bothered by the daily fights in Rashan's school, one of the state's toughest.

"My mom didn't want me to be around that," Gary said. "My grandparents, thank God, had a home in a better district, so I transferred school for seventh grade."

That required tests to place Gary in the proper classes—and that's when they discovered Gary was dyslexic, a learning disability that affects 20 percent of the population. The condition makes it difficult to connect letters on the page to the sounds they represent, which in turn makes spelling, writing, and reading fluently much harder. One reason dyslexia often goes undiagnosed is a simple paradox: people who have it are usually very fast thinkers, with strong creative and reasoning skills—which is also why it's so frustrating for them.

The confirmation was both helpful and hard to hear.

"That was a sad time," Gary said. "I was crying when we got the news. You think you're dumb, that something is wrong with you. But my mom had to be strong for me and wouldn't let me get down."

Instead, she focused on a farther horizon. She found

a dyslexia center where Gary attended classes from seventh through tenth grade. While dyslexia can't be cured, experts can show students how to manage it, and—just as important—reinforce the fact that its victims aren't stupid or slow just because they have a neurological disorder.

"You just got to get around it, day by day," Gary told me. "It was hard, but I had my mom by my side. She made sure I didn't get down on myself."

She also made sure her son was highly motivated to do his best, and she knew the best way to do that was to connect academics to athletics. She scheduled his appointments at the dyslexia center between school and football practice so he would always be at full energy for his lesson, then get in as much practice as he could.

"The second I heard that school bell," he said, "I *ran* to the dyslexia center. Sooner I got there, sooner I finished. Then I'd run from there to practice, whatever was left. If I had a bad session [at the center], I took it out on someone else. Anger drove me."

When Gary brought home a "C" in seventh grade his mom told him he couldn't play football that Saturday—denying him his oasis, the one place he felt confident and in control.

"What?!" Gary recalled thinking. "I couldn't believe it. I was crying. It was the *worst* punishment."

Gary's mother added to it, not allowing Rashan to watch TV or leave his room until the next report card. It worked: Gary has never received less than a "B" since.

"For me, it's always been connected, school and football," he said. "If I have a bad test, I feel like it affects my football. But when you start to get it, then it's actually fun. I can do this! And it carries over."

Gary had performed well enough on the field and in the classroom to earn a scholarship to Paramus Catholic School, a full hour from Plainfield. There he met Chris Partridge, a life-changing coach.

"He knew the type of guy I was," Gary said. "I could talk to him about anything."

When Gary graduated in 2016 with a 3.85 grade-point average, he had grown to 6-5, 285 pounds, and become the nation's number one recruit at any position. He could go anywhere he wanted but boiled his choices down to Clemson, Auburn, Alabama, Ole Miss, USC, and Michigan, the only cold-weather school on the list.

When I asked Gary about a rumor that one program had offered him $300,000, he chuckled and tilted his head, mulling over how much to say.

"Man, it was more than that," he finally said. "It

was more than just money, too. And it was more than one school. Man, I could tell you stories."

He named the schools on the condition they remain confidential.

Gary's decision was anything but easy. By signing day he had narrowed his choices down to Clemson, which had lost the national title game to Alabama just a few weeks earlier, and Michigan, which had just finished Harbaugh's first rebuilding year.

While a few thousand fans packed Michigan's historic Hill Auditorium for the "Signing of the Stars" event to celebrate Harbaugh's first full recruiting class, which included eight four-star players including Devin Bush Jr., David Long, Lavert Hill, and Ben Bredeson, Gary was riding with his family to ESPN headquarters in Bristol, Connecticut. After they applied Gary's makeup and told him he would be on TV, live, in 15 minutes to announce his decision, he sat up straight, panicked.

"No, no, no," he said. "I need more time!"

Gary recalled, "My family was looking at me like, 'What?'"

"You got to push it back," Gary insisted. "I still don't know!"

They gave him an additional 90 minutes, which he used to call both coaches one last time and think. Still unsure, Gary, now in a studio room by himself, closed the door and took a nap.

"I promise you," Gary told me, "I *promise* you, I saw maize and blue in my dreams. And when I woke up, I said, 'That's where I'm going.'"

Beyond Gary's sleeping vision a big factor was Harbaugh, his knowledge of the game and the NFL.

"I knew he's been around the best," Gary said, "and he'd run his program at that level. That was the level I wanted to be on. To get to be the best you've got to be around the best, and we had an amazing class coming in."

With Gary on board Michigan's 2016 class would be ranked sixth in the country, right behind Ohio State's. Perhaps a bigger factor was Gary's mom, who insisted he get his degree. Both felt Michigan offered the best chance for him to do that.

"Academics was big," Gary said. "BIG! I promised my mama I'd graduate, and the people here [at Michigan] impressed her. I've met a lot of genuine people here who want to see you grow off the field, too."

Gary's academic mentor, Brittany Papadopoulos, a petite woman less than half his size, built his confidence and pushed him to exceed his limits.

"She was great, man," Gary told me. "Kept me honest!"

When he confessed his goal of making the Academic All-Big Ten team she told him he could do it, but only if he was willing to work. On the Amazon series *All or Nothing* they showed Gary in a meeting with Papadopoulos, who reminded him, "NFL stands for 'Not for Long.'" Even the best players need a backup plan, she said, but added, "Rashan is one of the most dedicated and hard-working guys I ever met."

When most Michigan athletes take 12 credits per semester, and make it up by taking summer classes, Gary took 15—four to five classes per term. Every night after dinner at Schembechler Hall he'd walk across the parking lot to the Academic Center, where he worked until 11.

His mom was never far away. When the Amazon filmmakers entered Gary's South Quad dorm room, they found him calling her back in New Jersey. She asked him if he was eating right, if he needed any school supplies, and if he was still wearing his retainer. He was just 19 years old, after all.

"I'm proud of you, Rashan," she said, then added, "Would you *please* wear your retainer?!"

"My mom is my everything," Gary told me. "My right and my left hand. Anyone who knows me knows that."

The Amazon series also showed Gary and his mom

having dinner at a Red Lobster in town. On that night she took the opposite tack, worrying that he was working too hard, and urging him to take more time for himself.

"Rashan, you're nineteen years old, okay? To me, you're just a kid. You can't throw your teenage years [away] just grinding."

But exactly when a Michigan football player trying to get to the NFL while overcoming dyslexia to graduate, and maybe even make the All-Big Ten Academic team, might find a little time for himself was not clear.

"Do you ever talk to your dad?" she asked. Gary shook his head.

"Does he ever call you?" she asked.

Again, he shook his head. After a sad silence he explained, "At the end of the day, you, in my mind, passed his position. And nothing's gonna change about that. Nothing's gonna change about that at all."

"You keep saying he's not there," she said. "He's there for you as best as he can be."

"You keep saying 'There,'" he replied, tears rolling down his cheeks. "Where?"

She had no answer.

"You never need to worry about nothin'," she finally said, "because I got your back!"

Then she reached out with a napkin to wipe his tears.

Minutes after the same practice that injured both Tarik Black and Rashan Gary, the players settled into the team room to vote on captains. But this season Harbaugh decided to select captains a little differently. Because Harbaugh's first recruiting class of 2015, put together in his first month on the job, consisted of only 14 players, ranking 37th, while his 2016 class had 28 and ranked sixth, the 2018 team naturally had more starters from the junior class than the senior class. So Harbaugh decided they needed leadership from both classes, and would vote for two seniors and two juniors.

The players voted for senior tailback Karan Higdon and junior offensive lineman Ben Bredeson to serve as the two offensive captains, and junior Devin Bush Jr. a defensive captain. No surprises there.

"Devin's the heart and soul of the defense," long-time PR man Dave Ablauf told me. "His engine runs in overdrive, 24/7, and his teammates clearly recognized he was worthy of that selection."

If the players weren't surprised by the picks, Ben Bredeson's parents back in Hartland, Wisconsin, certainly were.

"Ben called as soon as he could sneak out of the room," Deb Bredeson recalled. "We were all sitting in the kitchen. He could only talk for a second. He was trying to be quiet, saying 'I'll call you back later—but I was just voted captain!'"

"Ben's captain!" Deb announced to her husband Mike and Ben's brother Max at the kitchen table.

"Oh, that's just for one game," said Mike, who had played at Illinois State.

"No, he's captain!" Deb insisted.

It was perhaps more surprising when Harbaugh announced senior defensive back Tyree Kinnel would be the fourth captain, not senior defensive end Chase Winovich, one of the returning stars who came back partly in hopes of earning this very honor. Getting over the disappointment, and learning to lead from another seat, would be Winovich's first challenge of the season.

"I relate a lot to Chase," Harbaugh told me in his office, where he was joined by his father. "The energy, the competitiveness, the confidence. I always wanted my dad's approval and my mom's approval, too, and I know Chase does."

Harbaugh then turned to Jack. "I knew I was giving you something! You were happy. Chase makes his parents happy! No one gets more joy out of watching their kid play than Chase's parents. They all come wearing his jersey, and his dad even wears the long blond wig under his hat. They love it. That really drives Chase in a great way."

"That's a great example of what football teaches you," Jack said. "You're broken-hearted, you feel like you've disappointed your parents, but then you wake up, and you go back to work."

As luck would have it, Harbaugh and Warde Manuel had decided weeks earlier to schedule an open practice at the Big House for the next day, Sunday, August 26, as a gift to the fans, allowing them to take the field when practice ended. What seemed like a simple gesture when they planned it now looked like a major PR problem. Try as they might to ignore the Twitterverse, communications man Dave Ablauf knew the internet had already been blowing up with speculation about the injuries to Black and Gary, but it would be hard to cancel the public practice now without a lightning storm to blame it on. Harbaugh and Ablauf decided to announce the injury to Black, who wouldn't be playing in any case, then sit out both Gary *and* Winovich as a smoke screen, explaining that both were simply taking the night off to save themselves for the big week ahead, to avoid tipping off Notre Dame.

I couldn't make it that night but my wife and almost-three-year old son Teddy joined the crowd. When practice ended the fans cheered and Harbaugh waved the entire team over to sing "The Victors" with the crowd, on a night free of criticism and cynicism.

Several thousand fans poured onto the field, tossed footballs, ran down the sidelines, sat on the players' benches, and gaped at the immensity of the place, which you can only fully appreciate from the field level. They were soaking up the rare opportunity to see things from the players' perspective.

"Teddy *loved* it," Christie said. "He looked so natural and comfortable on the field. Our boy, so often shy around strangers, suddenly became outgoing, saying hi to other kids, and even trying to get a bigger kid to throw him a football."

A football crowd has the power to turn strangers into neighbors and friends in an afternoon.

"He ran in circles and up and down the field until he scored a 'touchdown,'" Christie said, which she recorded on her phone. His joy is infectious.

The reader might not believe me, but I've always said Teddy will be free to attend any college he desires that will admit him. I've never pushed the Michigan mantras on him—he's only three, in any case—but it's probably no accident that after that night, he started teaching himself to sing, "The Victors." He mangles a few words, but does so with unbridled enthusiasm, punctuated by his little left fist punching the sky on "Hail!"

When my wife titled her notes, "How fans are made," that is what she was talking about. But this raised a follow-up question: if Teddy grew up to be a lot taller than his 5-foot-8 dad—and faster, too, and more talented—and he wanted to play football, would we let him? In August 2018, we did not have an answer.

PART II

September

Chapter 6
Drowned Out by the Echoes
At Notre Dame, September 1, 2018

The Michigan–Notre Dame football rivalry is as big as it gets—almost. Interest was sky-high, with the *average* ticket price on the resale market going for $948, highest in the country. Its status as the opening weekend's marquee game was confirmed by the arrival of ESPN's College Gameday.

While no one in Ann Arbor confused Notre Dame for Ohio State, the Notre Dame game always drew the national spotlight. A win would propel the Wolverines into the top ten and immediately spark talk of Big Ten titles.

"Man, there's a *lot* of hype around this game," said fifth-year senior Jared Wangler, son of celebrated Michigan quarterback John and brother of Jack, who

had just finished his career as a walk-on the year before. Jared had earned a scholarship out of high school,
playing defense and special teams his first three years
at Michigan before switching to fullback in 2017. But
when he learned he would not be getting a scholarship
for his fifth season he debated transferring to Indiana
before special teams coach Chris Partridge, Rashan
Gary's former high school coach, persuaded him to stay.

During August practice Wangler felt like he was
playing the best football of his life. He was looking forward to making a big contribution on offense, and playing against Notre Dame for the first time. He thought
he might even pick up one of the "leftover" scholarships. But during a live scrimmage on August 11 he
caught a pass out of the backfield, got wrapped up by
a defender, then twisted his knee trying to break loose.
Two days later Michigan's doctors operated on his knee
and told him the best he could hope for was returning
to the lineup by the end of September.

Wangler, whose father proved the doctors wrong
when he overcame his own knee surgery to lead the
Wolverines to a 1981 Rose Bowl victory, was having
none of it.

"I told them that I *needed* to play in the Notre Dame
game," he said. "This is my last season, so sitting out
for any game is not an option—and especially not Notre

Dame. This is a prime-time match-up between two of the biggest teams in the country."

The medical staffers smiled and shook their heads. But two and a half weeks later there he was: eating with his teammates at the Blue Chip Casino, preparing for Notre Dame.

The stats rolled on the sports stations and websites all week.

After a traveling band of Wolverines literally taught Notre Dame how to play football in 1887, Michigan won the first eight games. But since the series resumed after a 35-year hiatus in 1978, the two teams were deadlocked at 15-15-1.

Both claimed 11 national titles. For years they were neck-and-neck in both all-time wins and winning percentage, some years so close that the game's winner would regain the lead. But after Notre Dame self-reported that a student manager had helped eight football players cheat in 18 classes, the NCAA vacated 21 Irish victories from 2012 and 2013, and Michigan widened its lead in total wins over Notre Dame to 943–886, and in winning percentage to .729 to .724, still leading the nation in both categories.

But there were a few ominous statistics for Michigan, too. Since 1978 the home team had won 22 of the 31 contests. The Wolverines had won at Notre Dame only once per decade—and they had already won in 2010. Worse, when playing under the lights, as they would be on September 1, 2018, the visiting team had lost all eight games.

Notre Dame fans were optimistic their head coach Brian Kelly, entering his ninth season in South Bend, could improve upon 2017's 10-3 record and return the Irish to the national title game for the first time since 2012.

The next day's game would have something to say about all of it.

From 1995 to 1998 Michigan All-American offensive lineman Jon Jansen started a record 50 games, then played 10 years with the Washington Redskins and Detroit Lions. In the summer of 2018 he started producing a weekly podcast for Michigan's football program called "In the Trenches," and broadcasting the games with Dan Dierdorf and Jim Brandstatter. Talking with the coaches and players and visiting practice every day, he was probably as piped in as anyone not wearing a helmet.

About Notre Dame Jansen had entirely mixed feelings. On the one hand, he told me, "It's too big of a game for an opener. We haven't beaten a ranked road opponent in years. Hell, we haven't beaten anyone good in over a year. And we're going to start with Notre Dame in South Bend? That's asking a lot—but I think we can."

Because, Jansen reasoned, Notre Dame had just lost three of the best offensive linemen he'd seen in ten years, and had to replace them with two untried red-shirt freshmen.

"You haven't played a game yet, and now you've got Chase Winovich and Rashan Gary coming after you? Now suddenly the opening game looks a little bit different."

Jansen was certain Michigan's defense would be the best unit on the field, and he had plenty of evidence. In 2017 Michigan's defense finished in the top three in the country in five defensive categories, including number one in pass defense.

"We've got depth, now, real depth. It's almost sick. Chase, Gary, Devin Bush, Khaleke Hudson. I think our *defense* is going to score two touchdowns against them."

The 2018 team reminded him of his 1997 squad, which was coming off four straight 8-4 seasons. "We were hearing the same things they're hearing now:

'M stands for Mediocre.' Ohhhhhhh, you want to talk about getting your blood boiling?!"

The 1997 team also had questions at offensive line and quarterback. Brian Griese almost skipped his last season to work at a bank in Bolivia. But after Michigan opened with a win over 8th-ranked Colorado, "the momentum starts to build and build," until they found themselves the undefeated national champions.

Switching back to 2018, Jansen said, "If we beat Notre Dame on the nation's biggest stage, all of a sudden you're feeling pretty good about yourself. You kick some ass on September first, and the world looks different Sunday morning.

"But it's opening night, so who knows? In this game, of all games, anything can happen, because both teams are going to make mistakes. We'll see who can handle it."

Ben Bredeson's parents drove four hours from Hartland, Wisconsin, just to see their son for a few seconds on his way into the stadium. Deb Bredeson "very cautiously" asked him, "How do you feel?"

"Mom, we've got this," the newly minted captain said. "There's no doubt."

"He believed in his heart they had planned well," Deb said, "they were as prepared as can be, and they were going to win."

While the players warmed up with dusk settling in a classic stadium on a gorgeous night, the reporters in the press box scanned the TVs. The night before Michigan State struggled to shake a mediocre Utah State team, 38–31, at home no less. The Spartans certainly didn't look like the nation's 11th best team. In Columbus, with Urban Meyer serving the first of his three-game suspension, the Buckeyes blew out Oregon State, 77–31, looking every bit as fearsome as expected.

But the reporters focused on Penn State coming from behind to beat Appalachian State in overtime—yes, the same school that upset Michigan in 2007. Why any school still invited the Mountaineers to play their home opener was a mystery.

Perhaps Michigan's schedule would not be as tough as advertised. But, as Jansen said, "On game night, who knows?"

With a stout defense but an untested offense, the Wolverines' best chance to win seemed straightforward: hope their defense could hold off Notre Dame for the first quarter, while Michigan's new quarterback settled in to score some points in the second. And that's exactly what didn't happen.

Notre Dame started on its own 25-yard line with a

basic running play, getting stuffed for no gain. On second down Fighting Irish quarterback Brandon Wimbush's pass was broken up by Lavert Hill, and almost intercepted. After nine months of hard work preparing for this moment, the game was starting exactly as Michigan had hoped.

Then on third and ten Notre Dame ran a motion, a basic play Michigan had practiced defending "15 to 20 times every week, something we do every day in practice," defensive back coach Mike Zordich told me. "We were supposed to trade guys off, and we didn't, and everything goes haywire. Their guy is open, Wimbush hits him. First down."

Instead of starting the game with an authoritative three-and-out, which would have silenced the home crowd and sent Michigan's defenders running off the field in triumph, the Wolverines gave the Irish a 16-yard gift, and their fans reason to cheer.

"I blame it on first game jitters," Zordich said. "It's impossible for me to explain it any other way. And it triggered an avalanche—an absolute avalanche."

On first down from Notre Dame's 41, Wimbush threw to Miles Boykin, covered by Lavert Hill.

"Lavert's one of our best guys in cover," Zordich said, "but he looked like he'd never been in man coverage before in his life. It was pass interference or holding [on Michigan], take your pick, and their guy caught the ball anyway."

Boykin got 28 yards to Michigan's 31. Two plays later, plus one face-masking penalty against Michigan, the Irish scored, covering 75 yards in a mere 1:25.

Michigan's Karan Higdon responded with three straight runs for 14 yards out to the 49-yard line, followed by Shea Patterson, attempting his first pass as Michigan's quarterback, hitting Nico Collins for eight yards to Notre Dame's 43. Even with Tarik Black out the promising early start tempted Michigan fans to believe the offensive line had been fixed, and Michigan's offense could go toe-to-toe with the Irish.

On second-and-two Michigan called for Higdon to run again, but the Irish caught him for a one-yard loss, then stopped him on the next play two yards short of a first down. Michigan's promising first drive had fizzled.

Will Hart's punt pinned the Irish on their four-yard line, giving the defense a great chance to show off. On third-and-nine Wimbush threw 26 yards to Alize Mack on the right sideline. The officials called Michigan's Josh Metellus for targeting, and after a lengthy review, ejected him from the game.

After failing to stop the Irish on another third-and-long, Wimbush threw a hanging long ball to the end zone. Metellus's replacement, Brad Hawkins, playing his first snaps in the secondary, had followed his man, Chris Finke, turned toward the ball and was waiting for it to come down. But what looked to be a sure interception slipped through his hands straight to Finke behind him for another Notre Dame touchdown.

Notre Dame 14, Michigan 0, with 7:09 left in the first quarter—the one scenario probably nobody expected to see.

"What happened? I don't know!" Zordich told me. But having been an All-American at Penn State before playing 12 years in the NFL then coaching high school for six years, the NFL for four, and Michigan for one, he knew one thing: "There's definitely more emotion in the college game than in the pros. The college crowds are bigger and more passionate, the players are younger and more emotional, and momentum is real. It can save you or kill you. The momentum was definitely swinging Notre Dame's way, and they rode it."

That resulted in the kind of opening game mistakes Jansen had feared, and Devin Bush Jr. witnessed. "First seven minutes we had a lot of unfortunate penalties," Bush told me. "We had the pass interference, the targeting, and then they got a cheap one to extend the drive. It happens."

Jon Jansen agreed. "You give Notre Dame that confidence early on, and they start thinking they can do anything. But they gained 233 in the first half, and 69 yards in the second. If we don't get down 14 points, that game is completely different."

After the disastrous start Michigan's defense returned to form, allowing only 10 points over the rest of the game—but those were 10 painful points. The Irish scored their third touchdown on a second quarter drive kept alive by two Michigan penalties called on incomplete third down passes that should have ended the drives, and a 48-yard field goal after the play clock hit 00 before the snap.

Michigan's offense showed some life, and a surprising inability to finish drives. Patterson hit five passes to get to Notre Dame's 25-yard line before a 16-yard sack took them out of field goal range. Another drive set up a second-and-goal from Notre Dame's two-yard line, but instead of smashing it in Michigan tried to pass, got sacked again, and had to settle for a field goal. In the second half, after another drive stalled at Notre Dame's 16, a botched snap-and-hold killed a field goal attempt. In a tight rivalry game, leaving points on the field is a good way to lose it.

Down 21–3 in the second quarter, the Wolverines received a shot in the arm when Ambry Thomas returned the next kickoff 99 yards. In the fourth quarter, with Michigan now behind 24–10, Patterson briefly went out with cramps. Dylan McCaffrey entered the game with no warm-up or warning, and delivered surprisingly clutch passing to keep the drive alive. After Patterson returned he hit three passes for 48 yards, followed by a short touchdown run by Higdon to cut the lead to 24–17, with 2:18 left.

For all the troubles the Wolverines had that night, this was their chance. Their defense did what the defense was supposed to do, shutting down the Irish offense in three quick plays to give Michigan's offense the ball back on its own 25, with 1:02 remaining, and no timeouts.

But four plays later at mid-field, Patterson was sacked, fumbled the ball, and Notre Dame recovered. Game over.

We finally were able to stop them," Zordich said. "But the game is four quarters, not five."

"There wasn't a whole lot of conversation in the locker room," Zach Gentry told me. "Very quiet. Coach stood up and said, 'They beat us. Now it's time to fight.' And that was about it."

After a big Irish win the concourse of Notre Dame Stadium usually echoes and vibrates with the cacophony of fans cheering and singing. But on this night there was surprisingly little of that. Perhaps they were tired from a long day of partying, relieved to escape with a win, or simply expected to win.

But the relative quiet didn't make Michigan's press conference any less morose. Held in a gray little cinderblock side room with gray plastic chairs, fluorescent lighting, and the humidity of a sauna, it would make a fine place to interrogate terrorists. That's about what it felt like when reporters questioned Michigan's players about the loss they had worked nine solid months to avoid.

Karan Higdon appeared wearing a Michigan football T-shirt and his hat on backwards. His face tight as a drum, he clutched the podium, and pursed his lips between every answer. After giving credit to Notre Dame's defense he concluded, "This game won't define us," nodded for punctuation, and departed.

Even in defeat Winovich brought personality to the press conference. When a reporter said, "I like your hair, man," he grinned and pointed and said, "I like yours, too."

"No matter how hard your [training] camp is," he said, "that first game is always tougher . . . To be honest, I'm not really sure where they beat us. I didn't feel like they had dominated us in any aspect of the game. We had a lot of penalties."

Seven, in fact, totaling 52 yards, often negating successful plays in crucial situations. When the *Detroit News'* veteran reporter Angelique Chengelis asked about Winovich's pregame quote—"you said this game would have a lot to say about the trajectory of your team"—Winovich replied with a grudging grin, "Sometimes quotes don't age very well."

Everybody laughed, then Winovich turned serious, listing some encouraging signs: Michigan's 2018 offense already looked better than last year's, and the team seemed mentally tougher. Down 21–3, "We didn't falter. That's different from last year. When things went astray, we had that kind of mindset last year, and this year it was kind of opposite. We had given up some points, and we regrouped.

"My personal take on it—I can't speak for the other guys—there's an expression: burn the boats. And that's what we're going to do."

Harbaugh exhibited a carefully controlled frustration.

"Guys really, really prepared well for this ballgame," he told the press. "It's not the outcome we anticipated or wanted. No excuses. Give credit to Notre Dame, and move on to next week."

What would that take?

"Good, old-fashioned resolve," he said, jaw clenched,

before adding: "This will be a very good football team. We're at the beginning, not the end."

Michigan color commentator Dan Dierdorf gave Michigan's effort the most positive spin possible, within the indisputable facts.

"Our defense rebounded for the last three-quarters," he told me, "but we lost the offensive line of scrimmage from the start. We couldn't block their defensive line. They knew it. Our guys knew it. It was pretty clear Notre Dame has a quality D-line and they took it to us."

If Michigan's offense already looked better than 2017's, that was mainly because of Shea Patterson, not the offensive line.

The players' parents could not afford to keep a professional distance. These were their boys.

"That was awful," recalled Deb Bredeson, Ben's mom. "That was heartbreaking for us, because Ben was so certain before the game that they had it.

"As a parent to have to sit outside the locker room waiting for your son, knowing he's going to come out heartbroken, it's hard. When he came over to us, I don't think he even said a word—and Ben's a talker. He just nodded, gave me a hug, and got on the bus."

"It was a very sour taste for everyone on this team,"

Shea Patterson told me. "It stings—it *really* stings—but you can't go back and change it. After the game I was just thinking to myself, 'We'll just keep getting better. We'll just keep getting better.'"

The bus trip home would take about three hours, ending at Schembechler Hall in the small hours. "We were all just thinking about what happened," Devin Bush Jr. told me. "It was one of those games where you lost, but you learned a lot about how much better you can be. Now's not the time to cover up and go into the tank. Now's the time to double down."

The players' resilience would come in handy that week. On Twitter plenty of people reminded Michigan fans that the Wolverines were the only Big Ten team to lose a bowl game the previous season, the only Big Ten team to lose a non-conference game opening weekend, and the only one riding a four-game losing streak.

Predictably, Harbaugh took the most shots.

-"After a 24-17 loss to Notre Dame, Michigan is 9-9 in its last 18 games under Jim Harbaugh after starting 19-3. The Wolverines have now lost 17 straight road games against AP-ranked opponents."

-"Jim Harbaugh is 8-8 in his last 16 games at Michigan. Urban Meyer has lost 8 total games in his six years at Ohio State."

If the statistics looked grim, they paled compared to the comments. Believing in the team's offseason promise, Michigan fans felt like Charlie Brown trying to kick the ball only to see Lucy pull it away yet again.

"Michigan SuperFan" wrote, "Fool me once shame on you . . . Fool me 14 years in a row. . . . well maybe I'm just a stupid asshole. #fact. What honestly rips my heart out is that my children have absolutely no idea what Michigan Football is supposed to be."

There are times it's tempting to believe college football is not actually a competitive sport, but a longitudinal psychology study to see the impact of endless anguish on millions of fans. As Elika Sadeghi, a blogger for the Ohio State fan website, *Eleven Warriors,* wrote, "How do people who don't watch college football know what it's like to simultaneously feel alive and like you want to die?"

Even the Indiana toll road ticket takers at the Angola exit, where cars, SUVs, and RVs were backed up at 1 a.m. on their way back to Ann Arbor and Detroit, got some of the blowback from Michigan fans.

"Man, I've been hearing it all night," one toll taker told me, with a chuckle. "They don't seem too happy."

But if Michigan's performance made many Michigan fans mad or miserable or both, they weren't indifferent—perhaps the biggest existential threat to the future of Michigan football, a condition that peaked in the waning days of the 2014 season. The ailment was thought to have been eradicated for good by the overpowering antidote of Jim Harbaugh's arrival, but there were some signs that it was still out there, poised to spread.

This malady was perhaps best expressed by Brian Cook, the founder of one of the nation's most popular fan blogs, "MGoBlog."

"Ah so it's this bit again. The bit where some people pick up on a factoid and yell about it a lot and other people yell at them about it. The bit where everyone's mad and trying to take it out on someone.

"I mean, I get it . . . But I don't want to do it again . . . If you're mad, fine. If you're mad at the people who are mad, fine. I'm not going to argue with you."

While Cook and the others above stuck to the facts at hand, it was amazing to see how one close opening loss spawned a legion of unsourced rumors, suggesting everything from a mysterious "dark dysfunction" within Schembechler Hall to some unnamed health problem for Jim Harbaugh that would require him to retire in

December, and just about every conspiracy theory you could think of.

But even the most negative critics missed something: the game earned a 4.51 overnight rating, meaning 4.51 percent of active televisions were tuned to the game—the highest rating for any football game that day, and the highest since the Michigan-Notre Dame game set NBC's record twelve years earlier in 2006. (The only market to top Detroit's 15.4 rating for the 2018 game was Columbus, at 16.2. The Buckeyes were watching the Blue, too.)

If that many millions were still watching the Wolverines, you couldn't say they didn't care. The internal battle among anger, apathy, and optimism would continue in the weeks ahead.

But the players did not have the luxury of indifference, despair, or self-pity. They would get home at 2 a.m., wake up Sunday morning, and dive into their homework. It was time to return to the other 8,700 hours of their lives.

They had work to do.

Chapter 7
The Gambler
Karan Higdon

Nine months earlier, in January of 2018, Michigan's leading tailback Karan Higdon woke up in his Ann Arbor apartment with a big decision to make: declare for the NFL draft, or return to Michigan for his senior season?

It wasn't his first big decision, and it wouldn't be his last, but this one would affect not just him and his family—including his three-year-old daughter, Kiyah—but his teammates, who knew they needed Higdon to avoid another 8-5 season. But simply to get to that precipice Higdon had already beaten the odds, and made a few crucial choices that ran counter to conventional wisdom.

Like thousands of kids in Florida, where football is

still king, Higdon joined his first organized team when he was just five years old. But his first practice for the Sarasota Redskins was not love at first sight.

"It was hot as *hell*," Higdon told me. "It was in the nineties, easily, and humid, like only Florida can get. The coaches were playing favorites, hard, giving their kids the ball, and I was getting tired of it. So I quit!"

But quitting was not something Higdon's mom, Christian, took to kindly.

"My mama told me to go back," Higdon said, "and to keep going back, so I did."

After a few practices the coaches finally listened to Higdon's pleas and moved him from center to tailback. With the ball on the 20-yard line, the coaches called his number.

"I got the ball, and man, I took off!"

Higdon could see immediately he had a clear path to the end zone but was so determined to prove himself he dared not crack a smile until he reached pay dirt.

"I remember being *so* excited," he said 16 years later, his thousand-watt smile on full display. "My adrenaline was sky high. I *knew* I could play this game."

His mom had to answer the next question: Where should he play? In 2006, when Karan was just ten, *America* magazine named Sarasota "America's meanest city"—not the kind of place Christian wanted to raise her oldest child. So they moved to Palmetto, 20 minutes away, where Karan continued his football career.

In fourth grade Higdon was already wearing size nine-and-a-half shoes, a big kid for his age. He spent his weekday afternoons at the Boys and Girls Club and his weekends playing Pee Wee football for the Port Charlotte Bandits. By the time he was 12 he could run around defenders with his speed, or run over them with his size, which earned him the nickname "Nightmare." But at his first practice at the next level for the Palmetto Trojans he couldn't hang on to the ball, fumbling again and again.

"Not a good start!" he recalled.

But on the opening kickoff of his first game that weekend Higdon caught the ball near the right sideline, "And I just *ran*. I hauled tail, making cuts down the sidelines. I don't even think I was touched!"

At halftime Coach Ernie said, "I don't know how the hell this kid fumbled all week long, and in the game, boom, not once."

Higdon was developing the habit of overcoming his doubts, and his doubters.

With ninth grade approaching Higdon had to make another decision. While his classmates and teammates would be attending Palmetto High School, he wanted to attend his mom's alma mater, Riverview High School, 40 minutes away in Sarasota.

When Higdon enrolled at Riverview, "I was the outcast. I thought I was being loyal to my family, but my neighbors [back at Palmetto] thought I was being a traitor to my town. I said, 'Hey, you got to realize, this is about my future, not yours.'"

Riverview head coach Todd Johnson had played at Riverview before starring for the Florida Gators, then played seven seasons in the NFL. He made his players earn everything.

"Coach Johnson was the first coach who didn't just give the starting job to me based on my talent," Higdon said, proving John Harbaugh's theory that high school coaches are more important than college coaches. "I've always worked hard, but coach Johnson brought my mindset to a completely differently level. I would do anything for him. If that meant sacrificing for my team, then that's what I did."

As a freshman Higdon outrushed the starting running back every game, but coach Johnson still refused to start him.

"Some games he wouldn't even play me," Higdon said. "The whole county thought I should be starting, but he was immune to it all. People on the sidelines were going crazy, cussing him out, and we'd hear it. I can't say if he heard it, but everyone else did! It was in the papers, too. Public opinion did not affect him.

"But he not only taught me a lesson—that you're given nothing, sometimes you have to wait, and the only solution is to keep working—he prepared me for my future. Coach Johnson is one of the strongest guys I know."

After Higdon's freshman year Kentucky and Tennessee both gave him verbal offers.

"And I hadn't even started yet! That showed me the future I could have. By my sophomore year, there were no questions. The job was mine. But it felt better than it would have if I'd been given the job as a freshman, because I had to develop a different mentality. When I wasn't starting, I decided I was going to grind each and every day no matter what it takes. Coach Johnson brought out the best in me."

"Karan was a guy who was always around," Johnson told the *Toledo Blade*'s Kyle Rowland. "He stayed after school and was doing something to improve himself and get better every single day."

That included the classroom, where Higdon earned a weighted grade-point average above a 4.0 in the rigorous International Baccalaureate program. "I took school seriously, every day. Oh yeah—start to finish."

When other high schools tried to lure Higdon away, he returned Coach Johnson's loyalty.

"Coach, I'm a [Riverview] Ram from now until forever," Higdon told him. "I will never leave here. I started here, and this is where I'm gonna finish. I told you that I'd be here for four years, and that's not going to change no matter what."

But Higdon's devotion did not extend to Johnson's alma mater, the University of Florida. "I told Coach Johnson I was never going to Gainesville. I just didn't like [the University of] Florida, didn't like it at all, and it just didn't feel like it was a fit for me."

Some of Higdon's friends signed with the University of South Carolina, but that didn't excite him, either. To just about everyone's surprise, Higdon clicked with the University of Iowa.

"I picked Iowa based on the relationships I built with the coaches and the players and the fans there," Higdon told me. "They are *invested*, something I loved. They pack Kinnick Stadium, one of the loudest stadiums I've ever played in."

But Higdon had also been building a close relationship with Tyrone Wheatley, Michigan's star tailback who played 10 years for the New York Giants and Oakland Raiders before returning to coach Michigan's running backs in 2015. Higdon's visit happened to fall on Sunday, February 1, 2015, the day of Super Bowl XLIX, which featured Michigan's own Tom Brady leading a fourth-quarter comeback for his fourth ring—and plenty of snow in Ann Arbor.

Unlike most Florida kids, who would probably have taken the next flight home, "I was in heaven," Higdon said. "I was in the Academic Center parking lot making snow angels, with Coach Wheatley just shaking his head."

But Higdon had to consider his mom and his pregnant girlfriend. What would be best for them? He knew he had to get more out of college than just a shot at the NFL.

"At Michigan, I was blown away by what they had to offer me academically," he said. "The reputation, the resources, the academic center, the tutoring, the classes, all the top ten departments, and what they could offer as a whole. I just felt like I fit here."

Just minutes before he was expected to fax his Letter of Intent to Iowa, Higdon decided, "I had to trust my heart. Really, I was just thinking about my future, and my daughter's future. I was getting no sleep, not at all."

He faxed his letter to Michigan instead, and slept well that night for the first time in days.

When Higdon moved north his family moved with him, including his mother, father, two younger brothers, his girlfriend, and their daughter, and set up house in nearby Sterling Heights. Karan lived in Ann Arbor and visited them every weekend, while Christian tried to give him his space, only coming to town on game days.

"I wanted to make sure my child succeeded," Christian told the *Toledo Blade*. "I wanted to make sure there were no hiccups, no barriers in his way from completing his education. Statistically, kids from Florida who go out-of-state with no support system, a great majority go back home. I didn't want that to happen to Karan."

It easily could have. Higdon suffered a serious ankle sprain his freshman year, getting only 11 carries, then interrupted a promising sophomore season when he popped his meniscus in the 2016 Penn State game, which required postseason surgery. But with his mother's help he stayed in school, got decent grades, and got healthy for his junior year, 2017. Although he had already scored eight career touchdowns on 124 career carries, Higdon didn't become the team's starting tailback until the fourth game of the 2017 season, when the coaches put him in against Purdue. Thanks to Coach Johnson's preparation Higdon hadn't lost his confidence waiting for his chance, and he didn't get nervous when it finally arrived.

"I've seen this story all over again," he told me. "When I was five, nine, 15, and now. Same thing. I've seen adversity before, and I know what to do. You don't panic. You just focus on being consistent, and you'll get your chance. I'm almost like a snake, who waits and waits for its prey—then snap! When your time finally comes, you jump at it, and you don't let go until it surrenders, and it's *yours*."

Higdon took full advantage. In his third start, against Indiana, he ran wild for 200 yards and three crucial touchdowns, including the game winner in overtime, to beat the Hoosiers 27–20.

"It wasn't shocking to me," he said. "It was nothing special in my eyes. For me, I was just meeting my bare minimum standards. I wasn't patting myself on the back. I'm thinking, Let's go! Let's hit it again."

The next week Higdon ran 15 times for 45 yards against Penn State, then 158 against Rutgers, and 200 again versus Minnesota, for 603 total yards, an average of 151 a game. After two and a half years of clawing, the job was his.

"My mind was clear," Higdon recalled, "because I didn't feel like I'd done anything yet. I was just hungry. I wanted more and more and more—and nothing seemed like it was enough. I knew I'd been waiting for this opportunity, and here it was. To everyone else [my performance] was shocking, but it was not shocking to me. I knew what I was capable of doing."

With three games to go in the 2017 regular season Higdon had already accumulated 804 yards. If his average was cut in half for the last three games, he'd still easily become the first Michigan tailback to break 1,000 yards since Fitzgerald Toussaint did it in 2011—a yawning gap by Michigan standards. But after Higdon suffered a high-ankle sprain against Maryland his carries and production were cut, finishing with 50, 20, and 55 yards, for a total of 929 for the regular season. Needing 71 yards in Michigan's bowl game against South Carolina, where some of his old high school teammates were playing, Higdon could muster only 65 yards, leaving him six yards shy with 994.

Despite his late start that season, Higdon's 6.1 yards per carry ranked third in the Big Ten behind only Ohio State's J. K. Dobbins and Wisconsin's Jonathan Taylor. When Higdon tested the draft market that winter, they told him he was a projected fourth-round selection.

Higdon was on track to earn his bachelor's degree in December 2018. He had also seen just how fragile his body could be. Having suffered a significant injury each season, he knew the next one could be his last.

"I'm running for more than just myself," he said. "It's more than just me when I play this game."

Just about everything, including his three-year-old daughter, seemed to be pushing Higdon to leave Michigan and enter the draft.

"But before I made my decision," Higdon recalled, "a great man, my old [7-on-7] coach, told me something important: 'If you can do it once, you can do it again. So go do it again.'

"I decided he was right. I can do this again. And next time I'll be better, and it'll be more money! And if I come back, I could be a leader, maybe team captain, and represent Michigan at the Big Ten Media Days in Chicago. I could perfect my craft, put more film out there, and make a statement, leaving no doubt. For me it was an easy decision.

"It's like gambling. I'll have my degree, so I'll secure, but if you're going to do it, go for all the marbles, don't just settle. This is a smart gamble," he said, then quickly knocked on wood. A smart gamble is still a gamble. If Higdon returned he would be risking his entire football career, something he had sacrificed to build since he was five.

Like everyone else on a football field, he would also be dependent on his teammates. If Michigan's 2018 offense was no better than the 2017 model, Higdon would be hard-pressed to run for 1,000 yards again when teams would be waiting for him.

What they lacked in 2017, Higdon believed, was consistency.

"All four losses we lost in the fourth quarter, and all but one of them were close. It wasn't that we were a bad team. It's just that we couldn't consistently finish. It was like a track race: when you're close it comes down to who's going to give up first. And it was us, too often."

So what reasons did he have to believe that this season would be different? For Higdon it started with Harbaugh. After the season Harbaugh sat down with a few of the older players and asked them what was working, and what wasn't.

"It was awesome," Higdon told me. "The minute you see coach in a vulnerable moment, asking us what needs to change, and honestly seeking our answers, it's impressive. Not many coaches would be willing to do that. He told us to speak freely, and we did. We laid it out on the line. And if you can't, what's the point of talking? Where are you going to go?"

When Higdon, Winovich, and others told Harbaugh they wanted improvements in training and eating, Harbaugh hired a new strength coach and a new nutritionist, both of whom proved immediately popular.

"That takes everything to a whole new level," Higdon said. "And that's why I think everything looks different this year. The team feels like less of a dictatorship and more of a relationship. Guys actually *want* to be here working out, watching tape, whatever it takes. There's no bitching."

Higdon was particularly interested in the much-maligned offensive line. When Tim Drevno, one of Harbaugh's closest coaching friends who shared the play-calling duties with Pep Hamilton and offensive line coaching with Greg Frey, decided during spring of 2018 to leave for USC, Harbaugh didn't stop him.

Harbaugh likes to say, "More is more," and in college football, that's usually true: more work, more preparation, more four-star recruits, and more top coaches generally equals more points, which means more wins. But not always. In this case splitting play-calling duties with two men created more chaos than accountability. When the dust had settled on the 8-5 season Drevno had returned to USC, Frey had left for his alma mater, Florida State, and Harbaugh had promoted Ed Warinner, who had served as Ohio State's co-offensive coordinator and offensive line coach for their 2014 national title team, before joining the Minnesota staff, and then accepting a job at Michigan as an analyst.

"He was coming here to be a $250,000 analyst," Harbaugh told me, which represents a significant cut in pay and profile. "He wasn't about the money. He wasn't about the title, or the power. He wanted to be at Michigan. He came here for the right reasons—and as things worked out, we needed him to coach our offensive line and help with the plays."

At the completion of 2018's spring ball Warinner was already the talk of the offensive and defensive players alike.

"I love the way he's attacking things," Higdon told me. "Those guys on the O-line only have a split second to make decisions. You can't hesitate. If they don't know what's going on, or question what you're doing, you can't be confident, and confidence is key. He's making things so much simpler, which makes the guys a whole lot more confident."

The next upgrade was Mississippi transfer Shea Patterson.

"He's the type of quarterback who can keep plays alive, not just with his arm but his feet, too," Higdon said. "He's got great confidence. Look, if you're going to play quarterback at Michigan, you gotta know you're the best. If no one else is going to make something happen, your ass is going to make things happen. Shea feels that and brings it out in other guys, and now everyone knows you have to step up your game to play with him. I like every part of that."

It was a maxim that applied to everyone inside Schembechler Hall: if you're trying to be the best, you better believe you are. And if you believe you are, and are willing to work to prove it, that can make even hard decisions easy.

Chapter 8
Growing up Harbaugh
1973–1977

What Karan Higdon said about Shea Patterson in 2018 was just as true of Jim Harbaugh forty years earlier: if you're going to play quarterback at Michigan, you better think you're the best. Harbaugh believed that long before anyone else did.

The Harbaugh brothers learned the game by playing in backyards, schoolyards, junior football fields, and alongside one of college football's best teams—a life-altering experience.

"My impressions of Bo started when I was nine years old," Jim told me a few years ago, "and my dad was a secondary coach on his staff. During practice, the coaches' kids played our own game of football, and whenever an errant kick or pass landed on Bo's field, he'd blow his whistle and scream, 'Get those damn kids off my field!'"

Recounting this, Harbaugh couldn't help but grin.

"Quarterbacks are a special breed," Schembechler told Mitch Albom for their book, *Bo.* "They need to be cocky, and the cockiest I ever had was probably Jim Harbaugh. You know how he got that way? By hanging around my practice field as a kid, waiting for his dad, Jack, to finish work . . . Even then, [he] was a devil, running on the field when he shouldn't, playing with his friends."

Jim's brother John remembered it, too. Ohio State week, 1975, was one of the most pressurized of Schembechler's career. Michigan hadn't beaten Ohio State since 1971—and hadn't lost or tied to anyone else in six years.

"We were out there on that little side turf where they worked the offensive line," John Harbaugh told me. "We were playing with the other coaches' kids, three on three. Well, the ball goes flying onto the practice field, into the starting backfield. *Not good.* I look at Jim, and just give him the nod, and he knows he's the anointed one. He was probably the one who kicked it over there. So he goes and gets the ball, and Bo sees him and yells, 'HARBAUGH! GET YOUR DAMN KID OFF THE FIELD!'"

"I think he was ten years old," Schembechler told Albom. "So, for the record, that is the youngest I ever yelled at one of my quarterbacks."

Far from offended, young Jim delighted in the attention—*any* attention—from this godlike figure. When Schembechler would run into young Jim in the hallway, he would say, "You're a cocky little guy, aren't you?"

"Sometimes, I guess," Jim would say.

But years later Harbaugh told me, with a wistful grin, "No matter what he had to say to you, it always felt great to be noticed by Bo."

It's not surprising that John, being the older brother, impressed people as more mature, while Jim usually came off as feisty, brash, and less concerned with public opinion—all typical of younger brothers. But their father believes the differences between his sons are largely superficial.

"I've always said John and Jim are the same guys, just wrapped differently," Jack told me. "But oh, they fought—and Jackie had to break those up. Glad I was working!"

"We fought like crazy about everything and anything," John told me. "I think the younger one starts it most of the time. Fifty-fifty was never an even split for Jim, whether we were cutting cake or dividing the backseat. He always tried to make a strong case for a little more for him, but I never bought it. When it was just the two of us in the backseat, he rationalized that he was bigger, which I disputed, so he deserved two-thirds of the backseat. 'How do you figure? No!'"

Everything was contested, even the mowing duties. Because their backyard was three times bigger than their tiny front yard, they alternated who mowed which side every week. John recalled, "It was *amazing* how many times Jim thought he had just cut the back yard last week, when I was *sure* that I had."

Their beleaguered mother usually stayed out of their squabbles, but sometimes she couldn't help but get involved. Most of their fights were glorified wrestling matches, but they both remember an epic battle at the home of Bill McCartney, Michigan's defensive coordinator and future national title coach at Colorado.

When the McCartneys moved to town in 1974 Bill encouraged Jack to bring his sons over to their house. "It'd be good for my kids," McCartney said. John was about to turn 12, Jim was 10, and the McCartney kids were a few years younger.

"Jim liked to go over to their house because they had the best cereal," John said. "Our mom bought only the healthy ones, like Wheaties and Shredded Wheat—no fun. The McCartney's had all the good ones: Honeycombs, Coco Puffs, Apple Jacks—those were big. So we went over there a lot.

"One time when we were playing basketball on their hoop we got into this huge, huge fight—*huge.* I mean, knock-down, drag-out, throwing punches, the whole thing. That was actually pretty rare for us. There was no stopping us. It was bad. Their mom, Lindy, sent us home, and Dad gets word that we're not allowed to go over to the McCartneys' house anymore. Didn't bother us too much except for the cereal. But we stayed friends."

Everybody remembered Jim always played with John and his friends.

"There was never a question," John said. "Jim wasn't tagging along. He was part of our group."

Competing with the older boys required Jim to adapt to survive.

"You know how the older kids are, testing the little brother, teasing him, putting him down," Jack said. "And John's friends were usually good athletes, too, and two years older—big advantage. So if you're a young kid and want so much to be a part of your brother's gang, you need to develop your confidence. I think that's where the cockiness came in. Jim had to believe he could keep up with those guys."

Jim recently told his dad he noticed the same syndrome in his Michigan freshmen. They come in as highly recruited stars, but they're still just freshmen, and they wonder if they really belong.

"The way you notice," Jim told Jack, "is they don't give you eye contact. They look at their shoes. What they need is confidence. And some reach it sooner than others."

"And when they do," Jack said, "they give you this," looking me right in the eye and nodding. "That's confidence, and to play at this level, you better have it."

Jim Harbaugh learned that lesson before he knew he was learning that lesson.

For those of us who grew up in Ann Arbor during Schembechler's heyday it's difficult to explain just how consumed our childhoods were with Michigan football. It probably helped that in the entire decade of the seventies, Detroit's four major league teams combined for exactly one division title out of 40 chances, leaving a large vacuum that only Michigan football filled. Like fish unaware they're swimming in water, we didn't know obsessing over the Wolverines was a choice. It was something we all did—abetted by our teachers who would hold contests on Fridays to see who could pick the Michigan score that Saturday, with prizes awarded on Mondays.

Those kids who didn't care—and there must have been some—probably kept it to themselves and played along, because I can't recall a single dissenter. In the early days of Michigan merchandising, we bought it all—the shirts, the jackets, the hats, and whatever they came out with next.

Bo—as almost everyone called him, whether they knew him or not—was the unquestioned spiritual leader of this tribe, with Bob Ufer providing the voice-over. In 1943 Ufer, running for Michigan, set a world record in the 100-yard dash at Madison Square Garden. He started broadcasting Michigan football games in 1947 and didn't stop until the fall of 1981, 34 years later, broadcasting his 362nd consecutive game just weeks before he died of cancer. He covered the play-by-play and the color commentary and served as his own stat man, spotter, and producer. Five people do his job today.

Ufer had unparalleled reach, partly because the Big Ten allowed teams only two television appearances a year until the early eighties. If Michigan wasn't playing Michigan State or Ohio State, you were listening to Bob Ufer—and even when the games were televised, most Michigan fans would silence the TV broadcasters (with the possible exception of Keith Jackson) to listen to Ufer call the game.

Ufer was scrupulously well-prepared, filling in his file cards during the week on every player who might see the field. He coined colorful lines, like "He's running like a penguin with a hot-herring in his cummerbund!" "God bless your cotton-pickin' maize and blue hearts!" and "Yessirree, football fans, this weekend in the hole that Yost dug, Canham carpeted, and Schembechler fills every home Saturday, there will be another great Meeeeeeechigan victory!" The Meeeeeechigan, by the way, was how Fielding Yost pronounced it, and the guys on ESPN repeat it every Saturday—though they probably don't know why.

But Ufer made his name by being the homer's homer, bringing such unabashed enthusiasm to his broadcasts that, when Michigan missed a big field goal or the Buckeyes tried to take down the famed M Go Blue banner, you worried about his well-being.

"And they're tearing down Michigan's banner!" he screamed. "They will meet a *dastardly* fate here for that!"

But his best line was a sweet homage: "Michigan football is a religion, and Saturday is the Holy Day of Obligation."

In the seventies, when Schembechler's teams went nine years without losing more than one regular season game, and the string of 100,000-plus crowds started, Ufer's claim seemed less like hyperbole than plain common sense.

In the epicenter of this maize and blue storm system lived the Harbaughs. They played alongside the Wolverines during the week, listened to Bob Ufer's broadcast on Saturdays, then went to sleep to his greatest hits' album at night.

"Whenever there was an away game we would gather in the Harbaugh house, in the living room, playing the game as it was being described by Bob Ufer," Jim Harbaugh told filmmaker Dan Chace, on his Ufer documentary. "It was a *happening* when Bob Ufer did the game. It was as good as going to the game itself. That's how much of a picture he painted. And the enthusiasm just poured out of the radio, and we were giddy. And at halftime, we'd pour out of the house and be playing the game in the front yard, then back into the house to listen to the second half."

Ann Arborites all seemed to be crazy about Michigan football, but Jim Harbaugh might have been the only one who could match Ufer's enthusiasm.

"[Ufer] felt like the Harbaugh family felt, just how important that [game] was," Harbaugh said. "If we won, it was the greatest hours that there could *possibly* be. And if we lost, I mean you didn't quite know if the sun was going to come up the next day."

In the fall of 1973, the Harbaughs' first season in Ann Arbor, the boys watched the home games from the stands. But in 1974, when Jim was in fifth grade, he joined the Ufer team, playing a small but vital role as a "plugger" on the sidelines, plugging in the cords to transmit the sound from the field to the booth.

"When the play would move from one end of the field to the other end," Harbaugh recalled, "from north to south, occasionally I would have to go run back, unplug the plug and plug it in at the 30-yard line on the north end. I was *part* of it. It was as good as it got for a fifth or sixth grader. It made me want to be like the heroes that I saw on Saturday afternoons, like Rick Leach."

When Leach, the All-American quarterback of the top-ranked Wolverines, scored a touchdown against Duke in 1977, Harbaugh "was down there in the north end zone and ran out there real fast and patted him on the back, and ran back to the sideline. And I was so excited, the next day in the *Ann Arbor News*, they had a picture of it, and I cut it out and hung it on my wall, right above my bed. I made the paper! That was just a cool, cool moment. That means a lot to me."

It apparently means a lot to Rick Leach, too, who has saved that photo on his phone, and often shares it with his friends.

If the Harbaugh boys couldn't get their fill of Michigan football during practices or games, their parents found the solution when they gave them an album of Ufer's "greatest hits" for Christmas.

"My brother had a stereo, and we would listen to it at night," Jim recalls. "Visions dancing in my head . . . and I just wanted to be a football player. We listened to this every night, until my mom would come up, and tell us for the third time, when she was really mad, to turn it off. And then we'd turn it off. But then we'd wait a little bit and then turn it back on."

In an era that celebrated the antihero—*Easy Rider, Bonnie & Clyde, Butch Cassidy & the Sundance Kid*—Ufer sang the praises of the old-school football heroes and their old-fashioned values: toughness, teamwork, and competitiveness, without irony.

And that's how Harbaugh grew up admiring the "football gods," he said, who taught "the game the way it should be played: Bo Schembechler, Woody Hayes, Bear Bryant, Bob Ufer."

Jim Harbaugh learned the lessons well. Long before reporters or scouts were watching young Jim Harbaugh, he was already an exceptionally tough kid. Ann Arbor native Ken Magee, who rose to direct the university's Department of Public Safety, recalled a scene from his high school days when he, Geoff Schembechler, Bo's second son, and a few friends were watching the Michigan spring game in the mid-70s, when Harbaugh was still in grade school.

Magee's crowd had gathered in the north end zone and sat close to the field. Behind them they saw some kids tossing a football about halfway up the stands. Geoff Schembechler told Magee the little kid was Jimmy Harbaugh, Jack's son. Magee thought the kid had a pretty good arm, but didn't give it any more thought until one of Jim's friends overthrew the ball, which bounced around the first rows of seats.

"That's when I saw Jimmy Harbaugh start running down to get the ball, at full speed," Magee recalls. "I mean he was *running* on the aluminum blue bleacher seats, as fast and fearless as possible. As he began to pick up speed, I thought, 'Wow, he is running really fast, downhill, and on the bleachers'—and then 'BAM! All of a sudden he slipped, and his head smacked on one of the bleachers. It was loud—I mean *loud*—and I thought he was going to need an ambulance. Seriously, with all the momentum taking him forward he hit that *hard*—the hardest hit I ever saw.

"What did Jimmy Harbaugh do? He got up quickly, and got the ball, and tossed it back up to his friends. I know he was dazed—he might have been out cold for a second—but he had the guts to ignore the pain, and get right back into the mix.

"I said to Geoff, 'That is the toughest little kid I have ever seen.' I always remember that day, and I've followed his career ever since."

The Harbaugh boys played every sport they could. They were both great at football, basketball, and baseball, and good at the rest. That included hockey, Jim's fourth sport, which often conflicted with basketball.

Dave McGuigan coached Jim's first Ann Arbor hockey team, Whittaker Gooding, for fourth and fifth graders. McGuigan's memories of Jim are vivid: "It was Jim's first year playing organized hockey, and he wasn't a very strong skater, but he was elected as the team's captain because everyone could see, even at nine years of age, that he had the heart of a champion. He gave maximum effort all the time."

While John played football, basketball, baseball, and track well enough in ninth grade to be voted Tappan Junior High School's Most Athletic, he still wasn't as good as his younger brother.

"Jim was the natural," Jack recalled. "John, he was a grinder. Decent athlete, and well-coordinated, but I don't think it came naturally to him the way it did to Jim. But boy, was he a worker!

"In all that time, seeing Jim do so well, John was always Jim's biggest cheerleader. He never said, 'Why not me?' John would cheer Jim, then go back to work."

Jim was a solid if unspectacular student, more interested in athletics than academics, with one notable exception: history.

His fifth-grade teacher at St. Francis, Mrs. Hiller, sparked a lifelong passion for the subject. To this day Harbaugh readily quotes Churchill, and if you drop a line from John Adams—"Facts are stubborn things"—he will start a conversation about Paul Giamatti playing the second president in the HBO series on him, which Harbaugh devoured.

"Mrs. Hiller was a really great teacher," Jackie Harbaugh said. "She kept the kids interested and attentive. That to me is one of the signs of a great teacher: she could get them hooked lots of ways, instead of just reading the textbook. She might have been the first person who really believed in Jim, academically."

They would need that ally when the principal phoned

Jackie to tell her she and four other parents were being called in because their sons were too loud. When she got there, she saw the principal looking as grim as a doctor prepared to deliver a horrible diagnosis. When she noticed she was the only parent summoned by the principal and the P.E. teacher, she asked, "Where's everyone else?"

"We want to talk about Jim being too competitive in the field," he said. It was an ambush.

"Is he being mean or hurting the other kids?" Jackie asked.

"No," he said.

"Is he cheating?"

"No."

"Then what's wrong with being competitive?" Jackie asked. "You're not going to make Jim less competitive. That's not going to happen."

She then turned to the P.E. teacher. "And you of all people should be the first to defend him!"

The teacher sat there, motionless and mute.

"It's interesting to me that Jim doesn't have any problems in Mrs. Hiller's class," Jackie added. "Maybe she challenges him more and keeps them interested in the topic."

Jackie was taking the long view: trying to avoid as

many current problems as possible, while not stunting the traits that she believed would allow her son to succeed years later.

Nonetheless, Jackie took Jim to their family pediatrician, Dr. Bill Graves, for an evaluation. After talking with Jim for a while, Dr. Graves told Jackie, "There's nothing wrong with your son. There's something wrong with your principal."

Driving the family Dodge on the way home Jackie told Jim, "You can't play dirty, and you can't cheat. You have to play fair, you have to play by the rules, you can't be a bully. Keep it between the lines. You know that.

"But you will be yourself. There's no need to hold back."

Jim took his mom's advice to heart. Everyone who knew him then remembers him as incredibly tough, competitive, and cocky—something Schembechler himself noted at an early age.

"Tiger" Ray Howland played baseball with Harbaugh at Tappan Junior High School.

"Jim came over to my house a lot to watch the Stanley Cup playoffs, and we'd have table hockey tournaments," he recalled. "But Jim could never just play to play. Nothing could be just for fun. He always had to keep score, and there always had to be a clock. So

I got an egg timer from upstairs, and we went at it. We're jamming the table around pretty good when we knocked a lamp over. Jim *catches it,* one-handed, at the exact same moment he says, 'Stop the clock!' He put the lamp back and we resumed play. That was Jim."

Jay Nordlinger, another friend from Harbaugh's neighborhood basketball and baseball teams, and now a senior editor at *National Review,* recalled a baseball practice in sixth or seventh grade. When a hot grounder went to Harbaugh at shortstop he fielded it between his legs, then fired to first base without missing a beat.

Coach Zuckerman, standing next to Nordlinger at first base, barked, "Hey, no hot-dogging! Cut it out!"

But then, Nordlinger recalled, he and Coach Zuckerman looked at each other, grinned, and agreed, "That was pretty damn impressive."

Jack and Jim both like to tell another story from the same baseball team.

"I got picked off first base," Jim told me, at his parents' kitchen table. "And I jumped up and turned to the umpire. 'What?!?'"

"You were show-boating, dancing back and forth off the bag," Jack said to Jim. "You never mentioned that."

But they agree that Jim then took his batting helmet off and whipped it like a Frisbee, skipping it along the dirt. "Went pretty far, too," Jim said.

Seeing this display of poor sportsmanship, Jack jumped from the stands down to the fence and actually started climbing it, trying to get to Jim.

Coach Zuckerman turned to Jack and said, "Jack! Jack! We've got this under control. I'm going to talk to Jim and work this out. He's staying right here."

"The hell he is!" Jack said, then turned to Jim. "Get your little ass in the car!"

"I can't!" Jim protested. "I rode my bike!"

"I don't care! Let's go!"

Jack tossed Jim's bike in the back of their yellow Dodge station wagon, and launched into his lecture on their way home. "He was trying so hard to get at me," Jim recalled, but Jim absorbed his father's berating with surprising calm.

"I got you figured out," Jack told him. "Right now you're the biggest, the strongest, the fastest kid out there, so you can beat those kids. But as soon as some *other* kid shows up who's bigger or faster or *better* than you, you're gonna fold your tent! You're gonna quit!"

"But dad, I think I'm *that kid*—the bigger, better one you're always talking about."

Jim's response stopped Jack short, forcing him to turn to the window to conceal his grin.

Like Jackie, Jack decided to let Jim be Jim, and see where it led.

"**Jim was** always the guy who could wear his welcome out in elementary school—and even here at Michigan," Jack told me. "But the guy who always brought him back and grounded him was John."

"I don't remember any big discussions, any heart-to-hearts," John said. "But every day, we were together. It was automatic. We never thought about it, never even discussed it. We were just always together. I can remember him rubbing people the wrong way, too, but never picking on anyone, never being a bully. He had friends, he was nice to girls, and a lot of his friends were girls. He was genuine, always."

Harbaugh's uncommon talent, world-class competitiveness, and unapologetic swagger could alienate people, but I've never witnessed nor heard anyone say Jim Harbaugh tormented anyone, played dirty, or cheated. Almost everyone who got to know Harbaugh well described him as surprisingly vulnerable, genuine, and kind.

Harbaugh naturally became friends with one of Tappan Junior High's best athletes, Brian Weisman, who stood only 5-8 but started in football, basketball, and volleyball, and was one of the city's best runners.

"I don't know if Jim had a lot of close friends," Weisman said, "but he was friendly with a lot of people.

People generally liked him, even though some wanted to bring him down a peg. He was both full of himself, and able to make fun of himself. At school he was overly confident, but when you got him alone, one-on-one, he was a different person. He was funny and just a nice, warm guy. I didn't know what to make of him, but I liked him.

"But I mainly remember being impressed that he tended to look out for people who were different than him. Jim often befriended guys who weren't always popular, guys who often had some issue they were trying to overcome—which belied Jim's 'Big Man on Campus' image."

When I mentioned this insight to Harbaugh, he replied with a self-effacing grin, "I wasn't a real popular guy either, so maybe those guys were doing me the favor."

Niel Rishoi, a neighbor and classmate, remembers being one of those "different kids" Harbaugh took under his wing.

"Jim was the most fearless kid I ever knew," Rishoi said. "He charged through life as he charged through the fields—with gusto, confidence, and a sure sense of his destiny. Out at recess, or in gym class, he automatically took charge of whatever game or sporting event commenced."

Author John Feinstein once wrote that Bob Knight took losing not merely as a setback, but as a personal shortcoming, convinced each loss diminished him in some way. Talk to enough world-class coaches and athletes, however, and you realize that could be applied to almost all of them. Yet, even by those standards, Harbaugh stood out.

"Jim did not take losing—in *anything*—gracefully," Rishoi said. "He took it as a personal affront, and his self-disgust was made acutely manifest as he agonized over lost or fouled plays. He was an arguer; Jim never held back when he had a point to make or if he felt a ruling was unjust or wrong. His scrapes—verbal and physical—with some of the other boys who took issue with his cockiness were legendary."

Although everyone describes Harbaugh as a charismatic leader with plenty of friends, "A lot of people resented him—probably his success," Rishoi said. "I was not one of them. I was not much liked either, but for different reasons. I had a hearing impairment, and a lisp that went with it, and I felt like I didn't fit in. Jim lived in my neighborhood, and I used to run into him walking home after school, and he was always— *always*—unfailingly nice to me."

Because no one could bully Harbaugh, having him defend you against the bullies meant everything. When

Rishoi told his younger brother, Jan, about our conversations, Jan told Niel a story he had never heard before.

"Apparently," Niel told me, "Jan witnessed Jim defend me against one of the school bullies, who was making fun of the way I talked. Jan said Jim confronted the guy and told him, 'Niel's a cool guy. Shut your goddamned mouth!' And I think that ended that.

"One thing you can say for sure," Niel Rishoi concluded. "Jim definitely wasn't a bully. In fact, he was usually the one who was targeted because of his overconfident bravado—but he could take it. I witnessed a pretty brutal slugfest one day between Jim and a big hockey player, who was built like a brickhouse linebacker. Man, they were really beatin' the living shit outta each other. But Jim never backed down.

"Perhaps it was because I wasn't threatened by Jim's supreme self-confidence and athletic prowess that we got along. I admired his singular self-possession, his ambitious drive to be the best, and if that was misunderstood and he rubbed some people the wrong way, that was none of my concern."

The American playwright and painter Lorraine Hansberry said, "The thing that makes you exceptional, if you are at all, is inevitably that which must also make you lonely."

How many truly great achievers fit in perfectly in

junior high? Harbaugh was an outlier, someone whose oversized personality portended future greatness, but was too big to be confined by the conventions of junior high school. For this, he paid a price.

"I've no doubt," Rishoi said, "that internally, at least, Jim felt lonely at times because he was so . . . almost alienatingly different from everyone else in his midst. But that usually happens to people who are not conventionally normal."

Perhaps Harbaugh was searching for something a force of nature like him can't find in junior high: a challenge big enough, a world broad enough, to accommodate his outsized abilities and ambitions.

"Jim thought bigger, wider in scope, keener in focus, than just about anyone I knew at that time," Rishoi said. "People like that are *not* normal. They are crazed with desire to succeed and allow nothing to disrupt their dedication and perseverance. Even if Jim had not become famous, he'd still be the person people remembered most vividly from school. Harbaugh wasn't a ripple in a pond; he was a meteor that caused a tsunami in the ocean."

For all Harbaugh would achieve years after leaving Tappan Junior High School—a laundry list including Michigan starting quarterback, Big Ten MVP, first-round NFL draft pick, a 14-year NFL quarterback, and a turnaround specialist coach at both Stanford and the 49ers—every success achieved against long odds, it could be argued that Harbaugh had not found a challenge worthy of his ambition until he returned to his alma mater as the program's head coach, to duplicate or even surpass what his greatest mentor, Bo Schembechler, had accomplished when Harbaugh was a kid—and not just on the field, but off it, too.

"Jim is right where he wants to be," Rishoi said, "and what was evident early on panned out exactly the way he wanted it to."

Chapter 9
Friday Nights, No Lights

The Graduate Hotel, Ann Arbor, September 7, 2018

The loss to Notre Dame dropped Michigan from 14th to 21st in the media poll, reflecting the media's predictions of Harbaugh's demise at Michigan. A good portion of Michigan fans feared this season would be as miserable as the last.

The players didn't give any of it much thought. Until the gauntlet arrived in October they knew they'd be playing under the radar, facing five straight teams they'd get no credit for beating, but losing to any of them would cause the sky to start falling. All they could do was stick together—a strength that appeared early with this squad, even in defeat—focus on the work ahead, and let the rest take care of itself.

And they had plenty of work to do. That week they had to adjust to something the fans and media don't consider much, if at all: the other 8,700 hours of the year. The rigorous routine the players had mastered during "fall camp" (which actually begins at the end of July, in the heart of the summer), when they worked on some aspect of their sport virtually every waking hour, got thrown out the window three days after the Notre Dame game.

Instead of two-a-days they started squeezing in three classes a day, usually between 9 a.m. and 2 p.m., plus weightlifting, physical treatments, film, meetings, and practice, while their homework piled up with stunning speed. Veteran coaches knew to keep their eye out for a different kind of fatigue. For a team with 48 Academic All-Big Ten players, the first week of classes took a toll.

"Usually the first practices during school are horrible," Higdon told me, "but this week was amazing. Just another sign we did a great job preparing this year."

Instead of getting down over the Notre Dame loss and obsessing over the negative pressure that went with it, when Monday practice arrived, "We were a hungry team," Higdon said. "We really needed a win, and we came ready to work."

They were convinced they were better than advertised, and they were eager to prove it.

"People can say what they want, but I'm telling you the offense is *dramatically* better than last year's," Jansen said. Offensive line coach Ed Warinner "has improved the O-line, and you're going to see that. And every mistake we made was self-imposed, and correctable."

The Wolverines would get their chance that Saturday against Western Michigan. Two years earlier the Broncos won 12 straight games, including wins over two Big Ten teams, before losing to Wisconsin in the Cotton Bowl—a run that boosted P. J. Fleck to the head coaching position at Minnesota. Following that miracle season the Broncos went 6-6 the next year and opened the 2018 season with a 55–42 loss to Syracuse, a team that would finish 10–3. While the Broncos certainly weren't the Fighting Irish, it would be foolish to dismiss them as a walk-over.

For Devin Bush Jr., however, it didn't matter. "Treat your opponent how they're supposed to be treated," he told me. "Don't think more of them than what they are, and don't think less of them either. Your job is to play your game, test your will and character as a unit, and go out there and perform."

There are a lot of reasons why the Wolverines prefer playing at home, but one you might not guess is the team hotel.

On the Friday before a home game, the players conduct a walk-through at Glick Fieldhouse at three, eat a big dinner at Schembechler Hall Commons at 5:30, then board two university buses at 7:30. As the buses crawl up State Street to the hotel on the far side of campus, the players look longingly out the windows at their classmates in shorts and T-shirts blaring music, quaffing beer from big red cups, and playing cornhole or beer pong.

If Michigan football has cost the players such quintessential college experiences, they do get a little time to kick back on game nights at the Graduate Hotel. Known for decades as the Dahlmann Campus Inn, the downstairs bar there features a picture of Desmond Howard mimicking the Heisman Trophy hanging on the wall with the inscription, "Before I struck this pose, I enjoyed a good night's rest at the Campus Inn."

They watch a movie as a team, followed by one of their favorite times of the week.

"On the road, everything's different," Jon Runyan

Jr., said. "Your room is different, the food is different, and you get lost trying to find the meeting rooms. Here, we stay in the same rooms every night, we like the food, and they know us. It's the difference between staying at someone else's house and your own. So you're more relaxed, and you feel like you've got more time to catch up."

For the past few years a fluid group of players had been holding a friendly vigil in the far right corner of the team dining room, where they swapped stories for an hour or so until lights out at 10:30. This informal gang usually included offensive linemen Ben Bredeson, Jon Runyan Jr., and Juwann Bushell-Beatty, tight ends Zach Gentry and Sean McKeon, linebacker Noah Furbush, plus Jared Wangler, Joe Hewlett, and Jack Dunaway—all sons of former Schembechler players—among others.

It's not much, just an hour or so sitting together at a cloth-covered table, snacking on pretzels, chicken fingers, and burgers, and washing them down with tall glasses of milk (plain or chocolate). But in their intensely regimented lives that unscheduled window represents an escape, a rare moment to let their hair down with nothing to do or accomplish, and simply savor one another's company.

"Instead of going back up to your room and watching TV," Joe Hewlett said, "we can sit around and talk about all the things we've done together, all the stories, without worrying about the game we've got to start getting ready for in 12 hours. We can watch TV any time."

"We do it on the road, too," Bredeson said, "but it's not the same."

"We talk about all kinds of stuff," fifth-year senior Noah Furbush said, "some of the most unforgettable stories we have. Comes with being a twenty-year-old college student, I guess. We talk about football, life, what guys are doing, what's next. Nothing's off-limits."

One of the most popular subjects: the team trips to Rome in 2017 and Paris in 2018—something any college students would talk about, but perhaps of greater value to these players because they all went together, without any real obligations, one of the few "quintessential college" experiences they're allowed.

The idea of a team trip to Europe grew from the fecund imagination of Jim Harbaugh, who comes up with a dozen ideas a day. In the course of a two-hour interview I had with Sarah and Jim in 2015, he excused himself a half-dozen times so his assistant could write down his latest notion on a legal pad filled with pages of them.

The players knew that, of all Harbaugh's "outside

the box" ideas, including conducting satellite training camps nationwide, producing a live theater show for national signing day, and taking a spring break trip to IMG Academy in Florida, the overseas trips were the most unpopular with the national media, who often described them as an attention-getting waste of time and resources. But the players loved them, and that's what he cared about.

"Not to sound too harsh," Jared Wangler told me, "but the people who say that, they just—they really have no idea what they're talking about. The trip is completely voluntary, and the cost is picked up by a donor. It's an extra thing we can do because we're Michigan. Then they say we're being distracted, but they don't realize we'd be going home that week anyway. Spring ball is done, finals are done. It's discretionary time. So everyone going home to play video games or party for a week, that's better?

"We really bond on those trips, because everyone has to get out of their comfort zone—we're not football players over there—and it's more organic. No schedule to most of it. That's rare for us."

The trips fostered bonding—important for any team—but more than, they broadened the players' horizons, helping them become more well-rounded people. If you were looking only as far as the next season, the trips might not add up. But if you were looking far out into the players' future, just like you promised their parents you would, the trips made perfect sense.

"I totally understand how an outsider can tee off on something like that," Furbush said. "But from the inside, those trips are easily one of the top five things I'll remember from my five years here, packed with so many experiences that I'll carry with me the rest of my life. And I know, from our Friday nights, the other guys feel the same way."

After each trip ended about half the players continued traveling, splitting up in groups to go to Iceland, Florence and Venice, Barcelona and Paris. The players had to book the hotels and trains by themselves—a rare experience for them, because so much of what they do is organized by others.

"This was really our first time out in the world by ourselves," Wangler said. "We're all like 20 or 21. This is what other students do all the time, but it's a big thing for us."

After the 2017 trip to Rome, Hewlett recalled, "Thirty or so guys spent more than a month traveling over there. Four or five guys went this way, a few went that way, and we'd meet up at various points. It was pretty unstructured. Some of us studied European

Union politics and economics in Brussels for one credit. We got a lot of stories out of that."

When Hewlett and a few teammates visited Brussels a Michigan alum recognized backup quarterback Alex Malzone, struck up a conversation, and invited them to a wedding the next day. The players put on their suits and joined the wedding party, then went to one of Brussels's most famous restaurants, Delirium—a day they'd be talking about for years.

"Coach [Harbaugh] really emphasized this," Hewlett said. "It was 100 percent what he wanted us to do. For me, it was the best few weeks of college—and a lot of guys would tell you that."

While the trips could not be rationalized solely as a team-bonding experience—they could have accomplished that on a canoe trip down the Huron River—the trips did help the players get to know each other better, essential for any college team.

"When we first got here in 2014," Wangler recalled, "we had black guys in that corner [of Schembechler Commons, where the team eats], and white guys over here, and it was bad. Not anymore. The bonding was amazing, and I think it changed our team the rest of the year."

Of course, when the 2017 team went 8-5 a few months after the first trip the media blasted Harbaugh,

calling it another of Harbaugh's stunts, one that produced more losses and fewer wins. But the players dis-
missed the critiques because they felt the purpose of the
trip wasn't to win more games, but to give the players
a reward for their hard work and help them become
better people and teammates.

"I'd say the same thing the players did," Harbaugh
told me. "The trips are partly a team-bonding experience. These things happen organically, when you're
not even thinking about it. It's experiential learning,
and we're doing it together. It's fun for me to see them
together, just hanging out or learning something. They
like being around each other."

One night overseas Harbaugh was having dinner
with a few players, getting to know each other outside
of football. After dessert Harbaugh thanked them.

"This has been just great," he said, feeling expan-
sive. "And the best part is, no one's been checking their
phones! That really impresses me."

"Uh, Coach," one replied, "we can't get Wi-Fi service here."

"Well, maybe that's the best reason to go overseas!"

There's bonding, and there are the beaches of Normandy, where Harbaugh's interest in history—thanks
to Mrs. Hiller—compelled him to schedule a visit.

"The whole trip was special," he told me. "I took this class in college, and I was enthralled with D-Day then, but to see it, to walk the beach—it's more than you can picture from the movies. Those guys fought on one of the greatest days in history, a day that changed the world so dramatically. The *magnitude* of that day!"

The players roamed the beaches then climbed to the platform, where they looked out on the beaches below, and the cemetery with the perfect rows of white crosses. It hit them that the men who made these sacrifices were no older than they were.

"I think that got to them," Harbaugh said. "It got to *me*."

When they played the national anthem and taps, Harbaugh recalled, "No one moved a muscle. No one sneezed or coughed. It was as still and solemn a moment as I've ever experienced."

These stories and more were the subjects of the players' Friday night gatherings at the Graduate Hotel. Furbush's favorite occurred back in Paris, where he, Jared Wangler, and a few others followed Pulitzer Prize–winning photographer David Turnley, who covers the team each fall, to a refugee camp under an overpass in the middle of Paris, filled with people from Syria, Iraq, and Afghanistan.

"I've taken David's photography class at Michigan,"

Furbush said. "He talks about how he can befriend a Muslim in seconds, and I saw it firsthand. He goes up to them, calls them 'Habibie,' and they trust him immediately. He handed them blankets and portable showers, and they were really grateful."

When the refugees invited them in Furbush followed Turnley's advice and sat down in whatever chair they offered, "like you're comfortable so they know you're appreciative of what they've given you. When they offer you this scalding tea in a Styrofoam cup that starts melting in your hand, you drink it like it's the best thing you've ever had. We couldn't understand their language, they couldn't understand ours, but you could tell we really made a connection with them.

"My biggest takeaway was seeing people my age and comparing their lives to mine. You work hard and you beat the odds to go to Michigan's engineering school and play on the football team, so you think you did it all yourself. But you see this, and you realize all you've been given, and how lucky you've been.

"Since I want to be a Marine pilot the odds of meeting more people like that are very good. That experience confirmed my decision to pursue that life for a career."

Mark Twain said it best: "Travel is fatal to prejudice, bigotry, and narrow-mindedness." Thanks to these trips the Michigan football players learned that in college—whether or not the media cared.

The next day they would put on their uniforms, sprint from the tunnel as a team—a team that had been to Normandy together—and become football players again.

Chapter 10
Stopping a Losing Streak

Western Michigan, September 8, 2018

In the off-season Harbaugh had learned about Brenda Tracy, her rape in 1998 by four men, three of them Oregon State football players, and her crusade to educate people about sexual assault. He invited her to speak to the team at the start of fall camp, and he was so impressed he brought her back for the team's home opener as the team's honorary captain.

When PA announcer Carl Grapentine introduced Brenda Tracy before the Western Michigan game, she walked to mid-field to a standing ovation.

Tracy tweeted:

I remember when tens of thousands of fans cheered for the men who raped me. Every Saturday they cheered. As Honorary Captain Sept 8, 2018 tens of thousands of fans cheered for me. I pray more survivors can experience that gift of love. Thank you @UMichFootball #SetTheExpectation @brendatracy24

Inviting Tracy to Ann Arbor wasn't intended to serve as a counter to the endless news coming out of Columbus about former assistant coach Zach Smith, his wife, and Urban Meyer's role in the controversy—but some Michigan fans took it that way.

Michigan's internet critics had focused on a statistic that Wolverine fans found more annoying every week it was extended: "It's been 364 days since a Michigan receiver caught a touchdown pass—almost a full calendar year. Kekoa Crawford and Grant Perry had one apiece, from Wilton Speight, against Cincinnati on Sept. 9, 2017."

On Michigan's first possession Patterson hit tight end Zach Gentry for a first down, but the Wolverines were penalized for a false start. Patterson handed off to Higdon twice for a total of four yards, then threw an incomplete pass. That series sparked a low roar of booing in the Big House—earlier in the season than expected, but also the product of eleven years of frustration. When the Broncos hit their first play for 25 yards, the booing returned.

Karan Higdon extinguished the brushfires of boos with a series of sharp cuts at full speed, dashing 43 yards to Western's 17-yard line. Two plays later Patterson hit wide open tight end Sean McKeon, who raced up the right sideline for a touchdown, Michigan's first lead of the season, and Patterson's first touchdown pass for his new team. But because McKeon is not a wide receiver, the stat still ran on Twitter.

On Michigan's next possession the offensive line created a huge hole for Higdon, who then cut left along the sidelines to go 67 yards virtually untouched.

14–0, with 4:11 left in the quarter. Not a boo could be heard.

Nick Bunkley tweeted that the second touchdown "thankfully quieted the cranky retirees behind me in section 40 who found it unacceptable that WMU was getting receivers 'wide open' for 1-2-yard gains."

On Western's next possession Devin Bush Jr. charged at the Broncos' quarterback, forcing him to throw off his back foot and underthrow his target. Outside linebacker Noah Furbush stepped up, caught it, and ran seven yards before hitting the turf.

"Devin was putting good pressure on the quarterback, like you'd expect, forcing him to make mistakes," Furbush said. "I was just doing what I was supposed to do."

Bush returned the praise, and then some. "Furbush, that's a super, super smart guy. Also an interesting guy. But the best thing for us is, he's a guy who knows his role and plays it and doesn't complain. You need guys like that."

After Higdon suffered a minor knee injury Chris Evans replaced him to score twice for a 28–0 lead. The rout was on.

Outside of the Wolverines' seven penalties for 55 yards there wasn't much for Michigan fans to complain about. Even the annoying stat was finally expunged when Patterson launched a rainbow to Nico Collins, who was so far ahead of his defender he could afford to turn around and wait for the ball to come to him for Michigan's fifth touchdown of the half: 35–0.

After Patterson threw another touchdown pass for a 42–0 third quarter lead he left the game with a gorgeous stat line: 12 completions on 17 attempts for 125 yards, three touchdowns, no interceptions, and a sparkling quarterback rating of 190.6—worthy of all the hype. When Michigan went ahead 49–0 with almost 9 minutes left in the game, the fans were satisfied, and headed for the exits.

True, they were playing the Broncos, not the Buckeyes, but the Wolverines did just about everything they had hoped to do. After Michigan had lost four straight games by 14 points or few, a good, old-school blowout was just what the doctor ordered.

"Man, that felt great to get the sour taste out of our mouth, and really come together," Higdon told me. "We practice hard all week, and the biggest thing we look forward to is to let our hard work show and take out our anger on those guys."

Did they hear the boos in the first quarter?

"Of course we did. You can't hide down there or cover your ears! But we don't care about that. At the end of the day, coaches coach, players play, and fans are gonna be fans. We don't lose any sleep over that."

Nor would they lose sleep over the rankings—a topic Michigan's coaches openly discussed with the players in 2017 but deemed off-limits in 2018.

"Rankings we discuss not at all," Higdon said. "Not a word. And we don't discuss anything else people are saying about us, either. Doesn't matter who's saying it. This year we don't give a damn about any of that. We just gotta play, we just gotta win, and that's what we're focused on now."

It was probably for the best since the Wolverines' 49–3 shellacking would bump them up only two spots to #19 in the media poll, while the coaches' poll kept them at #22. The nation's winningest program now lived on the fringes of the national radar.

Most of the players were not old enough to buy a beer but they were already learning how to define themselves, instead of letting millions of adults do it for them. They also knew not to take any win for granted, which they learned from their coaches.

"The Harbaughs celebrate all victories!" Jack told me. "We know how hard it is to win, and how easy it is to lose."

That's why after every win, no matter how small or ugly, the Harbaughs host a party at their home where not a discouraging word can be heard, at least for a few hours. In case anyone had forgotten that lesson the Michigan State Spartans provided a timely reminder when they blew a 13–3 third quarter lead at Arizona State, in 100-degree heat, and lost 16–13.

More shocking was Eastern Michigan. In 2017 the Eagles broke their 38-game losing streak to Big Ten teams, going back more than a century, by beating lowly Rutgers. On this day they played Purdue, which had finished third in the Big Ten West Division the previous year, with EMU freshman Chad Ryland kicking the game-winning field goal in the final seconds— all of which goes to show that the football is pointy, and no one knows which way it's going to bounce.

Noah Furbush celebrated the win and his interception by taking his parents back to his rented house on State Street, right across from the Glick practice field. There Furbush and family settled in on the wooden front porch, where he wolfed down "some great chocolate milk and mac-n-cheese and got some shout-outs from fans walking past."

Celebrate all victories.

Chapter 11
The Rocket Scientist
Noah Furbush

B ecause most of us see only 60 of the players' 8,760 hours each year, we miss a lot of good stories.

Noah Furbush had never given much thought to professional football before he arrived in Ann Arbor, and he would give it even less when he left. His mom, Martha, had enrolled at Miami University in Oxford, Ohio, graduated from Ohio State, then became a nurse in the Air Force. His father, Bernard, grew up in Kenton, Ohio, where he played linebacker in high school. After they got married they lived at Andrews Air Force Base, where Martha served as Captain Furbush. They returned to Mount Victory, Ohio, and raised two sons, a daughter, and then Noah.

"They did a really good job fostering creativity in all their kids," Noah told me, "by finding out what we wanted to do and helping us get there. They encouraged me to anything I wanted to do."

For their youngest son, that meant flying.

"I really don't know what it was that triggered my interest, but ever since I was a kid I loved airplanes. I drew them in class and sitting in the pews of the First United Methodist Church on the back of the sign-up sheet during the sermon."

Like most Ohio boys, Furbush loved football. But right before his senior year he broke his left wrist and played with one hand in a big club cast the entire season, then hurt his left shoulder badly enough to require surgery on that, too. He was still good enough to be named Ohio's Division IV defensive player of the year, attracting the attention of Ohio State but receiving no scholarship offer, leaving Furbush to pick among full-scholarship offers at Northwestern, Purdue, and Michigan.

Furbush began his freshman year, 2014, in Michigan's catch-all College of Literature, Science, and the Arts, where he took chemistry, calculus, and physics. Things weren't any easier on the practice field, where Furbush spent most of his time rehabilitating from his two offseason surgeries. Without getting into a game Furbush had to scratch his football itch with "hundreds of miles of sled pulls."

But that wasn't the hardest part.

"That year it just seemed like everyone was out to get us," he recalled. "The AD, the fans, the protests, the attendance streak. Just a lot of negativity."

Do the players feel that?

"Absolutely. I'm not sure people realize that. But because I was so far down the depth chart, I felt more like an observer. It was interesting to start off with that as my first college football experience. How low can you go? How bad it can get?"

Despite the inauspicious beginning, Furbush never doubted his decision.

"I knew right away I picked the right football program because of the bounty of resources at this university—second to none, a unique combination. Here we're competing to be the best on the gridiron, a top 25 program, trying to win a Big Ten title, a national title, every year, top tier. Then we're the number one public university in the world, with one of the top engineering schools in the world. If your work in football or school is lacking, you can focus on the other."

By that measure the end of the 2014 season marked a good time for Furbush to focus on his studies. But when interim athletic director Jim Hackett announced Jim Harbaugh would be Michigan's next football coach, Furbush and his teammates were excited for the future.

"Personally, I just wanted to learn what made him tick, and how he gets things done," Furbush said. "Well, I found out the hard way: he does it through a lot of hard work, like our four-hour practices that first spring. Man, that was a reality shock. Is this even possible?"

Furbush recalled the lowest moments during Harbaugh's first fall camp. "We were pounding away day after day. We're staying in South Quad, with 90-degree heat and no AC. I could barely walk when I got out of bed in the morning. It was tough as possible, by design. I started to question, 'Is this really what I want to do?' But day by day, we built that 'football callous' coach was always talking about. And you learn something essential: You don't know you can do something until you actually do it."

Furbush survived, and transferred to the College of Engineering, where he majored in aerospace engineering. On the Monday before the 2015 Maryland game Harbaugh set up a race to determine who would fill the two open spots on the kickoff team. Tyree Kinnel and Furbush won the final positions, giving Furbush's confidence a big boost. He started getting more time on special teams, playing regularly on all four units by the end of the season. The need to be on "full alert" the entire game appealed to him.

"When you play on special teams, you're always on edge to see what the offense and defense are doing every third down. A big moment happens in the game, and you're ready to go."

For the 2015 Ohio State game the coaches named Furbush the special teams captain. "That really meant a lot to me—here," he said, patting his heart.

The next season, 2016, Furbush carved out a niche on defense once he figured out his strengths. The position of outside linebacker requires a jack-of-all-trades, putting Furbush on pass coverage in the middle of the field one play then on the line to blitz the quarterback the next. He liked the variety, and the thinking it required.

"The stigma that football players are dumb brutes banging their heads against the wall—it's just not so," he said. "Everything is very calculated. Each play has a lot of moving parts and pieces all working together to produce the finished product.

"The way [defensive coordinator Don] Brown sets it up, on a given play you've usually got one or two guys you're looking at. If they do this or that, you react. In the simplest terms, if you see a tackle downblocking, that's a run play, and you respond accordingly. A lot of what we do is predicated on what their offense is doing, but at the same time we want to be the aggressors, because we want them to react to what we're doing. One of coach Brown's favorite philosophies is from Sun-Tzu: be the aggressor and force your opponent to react.

"He's got some passion, man! He brings it every day—and some days you really need that. It's week nine, you're tired, you're doing a lot of the same things every day, you're getting burnt out, and you're grinding to keep up with your homework. So if your coach is not into it, it's going to be tough.

"Another thing I've learned from coach Brown: he consistently critiques the performance, not the performer. He'll tell you when you screwed up your assignment, but not call you an idiot. At the end of the day you know he loves you, and we're all on the same team."

Furbush got more plays at outside linebacker in 2017, capped by an interception against South Carolina in the Outback Bowl. For 2018, his fifth and final year, he's working on his master's in space systems engineering.

"I kind of approach it all the same—grad school and starting on defense. The person I'm always competing against is the person we all compete against every day: the person inside of us, trying to get better."

The disparity between Furbush's two worlds was something he encountered daily. Since almost all engineering classes are on North Campus, a 30-minute bus ride from central campus, Furbush made the trek in 15 minutes in his 2009 Honda Civic.

"It's a good car, but I can't say too many nice things about it because I worked at Ford this summer."

Because his classes didn't start until 11:30 each day—much later than his 8:30 undergraduate classes—all the parking spaces had usually been taken by then.

"So you find someone walking in the parking lot with their backpack, and you slowly follow them with your car, which results in a lot of awkward eye contact. It's the strangest, creepiest thing.

"Last week I followed these two guys for five minutes, and they kept looking back at me. I ended up parking right next to their car. When I got out they saw my number 59 on just about everything I own—my sweat suit, my shirt, my backpack—and they said good luck. But most engineering students don't know I play on the football team. When I'm in the Climate and Space Research building, I'm in my own little bubble with the other space nerds. It's a pretty small group.

"On the other hand it's a lot like the football team. When I first got here, both were very humbling experiences. No matter how great you thought you were in high school, you get here and discover pretty fast that there are a lot of people here who can do what you can do. So you have to keep the wheel turning and get better the next day."

Furbush was one of ten students to join the Bio-Astronautics and Life Support Systems team (BLISS), a 20-person consortium of UM doctors, engineering professors, and a few students, all trying to figure out how to get a mobile space station to support four astronauts for 1,100 days—the time it takes to send the habitat to Mars, stay there for 500 days, and come back. BLISS is one of the few university groups to receive funding from NASA's Mars Exploration Systems and Habitation Innovation Challenge.

Yes, this really is rocket science. Furbush was not aiming for the NFL but the Marines, where he hoped to become a pilot, and possibly an astronaut.

"It's a lot tougher getting into the military than people think," he said. "To be a Marine pilot, they want the best of the best."

To help his chances Furbush applied to get his pilot's license the summer before his junior season, 2016. Because it's not offered on campus he approached Harbaugh to see if Michigan would pay for it.

"How much does it cost?" Harbaugh asked.

"Ten thousand dollars," Furbush said.

"Well, that's not cheap," Harbaugh told me later.

"And in any case, I figured there was no way compliance would approve it, with all the NCAA rules, but I promised Noah I'd ask. Well, they looked into it and called back and said they could pay for it."

Furbush successfully completed the course on Tuesday, November 22, 2016, four days before the Ohio State game that would go into double overtime. Furbush earned four credits and his pilot's license. When he asked Harbaugh if he wanted to go up with him, his coach didn't give it much thought.

"No," Harbaugh said.

"Why not?" Furbush asked.

"Well, I keep hearing Don Brown yelling, 'FURBUSH! You're lined up on the wrong side again!' You go the wrong way on a practice field, you live. You go the wrong way in the air, maybe not! So, I'm good."

Harbaugh later recalled, "Noah went up by himself."

Furbush knew his previous injuries might be a sticking point with the Marine pilot program—and for that matter, future injuries, too.

"It's a high-velocity, high-contact sport," he said. "But you can't think about that when you're playing. If you want to play it safe, you're not going to be flying around doing what you're supposed to do, and I suspect you're more likely to get hurt, not less."

A few weeks before his final season he visited the Military Entrance Processing Station (MEPS) in Troy, Michigan, where they ran preliminary medical tests for his Marine tryout, scheduled a few weeks after Michigan's 2019 bowl game.

"I'm an officer candidate, and I hope I look like an attractive candidate, with my schoolwork, an athletic background, and a pilot's license. Things are looking good right now, but anything could happen. I hope I'll know if I can be a Marine pilot before I graduate with my master's in space systems engineering in May [of 2019].

"I really have come to appreciate how lucky I am to know what I want to do and feel strongly and passionately about it. Even here, that's rare."

Chapter 12
Student-Athletes
Academics

S tudent-athlete. Is it an oxymoron?

Noah Furbush is clearly exceptional, but are players who take school as seriously as football the exception, or the rule?

The answer depends entirely on where you look.

It's no secret that coaches' overwhelming desire to win tempts many to cut corners. Of all the ways to cheat the easiest might be academics, where plagiarized papers, overeager tutors, and even cooperative professors can make the already subjective nature of grading vulnerable to manipulation.

Consider the University of North Carolina, one of the nation's premier public universities. In 2010, they discovered their school had been handing out As to students taking some 200 bogus classes, which didn't even meet. They had a high percentage of athletes enrolled, and had been doing so for 18 years—thus scuttling the "Carolina Way" of combining elite academics and athletics.

At this point many credible universities, caught running out of bounds, would admit the mistake, rescind the unearned grades and whatever went with them—including UNC's 2005 and 2009 national basketball titles. But UNC decided those banners were too valuable, so instead told NCAA investigators that because the fraudulent classes were available to all students, not just athletes, they were not NCAA violations. We may be a sham school, but we're a sham for all.

In 2017, the NCAA bought the argument.

Yahoo columnist Dan Wetzel wrote, "To defend the basketball team, the university had to claim it wasn't really a university." He added that not only was North Carolina not ashamed of academic fraud, "it's practically celebrating it," and then delivered the punch line: "Sure, they took a shotgun to their academic credibility, but, hey, those championship banners get to stay. The truth is, alums probably care more about hoops anyway."

Wetzel may well be right, but it must be said my mother, a proud UNC graduate, is furious.

UNC could fool the NCAA but not the Southern Association of Colleges and Schools Commissions (SACSC).

After debating dropping UNC's accreditation—which would end all federal funding, and all but close the school—it settled on the lesser sentence of probation for non-compliance with the principle "of academic integrity."

Consider that sentence for a moment. What other principle can any educational institution stand on other than academic integrity?

By the NCAA's own contorted logic, any team supplying steroids to their players should be exonerated if the illegal drugs were made available to the entire student body. Likewise, former Louisville basketball coach Rick Pitino's great sin was not hiring prostitutes for recruits and players but failing to make them available for the rest of the undergraduates. But then, logical reasoning was never the NCAA's strong suit.

To UNC's credit, they enacted serious reforms designed to ensure this never happens again—exactly as you'd expect from a first-rate university. But this episode shows parents of college athletes would be wiser to put their faith in their children's coaches than in the organization that oversees them.

When Jack Harbaugh became an assistant coach for Stanford in 1980, he saw the academic equation from the other side.

"The [football] staff was all over the board with regard to academics, and not always in a good place," he told me. "They were constantly *fighting* the issue. 'USC is getting these guys in with lower grades! We've got to drop our standards to beat those guys!' And there's your conflict. Then admissions started fighting back, and now you've got a bigger problem.

"When Jim went there [in late 2006] he was the first coach I think they've had who saw Stanford's academics not as a liability, but as an *asset*! Jim just said, 'This is who we are, and it's good! We're going to work *with* admissions. We're just going to have to cast a wider net and look at more recruits to find the ones who will fit in here—guys who can handle the football *and* the coursework.'

"Instead of trying to water it down or complain about it, Jim embraced it. The academics at Stanford set you apart, the thing that makes you different—that makes you better! And they've done it that way since."

By May 2007, six months into Harbaugh's new post as Stanford's head coach, he had learned enough about his new school to be impressed by his players, five of whom were engineering majors, and 20 more enrolled in Science, Technology and Engineering. When Glenn

Dickey interviewed him for the *San Francisco Examiner*, Harbaugh provided a seemingly innocuous off-the-cuff observation.

"College football needs Stanford," he said. "We're looking not for student-athletes, but scholar-athletes. No other school can carry this banner. The Ivy League schools don't have enough weight. Other schools which have good academic reputations have ways to get borderline athletes in and keep them in."

Dickey followed up by asking Harbaugh, who had earned Academic All-Big Ten honors at Michigan, about his alma mater.

"Michigan is a good school, and I got a good education there," Harbaugh said. "But the athletic department has ways to get borderline guys in and, when they're in, they steer them to courses in sports communications. They're adulated when they're playing, but when they get out, the people who adulated them won't hire them."

Former *Ann Arbor News* sports columnist Jim Carty wrote, "With fewer than 100 words, Harbaugh made himself a major topic of conversation on Web sites devoted to Michigan's sports programs and drew the attention and concern of school officials."

When Carty called Harbaugh's office, Harbaugh

quickly returned the call. No one could accuse him of ducking.

"Harbaugh not only stood by his comments," Carty wrote, "he expanded on them. When asked to defend his claim that Michigan pushes athletes into easy majors, he paused for a second, and then dropped a bombshell.

"'I would use myself as an example,' Harbaugh said. 'I came in there, wanted to be a history major, and I was told early on in my freshman year that I shouldn't be. That it takes too much time. Too much reading. That I shouldn't be a history major and play football.'

"'As great as the institution is at Michigan,' Harbaugh said, 'I don't think it should cut corners that dramatically for football and basketball players. I love the university. I got a tremendous education there. I think it should hold itself to a higher standard.'"

Eight years later, in 2015, Carty told me, "The only thing I can add is that there was a general attitude of 'Seriously? Am I saying anything that controversial here? Who are we kidding? Am I saying anything crazy?' No, he wasn't."

Because the comments came from Harbaugh, the very embodiment of the Michigan Man ideal, and also because he made them in May, perhaps the quietest month of the college sports media cycle, his quotes blazed on sports talk radio stations, blogs, newspapers, and magazines for weeks.

Harbaugh's comments also generated an indirect response from Lloyd Carr, who called them "elitist," "arrogant," and "self-serving." Mike Hart, who would become Michigan's all-time leading rusher the following season, said, "That's a guy I have no respect for. You graduate from the University of Michigan, and you're going to talk about your school like that, a great university like we have? . . . He's not a Michigan Man. I wish he'd never played here."

But when a Michigan Man sees another school doing something better than Michigan does, what, exactly, is a Michigan Man supposed to say? "That's okay. They're better. We could never catch up"? No, he wonders— perhaps aloud—"Why can't Michigan do that, and do it better than they do?" If it's elitist and arrogant for a Michigan Man to believe his school should aspire to be the best both academically and athletically, then every Michigan alum would qualify.

Harbaugh quickly recognized he had started a media storm, but he didn't back down. "My motivation was positive," he told the national media. "I see how it's done now at Stanford, and I see no reason to believe it can't be the same there. I have a great love for Michigan and what it's done for me. Bo Schembechler was like a second father. Michigan is a great school and always has been, and I don't see why they can't hold themselves to a higher standard."

For all the blowback Harbaugh suffered for his comments, much of it from the very people charged with keeping the Michigan Man ethos alive, no one made a dent in Harbaugh's argument. The exchange inspired *The Ann Arbor News* to launch a seven-month-long investigation into the Michigan athletic department's academic practices. The four-day series, which came out in March 2008, had its strengths and weaknesses. While it didn't expose fraud, plagiarism, grade-changing, and other practices so often found at other schools, it did reveal some surprising facts.

First, almost 80 percent of the scholarship players on the 2004 team—the most recent available with four years of data—were pursuing a bachelor of general studies degree program. Offered through the university's main college of Literature, Science, and the Arts, the BGS is similar to conventional majors, but doesn't require a concentration in any one discipline, or a foreign language. And second, 48 football players had taken at least two independent study classes, with nine taking three or more.

What should Michigan do about this?

Michigan athletic's Director of Academic Services, Steve Connelly, was raised by a single mom who qualified for welfare—but declined it. Based on Connelly's high grades and scores, Michigan offered him full financial aid in 1993, and he eagerly accepted. He has worked in the athletic department since graduating from Michigan in 1997, and rose to director of football academic services in 2010, two years after the *News* report came out. He now leads a staff of six full-time counselors and learning specialists for all athletes, and five interns.

When I asked him in 2019 about the *Ann Arbor News* report, Connelly assessed the strengths and weaknesses with admirable objectivity.

"Let me be clear from the outset," he said, "I have no problem with students taking any of our majors, including the BGS. We don't have any phony diplomas here."

Michigan's BGS alumni include Steve Nissen, the chair of the Cleveland Clinic's Cardiology Department; Rick Snyder, the recently retired governor of the state, who also served as Gateway Computer's CEO; Jim Hackett, the former Steelcase furniture CEO and UM interim athletic director, now the CEO of Ford Motor

Company; and current athletic director Warde Manuel, who went on to earn an MBA at Michigan. (Both Hackett and Manuel played football for Schembechler.) In short, the BGS major is not an escape hatch to avoid real study.

"But," Connelly added, "when you see 80 percent of any team in one program, it's worth looking into. Are the counselors doing some steering? *The Ann Arbor News* story suggested the counselors too often told the players to take this or that class, and major in this and not that."

That was exactly what Harbaugh had said: he had been discouraged from majoring in history, a genuine passion of Harbaugh's then and now.

"I can't speak to what they did when Harbaugh was a student here," Connelly said, "but my staff will never do that. That's a hard-and-fast policy now."

Soon after Connelly took over the division in 2010 they started tracking the players' majors, with good results.

"Since 2011," he told me, "the football team has never had fewer than 25 different majors, minors, and degree programs among the 60–70 upper-class students who've declared a major—a very healthy spread. In the fall of 2018, the football upperclassmen were pursuing 31 different degree programs."

On the 2018 team, only 6 were in the BGS program. Connelly then addressed the issue of independent studies.

"We now strongly recommend, before a player can take an independent study with a professor, the player has to have already taken another course with that same professor at least once. So, by and large, the ones who enroll in an independent study now tend to be seniors who have some electives left. Since we put that policy in place, we've never had more than ten players [out of 140], and typically significantly fewer than that, enrolled in independent studies at any one time. Independent studies are not safeguards for staying eligible."

These positive changes were prompted by *The Ann Arbor News* article, which was sparked by Harbaugh's comments back in 2007. You could therefore argue that, years before Harbaugh returned to Michigan's campus, he had already brought about many of the improvements he had suggested—though he was not likely to get credit.

Harbaugh's sincerity would be tested when Jim Hackett hired him to become the school's twentieth head football coach on December 30, 2014. At Harbaugh's opening press conference he demonstrated what the preceding few years had taught him about diplomacy when he invited Lloyd Carr to attend the event, and then went out of his way to congratulate and thank Carr from the podium.

"Jim is gracious like that in ways that people don't understand," John Harbaugh told me.

After a reporter asked Jim about the Stanford football program's academic standing, he achieved closure on his previous comments by simply replying, "I've learned never to compare great with great."

It's worth noting that, as congenial as Harbaugh's comments were that day, he was not taking anything back, either. He still believed in the way he approached academics at Stanford, and he was privately determined to achieve that and more at his alma mater.

"Since I've been in academics, Harbaugh is my fourth head football coach," Connelly said. "I've been fortunate that all four were serious about academics, and none of them even hinted about cheating. But we've never had a head coach who'd been an Academic All-Big Ten athlete here, either, who knows what it takes, and no one who took academics to the level Jim has. From the start, he wasn't just *interested* in his guys doing well academically. He was *adamant* about it."

On January 2, 2015, just three days after Harbaugh accepted the job, he met with Connelly. Harbaugh said that every new coach introduces a team-building exercise so the players get to know him, so they were going to do a team study table in the athletic department's Academic Center, a 38,000-square foot complex completed in 2006 for $12 million, with every player and every coach attending, for two weeks.

Connelly readily agreed. Two weeks became six weeks, with Harbaugh there every single night, doing his own work alongside the players.

"He wanted to send a very clear message that he would be prioritizing academics, and he meant it," Connelly said. "Once you set that up, you separate the players who are sincere about studying from those who aren't. Some guys 'opted themselves out' of the program and transferred."

Such turnover can put a temporary dent into a team's Academic Progress Report (APR) score, a formula the NCAA uses to reward and punish teams for their performance in the classroom. The APR gives one point for each scholarship athlete who stays in school and another for being academically eligible. That number is then divided by the points possible, then multiplied by a thousand to produce sums that typically fall between 900 and 1000. (The walk-ons, usually among the team's best students, are not included in this number.)

But in the long run, weeding out indifferent students and attracting the committed ones paid off.

"I think the word's gotten out to the recruits," Connelly said. "If you're not going to take academics seriously, you'll be better off going somewhere else."

But merely focusing on those who want to be Wolverines, and are willing to work in the classroom, isn't enough to guarantee success. Connelly recalled Harbaugh backing up his commitment from the first team meeting, when he made it clear that academics were going to be a top priority.

"Our rules are simple here," Harbaugh told me. "If a practice or a meeting conflicts with a class, we tell them to go to the class. They can't make up the practice, but they can make up the meeting.

"You think about a guy like Noah Furbush, just how hard it must be to be an engineer and play football here. They have labs, and you usually can't reschedule those. So we let them go to the lab—and we have 16 to 20 engineering students on the team, depending on how you count it. One thing we discovered, when an engineering student misses a practice, they don't miss much. They're smart, they pick it up fast, and they work hard to catch up. They're fine."

But the policy also applies to freshmen taking their first college classes over the summer, just after they graduated from high school and before the all-important "fall camp" begins in late July. Harbaugh meets beforehand with football's director of academic services, Claiborne Green, who reports to Connelly, to see how his guys are doing. If anyone is in danger of flunking a class he gives them time off practice to study. That might sound like a break, but to the players it's a punishment. They don't want to miss fall camp, when depth charts are established, so the policy also serves as a motivator: if you fall behind in the classroom, you won't see the practice field.

Connelly knows he and his staff are in the middle of a bigger battle. They work with students who often don't have the advantages many Michigan students enjoy: parents who make more than $250,000 a year and can send them to the best schools, some of which can cost $75,000, which can help them achieve grades and test scores to get into almost any university in America.

"The easiest way to get rich in America is to be born with it," Connelly said. "Sixty percent of wealth is inherited."

Likewise, the team's racial makeup is very different from the student body's. Among the university's 15,252 undergraduate males, only 531, or 3.4 percent, are African American. Eleven percent of those, or 57 total, are on the football team, where they comprise 42 percent of the squad. So an African American man can start his

day in the weight room, where almost half his teammates are African Americans, then walk to class where
he might see two African American males in a 100-seat
lecture hall.

It can be a jarring experience, especially if they've
come from schools with very limited resources, over-
whelmed teachers, and little support, where AP courses,
long term papers, and sometimes even regular homework
assignments are rare.

If the football recruits get a wake-up call in their
first Michigan practice going against dozens of fellow all-staters, it pales in comparison to the shock of
competing with the cream of the academic crop in the
classroom—top students who can study all weekend
and pull all-nighters if they need to.

When I asked former Michigan quarterback Devin
Gardner, who took his classes very seriously, what he
would be if he wasn't a football player, he thought about
it, then said, "An 'A' student."

"This academic center wouldn't exist if we expected
every student to come in with the same preparation as
everyone else," Connelly said. "Oftentimes their iden-
tities are so tied into their sport that they need to build
their confidence in the classroom. It's not about sliding
by with a 2.5, it's about embracing the challenge, and
excelling. And that's Jim's emphasis. When it all works

right, they start caring more and more about their own academic success."

So how can these students catch up and compete? In his 20 years working with athletes Connelly has learned the importance of giving the students the resources they need, while expecting a sincere effort on their part. That means providing support, not handouts—an approach that is not only easier to defend but produces better results. Connelly has found that when they increase the structure and accountability of the players' academic program, they are more likely to take ownership of their academic careers.

"And that's the key," he said. *"It has to be yours! If a student is making his own choices and taking responsibility, he'll do better work. Our job is not to tell them what they can or can't do but have a backup plan if their dream of engineering or business school doesn't work out. We want them to get out of this what they put into it.*

"We do our part, but if the coaches don't bring in the right men, it doesn't matter what we do. We can't save them. And Jim backs that up: 'If you miss your appointment with Steve, you lose access to Steve.' The resources here are pretty incredible, but they're a privilege, and if you take them for granted, you'll lose them.

"Jim is as sincere a human being as I've ever met.

That's who he is. He has not got any façade. You're going to know where you stand with him, like it or not, and I can say definitively I've never had a personal interaction with him or with his players or my staff where he has not prioritized academics. At this level, that's rare."

Put it all together, and they get results. After the football team finished the 2008–09 academic year with a school-low Academic Progress Report of 897, due partly to a spate of transfers after Rich Rodriguez started in 2008, the Wolverines teetered on the verge of NCAA academic sanctions if they fell under 925 again. They easily cleared that in the 2009–10 year with a 946, then—with Connelly now in charge—set a school record the next year, 2010–11, with a 984, just 16 points off a perfect 1,000, and followed it up with APR scores of 981 in 2011–12, 985 in 2012–13, and a flawless 1,000 in 2013–14, which would have been bumped to a 1,006 after points from two delayed graduations landed in Michigan's account, but the NCAA does not recognize any score higher than 1,000.

The total still inspired Connelly to coin a phrase that makes Michigan's rivals cringe: "There's good, there's great, there's perfect—and then there's Michigan."

Michigan's football program maintained these high standards the past three years with single-year APR scores of 985, 997, and 974 in 2016–17. Their multiyear APR scores, which combine the four previous academic years and is the figure the NCAA uses to rank programs, have come in at 990 in 2011–15, and 993 in 2012–16, finishing third nationally, two points behind Air Force and Northwestern at 995.

In 2013–17, the most recent data, Michigan football's APR slipped a little, thanks largely to the transfers who left when Harbaugh arrived in 2015, but still finished at 990—sixth place out of the 128 BCS football teams, behind only top-ranked Northwestern at 997, Air Force and Vanderbilt at 993, and Duke and Navy at 992.

Once again, Michigan beat Stanford, which finished tied for 12th, with a very respectable 985.

Harbaugh's comments comparing Stanford and Michigan, which had caused him so much trouble a decade earlier, had since proved prescient. The Wolverines could do better academically, and they were— emphatically.

Under Harbaugh, Connelly asserts, Michigan has had only a few students in eight years who completed their eligibility (who didn't transfer or jump to the NFL) and failed to graduate. Because they now go to school year-round, even those who leave early to the NFL usually graduate within a year.

"Everyone says to me, 'Your favorite day of the year must be graduation,'" Connelly said. "No, that's boring. I'm proud, but they *should* graduate. For me the best days are when you see the light go on, and they get it. They understand what you're telling them, and they see the value of studying, the importance of an education, *for themselves*. And they see they can do it.

"I know I'm biased, but I'm convinced we see as much or more growth from our students here in athletics as any other group on campus. We get a student who struggled to read or write or study at this level, and they leave competing with the guy who went to the expensive boarding school. In their four years they grow more than anyone else on campus, and that usually continues after they leave. They have a different trajectory, and will do more to make the world a better place because of where they're from and what they've seen. Now they have the power to make a difference."

While it's undeniably true that most of Michigan's players get scholarships and a high level of academic support because of their athletic prowess, and Michigan has a self-interest in keeping them eligible, it's also true that both sides take academics far more seriously than they need to if the goal were simply to play football that weekend.

"I'm proud of our students, and what they bring to

campus," Connelly said. "Diversity is more than just race. It's geography, politics, socioeconomics, and life experiences. I believe they're a valuable asset to the institution as a whole."

For all the noble reasons to run a program this way, Harbaugh's innate competitiveness plays a role, too.

"Every year I brought him the APR scores, the first question he asked, always, before he even opened the envelope, was this: 'Are we ahead of Stanford?'"

And the answer, every year, has been yes.

When a staffer from an elite football program in the South joined Michigan's staff, he was stunned to hear about a starting player who failed a class and got sent home during a bowl trip. The staffer said at his previous school if a starter flunked a class, "the professor would be run off—by the faculty!"

I've heard more such stories from those who've coached and played at the top programs, usually in the South, than I can count. At such programs such stories are not the exceptions but the rule—a noted contrast to how they do it elsewhere.

On this point I can speak directly. I've taught at Miami of Ohio, Northwestern University, and the University of Michigan, for the sake of doing something I think is important at three great universities. At Michigan, where I've taught since 2006, I have flunked two starting football players, one under Rich Rodriguez and one under Brady Hoke. In both cases I informed the player, the academic advisors, and the coaches about missed classes and late assignments, and what I would do if it continued: flunk the student. In both cases, everyone appreciated the notice, but the behaviors continued, and I ended up flunking both players.

One of them got his act together, graduated on time, and soon friended me on Facebook, where we've maintained a cordial relationship. He grew up. The other guy, a five-star player with tons of promise, did not, and soon transferred to one of the schools I've heard plenty of stories about, where his career fizzled. But in both cases no one at Michigan, inside or outside athletics, ever presented a too-fancy paper, urged me to give extra credit, or otherwise pressured me to do anything other than follow the policies I'd set up. I've never heard any teachers complain about such tactics, either.

"If anyone from our office ever *does* contact you looking for favors for a failing player," Connelly said, "let me know, and they'll be gone immediately."

Of course, as any student of logic can tell you, it is impossible to prove a negative. I cannot say with absolute certainty that no one on Michigan's 2018 football team ever took forbidden money or gifts, cheated on a test, or committed other sins. (Certainly some of Michigan's basketball players took money in the 1990s, which is why some banners are in storage today.) It may be that someday someone from this team will surface who has done these things, or even a UNC-sized scandal might erupt.

But I have found zero evidence of any of those violations occurring, and I've looked pretty hard. From my research, the football players' rental homes are every bit as beat up as the other students'; their cars just as old and unreliable—when they have a car at all; and their term papers as uneven as any undergraduate's. From everything I've seen, they're genuine college students, doing their best to do it the right way.

When they fall short—by getting in a fight outside a college bar, by taping a sex encounter, or by plagiarizing a paper—they're gone, immediately. I've seen that, too.

Crucially, Connelly is backed by athletic director Warde Manuel. "Cutting corners is not the path to sustained success—here or in life," Manuel told me. "If we let it go now, then for a lifetime you're not going to learn.

"I will never put any of us, a staff member or a coach,

in a position to defend or ask for anything outside the lines academically. It's never gonna happen. That was true before I arrived, and I don't see it changing after I leave. Our athletes have to work as hard as any students here, maybe harder.

"That was certainly true for me," he added, recalling a big kid from New Orleans who went north to play for Bo Schembechler. As a sophomore Manuel started at defensive end until a neck injury sidelined his career. In addition to bone spurs they discovered spinal stenosis, a narrowing of the spine between the sixth and seventh vertebrae, a condition he was born with.

His football career was over, but the program kept him on a medical scholarship that allowed him to get his degree. He went on to earn a master's in social work and an MBA from Michigan while working for the athletic department, where he served as the director of the academic success program from 2000 to 2002. During that time he hired Connelly as a full-timer, and helped raise the $12 million for the Academic Center, leading the design and construction phases before leaving to become the athletic director at the University of Buffalo.

"No one ever talks about it, but we currently have 20 former student-athletes on medical scholarship, including mental health. The NCAA doesn't require it, the Big Ten doesn't require it, a lot of schools don't do it. But we think it's the right thing to do. That's always been true here.

"If we say we really care about the athletes, we've got to care about everything. We can't pick and choose—we care about this, but not that—or wait until the timing's most beneficial to us. When I see kids on campus 99 percent of the time I ask them how're things going at school, how's your family, and third, how's the game. And that's the order it should be."

In Harbaugh's case, his innate competitiveness has not tempted him to cut corners academically, but to do the opposite: crank up the academic standards to beat his rivals in that field, too. To his way of thinking, much like his father's and Schembechler's, once you've cheated, you've conceded that you do not believe you can compete fairly and win. And, therefore, you've lost. Following the rules does not run counter to Harbaugh's competitive instincts but is an expression of them.

"It can be a rallying cry around here," Connelly said. "Yes, we lost, but we don't cheat. If we cheat and win, we didn't win. To me integrity is not flexible. It's hard to maintain it, but it feels worse when you don't."

This is a principle with a payoff, one anyone who

has ever achieved something competing honestly over those who weren't can appreciate.

"There's nothing better," Connelly said, with a chuckle, "than beating a team you know is cheating their asses off."

Chapter 13
The Victory After the Game

Southern Methodist, September 15, 2018

While the UNC scandal is widely considered the most brazen academic fraud in NCAA history, probably no team is better known for "cheating their asses off" than Southern Methodist University's football program in the 1980s.

The Mustangs were far from the only team to pay players—at one point, five of the nine Southwest Conference (SWC) teams were under NCAA probation—but they were the most famous for it, setting up a slush fund to buy their stars just about everything. Whenever the NCAA caught SMU the Mustangs simply doubled down, daring the NCAA to impose the "death penalty." The NCAA ultimately did just that, eliminating the SMU football program for the 1987 season.

The damage was lasting. The SWC soon imploded under the weight of its own corruption, disbanding in 1996, while SMU had only one winning team in its next 20 seasons. Now playing in the nondescript American Athletic Conference, SMU was no longer competing for national titles but paychecks, the kind Michigan gives to second-tier nonconference teams willing to visit the Big House.

For Michigan's coaches and players the victory over Western felt like a refreshing hot shower to clean off the grimy residue of the Notre Dame loss, while their next game against SMU felt like . . . neither. It lacked both tension and catharsis, from the desultory pregame feel of the tailgates to the lackluster atmosphere in the stadium that day. With just 25 minutes before kickoff, Jackie Harbaugh—who still sits in the bleachers with her husband—worried about the swaths of empty seats surrounding them, which didn't fill up until just before the 3:30 kickoff.

The game's first five possessions produced four punts and an interception from Patterson before Michigan finally scored a touchdown midway through the second quarter. Michigan would build a 35–13 lead at the end of the third quarter, prompting the wave to circle the stadium. It might not have been the most energized wave, but the players certainly preferred it to booing.

Fans headed for the aisles, their holy day of obligation completed. They didn't miss much: a lot more penalties (a staggering 13 for Michigan, for 137 yards), play reviews, and TV timeouts—all of which drew plenty of commentary on Twitter and beyond—and a 45–20 final score.

Still, the players had some good news waiting for them in the film room. Shea Patterson again showed why he was worth all the fuss, with 14 for 18 passing, 3 touchdowns against one interception, and a stratospheric quarterback rating of 232.3. Michigan also had 40 points in back-to-back games, which doesn't sound like much against Western and SMU until you consider that Michigan's highest point total the entire previous season had been 36 against Cincinnati.

The pollsters weren't watching, but the Wolverines were getting better.

When Michigan's players and fans went home to watch the night games they found a lot in the "Could Be Worse" category. On this day half the Big Ten teams not only lost, but lost to such lowly foes as Troy, Temple,

Akron, Kansas, South Florida, Missouri, and BYU. The losing teams happened to include Michigan's next four opponents:

- Nebraska, which lost to Troy to go 0–2 for the first time since 1957;

- Northwestern, which somehow lost to Akron, at home;

- Maryland, which replaced the high of beating Texas with the low of losing to Temple;

- And Wisconsin, a 21-point favorite against BYU at home.

Michigan's notoriously tough schedule didn't look so tough that week—with one notable exception: Ohio State dispatched 15th ranked Texas Christian University 40–28, marking the third straight game the Buckeyes won without head coach Urban Meyer. He would return to the sidelines the next weekend.

If Michigan's future looked a little easier, the sport's did not. College football faced big problems, and they weren't shrinking that fall. During the SMU-Michigan game D. J. Sparr tweeted, "People wonder why football is down. After every 7-second play is either an injury, a penalty, or a commercial. And the head on head bashing is really becoming more and more disconcerting . . ."

Another fan named Jeremy Shettler added, "Between CTE, players kneeling, and rampant criminal activity at a handful of prominent universities, does football really even matter anymore? Is this really a sport we should be worshiping?"

A few days after the SMU game Michigan received some good news. The Wolverines had been in the hunt for five-star defensive back Daxton Hill out of Tulsa, Oklahoma. He and his parents had driven 12 hours in the spring of 2018 to see Ann Arbor for the first time and were sufficiently impressed to arrange an official visit for the SMU weekend.

Michigan's coaching staff was impressed, too, and not just with Hill's eye-popping game film. Michigan assigned assistant coach Sherrone Moore, who played at Oklahoma, to be Hill's main contact.

"The football part was really important to them," Moore told me, "but his parents were more focused on how we were going to prepare their son for life after football. We spent a lot of time with the academic support people—and that's always a good sign."

By the end of the summer Hill had eliminated Oklahoma and Oklahoma State, where his brother Justice played, leaving just Alabama and Michigan—and Moore was convinced Hill was "trending toward" Ann Arbor. The night before the SMU game the Hills' plane was delayed, creating some other complications, but "they made the best of every situation," Moore said. "Daxton is more of a shy kid, but he came out of his shell."

Because Daxton's brother Justice would be playing for Oklahoma State that day, recruiting director Matt Dudek loaned the parents an iPad to follow the Cowboys, and made sure the Cowboys' score ran on Michigan's big screen throughout the day.

"They thought that was huge," said Moore, who carefully monitored their mood throughout the weekend. A few days after Daxton's visit, he called to say he was committing to Michigan. Moore was predictably thrilled, while Daxton seemed relieved to get the decision behind him.

"He's not the kind of kid who likes the attention recruiting brings," Moore said. When Hill's classmates wanted to put him up for homecoming king, he declined because he didn't like the spotlight.

Sam Webb, who co-hosts *The Michigan Insider* on WTKA, flew to Oklahoma to meet with Hill and his parents. "This quote from the father of Michigan's newest commit, 5-star safety Daxton Hill says it all," Webb wrote on his website: "'Of course [Michigan] wants to win, but it's about developing the person, not just the player . . . not winning at all or any cost. It's about winning in every area of your life.'"

But as they say, after a player commits is when the recruiting really begins. Taking nothing for granted, a handful of Michigan coaches would call Hill every week throughout the fall. The value of a five-star player like Hill to the program was hard to overstate. He not only could help secure Michigan's defense for several years but would immediately show the nation that Michigan could beat out Alabama for a top talent. And that, in turn, could result in more elite recruits coming to Ann Arbor.

For the long-term success of the program, recruiting Daxton Hill was probably more important than beating SMU.

Chapter 14
It Takes a Village

For the 67 people who work in Schembechler Hall the Wolverines winning or losing dramatically changes the mood of the building, but doesn't affect their hours or job descriptions. Whether they work in administration, operations, recruiting, or one of the six other divisions in the building, they invariably put in about 100 hours a week during the season, which scales down to about half that in the "offseason."

The reason harkens back to the Schembechler era.

"If they're in this building," he told me, "it doesn't matter if they're stuffing envelopes or taping ankles, they must be important to our success as a team, or we wouldn't have hired them. And they better want to win as much as everyone else in this building does, or we will not be successful. And they will be gone."

Schembechler explained that it wasn't the job description of his secretary, Mary Passink, to answer the phones.

"Mary's job is to help us win Big Ten titles, and she does that by being the best executive assistant on campus."

That's why, when Michigan wins a Big Ten title, everyone in the building gets a ring—or, if they prefer, a necklace with the same face. Schembechler died in 2006, but his philosophy is alive and well in his eponymous building.

"That's what we have here," Harbaugh told me, "people who are really passionate about their work, who take it seriously, who do it well, and are fun to be around. They're problem solvers, instead of just dumping everything on my desk.

"You don't see the water cooler talk around here. We don't have time for it. This place is *humming* with people being good at their jobs."

"This job is not for clock-watchers," Harbaugh's executive assistant DeAnna McDaniel told me—and that applies to, well, all of them.

McDaniel grew up in the tiny town of Thermopolis, Wyoming, before moving to Northern California, where she started a company that helped clients with finances and administration. After she helped the Harbaughs organize their hectic lifestyle, Harbaugh hired her as his executive assistant with the 49ers, where she worked for two years until Harbaugh left at the end of 2014 to come to Michigan.

Before the 2018 season Harbaugh asked her to take the same position at Michigan, where she was struck by the difference between Michigan football and the NFL.

"The intensity of college football is much greater, and the fans are much more passionate," she told me. "They're extremely attached to the team."

Of McDaniel's dozens of duties her most consuming task is handling the various schedules that rule the denizens of Schembechler Hall. These include the monthly coaches' schedule, the weekly recruiting schedule—for coaches and recruiting staffers alike—and a daily schedule for all coaches, including Harbaugh, which is the most complicated of the batch.

During the season juggling the schedules gets more convoluted, with daily media schedules for all the coaches, workouts, meetings, and practice schedules and scripts, plus game schedules with every minute of travel, meetings, meals, treatment, and preparation accounted for. All these schedules can change many times during the day, and each time they do, McDaniel makes the changes, makes sure everyone affected is aware of the changes, and handles all the unintended consequences of each change. Screw up one element on that long list, McDaniel said, "and you get a domino effect that will create chaos throughout the building."

You get the feeling she's seen that happen, and does not intend to see it again.

In addition to the schedules McDaniel manages Harbaugh's off-the-field work, organizes his correspondence, and fields about 20 requests a day from strangers for "just ten minutes with Jim," plus invitations to birthdays, graduations, weddings, and anniversaries. After Harbaugh "responds to every letter," she said, former equipment manager Jon Falk, whom Harbaugh brought back after former athletic director Dave Brandon let him go, slips a special Michigan coin in each envelope.

When Harbaugh has a minute to spare he signs his autograph on more than 50 letters, photos, footballs, and helmets every week—almost 3,000 a year.

"Jim never, ever scribbles his autograph," McDaniel said, something he learned from Schembechler.

McDaniel also noticed Harbaugh was "different from the man I worked with at the 49ers." Perhaps that's partly because, according to the San Francisco sportswriters, Harbaugh's efforts were being undermined by the 49ers' owner and general manager—problems Harbaugh doesn't have in Ann Arbor.

While McDaniel recalled Harbaugh remained in control of himself in San Francisco, despite the bizarre situation, "when I see him working here, he appears very much at ease. And that's when his best sides come out. He's amazingly innovative, with a lot of over-the-top ideas—you have to keep up!—but it's amazing how many of them work out. He's very genuine, very transparent, very grateful—always please and thank you—and he likes to laugh. He's actually a very funny guy, but people don't believe me when I say that."

What hasn't changed is Harbaugh's competitiveness.

"Oh, boy, he can be competitive just chewing gum," she said. "When we lose, he never blames anyone else. He puts it all on himself, 100 percent. It's a failure to him, and it's his failure. You can see it's such a heavy load. The Notre Dame loss, that was a tough one. I could see the distress on his face. And he gets very quiet.

"But within about 24 hours, they're working on the next game. No one is looking back. It's not allowed!"

The reason is simple: if you spend your time griping about the last loss, you might lose the next one—which only makes everything worse.

"Winning is preferred," McDaniel said. "Trust me."

The two most prominent people in the players' daily lives might be strength and conditioning coach Ben Herbert and nutritionist Abigail O'Connor, whom they probably see as much as the rest of the staff combined.

That's why, when Chase Winovich and Karan Higdon both urged Harbaugh to make fundamental changes to their strength and food programs, Harbaugh took action, searching nationwide for the top candidates until he found exactly what he was looking for.

Show me a normal strength coach, and I'll show you someone looking for work. Manic energy is a baseline requirement for this unique position, and Ben Herbert more than exceeds it. He's in ferociously good shape, his face so tight it looks like someone is pulling his skin from the back of his head, and his tightly cropped, white-haired goatee and freshly shaved head add to the effect. But it's Herbert's eyes that get you, which look like they could burn through dry leaves.

Herbert comes from Pittsburgh, where his mother ran an antique store and a hair salon, and his father was a heavy equipment mechanic who fine-tuned bulldozers, backhoes, and excavators. Ben played linebacker on the West Allegheny high school football team, the first in school history to win the West Pennsylvania Interscholastic Athletic League, which covers the western half of this football-mad state. He laid a Penn State blanket on his bed every morning and was thrilled when Joe Paterno offered him a scholarship. But when Herbert took the first flight of his life to Wisconsin, the world looked a little bigger.

Herbert's high school friends gave him a lot of grief for picking Wisconsin over Penn State. But after the Badgers beat a great Penn State team in 1998 and went on to win two straight Rose Bowls, Herbert could quiet them simply by playing with his Rose Bowl rings.

After graduating Herbert stayed in Madison until he became the head strength coach under Bret Bielema. When Bielema left after the 2012 season for Arkansas, he brought Herbert with him.

"It was powerful to learn that what I knew was transferrable to another program," Herbert told me. "It gave me the confidence to know doing it this way can work anywhere."

After Arkansas finished 4-8 in 2017 Bielema was fired, so Herbert accepted Michigan's invitation to interview a few weeks later. When Herbert walked into the coaches' meeting room with Harbaugh, Don Brown, and five other staffers on the other side of the table, he was wearing a nice suit and a tie—but they would not last long. After handing out copies of his five-page program with the science behind it, with every question from the staffers he became more animated, loosening his tie, taking off his coat, and rolling up his sleeves.

When they asked how he would develop upper and lower body power, he said, "Let me show you," then dropped to the floor to demonstrate exactly how he wanted a push-up properly executed.

"I want feet *together*, touching," he said, looking up to them from his position on the floor. "Yes, it matters. *Attention to detail* carries over to everything you do! I could say it 5,000 times and it wouldn't be enough.

"My glutes and core muscles are engaged. My body is a steel plank—not sagging or dipping in the middle or peaking [raising his butt] to make a teepee. I want everyone to have a *steel-plank mentality*.

"My head is in line, not raised, and not dropping. You weren't given a chin so you could drop it. *Always* keep your chin up and your eyes up. This is very powerful body language for a variety of reasons, and it applies to push-ups too. When your chin drops, your lower back sags, and everything goes to shit.

"You'll see my hands are outside my chest, my elbows are six inches off my rib cage, up, and they are *never* flared out to the side.

"You lower yourself slowly to the floor, maintaining your form, until your chest and *only your chest* touches—not resting. You hold that position for *one second*, then you drive out, and stabilize."

After holding his push-up in perfect plank form for a second or two, he hopped up.

"And *that* is how we will do push-ups."

The coaches looked at each other, impressed. The job was his.

After Herbert eats dinner with his wife and two boys, he puts the kids to bed, and retires about 8:15—but not before setting his alarm clock, his phone, and his wife's phone for exactly 3:05 a.m.

"There's something about those extra five minutes that feels right," he said. He gets out of bed at 3:08 and walks to the bathroom, where his German shepherd gets up and takes his place on the bed. After a shower and a quick breakfast, he's out the door by 3:38.

He drives 8.2 miles to get to his office by 3:54, "at the latest," where he is soon joined by his four full-time staffers. He doesn't give his staff a set time to show up, because he doesn't need to. They're not stupid, and bring to their work the same intensity their boss does.

On Herbert's office wall he has posted a sign: "GET SHIT DONE." He explained, "I don't give a damn about anything else. Either you can or you can't. Stop thinking about all this bullshit—and Get Shit Done."

Suffice it to say, Herbert and his staff get shit done, spending an hour or so to set up each day's workouts by 5 a.m.

"Being organized allows us to work in a very fluid manner," Herbert explained.

Why does it take five men an hour to set up a two-hour workout? Because of the number of toys they have available in Coach Herbert's little shop of horrors. These include:

- 500 dumbbells, from 7.5 pounds to 207.5 pounds each

- 165 kettle bells, which look like cannonballs with large handles, and run from 26 to 203 pounds

- 20 standard benches

- 40 machines for arms, legs, torsos—you name it

- 16-multi-hip machines

- 10 inversibles, for inverse leg curls

- 10 dual-bend reverse hyper-extenders

- 32 mobility stations

"And a partridge in a pear tree," Herbert said.

But there's more: 26 two-inch thick ropes that run 50 feet long; 20 sets of Rotex foot rotators; and any number of other apparatus in the back room—all organized with military precision.

When you walk into the state-of-the-art weight room, 32,000-square feet of open space that looks through a three-story wall of glass onto the outdoor practice fields, all recently rebuilt at a cost of $36 million, the first thing you notice are the 32 racks for squats, bench press, and other lifts. These carry more than 1,000 plates total, about 30 per rack, from 10 pounds to 100.

"Sorry, no five-pounders," Herbert said, with an evil grin. "You can find those at your local Y."

In case that's not enough to work with, on each rack the staff hangs super-thick six-foot chains, about three-inches wide, which they can attach to the bars for a bigger challenge. Attached to each rack you'll also find an "Elite Form Unit," fancy key pads that the players sign into to track their workout, including the bar weight, number of sets, number of reps, the bar speed, the power they produce in watts, and the amount of work they do in joules.

Whatever happened on Saturdays, no one could say Michigan was not invested.

"Some people believe if we don't win, there's something we're not doing to win," Warde Manuel said. "But these young people are working as hard as they can, and so are the coaches and the staffers. You just can't do any more, or work any harder."

After Herbert and his staff set up the day's workout, they have a little time to themselves before the first of three groups of players start straggling in about 5:40, rubbing their eyes.

"I love watching them come in," Herbert said. "You can see where they are just from their body language. You can drastically improve a guy's attitude with just a few words. He's going to stand a little taller and work a little harder."

To avoid burnout they rotate three main position groups—the linemen on offense and defense; the "big skill" guys (tight ends, fullbacks, linebackers); and the "skill guys" (quarterbacks, running backs, receivers, and defensive backs)—at one of three different times each week: 6 a.m., 1:30 p.m., or 3:30 p.m. They also change up the workouts, and play everything from Migos to Celine Dion.

But work is work, and Michigan football players put in more work before breakfast than the average person does in a day. They spend the first hour on one of the practice fields doing "movement work" specific to their positions for strength and agility. This alone can make a rookie lose his breakfast, but then it's time for an hour in the weight room, where Herbert and his staff put them through a nonstop workout of weights, plyometrics, and more, with as many as 250 reps in one hour.

That often includes one of the simplest and toughest exercises: 20 sets of five pull-ups, each 45 seconds apart, using three different grips: overhand, neutral, and reverse.

"And it's strict," Herbert added. "You start out fully extended. You squeeze your way up, pause at the top, then come down under complete control. Rip it, stick it, and descend. Can't do all that, it doesn't count."

Don't be fooled by the number of reps, either. Some days they do as few as 35 reps—and those are the toughest days.

"On those days the volume of reps is low," Herbert explains, "but with heavy loads, it's very demanding. You get to 17 in the squat rack, and now you've got to go to another place if you're going to get those last few."

When they're done with that it's time for something you've probably never seen before: a ramp built at 30 degrees (which feels like 45) and runs 50 feet to the 17-foot-high second floor. Next to that are the "Plyo-Stairs," a set of seven gigantic steps, each 27 inches high (about three times higher than normal stairs). These are used for all kinds of diabolical exercises, including hopping on two feet, then one. After they master that they strap on a weighted vest with 10 to 80 pounds.

"Everyone can tolerate a certain level of stress," Herbert said. "Our job is to expose you to a level that stimulates your growth and development."

That's why the players swore by Herbert: they were convinced he had prepared them better for the 2018 season than they had ever been before.

Herbert admitted that he was particularly keyed up for the Wisconsin game four weeks later. His former Wisconsin teammate Ross Kolodziej had become the head strength coach at Wisconsin, and sent him a note before the season: "See you in October."

Herbert replied, "Yes, sir!"

It was on.

As DeAnna McDaniel said, "Winning is preferred."

Abigail O'Connor, from San Antonio, played catcher for the Southwestern University softball team in George-town, Texas, despite being "particularly undersized." Because she was constantly trying to gain weight and muscle, she educated herself about both. After earn-ing a master's degree in nutrition at Texas A&M she completed an internship at the University of Houston, where she also worked with the athletic department. A half year after the University of Minnesota hired her as a performance dietitian in June 2017, Harbaugh's newly minted strength coach, Ben Herbert, urged Harbaugh to interview O'Connor in early 2018.

After Herbert picked up O'Connor at the airport one evening for a full slate of interviews the next day, he gave her a couple of options: he could drive her back to the hotel to have dinner and talk about the position, or take her to the facility for a tour.

"Take me to the facility," she said—all but sealing the job with that response. It remains Herbert's favorite story about her.

"The Michigan football museum was great," she told me, "but every program has those. But when you walk into Glick [the indoor practice field] you see all those banners, and you realize, this is Michigan."

Running down the right sideline are eleven big banners listing Michigan's 42 Big Ten titles, four per banner. Across the field are another twelve banners listing Michigan's 47 bowl games, from the first Rose Bowl in 1901 to the 2018 Outback Bowl. At the far end hang eleven bigger banners, one per national title.

Wherever you go in that sprawling building you're surrounded by Michigan tradition: the three Heisman trophies upstairs, the 42 Big Ten titles wallpapered on the wall of the Commons, the team awards screwed into the walls, the framed pictures of every All-American ascending the ramp from the field, and the quotes from the greats. There is no escaping it—the blessing and burden of playing for Michigan.

That night the players happened to be doing baseline evaluations in the weight room. After they establish their current limits in various exercises, they build on that until final exams, then do it again for the summer, and again in the fall. O'Connor knew that for Herbert to take time off from this important night to pick her up, he must be serious about the nutrition program.

When receiver Donovan Peoples-Jones asked her, "What would you do if you got this job?" she replied: "What did you eat for dinner last night?"

"Chicken breast, brown rice, and broccoli," he said.

"Is that what you want me to hear, or is that what you ate?" she asked.

He grinned. "No, that's what we had upstairs."

"And the day before?"

"Brown rice, chicken, broccoli."

"And that was driving them nuts," she told me. "It's nutritionally sound, but not if they skip it and go to Pizza Bob's and crush a calzone and a milk shake."

After O'Connor got the job she shook things up, changing the menus for every meal to add more nutrition, more variety, and more of their special requests. She had the menus planned for the year by July. She switched the recipes from buttermilk to Greek yogurt, and started sneaking a cup and a half of vegetables in every ladle of marinara sauce. To date, not one player has noticed.

"I have to compete," she explained. "The person who fed them last was probably their mom. I have to convince them that what I'm offering is better than what your mom was feeding you. That's a hard sell."

O'Connor's department includes two full-time chefs and a staff who make the meals in a huge kitchen under the Big House stands, then deliver them to Schembechler Hall Commons by truck. When the Wolverines play on the road O'Connor gets to the hotel Friday morning to go over the menu and ingredients, make sure they have enough food so the lines don't back up, and sets up their extra "fueling stations" at the hotel and the locker room.

Because most athletes want to eat some meals away from the team training tables, Caroline Mandel, the athletic department's director of performance nutrition, set up a clever system she named Fueling Blue, which gives each athlete $60 of paper chits each week to use at local restaurants. Although the football team hadn't participated in the program, O'Connor thought it was a good idea. She tweaked it by limiting the restaurants to the healthiest ones near campus, including Chipotle, Potbelly, and Zingerman's Deli, and replaced the paper chits with a phone app. The players like the convenience, while she likes tracking their eating habits.

"Big Brother is watching," she joked.

Keeping the players properly fueled requires everything from bottles of multivitamins at every table to protein shakes and meals at the hotel the night before a game. While O'Connor and her staff go to great lengths to keep the cost down, there is no cheap way to feed 140 players between 3,000 and 10,000 calories a day. (Some of the biggest eaters are undersized freshmen in the 180–200-pound range.)

The team consumes 20 gallons of milk every day, and three pallets of bottled performance drinks each week. When O'Connor moves those loaded pallets into her office, she considers that part of her daily workout.

The players eat more than 70 dozen eggs every morning—so many, O'Connor doesn't bother ordering eggs by the dozen, but by the pound, about 100 pounds per day. All orders increase during August training camp, when the workload is greatest and they eat four meals a day. At a typical lunch the players will gobble down 15 pans of chicken wings, and the pans hold about 15 pounds of wings each, or roughly 225 pounds total. During the season a week of dinners costs more than $100 per player.

Where O'Connor has managed to save money is not on the quality or quantity of food—not a good way to make players happy or build winning teams—but by cutting dramatically on waste, thanks to her more popular menus, eating times, and Fueling Blue program. Because the players now eat more meals at Schembechler Commons, eat more each time they sit down, and eat the rest of their meals at healthy places on campus, food waste has been reduced from 40 percent during the season (which is typical of restaurants) and 75 percent during the August camp to less than 10 percent most days—about as low as you can go without running out of food.

It all makes a difference. Stand-out offensive guard Ben Bredeson said the addition of O'Connor, Herbert, and coach Ed Warriner had "transformed the O-line."

Even for a nutritionist, attitude goes a long way. O'Connor got a place in Canton, about 20 minutes away, "because I need that time to get ready for work. If I lived across the street and could roll out of bed, I wouldn't be as cheerful as I want to be, and they need that. They can be grumpy, but I can't."

During the season O'Connor gets up at 4:30, arrives at Schembechler Hall at 5:30, then spends her time at the meals with the players, with breakfast from 7:30–9:30, lunch from 11:30–2:30, and dinner two hours after practice ends.

Her favorite days are Mondays—but only after a win. When they lose they get a standard meal, still good and healthy, but they invariably eat less after losing.

But when they win the chef hand-cuts 200–250 steaks—about 1.5 per player, though some eat none and some eat three—served in a dozen huge pans, plus lobster, and a very rare treat, ice cream.

Winning was preferred.

Chapter 15
Harbaugh in High School
1977–1982

Through eighth grade Jim Harbaugh played at least four organized sports every year—specialization be damned. (To this day he strongly prefers recruiting two- and three-sport athletes.) Even then he was someone people noticed, remembered, and often told stories about.

I'm six months younger than Harbaugh, and grew up playing baseball against him, and during eighth grade, hockey with him. Hockey was my best sport, and I was a little better than he was (or so I claim, anyway). But hockey was Harbaugh's *fourth* sport, which he played on the side during basketball season. One of us was a great athlete.

In eighth grade I thought Harbaugh was the most competitive person I'd ever met. He still is, and I've met a few since. While the rest of us in the locker room were struggling to peel our eyes open before a 7 a.m. practice, Harbaugh arrived jacked, delivering motivational maxims at a mile a minute. On our hockey team I don't recall him being cocky at all, though perhaps that was because hockey was the only sport where he had to wonder if he was going to make the team.

I don't recall him trying to cheat, play dirty, or bully anyone. His peers consistently make the same observations. While we've always been cordial, we've never been close friends, but my four-plus decades of watching Harbaugh, often at close range, tell me he has always been authentic. Whether you like him or not, I've never detected a phony bone in his body.

From 1969 to 2009 Rob Lillie taught physical education and coached the varsity teams at Tappan Junior High, where they've named the gym after him. Lillie has an amazing memory for his former students, but the Harbaugh brothers still stand out.

"John was kind of quiet and subdued in his regular dealings throughout the school," Lillie told me, "but Jim was a character from the get-go. He liked to come down to the locker room to talk with me and Don Horning, the baseball coach. He always wanted to know what was going on, always had an opinion on it, and wanted to discuss everything with you. Don was great with historical trivia, and of course Jim had all the answers. He loved history, and he loved competing in everything."

Due to budget cuts, when the Harbaugh brothers arrived the only varsity sports the five Ann Arbor junior highs could offer were football, basketball, volleyball, and baseball—all for ninth graders only. In 1977–78, when Jim was still in eighth grade, he informed Lillie that he should be the starting quarterback on the football team.

"I'm better than all those guys," Harbaugh said. "I could really help your team."

"But only ninth graders can play."

"But I'm better."

"Doesn't matter. But Cesar Puente has got a soccer team, and he needs a goalie."

Harbaugh thought about it, then said, "Yeah, I could do that."

"Jim liked Cesar as his Spanish teacher because he was a great teacher, but always made Jim toe the line," Lillie said. "Jim respected that. One day Jim didn't have his homework done. Cesar had a simple rule: if they didn't get it done before class, they had to come in after school and finish it—on Cesar's time. So when

Cesar sees that Jim hasn't got his homework, he says, 'Well, I guess I'll see you at 3:10.'

"No!" Jim protested. "I've got practice!"

"Not today you don't."

"But I really can't miss practice!"

"So," Lillie recalled, "Cesar called Jim's mom, who told him, 'Yes sir, Jim will be there.' And he was—and he missed most of practice." Lesson learned.

After Jim agreed to play goalie, during one game Puentes, an Air Force veteran whose teams were usually far ahead of the competition, was watching his team attack the opponents' goal when his players on the sidelines started yelling: "Mr. Puente, Mr. Puente, look at Harbaugh!"

At the other end of the field Puentes saw Harbaugh lying down in front of the net.

"Harbaugh!" Puente yelled. "Get up!"

"I will, Coach, as soon as they cross the fifty!"

"I don't think they ever crossed the mid-line," Lillie recalled. "Jim always loved to be the center of attention. A lot of kids liked him. He was a charismatic guy, and I think he naturally liked people. But some of the other kids—well, they didn't dislike him, but they resented his cockiness. But I guess when you can back up most of what you say, you can say almost anything."

When students gave Puente their class pictures he saved them under glass. When Harbaugh gave Puente his, he told him, "Save that one. I'm going to play in the NFL."

In the spring of eighth grade Harbaugh told Lillie, "Coach, I'm the best player on the baseball team!"

"Jim, remember football? Same rule. You have to be a ninth grader." But, Lillie asked, why don't you come out for track, which accepted all grades? They needed a hurdler.

Once again Harbaugh decided, "Yeah, I can do that."

"He wasn't very good at it," Lillie said, "but he worked and worked and worked until he was pretty good. After losing to Connie Rush all season, he finally beat him for the city championship. Jim just never let up at all."

When ninth grade arrived Harbaugh was ready to star on all the teams he wasn't allowed to play on the previous year. After leading the Trojans' football team to the city title game, which they lost to Forsythe in a wild battle ("That didn't sit well with Jim," Lillie noted), Harbaugh starred on the basketball team as a power forward.

"Jim was an *excellent* basketball player," said Jay Nordlinger, Harbaugh's teammate in three sports. "A very good shooter, passer, rebounder—because of smart positioning—and floor leader. I thought it was his best sport, frankly."

"We had a great basketball team," Lillie said. "I'm not sure if Jim was the best player, but he was one of the best. One day [fellow teacher and coach] Dan Horning asked him, 'Say you're playing a basketball game and you're behind by one, and we get two free throws. Who would you want to take them?'

"Easy, Coach—me!"

"Why?"

"Because I know I'd make them."

Harbaugh wasn't certain he was the best but he already knew he was the most competitive—and he was right.

When Jim Harbaugh entered Ann Arbor Pioneer High School in the fall of 1979 as a tenth grader his most prominent traits were already well established: the world-class competitiveness that would make him successful, the swagger that would make him a lightning rod for critics, and the kindness that would make those who really knew him fiercely loyal.

Jim started August training camp as the junior varsity's starting quarterback, while John, a senior, was starting on the varsity, with a good shot at captain.

But during a pre-season scrimmage somebody fell on John's knee, partially tearing his MCL.

"I remember coming home, so distraught," John told me. "Heart-broken. They had me in a cast from my hip to my foot. It was the worst. But I still wanted Jim to come up as our quarterback. It wasn't even a question to me. I knew he was good, because I had to deal with him every day. We all knew he was our best chance to win."

The Pioneers opened the 1979 season with two dispiriting losses before winning their first game, 18-0, against a weaker opponent, while Harbaugh tore up the junior varsity. His former wingback, Derek Lee, recalled that on one of his first plays, if not his very first, Harbaugh threw a 60-yard wheel route to Greg Parham for a touchdown, and kept it going from there.

On the morning before the varsity's fourth game, against powerhouse Flint Southwestern, Harbaugh was sitting in class with the backup quarterback, Al Smith, when Pioneer's head football coach, Chuck Ritter, and the head JV coach, Paul Fuehrer, asked the teacher to speak with Harbaugh. When Harbaugh returned, he leaned over to Smith and said, "I'm going up to varsity."

Even in tenth grade Harbaugh's teammates usually found his brash confidence tolerable because he backed it up not only with success, but all the work that led up to it. That same fall, in the same class, Harbaugh wrote something on a note and passed it to Al Smith: it was Harbaugh's autograph, with his jersey number.

"I've been practicing that," he told Smith. "It'll be worth something someday."

"Al and I were equally amazed at Jim's confidence and cockiness," Derek Lee said. "One day he told us he was going to play quarterback for Michigan. I didn't think much of it since we had faced him for years in junior football and junior high. He was good, but who would recognize his greatness at that age? Only Jim.

"Of course, I should have given him more credit. Obviously he backed it up. Always did. He was called up to varsity, just like he said—the only sophomore who played up that year."

When the JV coach told the team Harbaugh was moving up to varsity, Al Smith recalled, "he was so upset, he was crying. Seriously."

Jim took the starting job and kept it the rest of the season, going a respectable 3-and-3 as the starter. When John came back from his knee injury to play the last two games, the Harbaughs led Pioneer to a 28-12 win over Jackson and a 20-8 win over cross-town rival Huron. With John at wingback the two connected for a couple of passes.

"No touchdowns," John said, "but it was pretty cool."

A few weeks later, Jim made the varsity basketball team.

"No other sophomores made either varsity team," said Derek Lee, whose dad coached the varsity basketball team. "I was jealous of Jim's abilities, especially since my dad brought him up to varsity and left me on JV!"

Harbaugh had a great chance to follow the path across the street from Pioneer to the Big House, worn by a century of local stalwarts like John Maulbetsch, Bob Westfall, Don Dufek Jr., and Keith Bostic, among others. But in the winter of 1980 Stanford head coach Paul Wiggin offered Jack Harbaugh a promotion to defensive coordinator, and he took it.

"Biggest mistake of my life," Jack said. "I fell into the 'title trap,' thinking a bigger title must mean a better job."

The family moved again—their ninth home in 20 years. While John had already accepted a partial scholarship to play defensive back at Miami, Ohio, the "cradle of coaches," Jim had to start over. Instead of being Ann Arbor Pioneer's rare returning starting quarterback as a junior—on a team that would go 8-1 his senior season without him—at Palo Alto High School

Harbaugh had to beat out a popular starting quarterback on a team that had won just one game the previous
year, and prove himself to new coaches and teammates
in football, basketball, and baseball.

Despite the public impression of Jim Harbaugh as
the golden boy who succeeded at everything and never
struggled, Jack and John see Jim's career very differently.

"Every step of the way he was the underdog," John
told me. "He had to battle for everything. There was
always someone ahead of him."

"Jim will tell you," Jack said, "Palo Alto was more
pressure than Michigan or the NFL! When Jim got
there he had to battle the starting quarterback—and
the whole community wanted the other guy. He was
already there, Jim was an outsider, so Jim had to play
that much better to get the job."

If Harbaugh failed, you might not have heard of
him. But Harbaugh edged out the incumbent then led
the team to a 9-1 record, and the team's first berth in
the state playoffs in years.

Harbaugh followed up his breakthrough football
season by leading Palo Alto's basketball team to the
semifinals of the Northern California championship.
The coach, Clem Wiser, "may have been the only
coach who really understood Jim," Jackie Harbaugh

said. "Wiser was for Jim at Palo Alto what Mrs. Hiller was for Jim at St. Francis. Wiser *got* Jim."

"Most teachers and coaches want to break a guy like Jim," Jack observed. "But the best ones want to work with him. They say, I like the energy, I like the confidence, let's re-direct it."

After Harbaugh put in another stellar season at quarterback only Arizona's Larry Smith and Wisconsin's Dave McClain—both former teammates of Jack's at Bowling Green—showed any interest in signing him.

"Not Michigan," Jack recalled. "Not *Stanford*—and I'm running their defense! I always felt like we were outsiders at Palo Alto. Man, *that* was pressure!"

Harbaugh had told his Pioneer JV teammates he'd play for Michigan. He had narrowly avoided having his dreams derailed by the starting quarterback at Palo Alto, and now he faced rejection from Stanford and Michigan.

In the fall of 1981, Harbaugh's senior year at Palo Alto, the only person who thought Jim Harbaugh might one day start for the Wolverines, let alone play in the NFL, was Jim Harbaugh.

When Jim Harbaugh returned to Michigan on December 30, 2014, against all odds, he was greeted not merely as a great coach but Michigan's Messiah. But after his team slipped to 8-5 in 2017, critics and even fans wondered if Harbaugh could turn the team around. *(Roger Hart/Michigan Photography)*

The Harbaughs' competitive spirit starts with their father Jack, an All-State football and baseball player from Crestline, Ohio. "Attack this day with an enthusiasm unknown to mankind!" (*Harbaugh family*)

In tenth grade at Pioneer High School, 1979–1980, Harbaugh was the only sophomore to play on the varsity football team: starting quarterback. A few weeks later he became the only sophomore to play on the varsity basketball team. He was an athlete. (*Harbaugh family*)

Jack Harbaugh made $16,000 when he joined Bo Schembechler's staff in 1973. The Harbaughs didn't have a big house, fancy cars, or fame, but they all remember their years in Ann Arbor as their happiest. "Who's got it better than us?" "Nooooobody!" (*Harbaugh family*)

After turning around a moribund 49ers team, Harbaugh faced his brother John's Baltimore Ravens in the 2013 Super Bowl. They hugged before the game, but after the 34-31 loss, Jim tried to refuse brother John's consolation hug—one of John's favorite stories. *(Harbaugh family)*

As soon as Harbaugh took over in Ann Arbor, he started challenging the status quo. His satellite camps in 2015 attracted thousands of high school players, not to mention his father, brother, and son Jay—and lots of criticism from southern coaches. *(copyright David Turnley)*

When Harbaugh met Sarah Feuerborn she had built a great real estate practice, and had no idea who the coach of Division II University of San Diego was. But they hit it off, got married, and now have four children who go to Jim's former grade school, St. Francis. *(Harbaugh family)*

Before the 2018 Michigan-Michigan State game, MSU coach Mark Dantonio had his players conduct their pregame march on Michigan's time, walking past captain Devin Bush Jr. "They really picked the absolute worst person to do that to," Ben Bredeson said. *(Eric Bronson/Michigan Photography)*

Devin Bush Jr. left the beaches of Florida for the snow of Michigan, "and I do not like the snow!" But he believed in Harbaugh and set his sights on the Academic All-Big Ten team. His teammates named him captain his junior year. *(Eric Bronson/Michigan Photography)*

Bush Jr. had great strength, speed, intensity, and game sense—but was considered too short for the NFL. He proved his critics wrong when Pittsburgh picked him 10th overall. Coach Brown said, "Now *that* is a *dude!*" *(Eric Bronson/Michigan Photography)*

With his long blond hair flowing from his helmet, his post-sack celebrations, and his taunting tweets, Chase Winovich was the Wolverine opposing fans loved to hate. But his teammates backed him, and his 2018 "Revenge Tour." "With Chase," Harbaugh said, "it's all about the engine." *(Eric Upchurch)*

"He's got some passion, man!" linebacker Noah Furbush said of defensive coordinator Don Brown. "He brings it every day—and some days you really need that. He'll tell you when you screwed up your assignment, but not call you an idiot. At the end of the day you know he loves you, and we're all on the same team." *(Eric Upchurch)*

Noah Furbush grew up obsessed with planes. At Michigan he pursued a master's degree in Space Systems Engineering, and worked on a team designing a ship to go to Mars. He hoped to become a Marine pilot, and possibly an astronaut. *(Furbush family)*

Rashan Gary was the nation's top recruit in 2016, and picked Michigan at the last minute after seeing "maize and blue in my dreams." Though dyslexic, Gary earned Academic All-Big Ten twice.

(*Eric Bronson*/*Michigan Photography*)

Karan Higdon fell just six yards short of 1,000 his junior year , 2017. Though close to graduating, with a 3-year old daughter, he decided to come back for his senior year, and was named captain. *(Roger Hart/Michigan Photography)*

Born in Toledo, Ohio, Shea Patterson went to Michigan games until he moved to Hidalgo, Texas, where won over his new teammates and beat out the starting quarterback. He would repeat that trick two more times. *(Patterson family)*

After winning two state titles in Shreveport, Louisiana, Patterson transferred to IMG Academy in Florida, where all four major scouting services ranked him the top pro-style prospect in the nation. *(Patterson family)*

"You want to play quarterback at Michigan, you better think you're the best, because that's a pressure cooker like no other," Winovich said. "Shea's got that, and he's got the team." *(Roger Hart/ Michigan Photography)*

"If you come here," Winovich told Patterson, in January 2018, "I'll come back." "If you come back," Patterson countered, "I'll come here." Both proved good on their word. *(copyright David Turnley)*

Despite losing 42-13 to Penn State in 2017, tight end Zach Gentry had invited a half-dozen relatives from New Mexico for the rematch. The Wolverines bounced back in 2018 with a 42-7 victory, including this Gentry touchdown catch. *(Eric Upchurch)*

Their fathers had battled to be Michigan's quarterback four decades earlier, and became best friends. In 2018, Jared Wangler and Joe Hewlett asked to be roommates, too. Critics ripped Michigan's foreign trips, but the players loved them. "We're not football players over there," Wangler said. "That's rare for us." *(Joe Hewlett)*

Jared Wangler's father John threw 26 touchdown passes at Michigan, but never scored a touchdown himself. In Jared's fifth year on the team, he made a little family history against Maryland. *(Eric Upchurch)*

Ben Bredeson played hockey, and was good at it, but whenever he hit someone he got a penalty for it. After his first football practice, he said, "I'm supposed to hit people—every play! My coaches love it!" *(Bredeson family)*

Coach Ed Warinner, Ben Bredeson and company were working to restore Michigan's reputation as "O-Line U." Against Wisconsin's famed offensive line, it was Michigan's that won the day. "It's the one position," Bredeson said, "where no one else is going to cheer for you and you're only as good as the weakest person." *(Eric Upchurch)*

"Fans don't understand what sacrifices these kids make," Deb Bredeson said. "Ben's whole life has literally been for this. He's learning to lead and handle pressure at a level most 50-year-olds never see—even when he loses. Where else can you get all that?" *(Bredeson family)*

Grant Newsome's father played baseball and football at Princeton, and hoped his son would stick to baseball. But Grant caught the football bug in ninth grade, and five years later was a serious NFL prospect. (*Newsome family*)

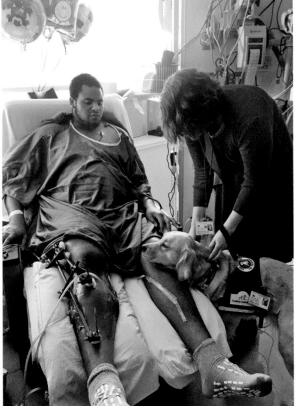

After suffering a gruesome injury in 2016, Newsome required emergency surgery to save his right leg. When asked if he would do it all again, he replied, "My answer is simple: Absolutely. In a heartbeat. Sign me up. I don't regret a second." (*Newsome family*)

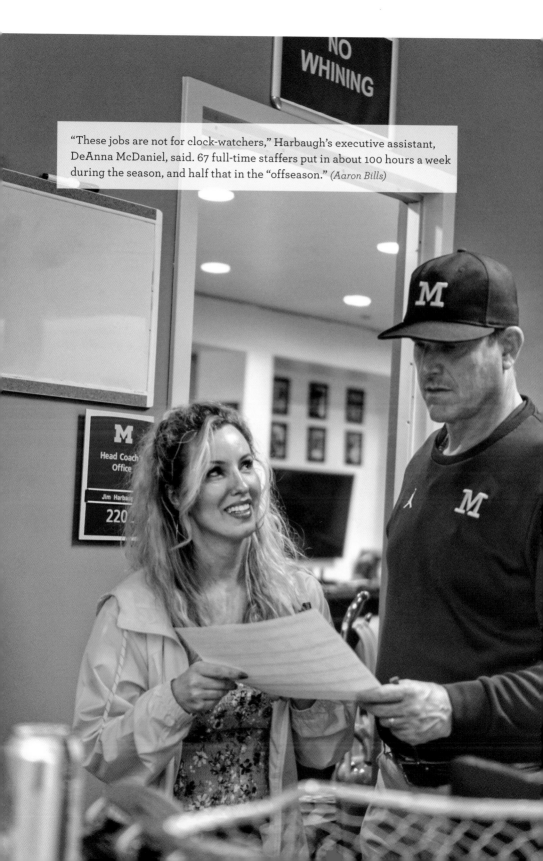

"These jobs are not for clock-watchers," Harbaugh's executive assistant, DeAnna McDaniel, said. 67 full-time staffers put in about 100 hours a week during the season, and half that in the "offseason." *(Aaron Bills)*

Michigan's players have great respect for their counterparts at Notre Dame, Wisconsin, Penn State, and Ohio State. Not so Michigan State. "We hate them, and they hate us," Furbush said. When they won in 2018, for the first time they celebrated with the Paul Bunyan Trophy on the field. *(Roger Hart/Michigan Photography)*

"We've had some happy locker rooms," Patterson said. "But Coach Harbaugh was almost in tears after that game. He got choked up a little bit— not common for him." *(Roger Hart/Michigan Photography)*

Despite late starts and big blow-outs against Wisconsin and Penn State, "No one left!" Bredeson said. "We love that—especially seeing the students stick around to sing 'The Victors' with us. That's pretty cool." *(Eric Bronson/Michigan Photography)*

"No one saw us getting blown out—not the way we've been playing," Karan Higdon said of Ohio State's historic 62-39 victory. "It kinda took your breath away." (*Jamie Sabau/Getty Images*)

When the nation's biggest stadium is filled to capacity with fans decked out in maize for a night game, it's something to see. For 2019, pundits were already predicting Michigan to win the Big Ten and make the College Football Playoffs. (*Austin Thomason/Michigan Photography*)

Chapter 16
Emptying the Bench

Nebraska, September 22, 2018

Michigan's win over SMU didn't impress the media pollsters, who kept the Wolverines at #19 for the second week. After the Wolverines lost to Notre Dame, in the media's eyes all they could do against their September opponents was tread water. Win, and they merely lived to fight another day. Lose, and all hell would break loose.

Those inside Schembechler Hall had to block out all such thoughts and set their sights on the Nebraska Cornhuskers. They were coming to town for their tenth meeting with Michigan stretching back to 1905, having split the previous nine, 4-4-1.

On paper this wasn't that big a deal. True, the Huskers had been a Big Ten rival since 2012, and this marked Michigan's Big Ten opener. If the Wolverines were serious about winning their first Big Ten title since 2004, it would have to start here. But the Huskers started the season 0-2 for the first time since 1957, and looked pretty bad doing it, with losses to Colorado and Troy. That their opening game against Akron, which would beat Northwestern in week three, had been canceled due to lightning now looked like a lucky break. Very little was expected from head coach Scott Frost's first Nebraska team—but that's not how college football works.

In the professional leagues rivalries are fueled by the fans, not the players, who have no problem jumping to the archrival if the money's good enough. As a result, pro rivalries tend to be passing fads based on personalities. When the players who battled in the rivalry between the Detroit Red Wings and the Colorado Avalanche in the late 1990s left those teams, so did the hatred between those clubs. Likewise, the finals between the Los Angeles Lakers and Boston Celtics in the eighties were classics, but when the NBA tried to market the Lakers-Celtics 2010 Finals as a rematch, no one bought it.

But when Alabama and Auburn lock horns, you

don't need Joe Namath or Bo Jackson to get fans excited. College rivalries run deeper than this year's rosters or records. So when the Cornhuskers came to play the Wolverines, they were not simply competing against this year's model. They were facing everything that has ever transpired between the two schools—directly and indirectly—from Fielding Yost coaching at both schools more than a century ago, to the 1985–86 Fiesta Bowl, when Harbaugh led Michigan to a victory and a #2 ranking, to the 1997 national title—split between Michigan (media poll) and Nebraska (coaches' poll).

Although the two teams never played each other that year, the split decision still bothered Michigan's players, particularly Scott Frost's role in it. Like Harbaugh, Frost is a former star quarterback and prodigal son returning to his alma mater to pick his beloved program off the floor. He was born in Lincoln, Nebraska, and raised a hundred miles away in tiny Wood River, where he set state records. But he turned down the Cornhuskers' Tom Osborne to go to Stanford, where he started only two games at quarterback and played five games at safety.

Realizing he'd made a mistake Frost transferred to Nebraska in 1995, but his teammates were so irritated by his big mouth that they tried to push him off the team. The next year, Nebraska fans—who are so nice they're known to cheer opponents—booed him after he lost to Arizona State. In 1997, however, Frost won over his Husker faithful by breaking records to lead the #2 Cornhuskers to the Orange Bowl.

The night before Michigan had finished its undefeated season by beating Washington State in the Rose Bowl, leaving the Wolverines at the top of both major polls. Frost recognized the Cornhuskers needed to do more than just beat third-ranked Tennessee to win their third national title in four years. They would have to crush Tennessee, and win some hearts and minds.

Just minutes after whipping Tennessee 42–17, Frost delivered a passionate speech through the stadium speakers.

"I don't think there's anybody out there with a clear conscience who can say that Nebraska and especially that great man Tom Osborne doesn't deserve a national championship for this!"

Just a few hours later, at 2:30 in the morning, the Cornhuskers' hotel rooms erupted when they learned the coaches' poll had bumped Nebraska ahead of Michigan by 1520 to 1516, a mere four points out of three thousand. To this day many Nebraska fans actually recall Frost's impromptu speech better than the game itself. Because of it, many believed he would one day coach the Cornhuskers. And they were right.

If the Cornhuskers never forgot Scott Frost's speech, neither did the Wolverines.

"When I see Scott Frost on TV, I still get mad," former Michigan linebacker Glen Steele told Bill Bender of *The Sporting News*. "I really do. It's more of the fact of the unknown. We'll never know what would've happened if we played them."

Frost added a little more to the rivalry when coaching his previous team, the University of Central Florida, against Harbaugh's second Michigan team in 2016. Despite losing 51–14, Frost said his team "out-hit" Michigan—a claim resurrected for fodder in articles and social media leading up to the 2018 Nebraska game.

At the 2018 Big Ten Media Days Frost admitted, "I know a lot of people in Michigan don't like me. But I will always have a lot of respect for the program."

Despite their grumbling, most Michigan players and fans would say the same about Nebraska.

"Michigan's not where it was in 1997, and Nebraska isn't, either," Jon Jansen said. "But it's still Nebraska. It's still Michigan. Put those two teams on the field and you're going to get good, old-fashioned midwestern football, how football was meant to be played."

The temperature was 58 degrees for the noon kickoff— perfect football weather. Most Michigan fans wore yellow for the "Maize-Out," especially thick in the student section, with plenty of Nebraska red scattered throughout the stadium. In only Nebraska's seventh year of Big Ten football, the Cornhuskers had already become one of the Big Ten's favorite fan bases.

The traveling Cornhuskers didn't have much to cheer about. On the third play Nebraska quarterback Adrian Martinez hit Stanley Morgan Jr. for 32 yards—which would be Nebraska's longest play of the day.

On the next play Josh Metellus intercepted Martinez to give Michigan's offense the ball on its own 36-yard line. After Higdon caught a pass for a 7-yard gain, they called "37-Niner," an off-tackle play they had run for 43 and 67 yards against Western Michigan. This time Higdon took "37-Niner" for a 46-yard ride before being brought down at Nebraska's 11-yard line. Michigan's battering ram, Ben Mason, finished the job for an early 7–0 lead.

Three plays later, Michigan's Jordan Glasgow sacked Martinez to send the Husker offense back to the sidelines. Before Michigan's offense could take over, a TV timeout gave Harbaugh a moment to gather the offense around him.

"We're gonna run 37-Niner again," he told them. "Let's see what they do."

Ben Bredeson turned to Higdon: "You better not get caught this time."

Higdon just smiled.

Patterson handed off to Higdon and faked a throw to get some defenders to hesitate. Michigan's offensive line gave Higdon another gigantic hole on the left side, and he took off. But about the time he reached the line of scrimmage a Nebraska safety who hadn't bought the fake was running toward Higdon at full speed—until Peoples-Jones stopped him cold.

"Donovan completely *annihilated* his guy," Higdon told me. "I got a front row seat. Seeing DPJ throw his guy down, now I *know* I've got to make a play out of this."

Higdon veered to the left sideline then ran for the corner in fourth gear, narrowly outracing three Cornhuskers. 14–0 Michigan, barely 6 minutes into the game.

After Higdon celebrated with his teammates he told Peoples-Jones, "You deserve my helmet sticker!" Then told his coaches: "Keep running that same shit, because they can't stop it!"

Higdon had one more message to deliver. "Karan came up to me," Bredeson recalled, "smiled, and said, 'Told you I wouldn't get caught!'"

After a sack by Rashan Gary and Carlo Kemp capped the defense's second straight three-and-out, the Wolverines returned to the end zone a few minutes later to establish a 21–0 first quarter lead.

The rest was just for fun—and there was plenty of it to be had.

By the end of the half Michigan had scored on all six of its possessions (minus a missed extra point) plus a safety, to take a 39–0 lead. The offense was riding a nine-possession scoring streak—eight touchdowns and a field goal—going back to the SMU game. After Michigan's fifth touchdown of the day, Nebraska had exactly two first downs. It was hard to tell how much Michigan had improved against fairly weak competition, but one thing was clear: this was not 2017's offense.

"This year," Bush Jr. told me, "you know when you give the ball back to the offense, they're going to do something with it. They put points on the board. When we go up 21–0 in the first quarter, you know Nebraska is gonna take chances they don't want to take—and we love that. That makes you feel good about your team."

While Patterson (15 for 22, 120 yards), Higdon (136 yards), Zach Gentry (three catches, one touchdown), and Ben Mason (three touchdowns) all had big games, the key was Michigan's improving front line, shoving the Huskers around and giving Patterson plenty of time to throw and Higdon big holes to run through.

Earlier that week, Jansen told me when you're playing offensive line and dominating, you can actually feel when the man across from you finally gives up.

"When your guy is just trying to do enough not to be called out and embarrassed on film the next day," he said, "or lose his starting spot, you can sense it. There's a difference between trying to win the game, and just trying to get through the game. I bet Ben Bredeson can tell you the exact play when it happened."

Sure enough, Bredeson said his counterpart cracked after Higdon's touchdown made it 14-0—just six minutes into the game.

"You can see it in his posture," he told me, "and you can feel it—and once you get close to his breaking point, you really just got to push 'em around and score again, and they'll shut down. Talk about the O-line winning the game within the game. That was the play that broke them. We just kept running it, because they couldn't stop it."

"That was one of those games where everything was executed, and went how it should," Bush Jr. told me. "Look what happens when we go out and execute! That was a big win against a Big Ten team."

Defensive back coach Mike Zordich was more direct. "The SMU game felt like a loss. I had a horrible taste in my mouth after that one. The Nebraska game was the opposite. Yeah, they haven't won a game, but they've got players. And I'm not sure it mattered who we played that day. We were getting after it."

"Against Nebraska," Winovich said, "it felt like we were playing on a completely different level. We didn't really have any of these wins last year. We had a great week of practice, and we got the result for all that. We just kicked their ass, top to bottom. This was a *team* win—all cylinders."

For the Wolverines, the best was yet to come.

After another Nebraska three-and-out the Huskers punted to Peoples-Jones on Michigan's 40-yard line. He cut back and to the right, got some great blocks along the sideline, then seeing his lane clogged, he cut hard to the left around the 25-yard line, picked up more blocks, and then executed a spin-o-rama right out of a video game to leave one defender in the dust before gliding the rest of the way to the left corner—then turned a somersault just for the heck of it.

Michigan had failed to return an unblocked punt or kick for a touchdown from 2009 to 2015. The 2018 Wolverines had scored one in each of its first four games.

Credit to Peoples-Jones, who scored twice, and special teams coach Chris Partridge.

The DJ played "Sweet Caroline," and the fans belted out, "So good! So good!"

As one loyal fan tweeted, "Football is fun again! Go Blue!

With Michigan up 46–0 just a few minutes into the second half the coaches pulled the remaining starters. Winovich usually got in for 60 plays but played only 19—with a sack. That sent some of the fans to the aisles, and the rest after the third quarter ended with Michigan up 49–3. They missed the players' favorite moments.

Matt Mitchell grew up in nearby Dexter, a former farm town outside of Ann Arbor, and enrolled at Michigan in 2014 as a preferred walk-on. He participated in every workout, practice, film, and study session, but had never gotten into a game in four seasons. His parents had attended every game hoping to see it. Mitchell, a business school student, decided to come back for one more year with a single goal in mind: get on the field for one play in the Big House—but it was hardly a given.

To improve his odds, Mitchell paid "extremely close attention" whenever Michigan scored, knowing his best chance to get in was on special teams.

"Every time we scored," Mitchell told me, "I would

sprint to the kickoff huddle and stand a couple yards away, hoping and praying that something would happen and that Coach Partridge would turn, see me, need me, and put me in the game."

It hadn't worked yet, but Mitchell kept trying. Mitchell had dressed for every home game his entire career, but when he checked the dress list Harbaugh posted that week, "I was shocked and devastated that I wasn't going to be dressing for the first time," Mitchell admitted. "I did the only thing I could think of, which was to work harder than I ever had before."

He also approached Harbaugh to ask what he did wrong, and if there was something he could do to dress for the Nebraska game.

"Well, you didn't grade out very well in the practice reps," Harbaugh told him, "so you need to improve your grade to dress."

Mitchell did as instructed, working so hard he earned the highest practice grade among the scout special teams players that week. On Friday special teams graduate assistant Greg Froelich, a good friend of Mitchell's, told him he was going to win the Scout Special Teams Player of the Week award. This both excited and confused Mitchell.

"Are you serious?" he asked. "I'm not even dressing for the game."

Froelich immediately went to talk to Harbaugh, who told him Mitchell needed to dress if he was going to win the award—which is how Mitchell found himself back on the dress list a few hours later. Still, Mitchell didn't have any reason to think his odds of playing against Nebraska were any better than they had been before.

"Some guys have put in four years here," Jared Wangler said, "waking up at 6 a.m. to work out like everyone else and leave the study center at 11 each night, guys who buy in to everything the coaches say, do everything right, and never see the field. That's happened. There's no guarantee. So when you see your friends play their first college snaps, everyone gets up to see it. It's one of the best parts of playing here."

After Peoples-Jones's touchdown, Mitchell sprinted over to the special teams huddle, like he always did. But for the first time in his five year career, he heard Partridge yell his name: "Mitchell! Get over here! We need you!"

"My heart dropped into my stomach," he recalled. "I had an adrenaline rush so strong I could barely contain it. In my shock, I could barely move."

Mitchell's best friend on the team, Chase Winovich, who roomed with Mitchell for three years, was standing next to him when Partridge called his name. Seeing his friend paralyzed by the news, Winovich grabbed

Mitchell and shouted, "BRO! THIS IS IT! GET IN THE GAME!"

Mitchell was so pumped he ran into the huddle and headbutted two coaches, and had a hard time hearing Partridge "over my thumping heart."

"Mitchell, you're going to be the rover," Partridge told him. "Line up at the five [position], and whatever happens keep your left arm free and angle your body to cut off the field."

When Mitchell jogged out to the field, his teammates—future NFLers and walk-ons alike—rushed to the edge to see history being made.

"Hey, those guys work just as hard as we do," Devin Bush Jr. told me. "We all remember our first play, what that felt like. But most of us don't have to wait five years for it! So when they get their chance to go out there and perform, you want to see it."

"That's something you see with our team," Joe Hewlett said. "Everyone knows everyone's story. We spend so much time together, and we've traveled together. So when you see someone like Matt Mitchell getting in for the first time, everyone knows it, and wants to see it."

Mitchell lined up in the five spot, waiting for the kick. With new rules added to limit special team play due to the injury rates, most kickoffs are not returned.

But Nebraska's J. D. Spielman caught this one on the three-yard line and ran out to the 27 before being tackled by Tru Wilson. Mitchell didn't make the play—but he was *in* the play, which was enough for his teammates to go crazy on his behalf.

"Chase ran onto the field and chest-bumped me so hard I was almost knocked off my feet," Mitchell said. "Next I was swarmed by at least 15 teammates, smacking me on the helmet and cheering and congratulating me."

When Mitchell finally got to the bench, he looked for his parents in the stands. "I could see the tears in my dad's eyes and pure elation on their faces."

His parents, the Winoviches, and other football parents started chanting, "Mitchell! Mitchell! Mitchell!" He couldn't help but shed some tears.

"It was one of my proudest moments in my life," Mitchell said, whose future is plenty promising without football. "I finally had achieved what I set out to accomplish."

Pete Winovich, Chase's dad, "swears that was the happiest moment of Chase's career," Mitchell said. "He never saw Chase smile so much or celebrate so hard, even when Chase himself made a huge play."

"We're playing a Big Ten opponent," Gentry explained, "one of the most storied programs in the country, and you just take it to them—both sides of the ball. You never go into a game like that expecting to blow them out 56 to 10. And then Matt Mitchell gets in, and that's about as good as it gets.

"To this point, that's the most fun I've ever had as a Michigan Wolverine."

Chapter 17
The Lightning Rod
Chase Winovich

In 1915 Chase Winovich's grandparents left Serbia for the United States. When they arrived at Ellis Island the agent changed their name from Avoinavich—which means "wolf-like"—to Winovich, and grouped them with people from the same region.

"I don't think my grandparents cared," Chase says. "They just wanted to get in."

Chase's father, Pete, who stands all of six feet seven, married the former Anina Brunazzi, and set up their home in Jefferson Hills, Pennsylvania, just outside Pittsburgh.

"It's a family-oriented place," Chase says, "and those traditions have always been important to us."

Pete is a real estate agent, and Nina, though a registered nurse, handles the office for Pete's business. They have four children, including Chase.

In football, Winovich didn't earn a starting position until his junior year. He was trying to follow in the footsteps of his brother, Peter III, who had been a three-year starter at quarterback and accepted a scholarship to Bowling Green in Ohio.

Peter's success in high school, Chase believes, "both helped and hurt me. He was a great role model, and I'm sure I got more eyes on me because I was his little brother. But the extra attention came with such high expectations, and I just didn't fit the mold. I stumbled a bit."

After struggling as a sophomore at safety and quarterback, Chase got a boost of confidence when he made the varsity basketball team, playing power forward and center, where he had to guard the opponents' most athletic player—improving his footwork in the process. Winovich got his chance on the football field the following fall, when a spate of injuries forced his coaches to switch him from safety, where he was a poor fit, to linebacker.

"They knew I loved to hit people, so they bumped me into the box—just what I wanted. Finally I get this break, and then I get hand-foot-and-mouth disease, and strep throat at the same time. I was pretty drugged up from the antibiotics. But I knew I might not get this chance again, so I wasn't going to let anything stop me."

Once he got into his first high school game as a starting linebacker—antibiotics and all—he felt unleashed, sacking the quarterback a couple of times. A long-time supporter of the program, Scott Breisinger, told Winovich, "Chase, a star was born tonight."

"It's funny the things you remember," Winovich said. "But that meant something to me."

Once Pitt offered Winovich a scholarship, "it set everything in motion," with Michigan State and others soon following suit. By the time Michigan football coach Brady Hoke visited his school office, Winovich was accustomed to being courted.

"At that point I really hadn't paid much attention to Michigan," he recalled, but he soon formed a relationship with Hoke and his staff. When he attended a Sunday Michigan basketball game during the winter of 2014, "I liked Michigan a lot, but I didn't *love* it right away. It was cold, and I don't even remember if we won the basketball game. My brother came up from Bowling Green and asked me, 'Could you see yourself playing here?' To be honest, I wasn't sure."

Like a lot of kids in Pittsburgh, Winovich grew up an Ohio State fan, so he was thrilled when Urban Meyer offered him a scholarship. Both Michigan and Ohio State were pursuing another linebacker, Carl Burger, but only after Burger committed to Ohio State did Michigan extend an offer to Winovich.

"To be honest, I felt offended by that," he said. "A day late and a dollar short."

Nonetheless, in the spring of Winovich's junior year he visited Pitt, Ohio State, and Michigan. "I wanted to have it done before my senior year, for sanity. [In Ann Arbor] I stayed with Jake Ryan, and he was great. Took me on my first moped ride. Jake played my position, and I liked the way he played—all out. I related to him right away."

While Winovich's visit to Michigan improved the Wolverines' odds, his visit to Ohio State lowered the Buckeyes'.

"I liked it," he said, "but one of the biggest things that turned me off was when Mrs. Meyer told me how nice it was to meet my family—and she hadn't met my family. She was busy with other families, but it just rubbed me the wrong way. It left a bad taste in my mouth. Nothing bad about the program. But I didn't buy into everything from that point on. I viewed it all with a jaundiced eye."

Winovich was also wary of programs that would

drop their offer if the player got injured in his last season of high school.

"You never want to worry that if you're injured your senior year, they'll leave you. A lot of schools would. I felt Michigan wouldn't."

And that was that: Winovich committed to Michigan. That was smart, because Winovich's last year did not go as planned. He played well at linebacker, but because their starting tailback quit, and the backup broke his collarbone, and then *his* backup broke his ankle, the coaches decided to use Winovich as a running quarterback. That took a toll on his body and his statistics. He finished with only a half-dozen touchdown passes, but he still managed to pile up 13 sacks as a linebacker. At the end of the season the prestigious Under Armour All-America Game did not invite him, a snub Winovich characteristically used as motivation.

On National Signing Day, February 5, 2014, Winovich was the first future Wolverine to fax his letter in, at 7:03 a.m. He knew what he wanted, and wasn't taking any chances.

Winovich's decision to attend Michigan didn't mark the end of his struggles, but the beginning. He arrived to play linebacker in Brady Hoke's defense but quickly discovered, even playing on the scout team, he was not ready for Power Five football.

"I was undersized, too skinny, and hadn't figured out the nutrition thing yet," he said. "Over the course of the season I actually dropped from 215 to below 200. I had to pump up to 201.5 pounds just to qualify to lift weights, and then threw up immediately. Then I lifted weights, because that's what you do."

While Winovich was trying to survive, both Brady Hoke and his boss, athletic director Dave Brandon, lost their jobs, creating "a winter of pure anarchy," as Winovich remembered it. When Jim Harbaugh took the mantle on December 30, 2014, everything changed again.

"Chase was just a little guy," Jack Harbaugh recalled, "maybe 200 pounds, when I saw him do the Oklahoma Drill," where one player simply tries to stop another in a narrow chute, about ten feet across. "Chase was up against a much bigger guy, going head-to-head. *And he knocks him on his ass!* The big guy turns and points and says, 'I want you again!' And Chase yells right back, 'You got me!' *And he did it again!*"

"With Chase, it always goes back to the motor," Jim Harbaugh told me. "His engine runs in overdrive, all the time. The effort he plays with is the most impressive part of his game."

When Winovich hurt his left PCL in the 2015 spring game he didn't think it was that bad at first, but a few days later he could barely walk. When he watched the tape, he realized his injury was a lot worse than he'd thought, and six weeks on crutches confirmed it. When he got off his crutches the team's starting tight ends, Khalid Hill and Jake Butt, were both injured, so the new staff asked Winovich to switch to tight end—not a small request, since the positions have so little in common, and Winovich had no experience at tight end.

"At linebacker, you're reacting a lot," Winovich said. "You might line up on the inside or the outside, but you're pretty much going where you think the ball is going to be. There's so much more in the offensive playbook than in the defensive playbook, just a ton to learn. And every single thing that everyone else does on offense affects the tight end. You have to know the formation, the route concepts, the coverages, and your responsibilities—and all that can change every week."

He learned, and was smart enough to watch the masters in front of him. "Jake was simply one of the best route runners in Michigan history," he said.

But no sooner had Winovich agreed to learn his new position during the first week of the 2015 fall camp than he pulled his left hamstring. Winovich found himself buried on the depth chart at sixth or seventh string—which is to say, a tight end in name only. His time on special teams was cut, too.

"It was a pretty rough start," Winovich recalled.

While the Wolverines were enjoying a renaissance during Harbaugh's inaugural season, 2015, Winovich was getting increasingly frustrated with his new lot. When he called his dad to complain, Pete told him, "Chase, this is what your coach wants you to do, so just be the best tight end you can be."

"Once I finally got my head around the offensive playbook," Chase recalled, "it started clicking, and I felt like I knew what I was doing."

But he wasn't getting any closer to playing at tight end, so he tried to crack the special teams lineup. With his hamstring still hurting, he lost a foot race for a spot on special teams, "but at least I went down with my boots on. Now, the guy who'd won the foot race against me, I think I'm better than him. When he broke his collar bone, they put me on the travel team. Then they put *another* kid in who was way slower than me, and he didn't do that good a job. Now I'm pissed!"

Winovich composed a letter to then–special teams coach John Baxter with an acronym spelling out each reason why Winovich felt he deserved to play.

"I basically begged for a spot," Winovich said. Baxter listened, putting him on kickoff coverage against

Indiana—a game Michigan won in overtime—and Winovich got two tackles on special teams.

"I pancaked a guy, which felt like a pretty big moral victory. I'd made my point and backed it up."

Winovich is no one's idea of the classic tight end, so he was relieved during December 2015 bowl practices when his cell phone rang in his West Quad dorm room, and he saw "Coach Harbaugh" on the caller ID. Harbaugh said they were going to put Winovich at defensive end for the 2016 season. With only 15 bowl practices—and a few already used up—Harbaugh put Winovich at his new position the next day.

"You could see his talent early," Harbaugh told me, "but we couldn't figure out where to apply it. He was kind of a tweener linebacker, he was okay at tight end, but not quite tall enough. So we tried him at defensive end, mainly to rush the passer. He was still a bit undersized, but it wasn't long before we saw the obvious: 'That's your position.' He saw it too—and he loved it. Ate it up."

"Man, the second he shoved me in there, it just felt like freedom," Winovich said. "Being back on that side of the ball gave me a special kind of energy. Attack!"

On December 12, 2015, in the middle of bowl practices, Winovich found inspiration from an unlikely source when he picked up an order of honey barbeque wings at Buffalo Wild Wings, near the main campus. Waiting at the hostess stand Winovich happened to look up at one of the 63 TVs lining the restaurant, where he saw an Ultimate Fighting Championship (UFC) battle, in which competitors are allowed to punch or kick their opponents during a furious five-round fight held in an octagonal cage—a futuristic gladiator contest where the normal rules don't apply—between Conor McGregor and Jose Aldo. But it wasn't much of a match, since McGregor knocked out Aldo thirteen seconds after the opening bell.

"Thirteen seconds!" Winovich said more than two years later, the image still fresh. "It was just dumb luck I saw it. I went home and looked McGregor up. In the post-fight interview the mental aspect he displayed completely grabbed me."

McGregor told the interviewer that before the bell he'd seen Aldo banging his fists, clenching his jaw, and glaring at him. McGregor realized how much Aldo hated him, which McGregor figured would make him too tense to react quickly. McGregor knew what was coming, so he decided not to wait but lead with his knockout shot as soon as they met in the middle.

"I loved that!" Winovich said. "I'm going to look like a fanboy, and this is gonna be corny, but to really reach your full potential you need a role model to aspire to. From that moment on Conor McGregor did that for me.

"I started researching him, reading everything about him, watching all his interviews. He was a no-name plumber who made the transition to Ultimate Fighting champion—and those guys are tough! I borrowed it all: his mantra—'There's no talent in this game, it's just outworking everyone'—his mindset, even his approach to workouts. He provided an example of how to view yourself in a positive manner, and how to revel in the process of becoming a champion. Not just a grind—but a thrilling journey. If it's not fun, all that work, all that pressure will wear you down mentally. I could repeat thousands of lines he's said on YouTube.

"And I decided, right then and there, that's what I wanted to be. Not a UFC fighter, but a champion: un-abashed, unapologetic, unafraid. His example encour-aged me not to be scared to take control of my life and set the bar high. Some guys don't need that, but I do. From that moment on, Conor McGregor was my inspiration.

"If you have courage enough to say your dreams out loud, they will come true. For me that meant having the courage to really buy into my dreams and invest everything I had into making them come true. He set the wheels in motion for me to define myself.

"That helped me a lot when I made the switch back to

defense. I wasn't going to wait for the coaches to anoint me a starter, or the media to discover me. On Twitter I already had a lot of critics: 'Can Winovich be an every down player, or is he just a pass rusher?' Well, I'm not gonna wait for you to tell me. I'm going to show you."

Winovich was a new man, and the coaches noticed. By the end of 2016 spring ball he had ascended from a bottom-dweller on the tight end depth chart to a defensive end rotating with the first string.

"Quite the turnaround," he said with a smile. "Playing tight end made me a better defensive end by forcing those neurons in my brain to work. I can read the play better now just based on how the offense lines up."

During the 2016 season Winovich earned starts against Central Florida and Colorado, and established himself as a pass rush specialist, finishing tenth in the country on the Pro Football Focus's Pass Rush Productivity Percentage. He had successfully rescued his career to set up a make-or-break season. If he seized the opportunity he would likely be a starter for a year or two and get the attention of NFL scouts. But if he let someone pass him by, he'd probably be watching his understudy from the sidelines for his remaining time in Ann Arbor.

Winovich started every game in 2017, working on

his rush defense while instilling fear into the hearts of quarterbacks everywhere and earning the enmity of opposing fans, who loved to hate the long-haired warrior. Despite Winovich's public persona, amplified by post-play celebrations, press conference quotes, and Twitter wars, his teammates maintain it's a mistake to dismiss him as an actor.

"Chase is a guy that is always focused, even when you don't think he's focused," Devin Bush Jr. told me. "He's always trying to get better on and off the field. He loves football, he loves living, and he loves to work."

"When we were on offense," Winovich said of 2017, "I couldn't wait to get back on the field. I wanted to play! It was fun to me. There's a big difference too, when you can tell what they're going to do before they do it. My time at tight end wasn't much fun, but it helped me accomplish my goals.

"I liked what I did that season. 'Can Winovich be an every down player?' After 2017, I didn't hear that question too often."

By the end of 2017 that question had been replaced by new ones: Was Michigan going to rebound from the 8-5 setback? Would Winovich, Higdon, and others stick around to be part of that renaissance, or would they jump to the NFL?

For Winovich the answer depended on a few factors that he discussed with his parents, his brother Peter, and Harbaugh in his office the day after the 2017 Football Bust, Michigan's awards banquet held a week after the end of the regular season.

"I wanted my family to hear what I heard," Winovich said, "because they're the one who're going to be in my corner, the people I'll be consulting to make this decision."

Like Higdon, who would meet with Harbaugh a few weeks later with several other players, Winovich raised two central concerns: nutrition and fitness. When it came to Michigan football's food program Winovich felt the team was spending too much money on food the players weren't eating.

"I think that came as news to coach," Winovich said. "But to his credit, he looked into it, and found out most of us were just showing up in the morning to get our names on the attendance list, blowing off breakfast, then eating at Coney Island."

Harbaugh soon discovered they were spending well more than a million dollars feeding the players, yet more than half the food was wasted. They fixed that by hiring Abigail O'Connor.

Winovich's second complaint also echoed his teammates': the all-important strength and conditioning program wasn't getting the results they needed. One of the reasons, Winovich told his coach, was Harbaugh's decision to turn everything they did into a competition. This was a far more sensitive issue than the food program, because competing in everything, all the time, was the driving force behind Harbaugh's incredible success as an athlete and coach. The constant competitions in Harbaugh's four-hour practices back in 2015 were widely credited by the players for turning them from a team that lost seven games in 2014 to just three each in Harbaugh's first two seasons.

But Winovich felt the approach had its limitations. During winter conditioning the team lifted on Mondays, Wednesdays, and Fridays, then had conditioning competitions on Tuesdays and Thursdays, with everyone's results posted on the wall. This had the unintended effect of encouraging players to go lightly on their Monday and Wednesday workouts so they could be fresher for the competitions the next day.

"You were trying to run your fastest sprints for the competitions," Winovich said, "so everybody was just sandbagging their squats the day before so they could show off during the races. I've never been in a weight room that was so unfocused on what we were doing, and so focused on what was looming ahead. There was a disconnect. When things have direct value to how we play on the field, it's easier for guys to buy into that. If it's unrelated, why put your all into it?"

"I wasn't the only one who felt this way, but I felt it was my job to speak up." Winovich bravely concluded his review by telling his coach, "We basically lost last winter."

Harbaugh listened. Nobody wanted to repeat 2017 less than the famously competitive head coach. He told Winovich he wasn't satisfied, either, and they'd already started interviewing strength coaches from the nation's best programs. This wasn't easy for Harbaugh, since he had brought the first strength coach with him from San Francisco, but because he believed Winovich was right, he hired Ben Herbert from Arkansas, who quickly became a huge hit with the players, and got results.

"You talk about me being open to the players," Harbaugh told me. "Well, I'm a lot more open to players who say, 'We want to eat better, and we want to train better, so we can play better,' than players who say, 'We want to work less and have more fun.' With the first group, we're willing to negotiate!"

In January 2018, months before they picked captains, Harbaugh knew that Higdon and Winovich would be team leaders—another reason to hear them out.

"Every team's different. I see the quality of the players here going up each year: guys who really want to make Michigan great, guys who are really trying to be better today than yesterday, guys who want to get good grades, work hard, and excel at football. They're really that way."

"Both my issues were fixed with flying colors," Winovich said. "Coach Herbert, he's one of the best in the business. We're making smart decisions, and it's giving us an upward trajectory, so it wasn't that hard to stay for my last year. Hats off to Coach Harbaugh. It takes a special kind of man who puts his pride aside. Having a say in the direction the team's going was a great feeling. Now it feels like it's our program too, not just Coach Harbaugh's. He's gone out of his way to make us feel that way.

"He also felt we weren't close enough. So he told us, 'When you see me don't just say 'Hi' and shake my hand. From now on, you see me in the hallway, come and give me a hug!' And we do.

"I think this is his way of being more than a boss. He's with us."

That would prove to be a vital asset when the team needed it most.

Chapter 18
To the Brink and Back

At Northwestern, September 29, 2018

After the Wolverines lingered for a few weeks between the 19th and 22nd spots in the national rankings, their thrashing of Nebraska earned them a bump up to 14th in the media poll. They benefitted from teams in front of them stumbling, but also from a serious effort over a serious program.

But a tougher foe was ahead—partly because it was undercover.

For decades the Northwestern game was as close to a bye week as Michigan could ask for—and perhaps better, since the Wolverines got credit for a victory, instead of just a week off. Under Bo Schembechler, the

Wolverines beat the Wildcats by scores like 69–0, 49–7, 38–0, 35–0, 31–0, 52–7, and—well, you get the idea.

One reason was Schembechler's paranoia about getting upset. He often warned his players, "The *upset* is in the mind of the *favorite.*" Meaning, the underdog can never beat the favorite so long as the favorite takes them seriously. Schembechler's teams always did—which drove his assistants and players crazy.

"God, we *hated* Northwestern week!" Jack Harbaugh told me. "In Bo's eyes, all week long, we couldn't do anything right—the coaches or the players. 'You're the worst coaching staff in America! You're not taking this seriously! Your D-backs are going to get shredded!' And so on, all week long—and the players got just as much. We couldn't wait to get that game behind us!"

Jim Harbaugh's 2015 Michigan team mopped up the Wildcats, 38–0, but Northwestern still managed to finish 10-3 that season, and again in 2017—two games better than Michigan. The Wildcats started the 2018 season with a win at Purdue, followed by ugly losses to Duke and the lowly Akron Zips, a team that shoots for mediocrity and only occasionally achieves it.

But since Northwestern stunned Michigan in 1995, the Wildcats have always played the Wolverines tough, and have often forced them to pull out dramatic, last-minute victories.

Michigan quarterback Devin Gardner faced the Wildcats in 2013 and 2014, and told me, "Northwestern is a team we respect. They're physically tough—very tough—and they're mentally strong, the real kind, not just the hoo-rah stuff. That's how they keep up with everyone else, with teams that probably have more talent. They can handle tough situations without breaking. They keep after you. That's a hard team to beat. If you're not at your best, they can beat you. Look at us. Look at Ohio State. Almost got us both. And with what? Players I bet neither team recruited."

Jon Jansen first played against the Wildcats in 1995, when they beat Michigan for the first time in 30 years, and has watched similar Northwestern teams since.

"You may be physically bigger and faster than those guys," he told me, "but they will not beat themselves. If they take a stupid penalty, or make a dumb mistake, those are rare exceptions, and you better be prepared to take advantage of it. They're smart, they're disciplined, they don't give up. They're *very annoying!*"

Since a career-ending knee injury relegated Grant Newsome to video analysis that fall, he saw more of Northwestern than his teammates had.

"Everyone knows they've had bad losses," he said, "so losing to them would be a disaster. But when I was watching them on tape, I'm thinking, 'This is *not* a bad team—certainly not a team that should've lost to Akron or Duke.'"

Newsome put together a seven-page analysis of the Wildcats' front seven defensive players, plus three backups, giving detailed bullet points on each player's strengths and weaknesses against both the pass and the run. He finished his report with this conclusion, all in capital letters:

THEY PLAY WITH EXTREMELY HIGH EFFORT AT NEARLY ALL POSITIONS. THEY NEVER ASSUME PLAYS ARE DEAD AND WILL RUN DOWN PLAYS FROM ALL SIDES AND ANGLES WHEN BLOCKERS DO NOT SUSTAIN. GOOD DEFENSE THAT IS FUNDAMENTALLY SOUND AND FORCES TEAMS TO EARN EVERY YARD. BETTER THAN THEIR RECORD IMPLIES!

"I knew they were going to make us earn everything," Newsome told me. "I was certainly not the first or only person in this building to recognize how good Northwestern really was, but I still felt the need to sound the alarms: heads up! These guys are going to be good, and they could beat us. And we're going on the road—the only place we've lost. So that's when you find out what a team is made of."

Ryan Field, built in 1926, holds 47,130 fans—the smallest stadium in the Big Ten, probably the most unassuming, and possibly the most charming. Since it's tucked into an old neighborhood, you don't see it until you reach Mustard's Last Stand, a great hot dog joint, in the front of the parking lot. On a wonderfully warm night, temperatures in the sixties, Wildcat fans filled the east stands, and Wolverines the west—packed house.

Northwestern was coming off a bye week, and it was clear just minutes into the contest that Pat Fitzgerald and his staff hadn't wasted the extra time. If the defense Newsome had analyzed was better than expected, Northwestern's offense was a notch above that. They had installed a series of quick, slashing, and crossing patterns designed to mitigate the damage Michigan's monstrous defensive line could inflict, while taking advantage of Michigan's preference for man-to-man coverage.

After Michigan's offense started with a three-and-out, Northwestern quarterback Clayton Thorson, a fifth-year senior who had started every game for three years, alternated three passes and three runs for a streamlined 56-yard drive for a quick touchdown. Northwestern 7, Michigan 0.

On Northwestern's next possession Thorson engineered a 10-play drive for field goal: 10–0. After Michigan failed to score again, Thorson led a 52-yard drive for another touchdown. In the game's first 18 minutes and four seconds, the Wildcats were already up 17–0. On ESPN's "Win Probability" graph, Michigan's chances quickly plummeted from 85 percent at kickoff to 31 percent.

"They jumped on us early," left tackle Jon Runyan Jr. told me. "We came out flat and didn't really move the ball at all. Then you look up at the scoreboard and you see they've already got 120 yards more than us, and they were moving it easily against our defense. And man, you just don't see that. They did exactly what they wanted to do, and they couldn't have been in much better position to pull the upset."

Jon Jansen, the All-American turned sideline announcer, reluctantly told me the Wolverines looked "lethargic." If the Wolverines didn't snap out of it they would return to Ann Arbor with a desultory 3-2 record, 1-1 in the Big Ten, far out of the top 25, and all but out of the Big Ten title race with the gauntlet and Ohio State still looming. This one loss would effectively put to an end all the hopes they had for this season—

with seven games left to play. It would also be the worst loss of the Harbaugh era, at arguably the worst possible time.

A fan named Ryan Fritz tweeted, "Can we admit yet that it's time to move on from the Harbaugh era?"

Michael Spath, a former Wolverine staffer turned WTKA noon-time host, added, "This team has a lot to prove in the heart department."

If the mood among Michigan fans was bitter, the mood among the coaches and players was surprisingly calm, confident, and determined, despite a light rain coming down, which would make a comeback that much harder.

"Even down 17–0, there was no doubting on the sideline," Gentry told me. "'Okay, we're going to come back and win this.' And we were all feeling and saying that before we did anything. First time since I've been here that I felt that."

"From the jump they punched us in the mouth, and they had us reeling," said Winovich. "But even then I thought there was zero chance we were going to give up, and zero chance we'd lose. And I wouldn't have felt that way last year."

"When you're down like that a lot of teams give up," Higdon said. "Maybe we would have last year. But not this year. You dig a hole like that, you have two options: go in your shell, or show up."

Another key: "Don't try to get them all back at once," Shea Patterson told me. "You panic, and you try to do too much, and you just make it all worse. You've got to trust your teammates, trust your defense to hold them, and go get one touchdown."

After the Wolverines took over at their own 21 the line gave Higdon room to run for 28 yards. Patterson calmly hit Collins for five yards, and third-string tight end Nick Eubanks for 21. Peoples-Jones ran a reverse for 25 yards and Higdon punched it in from the four-yard line. Not one failed play in the series.

Michigan 7, Northwestern 17. 9:14 left in the half.

The same defense that the Wildcats had shredded with a steady diet of slants and crosses in the first 18 minutes went on lockdown mode, sending the Wildcats to the sidelines on seven straight possessions, six of them punctuated by sacks. That was particularly surprising after Rashan Gary left the game with his right shoulder acting up again. While Winovich was getting double-teamed, Gary's replacements, Kwity Paye on most first and second downs and Josh Uche on third downs, accounted for two sacks each, while Winovich added one himself, despite the extra attention.

On offense the same line that the Wildcats' defense had pushed around for most of the first half seemed to grow up in unison, giving Patterson more time in the pocket than he'd enjoyed all year, and Higdon more holes to run the ball a personal record 30 times, for 115 yards—his third 100-plus game of the season. Michigan's first two drives of the second half both lasted 11 plays. Although they had to settle for field goals deep inside the red zone, which cut Northwestern's lead to 17–13 at the end of the third quarter, they had gained control of the trenches. Still, when the Wolverines had to punt a minute into the fourth quarter, their "Win Probability" had improved only slightly, to 34 percent—but that's not how they felt.

With 10:05 left in the game, still trailing 17-13, Michigan's defense gave the offense the ball once again. On the first snap from Michigan's 33-yard line, with the game and possibly the season in the balance, Patterson found fullback Jared Wangler on a play called "Rush Spittoon" for a nine-yard gain—Wangler's first career catch, only five years in the making. Then Patterson hit Gentry for 13 and 22 yards. On the five-yard line Higdon ran through a gigantic gap for his second touchdown of the game, fifth of his season, and 22nd of his career, completing a near-perfect drive.

Michigan 20, Northwestern 17, with just 4:06 left in the game.

The defense stopped the Wildcats once more, and after the offense knocked off another 2:28 but had to punt, the defense stopped them again, ending the game on Uche's second sack of the night.

Michigan's 20–17 comeback didn't impress the media, who would grumble about Michigan's near upset to 1-3 Northwestern the entire week, or the pollsters, who would drop Michigan one spot. But the narrow victory seemed to show a lot to the men in the locker room—starting with the head coach.

Though usually "excited but calm" after victories, "Coach Harbaugh was in rare form after that one," Runyan said. So much so, every player I talked to recalled Harbaugh's unusual demeanor—letting loose, whooping and hollering with the players—and could quote Harbaugh's lines.

"Gentlemen, that was a huge *program* win," Harbaugh told them. "We were down and out, on the ropes—and we didn't give up! There was not *one second* when we didn't believe in each other, didn't believe we would do it. We kept fighting—and that's a testament to your great spirit.

"You'd be hard-pressed to find a better half of football than the second half you just played against Northwestern. You just *shut them down*! You scored 13 points that we simply had to have, and you drained the clock.

"You've got to have a win like that if you're going to have a fantastic season—and you guys just got it. That is going to propel our season. I am *proud* of you!"

Harbaugh's message stayed with the players the rest of the season.

"Honestly," Bredeson said, "it was just like he was playing again, like one of us, such an emotional high. You really didn't see that energy level all last year."

"My favorite quote from Coach Harbaugh," Winovich said. "'We just ruined the best night of their lives!' We cheered and laughed—probably the greatest celebration I've been a part of in *any* sport."

"The road wins always make you feel the best," Harbaugh told me later. "You beat another team in their home with their crowd—and in that game, you beat the elements, too. That's a trifecta triumph. I was just *giddy*."

The players knew such a narrow victory over a battered opponent wouldn't play well with the public, but the Wolverines had secured the fourth-biggest comeback, and the second-biggest comeback on the road, in school history, going back to 1879.

"We know we're going to get ripped for barely beating Northwestern," Bredeson told me the next day. "Hell, we probably already are. We don't care.

"We know we're going down in the rankings. We don't care.

"Because *we know* we came together when we had to. We know how hard that was—and how we never doubted it. We know what that game meant to us. So it really doesn't matter what everyone else thinks."

"Our critics are always going to try to find reasons to take away from our success," Higdon said. "We knew that what we accomplished was special that day, and we had every right to celebrate the way we did."

With this victory they seemed to come to a crucial decision: they would concern themselves only with the people inside their room, and nobody outside it. They would write their story themselves.

PART III

October

Chapter 19
The Backup
Jared Wangler

"When I was playing on a fifth-grade AAU basketball team," Jared Wangler recalled, "I took a hand in the face and broke my nose. It produced a good amount of blood, so I had to come out of the game for a bit. But my dad was the coach, so I didn't cry. Stuck some Kleenex up my nose and went back in."

Jared's dad happened to be Michigan quarterback John Wangler, who overcame a blown-up left knee (courtesy of UNC's Lawrence Taylor in the 1979 Gator Bowl) to lead the Wolverines to the 1981 Rose Bowl victory, Schembechler's first in six tries.

On Michigan's 2018 football team ten players were sons of Michigan football players—probably the most

of any program in the country. Many of their fathers'
names are well-known to Michigan fans, like All-Big
Ten honorable mention tight end Craig Dunaway, All-
Big Ten second team running back Stan Edwards, and
All-American Brad Cochran. But perhaps the most fa-
mous of the football dads are John Wangler and Rich
Hewlett, who battled for the position back in 1979 and
1980.

It was a hard-fought, often tense competition, but the
two became best friends, and remain so today. Their
sons Joe Hewlett and Jack and Jared Wangler grew up
together and played for Michigan, with Jared Wangler
earning a scholarship. Jared and his teammates were
thrilled—and more than a little surprised—when Jim
Hackett hired Jim Harbaugh. They welcomed the end
of chaos and confusion and the return of order and optimism, but it came with a few adjustments.

"I thought I'd finally grasped how to be a college
football player under Coach Hoke," Wangler said, "and
then Coach Harbaugh brings in a totally different system and culture. Under Hoke, we thought we were
grinding, and the results just weren't coming. Then
Harbaugh comes in and we quickly realized we didn't
understand what it really took, what hard work really
looked like."

John Wangler had warned him, "Jimmy's gonna

push you farther than anyone you've had. You gotta be prepared for anything."

Jared's dad was right about that. At Harbaugh's first team meeting he gave the players a long list of new rules and a schedule that started with 6 a.m. workouts, when everything would be a competition: every rep recorded, with scores for wins and losses, and the results announced at the next meeting.

"Then he drops the bomb on us," Jared recalled. Four-hour practices. Honestly, we thought he was joking. Two and a half was as long as we'd ever gone before. But he definitely wasn't joking. It was a shock to a lot of people. I remember there was a lot of pushback from the older players, and Coach weeded those guys out—or really, they weeded themselves out. During my first spring practice guys were dropping like flies. But by the end of spring ball we were a different team."

With the help of their fathers, who recalled Schembechler's two-a-days during spring ball and three-a-days in fall camp, Joe Hewlett and the Wanglers stuck with it.

"You get used to the four-hour practices," Jared said. "And once you do it's kind of a nice motivational thing because you know damn well there's no other team in the country doing four-hour practices. So you figure we do this, we'll be more prepared."

Having survived 15 four-hour spring practices, Wangler and his teammates were in for another surprise.

"I thought spring was tough, but fall camp was tougher—the hardest I'd ever experienced. You look at the first day's schedule, you just *stared* at it, and you kept looking for a little pocket for a nap or something, until you realized there's no time left for anything else. Six in the morning to ten at night: workouts, practice, meetings. I don't know if we had a day off. The whole camp runs one month, but it felt like six months. This was not for the faint of heart, but the mental aspect really forms you."

Not only for the season ahead, but for the next level—whether it's the NFL or the working world.

"All the guys we still keep in touch with in the NFL, or the real world," Jared said, "they all say the same thing: when they left here there wasn't anything they weren't ready for. [NFLers] Mason Cole, Jake Butt, Ben Gideon—all those guys. They say Coach Harbaugh brought the NFL-type culture here: if you don't work hard, you're going to lose your spot. So when they got to the NFL, they had a leg up on the other rookies because they knew what to expect—from the playbook, to the practice field. Nothing threw them.

"Even in the real world, same thing. My brother Jack is at Ernst and Young now. He's a smart guy, but there are a lot of really smart guys from good schools all over the country in his office. But he says they don't know how to handle the workload, and the stress. Well, here, you're working and under stress all the time. So I'm not worried about what's next. I'll be able to handle it."

Wangler witnessed the difference after Harbaugh's first game as Michigan's head coach in 2015.

"We knew Utah would give us a good battle, but we still thought, 'We're Michigan, you're Utah.' We've got to be better than them, right? But we lose that game [24–17], so now we're down in the dumps. All that work, all those four-hour practices, for what?

"But when we got home, we made the rest of the season 'us against the world.' All the outside noise— ignore it or use it as motivation. The word was, 'Good coach, bad players,' but we knew we weren't bad players. That pissed off a lot of guys, and it became a big rallying thing. We're not going to wait for the recruits. We're good enough to win now."

Three straight shutouts proved that. Even after the loss to Michigan State on one of the craziest plays in football history, the Wolverines beat everyone left on their schedule but Ohio State to finish 10-3, twice as good as the year before.

"So that's what we learned: you do the work, at that level, you get the results."

The train kept rolling into 2016, starting with a top ten recruiting class including Rashan Gary, Devin Bush, and Ben Bredeson.

"Man, we had so much talent coming in," Jared said, plus eleven players who would be drafted after that season. "That whole season was about as fun as it gets. We just *beat down* a lot of teams. The current seniors, we still talk about that year. We felt like we were the best team in the country—a great senior class, so many physical players, we could just push teams around."

Two weeks after the 9-0, second-ranked Wolverines were upset at Iowa by a point they lost in double overtime at Ohio State, then lost again by a point in the Orange Bowl. Nonetheless, the 2016 season is still revered by the current players, while 2017 is not—a campaign filled with doubts, setbacks, and general unhappiness.

"But I think it says a lot that no one made excuses," Wangler said. "You never heard any of us say we were the youngest team in the country."

Of their five losses four were battles, including Ohio State, when Michigan jumped out to a 14–0 lead before quarterback problems cost the game. But when you lose four consecutive conference games to finish fourth-place in your division—and you're Michigan—you can expect the pundits to denigrate your coach, your players, and your program.

"Look, winning is part of the tradition here," Wangler explained. "No one came here to go 8-5. You don't do all this to lose five games. You come here to win. But all that kind of set us up for this year. In my five years here I've seen a hell of a lot, and I've come to believe it really boils down to experience and buying in. And we've got that. And if you don't buy in here, you find yourself walking out that door."

Wangler's personal resolve was tested when he learned he would not be getting a scholarship for his fifth year. He considered transferring to Indiana, where he would likely start, until Coach Chris Partridge "talked me out of that." Wangler decided to stay and pay his own way—no small thing when his graduate program in real estate development, through Michigan's school of architecture and the business school, costs $15,000 a semester.

Wangler also switched from linebacker to fullback—a position that barely exists in the NFL, but playing on Sundays was never his goal. He adjusted quickly, playing backup to sophomore starter Ben Mason. Wangler made his first career catch against Northwestern, but he still hadn't scored a touchdown. Amazingly, his father—who threw for 26 touchdowns—had never set foot in the end zone, either.

Before their fifth and final season, Jared Wangler

and Joe Hewlett learned their fathers had been room-mates on the road, so they asked to room together on Friday nights, too. When their wish was granted they called their room "The Old Man Suite," with fellow fifth-year senior Juwann Bushell-Beatty next door.

Jared Wangler also pined to wear his dad's number five, which he had worn throughout Little League and high school.

"I feel comfortable in it," he said. "It's a number I love. Putting that over your head—it just has a differ-ent feeling."

But because Michigan All-American Jabrill Peppers was wearing it, "that's a tough one to swing," Wangler joked. "I didn't quite have the pull to ask for it. But when Peppers left [for the NFL], I jumped on it."

In fall camp Wangler hoped to earn one of the scholarships that come available due to transfers and injuries, when Michigan players are put on "medi-cal redshirt." He had become a valuable contributor on special teams and a reliable fullback, taking all the snaps during spring ball while Ben Mason was out with a knee injury. But during a practice on August 11, Wangler tore his meniscus in his left knee, got it oper-ated on, and was told he would be out 8 to 12 weeks.

Wangler then had to watch teammates take his place on offense and special teams.

"I was infuriated," he told me. "The timing, the combination of everything. Maddening."

Wangler told the doctors they were wrong—he *had* to play against Notre Dame—and came back 19 days later, just in time to take the field on September first in South Bend. Despite the tough loss, Wangler was still grateful to get on the same field where his dad had competed—and also lost a heartbreaker, 29–27, on a last-second kick.

"You know you're going to get everyone's best game, always, because they're coming to play Michigan," Wangler said, "and that's the way you want it.

"That's why you come here."

Chapter 20
Tragedy at Maryland

The leading stories about Michigan's upcoming game against Maryland focused on two men who would not be participating, for very different reasons.

Rashan Gary would be wearing sweats on the sideline due to the shoulder he secretly injured in practice a week before the Notre Dame game, and re-injured in the Northwestern game.

The second would be Maryland head coach D. J. Durkin, who lost a player to heatstroke, and then was suspended with pay by the university before the opening game.

This became an ongoing national story, but also hit close to home for many Michigan men because Durkin had coached Jim Harbaugh's defense at Stanford for three years and at Michigan for one. Under Durkin

Michigan's 2015 defense rose from 41st to seventh—one of the biggest reasons the Wolverines doubled their win total from five in Hoke's last year to ten in Harbaugh's first year.

Among the Michigan players I interviewed, most didn't like Durkin but none thought he was dangerous.

"You'd never guess just looking at him," Jared Wangler said of the seemingly mild-mannered coach, "but when he puts that whistle around his neck, he becomes someone else."

Durkin's targets included Jared Wangler, Noah Furbush, and Brandon Watson, among the smartest, hardest-working, and most coachable players on the team, not prone to complaining about a hard practice. But they remember Durkin barking at players, "You will never play here at Michigan!" and worse. Perhaps more important was what they didn't recall: Durkin showing he cared about them.

"Bo would say things like that, but he'd love you harder," Jared said. "My dad'll tell you."

"Bo was tough," John Wangler confirmed, "but he was a players' coach. People don't believe me when I say that, but if you were trying, he was on your side."

Wangler's son did not feel the same way about Durkin.

"There's a line," Jared said, "but you can tell when

the guy pushing you cares about you or not. Coach Brown, yeah he's tough, and so's Coach Harbaugh, but you know they care about you. There's a way to do it—and this wasn't that."

Durkin's success at Stanford and Michigan made him one of the nation's hot young head coaching prospects, so it was not surprising when Maryland offered him their top spot the next year, 2016, and he accepted.

He had his work cut out for him. The Terrapins had finished dead last in the Big Ten East Division in 2015, their second in the Big Ten. In Durkin's first two seasons it looked like he was turning Maryland's program around. But during an intense conditioning session in the spring of 2018, a 19-year-old offensive lineman named Jordan McNair collapsed due to heat exhaustion. Medical staff and players witnessed him suffer an apparent seizure.

According to *The Diamondback,* Maryland's student newspaper, when the school brought in a professional trainer, Dr. Rod Walters, to investigate, one player told him head trainer Wes Robinson shouted across the field to "get [McNair] the fuck up!" Another player recalled Robinson yelled for them to "drag his ass across the field!" statements corroborated by ESPN's report. One hour later—yes, *one hour later*—somebody finally saw fit to call 911. In the hospital doctors discovered McNair's temperature had shot up to 106 degrees; 15 days later, he died.

To his credit Maryland president Wallace Loh gave the family an unqualified apology and took full responsibility, which seemed to come from the heart instead of a team of lawyers. But no similar sentiments came from the people who actually had been responsible.

As the weeks passed it was not clear what Maryland was going to do about the tragedy, if anything, until ESPN published a report in August, two months after McNair's death, exposing a toxic culture of Maryland coaches bullying their players and endangering their health on a regular basis. This forced Maryland to suspend Durkin and his strength coach, Rick Court, who was soon let go. The university put Durkin on paid administrative leave while conducting an 80-day investigation.

When Maryland's report came out on October 25 it largely confirmed ESPN's findings, which would seem to make the next step obvious: fire Durkin, and keep his interim replacement, Matt Canada, who had been doing surprisingly well under trying circumstances. The Terps had gone 3-1 under him, including a win over 23rd-ranked Texas in the first week, and morale seemed to be on the rise.

Instead, on Tuesday, October 30, the regents threatened to fire President Loh if he did not *keep* Durkin. President Loh told them he would resign instead of carry out their orders. To keep Durkin, the board accepted President Loh's resignation.

How Durkin's return would be received by the players, McNair's parents, the parents of future recruits, and the public were four considerations the regents apparently gave no thought. It is hard to fathom what they were thinking.

The board's decision was so careless and so heartless that it created an overwhelming backlash from Maryland students, faculty, alumni, and even the governor of the state—not to mention many of the players. That this surprised the trustees only confirms how out of touch they were. The tsunami of outrage was so great the university reversed the board's decision the next day, October 31, and proceeded to fire Durkin, leaving Matt Canada to coach the rest of the season.

In the past decade in the Big Ten East Division alone, we've seen: Penn State's trustees mishandle the Jerry Sandusky tragedy in 2011–12; Michigan's former athletic director blow the Shane Morris concussion situation in 2014; Michigan State's board, president, and interim president botch the Larry Nassar scandal repeatedly; Ohio State discover a team doctor abused at least 177 male athletes, and then mishandle their abusive assistant football coach, Zach Smith; and now this.

These situations have little in common except their responses, which were all as cynically self-interested as they were stupid—and utterly unhelpful. They also undercut the argument that university presidents are higher-minded than their athletic directors. In most of these cases, the presidents and trustees behaved far worse.

The Maryland leaders might have thought up worse ways to handle this crisis, but none immediately come to mind. It was no surprise when the national media argued they should all resign.

Just when you figured Maryland couldn't make it worse, a few days before the Michigan game Maryland football booster Rick Jaklitsch, a personal injury lawyer, told the student paper, "As much as we hate to say this, Jordan [McNair] didn't do what Jordan was supposed to do," blaming McNair for his own death for not hydrating enough—when evidence points to Maryland's staff for his collapse and their hour-long delay in calling for help.

When some Terrapin football players let it be known that Jaklitsch would not be welcome on the team plane heading to Michigan, the day before the game Jaklitsch decided not to attempt to board. The showdown proved the players had greater moral courage facing rich and powerful men than did their trustees.

Beyond the considerable damage to the sport, when it could ill-afford any more, this was largely Maryland's problem. But it still touched Michigan's players, especially those who had played for Durkin.

"Because of that," Wangler said, "we all came to the Maryland game with some extra juice."

Wangler had additional motivation. The coaches had installed a play featuring him called, "Right 30 U-Right Keep 97 F-Slide," also known as "U-47," for the sum of the two fullbacks' numbers, Ben Mason's 42 and Wangler's 5. The play sets up with both fullbacks in the I-formation, with Wangler taking a route to the right flat for a pass. If it all worked, Wangler would become the quarterback's first target.

Even if Michigan got into the national playoff, and Wangler stayed healthy, he would have a maximum of 10 games left, with 85 percent of his career behind him. If he wanted to be the first Wangler to set foot in the end zone, the clock was ticking.

And if that were not enough, Jared's Grandpa Wangler—whose wife, a vivacious former teacher well-known to Michigan tailgaters as "Mama Wangs," had passed away the previous year—had fallen the week of the Northwestern game and fractured his pelvis. The 90-year-old was recovering at Beaumont Hospital near Detroit when Jared visited him the day after the Northwestern game, fresh from a historic comeback and his first collegiate reception.

Grandpa Wangler had asked Jared, "If you do something special in the Maryland game, what are you going to do so I'll know you're thinking of me?"

"I'll point to the sky," Jared said.

Now he just had to do something special.

Chapter 21
Making a Little History

Maryland, October 6, 2018

After lightning delayed the noon kickoff to 1:10, the temperature climbed to the mid-70s, the sun came out, and a perfect stage was set for Michigan's third Big Ten game of the season.

Although the stakes for this game were not particularly high—another contest where the Wolverines had much to lose but little to gain—it was still a league game, and an East Division game at that. If the Wolverines got caught looking ahead to the upcoming gauntlet of Wisconsin, Michigan State, and Penn State, they could easily stumble against a team that had already knocked off a strong Texas team.

"We didn't go in lightly," Higdon told me.

When the Terrapins started trash-talking the Michigan players jogging by in the tunnel before the game, Higdon figured they wanted to take advantage of a trap game for Michigan, with Wisconsin on deck. If so, Higdon said, they had miscalculated.

"No way we were going to let that happen."

The Wolverines won the coin toss and elected to receive again, which seemed like an odd strategy for a team that often had trouble getting started.

It took Michigan three possessions to get on the scoreboard with a field goal—immediately followed by Maryland's 98-yard kickoff return to take a 7–3 lead.

Penn State beat writer Ben Jones, a cool-headed scribe, was moved to ask, "In all seriousness what has Michigan gotten better at since Harbaugh took the job?"

Michigan's fifth possession started on its own five-yard line, from which fewer than 10 percent of drives end up scoring any points. But after a bunch of basic runs and Patterson's 51-yard pass to Nico Collins, Ben Mason once again finished the job with a one-yard run—which was more impressive than it sounds, since Maryland's defender had stepped up to fill the gap, only to have Mason run him over.

It marked Mason's fifth touchdown on only 14

carries—an absurd ratio, made possible because his main role was to finish what Patterson and Higdon started. The 11-play, 95-yard drive marked Michigan's longest scoring drive since the first week of 2016 against Hawaii. The Wolverines had outgained Maryland 227–23 to that point—yet that was also the bad news, since all those yards had earned them a mere 10–7 lead midway through the second quarter, thanks to their inability to finish in the red zone.

Another Michigan touchdown and field goal gave the Wolverines a 20–7 lead midway through the third quarter, which still wasn't much for a team that had outgained its foe 335–43.

Patterson worked to expand that lead on Michigan's next possession when he twisted one way to avoid a rusher, then turned back to the Michigan sideline to avoid another before hitting People-Jones near the sideline, who split two defenders and eluded two more on his way to the end zone.

Maryland 7, Michigan 27. End of third quarter.

But Maryland came right back with another touchdown—the first allowed by Michigan's defense in 91:28, more than a game and a half—to cut Michigan's margin to 27–14 with 11:28 left in the game. Despite dominating the Terrapins in virtually every statistical category, the Wolverines hadn't put them away.

Taking over on Michigan's own 19-yard line, Patterson hit Gentry for 16 yards—he would catch 7 passes for a career high 112 yards that game—and Tru Wilson ran for 36 yards to get down to Maryland's 7-yard line.

When Harbaugh called for both Ben Mason and Jared Wangler to go in, "we knew what was coming," Mason said, "just based on where we were on the field. In the huddle, I could see in [Wangler's] eyes just how excited he was, because he's put in so much work."

And that's when Harbaugh sent the signal for U-47 into Patterson. When Patterson passed it on to his teammates in the huddle, Wangler and Mason locked eyes, nodded, and bumped their helmets together.

This was Wangler's chance, and everyone on the field knew it. Three of them lived in Wangler's house: Runyan at left tackle, Gentry and McKeon at tight end; plus one of Wangler's European travel buddies, Juwann Bushell-Beatty, at right tackle; and two more housemates, Jordan Glasgow and Brandon Peters, watching from the sideline.

With the play clock running down, they took their positions seconds before the snap.

"Mason's behind me," Wangler recalled, "and he slaps my ass and says, 'Let's go, bro!'"

Wangler saw that Maryland's strong-side linebacker was playing up so Wangler would have to go past him, not in front of him, before cutting right. This was crucial to the play, because if Wangler made even incidental contact with the linebacker he wouldn't be able to get to his spot in time, and Patterson would quickly switch to either Gentry or McKeon.

"I had a cool, confident feel," Wangler told me. "Confident in my hands, and my ability. I knew I could make this play work. And I *had* to make this play work because if I didn't, I'd never see a pass again! This was it."

Patterson walked up to the line, crouched under center, and barked, "Hurry-Hurry-Set-Go!"

Gentry, setting up on the right side of the line, blocked down on the defensive end, leaving an open path for Wangler to jump out past Gentry's man without making any contact. So far, so good.

Once Gentry finished his block, he ran beyond Wangler as the second option on the play. Wangler approached the strong-side linebacker, who remained up, so he made a hard cut behind him to the right—two yards into the new blue end zone.

"I was pretty open," Wangler said. "By the time I looked back Shea's rolling out and looking where to throw."

"I remember turning around," Gentry told me, "and seeing Jared was open, praying he'd get a good ball."

Patterson saw that Wangler, his first option, was open as planned, and fired. The ball was low and to Wangler's left, so he had to dive for it.

"But it's football," Wangler said. "You've been playing your whole life. So you're in the moment, just reacting, instead of thinking."

When the ball arrived Wangler trusted his instincts: "Catch it, cradle it, and let my momentum carry me out of bounds. I really didn't know I was in the end zone until I looked down on my way through, when I was skidding out, and saw the blue turf.

"Now the thinking starts. It was just one of those moments, only the second catch of my career, but a lot of hard work went into it. I'm a fifth-year senior, and this was everything I'd been working for."

"For everything to come together on that play," Mason told me, "for Jared to get that opportunity and seize the moment—that was not only great for the team, but his family too, because he really loves this program, and he loves this school. You don't turn down a scholarship to come back for nothing for any other reason."

Wangler's teammates mobbed him.

"We were all running into the end zone," Gentry recalls. "I was one of the first to get to him. We crashed face masks and screamed at each other. 'AHHHHHH!!!'"

Mason was the second teammate to find Wangler. "We were just going crazy," he recalled, "just yelling and screaming and going nuts. But we all knew how special the moment was for all of us. It was pure excitement and joy—a great moment."

"They all knew how much it meant to me," Wangler said, "something you figure you'll remember the rest of your life."

While his teammates ran down the sideline to join the mob, Wangler recalled a promise he'd made to his grandfather a few days before, and pointed upward to let him know he was thinking of him.

When Wangler got back to the sideline his brother Jack happened to be sitting in the front row, screaming at him to come over. They hugged, then someone yelled for Jared to return to the field, because Michigan was going for two.

"I was gassed after all the jumping around," Wangler recalled, "but still so fired up I sprinted back on the field."

Jay Harbaugh called the same play, U-47, but this time Patterson handed off to Mason for an easy two.

Maryland 14, Michigan 35. With 6:37 left, it was finally over.

If Wangler felt a twinge of revenge against Durkin's team, he was joined by cornerback Brandon Watson,

another target of Durkin's. On Maryland's next possession Watson followed his man closely, read the play
correctly, stepped up to catch the ball at Maryland's
45-yard line, and pivoted toward the end zone, where
he completed the pick-six with his hand in the air.

"Two guys that Durkin loved to pick on, putting the
nail in the coffin on his team," Wangler said. "I can't
lie: it felt good."

After Michigan closed out a convincing 42–14 win,
Wangler showered and changed, and started his cus-
tomary walk from the tunnel to his family's tailgate
a couple hundred yards away. On the way he ran into
a friend who had a brother on Maryland's team, who
confirmed the ESPN report was "100 percent accurate," Wangler recalled. "Who would send their kid
there?"

For four and a half seasons, after 32 home games,
Wangler's family and friends would always wait for him.

"They never missed," Wangler said, "and they
always greeted me with a smile. A lot of those games
early on in my career I didn't even sniff the field. So for
me to come back to the tailgate after scoring a touchdown, it felt extra special."

Long after Jared and his friends had gone home,
John Wangler and I were still talking in the parking

lot. John is anything but a braggart—he isn't even sure if he threw 25 or 26 touchdown passes—but he couldn't conceal his pride in what Jared had accomplished.

For John, it wasn't simply a matter of Jared getting into the end zone—something John was quick to point out he had never done—but all Jared's quiet battles behind the scenes that had impressed him. The touchdown was a delicious cherry on top—the symbol of a struggle completed.

When I asked John how Jared's one touchdown catch compared to John's 26 touchdown passes, he grinned, then pushed his lower lip up to control his emotions while shaking his head, his eyes suddenly glassy.

"Not even close, brother," he finally said, when he trusted himself to speak again. "Not even close. You can take my touchdowns and swap 'em for that one, and I'd be happy. I can't describe how it feels."

But any parent already knows.

We hadn't noticed the sunshine had been replaced by a gentle rain until we looked around and realized every sane person had already left, and we were by ourselves in the parking lot outside the Big House.

Football communications director Dave Ablauf once again picked Karan Higdon to be one of three offensive players to handle the post-game press conference. He had a lot to brag about. No one had run for 100 yards on Maryland's defense all year, and he had just tagged them for 103 yards on 23 carries—his fourth game in a row running for more than 100 yards. He was on pace to break 1,000 if he avoided injury.

But what he wanted to talk about was the offensive line. "They grow every single week," he told me. "They're getting better and better. They're really finding their groove."

Higdon hopped in his car for the drive back to Sterling Heights.

"The other guys like to party in their houses or in the bars, but I love going home to see my family."

They would relax and watch some football—but not before his daughter, Kiyah, who had just turned four, gave him her assessment of his play with a thumbs up or down. She's no pushover, having giving him thumbs down after a game in 2017.

As soon as Higdon got out of his car, "She's jumping in my arms, talking to me about the game. Thumbs up! Then she's telling me how she wants to get a Halloween costume. So we go get a costume at Party City—'Elsa' from *Frozen*—then we watched more football."

Kiyah fell asleep in her daddy's arms.

Chapter 22
The Eye in the Sky
Never Lies
The Video Staff

While Higdon relaxed at home with his family and his teammates went to the bars, met friends at home, or got some much-needed sleep, Phil Bromley and his assistant, Kevin Undeen, plus seven paid students, four student interns, and a few volunteers were breaking down video for the staff.

You can thank Sid Gillman, the only coach to be inducted into both the College and Pro Football halls of fame. His coaching tree has won almost half the Super Bowls ever played, and he was, by all accounts, a good guy and a superb coach. But his greatest epiphany came to him as a movie theater usher in Minneapolis in the 1920s. He realized this new technology could be applied to his real passion: football.

The game would never be the same.

Since then coaches have logged untold millions of hours—away from their wives, their children, and their beds—staring at flickering 16mm film, VHS, SVHS, Beta, and MII video tapes, DVDs, Blu-ray disks, and now processed computer video files sent to central services, where they can be downloaded by each team's video staff just minutes after every game. The coaches also watch their own practice video, and blurry recruiting footage sent by eager high school coaches, parents, and recruiting services. The average Division I coach probably watches 40 hours of video a week, every week, for half the year—almost a full-time job in itself.

Michigan's former offensive coordinator, Cal Magee, once told me, "When I close my eyes, I see little men playing football inside my head. That can't be good."

But try telling that to any self-respecting head coach, and he'll give you a dismissive snarl in return.

From the end of the Maryland game on Saturday evening to early Sunday morning, Bromley and Undeen were toiling in the film room, processing game video.

They're in charge of the 200-plus computer monitors and TV flat screens that cover just about every desk and wall of Schembechler Hall. In their windowless 20-by-25-foot office alone they've crammed 25 big screens, stacked three screens high at each seat. The room also features a Nerf hoop and a couch, but I've never seen any of them used either unless a visitor goads them into taking a few shots.

About half of the 200 screens in the building have been registered with a $2,500 license per computer to receive the XOS video program, which allows every subscriber to do just about anything they'd ever want to do with football video, including identify all 22 players on every play in practice that afternoon, then filter them so Chase Winovich can pull up every third-and-long play he participated in that day—all in minutes. It's not cheap, but if that's what it takes, that's what they pay. Why? Because most weeks the coaches spend more time watching video than everything else combined. Video is the lifeblood of the profession.

Bromley and his staff sift through thousands of hours of Michigan's practices, Michigan's games, and Michigan's opponents' games, then package them so the coaches, the players, and the recruiters get exactly what they want, when they want it. On a given day offensive line coach Ed Warinner might want to see how his guys have improved on third-and-short situations from Notre Dame through Maryland; defensive coordinator Don Brown could ask for Wisconsin's third-and-long plays in the red zone; Devin Bush Jr. might have 15 minutes after class to break down his plays against Maryland; and Harbaugh might ask to see what happened to Ohio State in their come-from-behind victory at Penn State, or the Buckeyes' wobbly win over Indiana the previous weekend.

Every coach, every night, watches that afternoon's practice, separated by offense, defense, and special teams. They take all this in while wolfing down their dinners in the coaches' main meeting room, where the blind has been drawn for years. If they ever painted that one window black, these guys would never notice.

Born and raised in Michigan, Bromley moved to Florida in grade school. At the University of Florida he started at center next to future seven-time All-Pro Lomas Brown, a lifelong friend. After Bromley finished playing in 1984 he stayed on as a graduate assistant, the lowest-ranked coaches who are paid in tuition, working with old-fashioned 16mm film. Learning that skill made Bromley more valuable than most G.A.s.

In 1988 Bromley got an interview with Bo Schembechler and the entire coaching staff to become a G.A. at Michigan. At the end, Schembechler asked, "What do you think about being a Wolverine?"

"I'm in, Coach! When do you need me?"

Michigan was still using 16mm film, which Bromley had to break down on an old Steinbeck machine. This required mastering a skill called "hot-splicing." If a coach wanted a reel of defensive goal-line stands, for example, Bromley would cut all those out of the printed copy reel, then scrape the chemicals off the first frame of the clip he'd just taken and the last frame of the film he was going to add it to, then glue the two pieces together, and finally seal the joints in the hot press. Once he got the hang of it he could finish a hot splice in less than a minute.

"And that's one," Bromley said. "We would do about 1,200 hot splices each week, every week." If they did a shoddy job on just one of those, the film would break.

"I'll paint the picture for you," Bromley said. "You're in the staff room. Lights out. Coaches sitting around the table. You run the 16mm film through the projector. There's a little blank window between each play. When you start cutting out each play, you've got to decide where you want to put it.

"The coaches say, 'We want this play to go with the goal line plays.' Or the pass plays, or short yardage, or blitzes, or different defensive fronts, or whatever. But you only have one printed copy, so you can only pick one group for each play."

Bromley would then cut that play out of the printed copy and pin it with a thumbtack into the wall next to the strips of other goal-line plays. Then he and his GAs would hot-splice one group together, using a hand reel. It took forever—but they didn't have forever so they worked fast as possible, often all night.

Then came the moment of truth when they showed a reel of plays for the coaches, with Schembechler almost always in the room, and everyone tired and cranky. If one of their 1,200 hot splices snapped the screen turned bright white, the film whipped around the reel, and Schembechler would interrupt himself midsentence.

"God daaaaaaaammmmn it!"

Bromley and the other GAs would jump up and work as urgently as a pit crew to make a new hot splice, while the assistant coaches would sneak off for a fresh cup of coffee or a bathroom break, relieved Schembechler wasn't yelling at them.

Bromley recalled thinking, "'Coach, you can stop yelling at this point, because I've identified the same problem you have. Also, could you please move out of the way so I can get some light and do this faster?' But I never dared say it."

While Schembechler barked, the graduate assistants sitting against the wall all looked at each other in silent reproof: "Who did it?" Whoever it was would get it after the meeting ended.

Mercifully, Michigan fully embraced the cutting-edge VHS technology the next year, 1989. No more hot-splicing.

It appeared Bromley had found his niche, until 1990, when the NCAA reduced the number of GAs each team could have from five down to two.

"I went home to our apartment that day and ol' Phil Bromley might have shed a few tears, knowing that my coaching career was over. 'Oh shit, this is done.' But sometimes fate works out the way it should."

Michigan could only offer Bromley a volunteer position, but he was now 27, and his wife Jill was working out of Washington, D.C., as a flight attendant. They hoped to have kids, and zero income was not a good start. But when Michigan realized they had to have a video director, and Bromley was good at it, they scraped together $24,000 to pay him as a staff member, not a GA, for his first year.

"I had excitement back in my life," he said. "I missed coaching players but I knew what I was doing was valuable to the program, and I saw the future. There was going to be more of this, not less. I liked the technology. I was part of writing the book, not just reading it. We were pioneers. At Michigan, if you can make a case that you really need it, you'll probably get it, and the people are the best. That's why I've stayed."

Bromley's life improved when Michigan embraced

videotape, but his hours didn't. Like most technological advances, every video invention saved time—and created more work, which invariably gobbled up those saved hours and then some. VHS ended hot-splicing but not the limitations of linear editing, which prevented videographers from skipping around within the game film for what they wanted, forcing them to run through the entire tape chronologically to find what they were looking for—then scan back to the spot where they wanted to move it.

With a staff consisting of two students, Bromley slept on the office couch three nights a week just to get the cutups to the coaches on time. By 1995 Bromley had a family, he was tired, and he knew he couldn't keep up that pace and be a decent husband or father. Once again the athletic department saved the day—and Bromley's job—by allowing Bromley to purchase a nonlinear editing system, even though it cost a gasp-inducing $600,000.

Bromley's load lightened a little more four years later when he took on a student assistant named Kevin Undeen.

"There's a bond there," Bromley told me, "a lot of trust, and that resulted in me giving him a lot of rope early on."

Undeen liked the work from the start—and it probably didn't hurt that the Wolverines won Big Ten titles in four of his first seven years, including one by a young quarterback named Tom Brady.

"I figured it happened all the time," he said, with a wry grin.

After filming the Maryland game from noon to four, Bromley and Undeen returned to the video office where they spent three hours processing that game, then turned to Michigan's next opponent, Wisconsin, processing the Badgers' game that night against Nebraska.

After a noon game, like that week's against Maryland, they usually returned Sunday at eight in the morning, but might come in as late as ten if Michigan played a night game and their work was in pretty good shape. After giving the coaches the basic game videos they'd spend the rest of Sunday breaking down the previous game, then put together files for the upcoming opponent into smaller components: offense, defense, special teams, plus game situations like third-and-long. The number of cutups they need to produce depends on the week, the opponent, and other variables. Michigan's defensive coordinator Don Brown might want cutups from the previous four games; the offense might want a cutup culled from four games the upcoming opponent played against offenses most similar to Michigan's; and special teams coach Chris Partridge usually wants all the opponents' special team clips from the previous few seasons to prepare for any trick plays they've run.

The videographers don't ask why the coaches or players want what they want. They just get to work preparing it.

Monday through Thursday Bromley arrives at 6:30 in the morning to serve the early rising coaches who want to watch tape on this or that, while Undeen comes in about 8 a.m. Bromley and Undeen usually try to go home by 9:30, but they can work remotely from home if need be.

"We just keep going until it's done," Bromley said.

From July to January, Thursdays are the closest thing to an off-day the video staff gets: 6:30 a.m. to 6:30 p.m.—12 hours of meetings, practice, and loading the equipment truck, before they return Friday at 8:30 a.m. to prepare for the next home game, or the next hotel if the team is traveling. On Saturdays, they arrive by 8 a.m. for all home games, regardless of start times, while the rest of the staff can come in as late as 4 p.m. for a home night game.

The video staff's ideal scenario: Michigan plays a

noon game, and the next opponent has a bye week that day. That way they can get all the video on the opponent chopped up before Michigan's kickoff and work on Michigan's game from 4 p.m. until they finish about 7, then get home in time for a late dinner.

"That happened once this year," Undeen said. "Northwestern. Doesn't get any better."

But if both Michigan and the next opponent have later games—which would happen the next week when Michigan hosted Wisconsin at 7:30, and Michigan's next opponent, Michigan State, played at Penn State at 3:30, too close to Michigan's kickoff to get any work done prior—"That will keep us up until 3 a.m., easily," Undeen said.

Worst-case scenario: The Wolverines play a night game at Minnesota, Iowa, or Nebraska, and don't get back to Schembechler Hall until 4 a.m. Even working on the plane ride home and getting to work immediately upon returning to make sure the video is ready for the coaches early Sunday morning, the sun will come up before they finish their work. They celebrate by moving onto their usual Sunday tasks.

"We don't get much sleep those nights," Bromley said. "Good times."

Add it all up, and just like almost everyone else in

the building, they're working more than 100 hours a week during the season, and 50 or so in the "offseason."

Phil Bromley is one of the warmest, friendliest folks you'll ever meet, a gentle bear of a man. Even at moments of high stress and fatigue, including long flights home after a loss, he never snaps. If a staffer is not meeting his standards, however, they're likely to see another side. Bromley's a genuinely nice guy—until he's not.

"You have to understand, everyone we bring in, we're relying on," he explained. "We don't have any extra personnel. If you have a job in this room, we need you to come through."

First, that means trust. If a player gets into a shoving match or throws his helmet in anger, the internet would love to see the film.

"That's all within our family," Bromley said. "We don't tweet or Facebook or post anywhere. You cross that line, I'm going to fire you immediately. No three strikes."

After bowl games the team truck drives all night to arrive at Schembechler Hall early the next day. Instead of waiting for everyone else to show up to unload it, which could take hours, Bromley tells his staff before the trip they will have to unload the entire truck immediately to get their equipment off in time to get their work done.

"We tell them all before we get on the plane," Bromley said, "'If you don't want to unload the truck, don't take the trip.'"

After the last bowl the interns showed up at 8 a.m.—groggy and hungover, perhaps, but ready, willing, and able to get the job done—except one. After they worked three hours to finish the job without him, the missing student "sauntered in," Bromley recalled, "acting like he'd forgotten the assignment."

Bromley was in no mood for lies or excuses.

"Get the fuck outta here," Bromley told him. "That's number one. Number two, I don't know if I want to see you again. We might talk later. We might not."

When Bromley took the others out for lunch, he asked them if they wanted the fired intern back. "Most said, 'Yeah.' If not, he'd be gone for good. Undeen is still fighting for him, asking me to give him some extra duties to get back in my good graces. We'll see.

"Look, this is Michigan football," Bromley concluded. "There's no halfway here. You're all in, or you're out."

Chapter 23
Michigan Man
1982–1987

At the end of Jim Harbaugh's senior season at Palo Alto High School, with only two serious scholarship offers—from Jack's old teammates now coaching at Wisconsin and Arizona, programs that had won exactly two league titles between them in Harbaugh's lifetime—Harbaugh held out hope Schembechler would come through.

Schembechler admitted, "We waited until the last minute. He came into my office, sat down, and I said, 'Jim, I want you here.' He nodded. That was that."

The conversation was so brief that a few days later, the Harbaughs recalled, Schembechler called the Harbaughs to talk to Jim. When Jackie answered she asked Schembechler if he was simply doing the family a favor, or was he sincere? When Schembechler assured her that such favors were not in his nature, and "every coach in this room feels Jim can play at Michigan," she was satisfied.

When Jim took the phone he asked Schembechler, "Is that a full scholarship?"

As Jack recalls, Bo barked, "Would I be calling you and asking you if I didn't have a scholarship for you? Come on!"

In the fall of 1982, Jim Harbaugh was returning to Ann Arbor.

Jack Harbaugh was returning to Michigan, too—Western Michigan, in his case, where he would take his first collegiate head coaching position, joined two years later by John when he graduated from Miami in 1984.

"The biggest advice I can give you," Schembechler told Jack: "Be yourself."

"I seemed to remember everything *but* that," Jack recalled. "I was trying to be Bo! And he was right: it doesn't work."

It wasn't due to a lack of focus. When Jack was working to get a Grand Rapids recruit named Kelly Spielmaker, the family dog decided to relieve himself right on Jack's pant leg. Jack never skipped a beat.

Jack's younger son wasn't faring much better down Interstate 94 in Ann Arbor, where the coaches had pegged Harbaugh dead last on the depth chart.

"It was sink or swim," Jack said, "and Jim was accustomed to that."

Harbaugh got off to a bad start when he showed up late to his first meeting—not the kind of thing Schembechler was likely to ignore.

"I can't *believe* you!" Schembechler shouted at him in front of the entire team. "Don't even *bother* coming into this meeting! YOU WILL NEVER PLAY A DOWN AT MICHIGAN!"

You could fill a few teams of All-Americans with the players Schembechler had promised would "never play a down at Michigan," but Harbaugh could not have known that as an 18-year-old. That was the idea.

"I knew exactly what I was doing," Schembechler told Mitch Albom. "In front of the whole team, I was saying, 'I don't care who you are, you follow the rules.' And you can bet those players watching took good mental notes; they didn't want to be the next guy yelled at."

Harbaugh's innate feistiness—which could oscillate between competitiveness, confidence, and cockiness—also got him in trouble early on.

"The consensus on Harbaugh," Schembechler said, "was that he was too temperamental to play quarterback."

During practice when a teammate hit Harbaugh

late, he got up and whipped the ball at the guy's head. But as Harbaugh learned to channel those emotions, he started passing the quarterbacks in front of him, until Schembechler named him the starting quarterback for the 1984 season, Harbaugh's red-shirt sophomore year. In Harbaugh's first game under center the Wolverines opened against the nation's top-ranked, returning national champion Miami Hurricanes—and beat them, 22–14, vaulting Michigan from 9th to 2nd.

They gave it back the next weekend by losing, 20–11, to 16th-ranked Washington, but followed it up with wins over Wisconsin and Indiana. The Wolverines took their 3-1 record and 13th national ranking into their rivalry game against Michigan State.

Trailing 13–7 in the third quarter, Michigan fumbled the ball. When Harbaugh dived for it, the Spartans' Thomas Tyree hit him and broke his arm. The Wolverines lost, 19–7—only the third time the Spartans had beaten a Schembechler team.

But in the process, Schembechler learned something about Harbaugh: "While he was cocky on the outside, deep down he was like the rest of us."

When Schembechler visited Harbaugh in the hospital that night, he found his former field general lying in bed, arm in a cast, with the eye-black still on his face.

"God, I hated to see him like that," Bo admitted, but he bucked up to give Harbaugh the news: "I got the report on the arm. Number one, you're out for the season. No bowl games, either. That's a fact. And you may not be able to participate in spring practice, you got it?"

Harbaugh just held Schembechler's gaze and said nothing.

"Now the other thing is this: I want a damn three-point average out of you this semester. You're not playing, so you'll have plenty of time for class. Understood?"

When Harbaugh again said nothing, Schembechler got up to leave. But when Harbaugh looked at Schembechler, "the tears started to well in his eyes," Schembechler recalled.

"Hey, Bo," Harbaugh said, "do me a favor."

"What?"

"Don't forget me, OK?"

Schembechler recalled, "I couldn't help it. I started to get choked up myself."

"'Jim,' I said, my voice cracking, 'how in the hell am I gonna forget you?'"

With Harbaugh out the Wolverines lost four of their next seven games to finish with a 6-6 record, by far the worst in Schembechler's 21 years at Michigan. It left Schembechler in a spot similar to the one Harbaugh faced heading into 2018: disappointing record, critics coming at him, rough schedule ahead. What do you do?

"Our challenge the next season, as I saw it, was to get back to the principles that we used to win all those Big Ten titles," Schembechler told me. "I decided to start over from scratch.

"Had I gotten soft? I doubt anyone on that 1984 team would call me soft—but I had to concede that I had not sufficiently reinforced all those things that make a Michigan football team a Michigan football team. My fault!

"I realized the solution was simple. Not *easy*, mind you, but simple. I decided that in 1985 we had to do what we'd always done before, just do it better. A LOT better!

"We also had to rededicate ourselves to the importance of The Team, The Team, The Team! Now, we'd been preaching that since 1969. But they'd heard it so often, maybe they took it for granted. Maybe I did, too. But starting that spring, we hammered that home like it was a brand-new concept. I was determined to keep that ringing in their ears until they were waking up in the middle of the night repeating it to themselves! Because, dammit, we're not going 6-6 again."

That offseason the critics had a field day with Schembechler's stumble: Michigan wasn't Michigan anymore, the game had passed Bo by, and they were going to crash.

"Well, we were going to see about all of that," Bo told me. "By the end of the summer I was already starting to think we might have something special, but you never know until toe meets leather—and our schedule that year was just brutal. In 12 games we were going to play *six ranked teams,* including our first three non-conference opponents. Holy smokes! NOT what you need when you're unranked and you've lost five of your last seven games. That schedule would have *crushed* a lesser team."

With Harbaugh back under center, the Wolverines opened against 13th-ranked Notre Dame, and won, 20–12. Then they traveled to play 11th-ranked South Carolina, and blasted them, 34–3, before hosting Bobby Ross's Maryland team, featuring Boomer Esiason.

"Didn't matter. We whooped up on them, too, 20–0."

After number-two-ranked Michigan lost to top-ranked Iowa, 12–10, and tied Illinois, 3-3, the Wolverines took an 8-1-1 record into its annual grudge match with 12th-ranked Ohio State, with the Big Ten title on the line.

After the Buckeyes closed Michigan's lead to 20–17 in the fourth quarter, Harbaugh approached Schembechler on the sidelines and all but repeated what he had told his ninth-grade basketball coach.

"Bo, whenever you need a play today, whenever this game gets critical, just make sure the ball is in my hands, OK?"

Two plays later Schembechler gave Harbaugh his wish. On second down from Michigan's 23-yard line, Schembechler called for a bomb to John Kolesar, exactly what Harbaugh was asking for.

As soon as Kolesar took off, Ohio State's strong safety came charging untouched "and headed straight for Harbaugh," Schembechler said. "I mean, he was just barreling in! And Harbaugh saw him coming—and he *ignored* him. He let go a bomb to John Kolesar a split second before that safety crunched him, head-on, an awful collision, and they both went down. Jim never saw where that ball went, but it landed in Kolesar's hands for a 77-yard touchdown that clinched the game for us, 27–17. A lot of people talk about Kolesar's catch, but Jim Harbaugh made that play. The best play I ever saw him make. If you only saw that pass alone, you would know this kid was something special."

Michigan would beat Nebraska in the Fiesta Bowl to

finish 10-1-1 and number two in the nation—the highest ranking Schembechler would achieve.

But that's not what Harbaugh took away from that game.

When Schembechler passed away in November 2006, just as we were finishing his last book, I decided to solicit stories from his former players. Harbaugh had just taken the job at Stanford, and was already working hard on recruiting, one of the busiest times of the year. But he stopped what he was doing to send me this piece:

"To this day," he wrote me, "I remember almost all of my encounters with Bo in great detail."

But the most memorable, he said, occurred the Monday after that 1985 Ohio State game. Bo had called him into his office, asked him to sit down, then stood up and put his fists on his desk and looked Harbaugh in the eye.

"That," he said, "was one of the finest games I've ever seen a quarterback play!"

Harbaugh had gone 16 for 19 for 230 yards and three touchdowns—but Schembechler focused on the pass to Kolesar. Bo leaned back in his chair and gazed upward.

"What it must feel like," he said, "to have a son play the way you did! To stand in that pocket with the safety bearing down on you unblocked and hit Jon Kolesar to seal the victory. UNBLOCKED!"

He then let loose his familiar chuckle, and said, "I'm proud of you, Jim."

Harbaugh closed his note by writing, "I felt as loved and appreciated as I have ever felt, like I was one of Bo's sons. In reality I was one of Bo's thousands of sons."

When Schembechler looked back on those two seasons, the faith-shaking 6-6 1984 campaign and the incredible 10-1-1 turnaround in 1985, he said, "I realize the secret was, there was no secret. We just remembered how we do things around here. Then we went back to doing those things better than anyone else. That's all.

"And that's how we went from being unranked one year to number two the next. I don't care what anybody says: THAT is a comeback!"

It's a lesson Harbaugh would take with him into the 2018 season.

Another lesson Harbaugh picked up from Michigan's renowned offensive line coach, Jerry Hanlon. Before the 1986 season, Harbaugh's fifth, he was concerned his last team wouldn't live up to the hype generated by the 1985 squad. So he asked Hanlon what kind of team he thought they were going to have.

"Hanlon gave Harbaugh the best answer to that question I have ever heard," Schembechler told me.

"Jim, come back in twenty years, and I'll tell you," Hanlon said. "Only then will we know how you and your classmates turned out. Did you get good jobs? Are you hardworking and honest? Were you good husbands and fathers? Did you contribute to your community? *Did you make the world a better place?*"

Schembechler and Hanlon won 13 Big Ten titles together, "But Jerry's right," Schembechler said. "That's not what matters. What matters is you grew up. You became men. And now you're raising your own children to do the same."

That season, 1986, Harbaugh led the Wolverines to a 9-0 record and a number two national ranking. They hosted an average Minnesota team for Michigan's last home game of the year—senior day—with Ohio State up next.

But on a rainy day the Gophers pulled the upset, 20–17—a devastating loss. At a press conference two days later, however, a reporter asked Harbaugh how Michigan would fare against Ohio State.

"We can still win the Big Ten championship," he replied. "We can go to the Rose Bowl, and we will. I guarantee you we'll beat Ohio State and be in Pasadena."

When Schembechler saw Harbaugh at practice that day he jammed two fingers into Harbaugh's chest and said, "Jim, are you crazy? Did you really *guarantee* a win to the press?"

"Yeah, I believe it."

"Well, damn it, you better be right."

When Schembechler addressed the entire team later that day, he told them, "Well, I know at least one guy believes we're going to beat them." They laughed.

The same day Jim Harbaugh made the infamous guarantee, Jack's athletic director at Western Michigan called him into his office. Jack didn't have to wonder about the agenda. After starting out 7-2-2 in 1982, the Broncos' win total had slipped one per year, to 6, 5, 4, and finally 3 in 1986.

Jack was not surprised when the athletic director told him, "We're going to go in a different direction."

"Which one?" Jack asked, tongue-in-cheek.

"Well, that was a day!" Jack said. "Jim and I were both in the papers the next day, and Bo had to defend us both! He publicly defended me, then invited me to join them for the Hawaii game after the Ohio State game the coming weekend."

After Jim backed up his guarantee with a gritty 26–24 victory in the Horseshoe, and another Big Ten title, the Wolverines flew to Hawaii for a bonus twelfth game to close out the 1986 regular season at 11-1.

When the team boarded the bus in Honolulu, Schembechler insisted Jack sit in the front seat with him.

"No, HERE!" Schembechler said, pointing to the seat next to his.

"That was Bo's way of telling me I would always belong," Jack said, "I would always be welcomed back. After I got fired that meant a lot. He told me, 'Do not take another job before talking with me!' He wanted to get me back on Michigan's staff."

While Jack and John Harbaugh were looking for new jobs, Jim Harbaugh, who would be named the Big Ten MVP a few weeks later, was looking at the NFL.

Their prospects couldn't have been more disparate.

Chapter 24
O-Line U

People call Penn State "Linebacker U," thanks to a long list of greats including Jack Ham, Shane Conlan, and Lavar Arrington.

Purdue is known as the "Cradle of quarterbacks," from Len Dawson to Bob Griese to Drew Brees, with plenty of great field generals in between.

USC's tailbacks alone have won five Heisman Trophies, more than all but three schools have won at all positions.

"If Penn State is 'Linebacker U,'" former Michigan great Dan Dierdorf told me, "then Michigan is 'O-Line U.' This is what we do."

Michigan's first consensus All-American lineman, William Cunningham, earned the honor in 1898. But

Michigan's reputation for producing a disproportionate number of elite players at the position started when a former lineman out of Miami Ohio named Bo Schembechler showed up in 1969.

Like most linemen Schembechler didn't choose the position; he just wanted to play. Because Schembechler had started playing for the high school junior varsity as a seventh grader, he knew by tenth grade, "There was no question I was going to be a starter on the high school varsity. But the question was where our coach, Karl Harter, was going to put me."

The young Schembechler asked Coach Harter, "Where do you need the most help?"

"Guard."

"Then put me at guard!"

"Hell, I didn't care," Schembechler told me. "I just wanted to play. And I started the next three years."

As a coach, Schembechler famously played no favorites—walk-ons and starters alike were left in the parking lot if they were even a minute late for the team bus—but even he couldn't deny his pet position group was the offensive line.

"If you want to know why I've always loved the big lugs on the line the most—well, you can thank Coach Harter for that."

Schembechler loved the O-Linemen because they represent everything he admired most about football players: they're tough, hard-working guys who sacrifice for the team, depend on each other, and never get any credit for their work while the guys they're blocking for get all the glory. If the quarterback is the lead singer and the tailback the lead guitarist, the O-Linemen are the bass players and drummers, providing the background out of the spotlight to let the others star.

After Schembechler took over in 1969, that's when Michigan became "O-Line U."

"If you're a Michigan fan you probably don't even notice," Dan Dierdorf told me, "but if you listed all the great O-Linemen under Bo, you'd be amazed how long that list is."

Michigan's talent was so deep on Schembechler's offensive lines that a player like Mike Kenn, who made first team All-Big Ten on a loaded line his senior year, 1977, alongside two first team All-Americans, would play 17 years for the Falcons, starting all 251 games, be inducted in their ring of honor, and is still a candidate for the NFL's Hall of Fame. Yet he was the third-best player on Michigan's offensive line that year.

"Bo played a very conservative offense for one simple reason: he knew he could make it work," Dierdorf said. "When you have more All-Americans and All-

Big Ten guys up front than anyone else, you can run the ball at will."

Schembechler had them. If you start with Dierdorf in 1970 and run through 1992, three years after Schembechler retired, when the players he had recruited and coached were still winning awards, during those 23 seasons Schembechler's offensive lines produced 10 All-Americans and 53 First Team All-Big Ten players, averaging more than two per season. Thus, every year almost half Schembechler's five offensive linemen earned First Team All-Big Ten status, and almost every other year one of them was named to the All-America squad.

No one did it better.

But after Schembechler stepped down, and his legendary line coach Jerry Hanlon retired soon thereafter, the fire hose of talent was reduced to a faucet, and finally a trickle. Counting the 25 years from 1993 to 2017, only four Michigan offensive linemen earned first team All-American status, and 32 first team All-Big Ten—roughly half as many as under Bo.

From 2014, Hoke's last year, through 2017, Harbaugh's third, Michigan produced exactly one first team All-Big Ten offensive lineman, and no All-Americans. That's when an abstract statistic becomes something you can feel. In 2014, when Dierdorf returned to Michigan as the radio team's color commentator, he was in for a shock—one that went beyond the team's 5-7 record.

"The record spoke for itself," he said. "But what surprised me the most were the fundamentals—or the lack thereof. It was a struggle all season long to consistently block for the running game and protect the quarterback. It wasn't what I expected—and really, it wasn't what I recognized as Michigan football, since historically it always starts with a dominating offensive line. This wasn't that."

Because O-Linemen are usually the position group that takes the longest to develop, they're also the group that takes longest to rebuild—a problem Harbaugh faced from the start, only exacerbated by Newsome's career-ending injury in 2016.

"Grant would have been a *terrific* pro," Jon Jansen told me. "You think about his injury, and the ripple effect it had on the O-line. When you've got him, you've got your lockdown left tackle. And you know he's staying."

Without Newsome the offensive line struggled.

"Just pointing out the facts," Dierdorf told me, "in 2016, Michigan's 9-0 going into the last four games. We lost three of those four, and I wasn't the least bit shy saying that if we'd have gotten *one more first down* near the end of all those games, we would have won all four, but they simply couldn't get it.

"You can't run and hide from that. It's a fact, as plain as the nose on your face. Everyone knew it. I could've glossed over it, and said the other team played really well—but no, we failed."

Seeing the same problem, Harbaugh made another bold decision: letting his longtime friend Tim Drevno return to USC, and giving the offensive line to Ed Warinner, who had built a national-title offensive line at Ohio State under Urban Meyer.

"It couldn't have been easy," Dierdorf said, "but if Jim hadn't done what he did, it would have been a real shortcoming. Not fun, I'm sure, but 100 percent necessary."

Jerry Hanlon, one of the position's greatest teachers, will tell you playing offensive line is a surprisingly complicated task, requiring precise posture—which looks like you're sitting in an invisible chair—positioning, footwork, and handwork. Not only does each lineman have to execute all those things in a flash, but *every* lineman does, or the whole thing breaks down very quickly, and then some big guys wearing the wrong color will be dancing in your backfield after sacking your quarterback.

For all the technical aspects of the position it still starts with an attitude, one particular to offensive linemen. Dierdorf learned this during his first game on Michigan's varsity, the 1968 season opener against California.

"It's the first quarter, and my head is spinning. So I turn to Stan Broadnax—a senior guard who became a doctor, by the way—and I ask him a question, I can't remember what. But I remember he turned to me and said, 'I've got problems of my own!'

"I knew at that moment, as I looked around the crowd at Michigan Stadium, that not one of them could help me. I looked over to the sidelines to the Michigan coaches, and all my teammates, and I knew not one of them could help me. I knew my mom and dad were in the stands, and they couldn't help me, either.

"So I realized at that moment, I was all by myself. And I either had to grow up and learn to take care of myself or find something else to do. I learned that the only friend you have is your technique. You can't freelance. When it gets tough, you fall back on the fundamentals.

"I tell you what that was: it was the day I grew up."

While the rest of the game has changed dramatically since 1968, with the introduction of the West Coast offense, the read option, and the wildcat, plus too many new defensive schemes to count, what it takes to play offensive line well hasn't changed much since then, if at all.

"If three wide receivers screw up their routes," Ben Bredeson asked me, "but one guy runs his right and he gets the ball, what do you care if the other guys screwed up? No one even sees it. Everyone's talking about what a great receiving corps you have. But if four O-Linemen do a great job, but one of us gets beat, the play's broken, you take a loss, and everyone says you have the worst O-line in college football. No one's going to remember that everyone else got their guy. So we're all in this together."

"Even if everyone does their job and the play works," Grant Newsome added, "you know you're not going to get credit. The guy with the ball is. But if he gets tackled behind the line, then you're probably going to get blamed—whether you screwed up or not. So I've got to know that Ben's got my back, and he's got to know I've got his. I don't know if that's true of any other position in football.

"That's probably why every football coach I've ever talked to said the same thing: The O-line is extremely violent, extremely thankless, and extremely close—and those things are probably not unrelated."

"The only guys who will know you just made a great

block are the guys next to you," Bredeson said. "And we're all each other's biggest fans. We have to be, because no one else is. It's the one position where no one else is going to cheer for you and you're only as good as the weakest person."

To get the horrible taste of the 2017 season out of their mouths for good, the offensive line would have to be the difference. There was simply no path to redemption that did not go through that group.

Warinner couldn't have devised a better test to determine how far his new charges had progressed than the one coming up against three big, tough teams with strong defenses: the famed "gauntlet" of Wisconsin, Michigan State, and Penn State.

If the Wolverines wanted to reclaim their crown as O-Line U, this was the time to do it—and the most likely candidate to spearhead that effort was a junior from small-town Wisconsin named Ben Bredeson.

Chapter 25
The Anonymous O-Lineman
Ben Bredeson

Michigan's offensive lines the past decade were far from the great ones of the past, but if Michigan had one current lineman who could play alongside those giants, that man was Ben Bredeson.

When Bredeson was growing up in Hartland, Wisconsin, he didn't know he'd want to play for Michigan one day. But he was certain of two things: he loved football, and he hated the Buckeyes—not a bad place for a future Michigan Man to start.

In eighth grade Bredeson wrote a paper explaining why millions of fans prefer college football to the NFL—a bold claim for a kid living two hours south of Green Bay. One reason, he argued, was the *American Idol* effect: "You get to watch these people coming up the ranks," he told me, "not just after they're in the big-time."

His teacher gave him an "A." But as an Ohio State graduate, "He kept bringing up the Buckeyes all the time, and it kind of made me angry. Even Badgers hate Buckeyes. Ohio State fans bother me."

Bredeson's mom is a breeder of high-end hunting dogs. His father played center for Illinois State's football team, then started building custom homes before becoming a salesman for a building supplies company. They have three sons. The oldest, Jack, is a relief pitcher for the Wolverines.

"Contrary to popular opinion," Ben said, "he didn't play as big a factor in my recruitment as everyone thinks. I would have ended up here just the same."

Ben's younger brother, Max, a high school sophomore, is showing promise in football and baseball. Ben excelled in those sports, plus hockey, playing for a top travel team in Milwaukee, 30 minutes away.

"Ben was good at hockey, and he liked it," Deb Bredeson recalled, "but he was twice the size of everyone else, so anytime he bumped into someone they called a penalty on him. Ben doesn't like taking penalties, so it was very frustrating for him."

The Bredesons made Ben wait to play football until

seventh grade. In his first week of football practice Deb was driving him home when she asked how he liked football.

"Mom, this is awesome!" he said. "I'm *supposed* to hit people—every play! My coaches love it!"

He made the Arrowhead High School varsity as a freshman, the all-state team as a junior, and the 2015 All-American team as a senior, when he was also named the state's best player. He fielded offers from Stanford, Alabama, Ohio State, Wisconsin, Notre Dame, and Michigan.

In the spring of 2014 the Bredesons made unofficial visits to Michigan, Ohio State, and Tennessee on their way to a Florida vacation. Ben immediately liked Michigan, where Brady Hoke was still coaching, and he liked Ed Warinner, when Warinner still coached at Ohio State, but he wasn't sold on Ohio State itself.

Their next stop, Butch Jones's program at Tennessee, only confirmed Ben's feelings about Michigan. Just a few minutes into their tour of the Volunteers' football building the guide showed them their "Academic Wall of Fame." When Deb Bredeson asked what it took to make the Wall, and their guide answered a 2.5 GPA— which will get you in the doghouse at Michigan—"Ben wasn't too impressed by that," Deb recalled. "He whispered, 'Let's keep this one short.'"

Fifteen minutes later they were back in the family van to start their vacation a couple of hours earlier than planned. Bredeson's later visits to Wisconsin and Notre Dame were good, but neither school captured his imagination. Warinner was not giving up so easily.

"He recruited me very hard," Bredeson told me. "He visited my high school more than anyone else. My mom works part time at the front desk in the afternoon, so he'd only show up in the afternoon so he could chat with her, too. I liked him a lot, but I just didn't fit their school. When I visited, it just didn't feel right.

"My parents didn't want to get involved in the whole recruiting thing. They felt I was old enough to handle it myself, but they wouldn't let me take shortcuts with it. They made me make every recruiting call. One thing my dad told me is: never burn a bridge. If you're not going to go, don't lead them on or drag it out or just ghost if you don't want to go there. Just tell them no."

That meant Ben, not his parents, had to call Warinner to decline—something he did not look forward to.

"It's nothing personal," he told Warinner. "Ohio State is just not a fit."

To Ben's relief, Warinner took the disappointment with good grace—something Ben would not forget.

Before the Bredesons drove six hours to Ann Arbor for Ben's official visit in June 2015, when Harbaugh was preparing for his first season in Ann Arbor, an assistant called Deb to ask what the family wanted to see. She told him, "I don't want to be carted around in a golf cart. I don't want any more cheerleaders following us. When I travel, I walk, because that's how you really get a feel for where you are."

What they did not anticipate was the blazing heat and stifling humidity that met Ben, Max, and their parents on their visit. As soon as they met Harbaugh, "He gave Ben a big hug and punched him lightly in the stomach," Deb recalled. "Everything with him is full speed ahead, every day."

"Let's go for a walk!" Harbaugh said.

"Everyone looked at each other like, 'You've got to be kidding!'" Deb Bredeson had forgotten her request, but Harbaugh hadn't. They started sweating as soon they headed up State Street and didn't stop until the tour ended three hours later.

During their walk up the hill they visited Bill Stolberg at State Street Barbers, then stopped next door to get milk shakes at Pizza Bob's, a classic campus joint whose walls used to feature a slab of corrugated cardboard with the message, "We Ain't Your Mothers—

Clean Up Your Own Mess." Even this mild bit of commerce made Deb unsure Ann Arbor was the right place for her middle son.

"We are from a really small town, with one stoplight. For Ben, Ann Arbor is a big city. I was concerned about him living in a more urban environment. I thought Notre Dame might be a better fit, with such a nice, tight campus where you can't get lost."

But her son did not share her reservations.

"The academic aspect hits you right away," Ben recalled. "It's one of the top public universities in the world. Later you realize how important the alumni base is: it's big, they're loyal, and those connections can be very powerful. I didn't realize how big a deal that was at first, but I do now.

"But honestly, it was just a feel-thing—something you get walking around. There was just something about it that felt right, like I belonged here. Coach Harbaugh and his staff were the final piece of the puzzle."

When they walked up State Street toward campus Ben turned to his mom, "and he gave me the nod, and whispered, 'This is where I'm going.'"

His parents told him not to make any commitments until they had toured all the schools and had had time to think about it. But on the ride back to Hartland, Ben repeated, "I'm coming to Michigan."

His father replied, "You've got two weeks to think about it. If you don't change your mind by then, you can do it."

When Ben started waking up at their home on Day 14, he knew what day it was before he opened his eyes.

"I figured I'd either wake up needing to psych myself up to go to Michigan, or wake up excited to go," he told me. "Well, I woke up and said, 'I'm good!' I went downstairs and told my parents and Max at the breakfast table. No hat stuff. I was never going to be a hat kind of guy. I didn't want to do that, and if I had, I don't think my parents would have attended. Not a big fan of that whole thing."

Ben recalled his parents telling him he couldn't commit to Michigan until he called Wisconsin and Notre Dame, but Deb Bredeson is not sure they ever had to tell him.

"Ben was born this old, wise man," she said. "He's been like that since he was little. He's always known the right way to do things, and he's never shied away from doing the hard things."

So, Ben Bredeson started one of the best days of his life sitting on his front porch calling the coaches at Wisconsin and Notre Dame to give them bad news. When Bredeson called Harbaugh with the good news, he was in a meeting with the university's president, Mark Schlissel, and couldn't pick up. By the time Harbaugh returned his call Ben and his brothers were chowing down at the local Qdoba.

"Love the family," Harbaugh told me. "Ben's one of the most rock-solid guys who've ever come through a program, anywhere, from a maturity standpoint. He's everything a coach could want from a player. To be all that at that age, that's very rare. Tough to take credit for that! He came here that way."

In the fifth game of the 2016 season, Bredeson's first at Michigan, the Badgers knocked out left tackle Grant Newsome. The coaches moved Ben Braden from guard to left tackle and put Bredeson in Braden's spot at left guard—a position Bredeson had never played before.

The Wolverines started the season with nine straight victories, including a personally satisfying 14–7 slugfest over 8th-ranked Wisconsin in that first game.

"We had an incredible team full of leaders," Bredeson recalled. "Jake Butt, Chris Wormley, Amarah Darboh, Jehu Chesson. They carried us through those tight games. Everybody picked each other up. They were some of the hardest working guys I've ever seen, and they had a killer instinct. But for all the success they had they were always so humble about it.

"My first week here I was walking up to campus with Rashan [Gary], and Jehu stops his car—a family sedan, probably ten years old, but kept in good shape—and offers to take us up to Couzens Hall [Bredeson's dorm]. And the thing is, I've never seen Jehu before in my life, and he's never seen me. That really showed you what an older guy should act like around here."

That's why it was particularly painful when they lost three of their last four games by a total of five points.

"Man, that was hard to swallow," Bredeson said. But the next season was tougher.

Bredeson carefully described the 2017 team, as most of his teammates do, as "a different group. I don't want to sound like they were bad or anything. We had a lot of great leaders, too: Henry Poggi, Mo Hurst, Mason Cole, Mike McCray. But it was not the same as 2016. The team wasn't as talented, and the season went a different way. Eight-and-five is awful here—and it *feels* awful. You walk around campus when our hockey and basketball teams are going to the final four, and everyone's asking, 'You guys gonna be any good next year?' I didn't like it. None of us did."

It didn't help that the offensive line was considered the team's weakest link, though Bredeson still earned second-team All-Big Ten as a sophomore, a minor miracle. Before the 2018 season started Bredeson was already encouraged by the team's improved attitude, work ethic, and willingness "to communicate with the coaches, and each other, about what we needed to do differently."

After Harbaugh announced the four captains for the 2018 team he invited each one up to say a few words. Bredeson kept it characteristically short.

"I just want to say what an honor it is for all of you to trust me with this. I'm extremely humbled by it. Thank you."

There would be no hat ceremony on that day, either.

Chapter 26
The Revenge Tour Commences

Wisconsin, October 13, 2018

The Wolverines' win over Maryland stretched their winning streak to five games, moved them up three spots to number 12, and set up a huge game against tenth-ranked Wisconsin—in some ways bigger than Michigan's opener against Notre Dame. The TV gods deemed it worthy of ESPN's College Gameday, and a slot in prime time.

With each victory fear faded and excitement grew among Michigan fans, while interest built among the media. But you got the feeling everyone watching the

Wolverines was still holding something back, reluctant to jump on the Michigan bandwagon with both feet until the Wolverines knocked off a serious squad like Wisconsin. After 2017's 4-0 mark crashed against the shores of Michigan State, Penn State, Wisconsin, and Ohio State, they had reason to be hesitant.

The players didn't care. They had started believing this team was different in January and had become more convinced of that every week—even after the Notre Dame loss.

"It manifests itself in practice," Winovich said. During Wisconsin week defensive line coach Greg Mattison said "this is the best three days of practice we've had since he's been here. That's a pretty big statement."

They would need to throw everything they could at the Badgers, who entered the game with a 17-game Big Ten winning streak, and ten straight road wins. In August *Sports Illustrated* featured Wisconsin's offensive line on one of their "College Preview" covers, with the title, "BIG IS BEAUTIFUL: Can Wisconsin Take The [National] Title? The Country's Best (and Best-Fed) O-Line Says Yes!"

"All the hype for the 'Heavy-weight matchup between Wisconsin's great O-Line and Michigan's great D-Line,' yeah, we heard it," Winovich told me. "Hell, I welcome it. Let's find out! If we can't beat them at our best, then we're never going to beat them. It's now or never."

That meant Winovich and others would have to overcome some minor injuries.

"My left hamstring is pretty sore," Winovich said, "but you suck it up. If I can't beat them today, when everything else is feeling good, then I'm not who I think I am."

His teammates understood the stakes, too.

"It feels like a win over Wisconsin should wipe the Notre Dame game out," Zach Gentry told me, "especially given how good Notre Dame is going [7-0, ranked 5th] and how Wisconsin plays year in and year out. Always solid. We all feel the magnitude of this game. A win over Wisconsin will just propel us forward to the rest."

Because Gentry hoped to see some passes that weekend, he was obsessing over the weather. "Accu-Weather, Apple Weather, you name it, I'm checking it out constantly. I want to make sure we can throw the ball."

Harbaugh underscored the offensive line's central role in both Michigan's rich tradition and its upcoming game against Wisconsin by naming Michigan's former offensive linemen the honorary team captains against

Wisconsin. Athletic director Warde Manuel invited dozens of them to a reception Friday night at the Chop House on Main Street, which has a New York–style steakhouse on the first floor, and a combination speak-easy, cigar bar, and Michigan football museum in the basement, where they hold private parties.

Black-tie waiters carried hors d'oeuvres, the bar-tenders served high-end vodka, and a glass-enclosed room housed heartier fare. Department staffers min-gled with former All-Americans like Jon Runyan Sr., George Lilja, and Ed Muransky.

From 1980 to 1984 former captain Doug James's teams went to five bowl games, including two Rose Bowls and a Sugar Bowl, and won two Big Ten titles. But he's been more impressed by how successful his line mates have been after hanging up their helmets. James worked as a radio executive in New York and most recently president and general manager of Radio One in Charlotte, North Carolina; guard Jerry Diorio became a high school football coach in Michigan, win-ning regional Coach of the Year honors; he split time with Art Balourdos, who is now the president of JB Realty in Chicago, which owns properties on Michi-gan Avenue; All-American center Tom Dixon earned his law degree from Notre Dame before joining one of Michigan's largest law firms; All-American guard Stefan Humphries won a Super Bowl with the 1985 Chicago Bears before completing his medical residency at the Mayo Clinic; and first team All-Big Ten and Academic All-American tackle Clay Miller earned a law degree from Northwestern and an MBA from Harvard before starting his own private equity firm, then created a substantial mentoring network for the current players.

Jerry Hanlon was right: you don't know what kind of team you're going to be for at least 20 years. So was longtime football PR man Bruce Madej, when he said, "The best ambassadors of Michigan football are Michigan football players."

As the big men reconnected that Friday night, October 12, 2018, everything was back on the table for the Wolverines: a shot at a Big Ten title and a national title on one side, or a demoralizing repeat of Michigan's losses to Wisconsin, Michigan State, and Penn State on the other. The Wolverines' winning streak wouldn't mean much until they beat a top team like Wisconsin.

"We're supposed to think, every week, 'Just another game,'" Winovich told me. "And you have to take that approach. You can't change your routines just because you're playing a top team.

"But certain opponents require your full attention, and Wisconsin's one of them. I watched a lot of Wisconsin film this week, and I saw some thick, thick mo-fos. Their O-line got all that hype for a reason—so let's go.

"This is the first part of the Revenge Tour. There are certain teams that have been kicking us around, taking our lunch money—and now we've got three of them in a line: Wisconsin, [Michigan] State, Penn State.

"I want our lunch money back. Plus interest."

At 7:42 on a cool Saturday night, Michigan's Jake Moody kicked off to Wisconsin under the lights on national TV.

"College Game Day, the atmosphere in the Big House, being on ESPN in prime time," Jon Runyan Jr. said. "You grow up dreaming of being part of it."

"We were jacked," Higdon said. "A lot of guys took this game personally. A lot of people were talking about us not being able to show up for big games, against ranked opponents, big lights. Well, here it is, all of it. So let's go do this!"

"We all heard a lot of talk about Michigan not showing up in big games," Patterson told me. "And Wisconsin had only given up 14 points on the road so far. So we knew it was a statement game. We were just pissed off. Just *pissed off*!"

But probably no Wolverine had greater motivation than Ben Bredeson, the former top recruit out of Wisconsin. In 2017 Wisconsin scored a third quarter touchdown to take a 14–10 lead when Michigan backup quarterback Brandon Peters went down, taking Michigan's chances for a comeback with him. The 24–10 loss marked a bad memory for all the Michigan insiders but especially the Bredesons, who received additional grief from their neighbors and strangers in the days that followed.

Before the 2018 game in Ann Arbor, Ben's mom, Deb Bredeson, gave him some additional motivation: "Ben, we must win," she told him. "We don't want to have to sell the house."

He wasn't sure if she was joking—but then, neither was she.

Bredeson's immediate family, aunt, uncle, and grandmother arrived en masse to Ann Arbor, plus five friends—all carefully screened to ensure they'd be wearing maize and blue. But that only added pressure: who would want to face their family and friends who just made a six-hour drive after a devastating loss?

Looking at the bigger picture, Bredeson said, "In 2016 I felt like we had support from everyone, but in 2017 it was the opposite, and I still feel like we're tacking into that headwind. But you win a few big games, and it'll switch right back.

"Well, the gauntlet is here. These are all the must-win games, all back-to-back-to-back. So we're about to find out who we are."

The game started out exactly as you'd expect: a no-frills contest of old-school football. Big linemen battling for small yards, with a lot of downhill running and no trick plays. Smash-mouth football at its best.

"A lot of ground and pound," Furbush said. "Great midwestern values—expressed on a football field. You know what's coming, so stop it. It's so much fun to play that style. The first quarter flew by.

"There's so much going on in everyone's life, it's a great outlet to smash into someone and get some frustrations out. Very therapeutic."

Neither team scored in the first quarter but Patterson had been setting the Badgers up for a big play, and finally pulled the trigger to start the second quarter. On Patterson's previous read options, a play he and Higdon had practiced countless times, he had given the ball out to Higdon for small gains. But this time Patterson kept the ball while Higdon sold the fake perfectly to allow Patterson to start off down the left sideline unnoticed. Even with Patterson's surprising head start, it was amazing to see *the Badgers were not catching him.*

"The play started out so well, I knew I was going to get some yards," Patterson told me. "I never thought it'd go for a touchdown. But after I crossed mid-field or so, I thought, 'I could take this one in!'

"From the time I started playing as a little kid, I'd never run that far before—so I had no idea I could run out of gas! But that's what happened. About the 15-yard line, I ran out of gas, and I thought, 'They're gonna catch me.'"

They did, pulling even at about the 10-yard line, where they shoved him out of bounds. But Patterson's 81-yard run set up a short touchdown for Higdon to give Michigan a 7–0 lead, with 13:33 left in the second quarter.

Michigan's joy was short-lived. The Badgers came right back with a quick four-play touchdown drive to tie it up, 7–7, while two of the Wolverines' next three drives stalled deep in Wisconsin territory, forcing them to settle for two field goals and a narrow 13–7 lead at the half.

In the second half, on third-and-one, Higdon cut through the line before Wisconsin's Reggie Pearson popped the ball out of his hands at the 44-yard line—Higdon's first fumble of the year. Michigan managed to recover the ball, but Higdon assumed his day was done. When Higdon returned to the sidelines he asked running back coach Jay Harbaugh who would be going in on the next possession.

"This is one of my favorite stories of the year," Higdon told me. "If you watched us last year, whenever you see a guy make a mistake, you see him get pulled out—no questions."

But this time Jay Harbaugh said, "You're in. What do you mean?"

"Man, that's all I needed to hear!" Karan said. "That was the pivotal moment—knowing I could capitalize on a second chance. I felt free, I felt trusted, and there's nothing better than when your boss has faith you can get the job done."

Despite a slow start—in the first quarter Higdon ran 7 times for just 18 yards—after Jay Harbaugh put him back in after his fumble Higdon ran 8 times for 91 yards, for a 11.4 yard per carry average, to finish with 144 yards.

Michigan bolstered its 24–7 fourth quarter lead when Lavert Hill intercepted Alex Hornibrook's pass at Wisconsin's 21-yard line and returned it for a touchdown, and a 31-7 lead. Michigan's defense had matched Wisconsin's offensive output.

"They've got a serious offensive line," Winovich said. "But once we got ahead of them 24–7, they fell apart. They really didn't want to be out there with us. I think they didn't even know how to come back. In the third quarter I felt their O-line break. We were just on another level. It's not just me. These dogs are hungry, man. They're starving. Just like coach says: Hungry dogs hunt best."

But the story of the game would be Michigan's offensive linemen. The same unit that had been disparaged throughout the 2017 season right up to the middle of 2018 had now became an asset.

"Everyone likes to talk about Wisconsin's offensive line," Jon Runyan Jr. said. "People overlooked us to that point, but that's the game we started getting credit. It was the *way* we won that game—running downhill— that felt so good."

"We all saw how hard [the offensive linemen] worked in the spring," Patterson said. "They were pushing tank sleds every day. Some of them had 800–900 pounds on them. But it's all paid off. Look at them this year—and it's like they're night and day."

"There was *visual displacement*," Bredeson told me. "That means you could see our guys push their guys out of the way, where they didn't want to be. [The Badgers] were classy guys, no trash talking. It was a very serious game. Nothing really needed to be said. But you could see their D-line just cave where you wanted them to. From an O-line standpoint, that's about as good as it gets."

Late in the game backup quarterback Dylan McCaffrey exploded on a 44-yard run to put some icing on a great performance: 38–7, with 5:16 left in the game.

"When they're down by 20 or 30 and they're punting on fourth and two, you just know they just want to get out of the stadium," Higdon said. "They wanted those gates opened so they could get on the bus."

With a few minutes left in a blowout on a chilly night, Michigan fans normally would head for their cars to get a midnight snack or start driving back to Detroit, Grand Rapids, or Chicago. But not this time. They stayed, soaking it all in, and they cheered—perhaps the most raucous Michigan crowd since the stadium's first night game in 2011, when Michigan overcame a 17-point deficit to beat Notre Dame.

The fans were celebrating a good, old-fashioned butt-kicking, the kind they'd grown up watching at the Big House. The coaches and players were celebrating that, too, but also all the work they knew went into that game—from the 6 a.m. lifting sessions to the 10 p.m. coaches' film sessions and countless recruiting calls.

But when the players ran to the packed student section to sing "The Victors," it felt like one big happy family. As much as the players tried to insulate them-selves from the rankings, the media, and the Twitter-verse, they loved the fans, and on some fundamental level, they needed them.

"No one left!" Bredeson said. "Everyone wanted to watch this finish. We love that—especially seeing the students, late on a Saturday night, stick around to sing 'The Victors' with us. That's pretty cool. It's like Coach Harbaugh said: you work 12 months a year for 12 games. You work 30 hours a week for 60 minutes of football."

The players spent much of that time in Ben Her-bert's weight room. His hiring was clearly paying off—witness the Wolverines pushing around the famously physical Badgers—and they wanted to thank him. After Harbaugh sang "The Victors" with his team in the locker room, he grabbed the game ball and said, "I'd like to give something to a guy who's impacted us in a really positive way. Coach Herbert, come up here!"

Harbaugh handed him the ball, the players cheered, and Herbert got choked up.

"I'm a very passionate guy," Herbert told me, "and as I've gained more confidence, I'm not afraid to let that shit out, and shed a tear."

Herbert walked out the tunnel to the parking lot to meet his parents, sister, brother-in-law, and their kids, with the game ball in his hand, "and a big smile on my face."

His former teammate, the Badgers' current strength coach, would be hearing from him.

"That was one of our happiest games for Ben," Deb Bredeson said. "We knew, after the heartbreak at Notre Dame, how badly he wanted to beat the Badgers. He always takes a little ribbing from his friends back from home about going to Michigan, and a lot more after we lost to Wisconsin the year before. He needed to prove that he was in the right place, that he'd made the right choice.

"I felt enormous relief that he could walk off the field proud of what he'd done. When I saw him outside the tunnel I told him, 'Oh good, we don't have to move!' That was fun—oh my."

Bredeson got home after midnight to find his family and friends waiting for him. After they had a few beers while reliving the game, Bredeson started a euchre tournament, largely to make sure everyone else stayed up, too.

"I didn't really want to go to bed," he said. "I didn't want the night to end. I was just living it. We all were."

While a victory over Ohio State is always the crown jewel for the Wolverines, they were not about to take their next opponent, Michigan State, lightly, because they had found losing to them so painful.

Minutes after the game Winovich announced, publicly this time, "The revenge tour has officially commenced."

Chapter 27
The Can't Miss Kid
Devin Bush, Jr.

The media pollsters rewarded the Wolverines for blowing out Wisconsin on a big national stage, 38–13—Michigan's biggest win in two years—by catapulting them from 12th to 6th. With five regular season games left, the Wolverines were well within range of the top four spots that would likely lead to a berth in the college football playoff.

They would not be in that position without top recruits like Rashan Gary and Ben Bredeson, but many of Michigan's best players, including Karan Higdon and Chase Winovich, were relatively unheralded three-star prospects who had to work their way to prominence, often surpassing higher-rated players to get there. Wherever they ranked, almost all Michigan's players—from Gary to Furbush to Wangler—had to overcome some unexpected obstacles just to find their place on the team.

But if any player on the roster was to the manor born, it was Devin Bush Jr. His father, Devin Bush Sr., had starred at safety on Florida State's 1993 national title team, was drafted in the first round by the Atlanta Falcons, played eight years in the NFL, and won a Super Bowl in 2000 for the St. Louis Rams. Devin Sr. and Kesha's oldest child, Deja, played center field on Florida State's national title softball team in 2018.

If you're looking for a world-class pedigree—and what college coach isn't?—Devin Bush Jr. had it, right down to the name. He drew attention in the hotbed of Florida football from pee wee football to high school, where scouting services ranked him a four-star player, and the nation's 13th-best linebacker.

Even Bush's journey had some twists and turns. He received a scholarship offer from most major southern schools, including his father's alma mater. Unlike Higdon, who reveled in his first snowfall, Bush had no affection for Michigan's notoriously cold, gray winters.

"I do *not* like the snow," he said. "I'll just tell you that!"

But when Florida State courted Bush, Harbaugh was not discouraged by the long odds of getting a Florida blue-chip to leave the Sunshine State for Ann

Arbor, and went after him hard. For those players and families who won't consider cold weather, or don't like school, or want to get paid—with the majority of blue-chip players fitting at least one of those categories—Harbaugh has little chance to convince them to come to Michigan, thereby taking at least two-thirds of the prospects off the table before recruiting even begins.

But for those who value academics, Harbaugh has a considerable edge: the university's reputation in general, and the academic success of his players in particular. When Steve Connelly and Claiborne Green explain their program and tell recruits (and their parents) if you're serious about school, you will get a good degree from the University of Michigan, Michigan suddenly has a leg up.

But Devin Bush Jr. was a special case.

"I wasn't a big academic guy in high school," he told me. "If I had a good enough GPA, I'd just keep it there. I didn't need to be on the honor roll. School was never hard for me. I just did it to get by."

His attitude changed, however, when he considered where to go to college.

"I wanted to test myself to see what I could really do in the classroom when I actually put forth my full effort," he said. "Academically, I know how much this school weighs, and what it means, to anybody. So if I have this chance why shortchange myself and go to a school like Florida, Florida State, Auburn, or Georgia and get a degree that really doesn't mean anything, and end up doing something after football I don't want to do? If I can get a Michigan degree, I can do something with it, and have that advantage over others."

This was music to Harbaugh's ears, but he knew it wouldn't be enough to lure a star like Bush without a strong football program behind it.

"When I looked at the football part," Bush said, "I saw what Coach Harbaugh had done in the NFL as a player, and coaching Stanford and the 49ers. Okay, here's a guy who's been where I want to go, so he knows what it takes and probably knows a lot of people who could help. He could be a person who could vouch for you."

During the Bushes' visit to Ann Arbor, "I saw how he ran his practices and how he ran his team—and he was *tough*. Nothing easy about a four-hour practice. And that's what I wanted: a real test to get better, to get ready for the next level."

After Bush committed to Michigan he helped recruit teammates Josh Metellus and Devin Gil to complete the nation's sixth-ranked class, Michigan's best in four years. Bush also caused more than a few jaws to drop among his Florida friends.

"A lot of people were like, 'What are you doing?' Even a lot of people up here, when they ask, 'Where you from?' They look at you like you're crazy, and say, 'What are you doing up here? You left Miami's beaches for this?' Some days I wonder too! But I had a plan from the start, and I knew this was the place."

Six weeks after Devin Jr. enrolled Harbaugh had an opening on his analyst team. After Devin Sr. had transformed his son's high school team, which had never made the state playoffs, into a state champion, Harbaugh hired him to do a job he's good at, takes seriously, and still holds after Devin Jr. left for the NFL.

In Bush Jr.'s first fall, 2016, he couldn't crack the starting lineup, loaded with experienced players, so he started on special teams and got mop-up duty at linebacker. But he kept his promise to himself and worked just as hard in the classroom.

"I wasn't playing much, so I needed something to boost my confidence," he recalled. "So I said, 'Let's do this.'"

One day that fall, driving with his dad, he blurted out, "I'm going to make the Academic All–Big Ten team."

His dad was surprised—his son had never announced academic goals before—but supportive. "You do that, you could tell your grandmother about it. She'd be thrilled."

Devin Jr. went to work. "Fall semester is a long semester, man. It was cold, and I had to be at the Academic Center every night until 11, then walk back up the hill to my dorm. Then I'd go back there on Sundays, then Mondays, and I just kept going back."

When Bush grew fatigued, he thought, "Maybe I'll do it another time. I don't care for this anymore."

But Claiborne Green, Michigan football's academic advisor, would tell him, "D, if you do this now, no one can take it away from you, and the coaches will see you can handle yourself off the field, too. You're going to get the best of all worlds."

Bush is no fan of Ann Arbor's climate, but he had to admit, "Up here, it's quieter than Florida. You got your parties here and there, but clubs close at 2 a.m., and you can get your work done without so many temptations. That's one thing I do like."

At the end of fall semester, Bush was in his dorm room when Green called.

"Man, you said you were going to do it, and you did it!" he told Bush. "You made the Big Ten All-Academic team!"

"I was shocked," Bush confessed. "And I was proud!

I'd never made the honor roll in high school—but I never worked that hard, either. It was a real confidence boost—and I needed one."

In 2017 Bush became the starting middle linebacker, but the team stumbled to fourth place in the East Division. When asked to explain the drop-off, Bush didn't hesitate. "Experience. We lost a lot of great players, so we were learning as we went through the season, facing different situations and scenarios, and obstacles we'd never seen before.

"But none of that really matters. We knew as a team what we had to do to get over that hump. Everything was elevated this off-season—the workouts, the focus. I didn't come all this way to win eight games. I don't think anyone did. So we're determined."

Bush entered 2018 as a preseason All-American—and a two-time Big Ten All-Academic Team member.

"Two for two!" he said. "Every time I do that, my confidence goes up. And this is a place you need some confidence in the classroom. I'm getting a bachelor's in general studies. I'm studying sales and marketing, with a minor in entrepreneurship. I got a couple classes in the business school. These guys come to class wearing suits and ties and skirts and stuff. It's a different world, man! But I know I can handle it now, and that's cool. I don't think I could have when I first got here."

Bush feels his decision to come North has been vindicated. Even undrafted players find the NFL lifestyle much easier than Michigan's. Khalid Hill, who played for the Seattle Seahawks, told Bush, "The league is a cake-walk compared to Michigan. You wake up, get treatment, lift, practice, and you're home by 5 or 6 p.m. You're done!"

Henry Poggi had a stint in the NFL before returning to Michigan as a graduate assistant, and told Bush, "You're not going to believe how much more prepared you are than the guys from other schools."

"These guys would know," Bush concluded. "It doesn't get any harder than this. If I had to do it all over again, I'd make the same decision.

"But I'm gonna tell you right now: I'm not leaving this place at 8-and-5. Uh-uh. That is just not acceptable."

Chapter 28
Bad Blood

When reformers turn their attention to college athletics, they invariably insist the key is to take power from the athletic department and give it to the trustees, the presidents, and the executive officers. But time and again we see these leaders do no better, and often far worse.

There is no better example than the scandal at Michigan State. Let's be clear: Michigan State is not merely a good school, but a world-class research university. It's one of only 62 in North America to be admitted to the Association of American Universities, the highest status a research university can achieve.

This makes it even more painful to see Michigan State's reputation forever tarnished by Larry Nassar, a team doctor who pled guilty to sexually assaulting ten girls and young women. His victims actually numbered in the hundreds, many of them athletes at Michigan State University.

It's worth noting that the Michigan State students, faculty, and alumni all "got it." They were outraged, demanding accountability and real reforms to make sure this never happened again. It was the leaders who failed so badly.

So where were the adults? *The Detroit News* reported Nassar's victims told at least 14 Michigan State employees about his abuse, yet they proceeded to do little or nothing about it. The scandal prompted the conviction of the dean of the medical school, Dr. William Strampel, and the resignation of President Lou Anna Simon, who was later arrested for lying to law enforcement. Her case is in the courts now.

"Larry Nassar's sexual abuse of more than 300 young gymnasts is a crime, not a scandal," wrote Jenna Glass, author of *The Women's War,* in the March 2019 issue of *The Atlantic.* "But the massive coverup; the length of time it went on; and the number of adults who made excuses, ignored complaints, and chose to protect institutions instead of the gymnasts? That's the biggest sports scandal ever."

An unpleasant lesson had been relearned. These great state universities were set up for the express purpose of developing young adults, and on the grand scale have done a remarkable job. Yet when conflicts arise the first victims are often the very students the school is supposed to be developing, and the enablers are too often the very people charged with protecting them.

Nassar's sins wouldn't affect the football game between Michigan and Michigan State, of course, but the leadership surrounding Michigan State athletics would. Every team has players who go astray, including Michigan's. The question is how the program leaders respond when that happens.

Sparked by the Nassar scandal, in January 2018 ESPN's *Outside the Lines* investigated the university's inactivity to complaints by women. *OTL* reported that, since Michigan State named Mark Dantonio the head coach in 2007, at least 16 members of the Michigan State football team had been accused of sexual assault or violence against women. It's hard not to conclude that the same leadership that made Nassar possible enabled football.

On Friday night, October 19, 2018, in the banquet room at the Ramada hotel in Lansing, Michigan, a couple hundred yards from the state capitol, the subject was not politics but football.

When Harbaugh stood up to address his team, the stakes barely had to be mentioned: The Wolverines, now 6-1 overall and 4-0 in the Big Ten, had a clear shot at a Big Ten title—and with it, a likely berth in the College Football Playoffs. What fans feared was going to be another throwaway season five weeks earlier was suddenly inflated with great expectations.

For the players the State game was personal, brimming with intangible benefits that couldn't be quantified in an AP ranking, including the bye week that would follow. These could cut both ways. If you lost to MSU right before the bye week, as Michigan did in 2015, you had to answer questions about it for two weeks before you had a chance to redeem yourself and change the subject. But if you won, you could actually bask in a big victory while taking a few days off for the first time since July.

Then there were bragging rights. Since fifth-year seniors like Wangler, Winovich, and Furbush had beaten the Spartans only once in four tries, the last thing they wanted to hear about the rest of their lives was how the Spartans dominated their teams.

Since 1953, when Michigan State started playing in the Big Ten, the winner of this contest has been awarded the Paul Bunyan trophy, which Lloyd Carr described as the "ugliest trophy in college football. But when you don't have it, you miss it."

Dantonio had already established himself as one of Michigan State's greatest coaches, with three division titles, three conference crowns, and even an appearance in the new four-team national playoff—prizes no current Wolverine had ever claimed. But Dantonio had raised upsetting the Wolverines to an art form. After the Wolverines had taken Paul home in 30 of 38 games played between 1970 and 2007, Mark Dantonio's teams won eight of the next ten—something even MSU's national champion coaches Biggie Munn and Duffy Daugherty never did—despite being favored to win only four of those contests.

If it was personal for the players, it was more so for Harbaugh.

In 2015, Harbaugh's first season back in Ann Arbor, the Wolverines had recovered from a season-opening loss at Utah with a five-game winning streak, including three straight shut-outs for the first time in 35 years, two of them over ranked teams. Against 7th-ranked Michigan State the Wolverines held a 23–21 lead with just ten seconds left. All they had to do was get off a "game-winning punt," and Paul Bunyan would be sent rolling across the tunnel to Michigan's locker room.

What followed was one of the craziest plays in the

history of college football, just this side of the infamous Stanford "Band Play." After punter Blake O'Neill dropped the snap, he spun around and tried to kick it sideways. But a Spartan grabbed his elbow, causing him to pitch the ball right in the belly of Jalen Watts-Jackson, who narrowly outpaced Jake Butt to make it to the end zone right as time ran out.

After the play Harbaugh's wife, Sarah, walked out of the VIP's skybox and slid down a pillar. She could hear the Spartan coaches in the visitors' skybox erupt in cheers across the hall. When they opened the door and all but skipped out, one of them walked over to her, read her name tag, and mimicked a baby crying, rubbing his fists in his eyes, and saying, "Boo hoo."

Sarah did not respond—until now.

"If a Michigan coach had done that," she told me, "it'd be national news, and the head coach would have to apologize for it. But that's not how it goes with the Spartans."

In the Spartans' first five games they suffered bad losses against Arizona State and Northwestern, while notching three unimpressive victories over weak teams. The week before the Michigan game they traveled to Penn State, one of the nation's toughest places to play, looking for a miracle against the eighth-ranked Nittany Lions, which had turned a 26–14 fourth quarter lead over undefeated Ohio State into a 27–26 loss previous week.

The Spartans pulled off a 21–17 upset, slipping back inside the top 25 at #24. That was important because it presented the Wolverines another chance to break their ignominious 17-game losing streak against ranked opponents on the road—a fact that seemed to run on ESPN every half hour.

But all that would be eclipsed by whatever happened the next day, the 111th meeting between these sibling rivals.

There has been enough adolescent sniping between Michigan and Michigan State to fill a book—in fact, several. It started before Michigan Agricultural College opened its doors in 1855. After the University of Michigan lost its bid to start the new agricultural college in Ann Arbor, a Michigan professor warned the new school "cannot be more than a fifth-rate affair."

Michigan athletic director Fritz Crisler followed up a century later by actively lobbying to block Michigan State from joining the Big Nine, as it was called after Crisler's alma mater, Chicago, had dropped out. When that failed the Wolverines publicly pledged that if they won the new Paul Bunyan Trophy, they would leave it on the field. No matter: Michigan lost, 14–6.

In 1973, after Michigan and Ohio State tied 10–10 to finish with identical 10-0-1 records, the league left its Rose Bowl invitation up to a vote of the athletic directors. When Michigan State's Bert Smith explained why he cast the likely deciding vote against their sister school at a Spartan banquet, he received thunderous applause.

After a relatively calm period, the pettiness between the programs picked up in the past decade. When Appalachian State stunned the Wolverines in 2007, Mark Dantonio sarcastically asked for "a moment of silence." Michigan's Mike Hart returned the favor by referring to the Spartans as "Little Brother."

In 2013, former Michigan athletic director Dave Brandon hired a skywriter to spell "GO BLUE" over East Lansing—then lied about it, until records proved his department had paid for it. Before the Michigan State game that year a couple dozen Michigan players made a show of plunging a big tent spike into the Spartans' field—only to get crushed, 35–11, and prompt Coach Hoke to apologize the next day.

If you added up all the slights and cheap shots they would probably shake out about even—though the final tally would likely depend on who was doing the adding.

Michigan football has three main rivalries and they all function differently, starting with reputations—

including Michigan's. While Michigan's rivals often consider Michigan fans arrogant—as one former MSU coach said, "AA doesn't stand for Ann Arbor, but Arrogant Asses"—they're not typically violent or rude. Rival fans who go out on the town after beating Michigan, from Appalachian State to Penn State, are generally well received.

With the Notre Dame rivalry, the fans on both sides are respectful, and so are the players. With Ohio State, the players are respectful—many of their lettermen are among the finest men I've met, from John Hicks to Tom Skladany to Archie Griffin—while a portion of their fans are considered among the worst in college football.

With Michigan State the fans are generally respectful toward each other, with Spartan fans among the friendliest in the country. Almost everyone in the state has friends who went to both schools, creating a week of harmless ribbing between them.

But the respect stops with the spectators. The players have harbored a genuine hate for each other going back at least to 1953—a noted contrast to the mutual respect between the schools' basketball coaches and players. Michigan football players, past and present, consistently report no one hits them harder, later, or cheaper. They'll tell you the Spartans' trash talk is constant, and when the play ends, the extracurriculars start, including spitting, scratching, and punching where it hurts most.

Perhaps the most egregious example in recent memory was a play that occurred during the 2011 game in East Lansing. After four Spartans gang-tackled Michigan quarterback Denard Robinson at midfield, leaving him facedown and immobilized, William Gholston jumped on the pile, which marked one offense, however common. But then he grabbed Robinson's face mask from behind with both hands and twisted it as hard as he could, torqueing it more than ninety degrees, in an apparent attempt to break his neck.

It was the most grotesque act I've ever seen on a football field. Fortunately Robinson was not injured, despite Gholston's best efforts. When the normally mild-mannered Robinson got up, he turned to the refs, arms outstretched, outraged. Gholston would later be suspended by the Big Ten for one game—not for twisting Robinson's helmet, but for punching Michigan offensive tackle Taylor Lewan later in the game, a violation that was more obvious than it was dangerous.

After the game, then–MSU defensive coordinator Pat Narduzzi said, "That's what we try to do. 60 minutes of 'Unnecessary roughness.' I'm just happy it didn't get called on every snap."

Later that week the *Wall Street Journal* ranked the dirtiest college football rivalries, as determined by personal fouls. While the Michigan–Michigan State rivalry ranked only sixth, it was also the most lopsided, with MSU being called for 80 percent of the personal fouls between them over the preceding five seasons.

Michigan alum-turned-political analyst Jonathan Chait, after acknowledging the Spartans flat out kicked Michigan's tail in that 2011 game, 28-14, wrote in *New York* magazine, "Thuggery is a foundational element of the program culture of Michigan State football," a belief firmly held by four decades of Michigan players.

Grant Newsome's father, Leon, who played at Princeton, was struck before the 2018 game in East Lansing by the easy camaraderie between Michigan and Michigan State fans. "You see them all tailgating together—no fights, no yelling—something you'd never see at Ohio State. But then the game starts, and on the field you can *feel* it—the animosity between the teams, the hate. The contrast between the fans and the players was stark."

Grant added, "This year we realized, it is okay to hate this team. They're not interested in playing us on a sporting level. They want to hurt you. That's what their season is about. Well, this year we showed up ready to respond."

During Michigan's Monday team meeting, which sets the tone for the rest of the week, Harbaugh addressed these issues directly. Harbaugh grew up hearing his dad's stories about the Michigan State games; Jim had started three games at quarterback against the Spartans, breaking his arm in the first; and he'd already coached against them three times, two of them heartbreaking upsets. He knew more than enough about this rivalry to speak without euphemism to his players.

"I don't think I need to tell you much about this game," he said. "It's Michigan State week, and we know what that means. We know what's at stake. We want what's ours. We're coming for everything."

"The look on Coach Harbaugh's face during that meeting, you don't forget," Shea Patterson told me. "You could see and feel how much he was pissed off and how much he wanted this one. He said we usually we take the high road. Well, this week we're taking the low road. But we're going to take it on game day. Let them talk their shit to the media all week, and we'll talk ours on the field."

Harbaugh then told his team that, for the first time in the trophy's 65-year history, if the Wolverines won it back Saturday they would take Paul off his stand and march him onto the Spartans' field, as the Spartans had started doing in Ann Arbor in 2008.

He then added a warning: "For you guys who've played in this game, you know what it's all about, you know what it's going to take, and you know what's going to happen. So after the play ends, you need to remember it's not over. If you're in the pile, you're going to get it. If you're standing near the pile, you're going to get it. So be ready, be smart, be tough, and play to the 'echo of the whistle.' And bring Paul back where he belongs!"

Harbaugh had lit a fire—then doused gasoline on it Friday night at the hotel.

"Coach is not a big rah-rah speaker," Winovich told me, "but that inspired us. I was ready to go! This is always a scrappy game, which is great for me. I'm a scrappy player. I'll outscrap anyone. You want to go there, I'll go there.

"It always seems like we try to take this moral high ground. But the way I took it is, okay, this time we're going to roll our sleeves up and get a little dirty. This is going to be a fight—so we're going to fight.

"They want to stay on that low road? Let's take a little visit! We're not going to spend a lot of time down there. Ultimately that's not who we are, but given the circumstances, we have to respond differently. If you don't want us to go there, don't pull all the antics you pull. You wanna start this? Fine, we'll finish it. That's the way we were feeling as a team."

After Winovich had publicly declared the Wolverines' "Revenge Tour" had officially commenced minutes after the Wisconsin game, at least a dozen teammates told him they supported everything he'd said.

"And that's how I feel," he said. "It wasn't for effect. My objective isn't just to *beat* State. My objective is to take the low road and *kick their ass.* I genuinely want to embarrass State. I want to run the score up on them."

"Wisconsin, I've got respect for those guys. Old-school football—nothing extra, no talking. Penn State, same thing. But Michigan State plays you differently. They push you in the back, push you after the whistle, they'll say a lot of derogatory things, they'll flop for a flag. Playing them is a completely different beast than any other team in college football. I've never played another team like them. If you get afraid to play this game, you're in trouble.

"You have to strike a balance between not getting distracted from playing your game, and not backing down. And I think we've got that.

"The mood is good. Our confidence is in full swing. It's a fine line, because sometimes a win can hurt you more than a loss, if you let it go to your head. But I don't feel that way this time. We're not complacent, we're hungry.

"This year we're not going to give anybody anything."

Chapter 29
"Cavalry's Coming"

At Michigan State, October 20, 2018

The one-hour drive from Ann Arbor to East Lansing is a beautiful run through rolling cornfields, with mature tree groves in the median. To avoid game traffic you can take the backroads through pretty little towns, taking you past the Bloated Goat in Fowlerville and a body shop advertising the "Deer Hit Special."

On the way I listened to WTKA's *Countdown to Kickoff* show, this week featuring a conversation with host Sam Webb, former Michigan tailback Jamie Morris, and his counterpart at Michigan State, Lorenzo White, who battled Morris three decades ago. When Webb asked White about steroids in the MSU program, White chuckled and admitted they had a popular "team chemist."

According to ESPN, Bo Schembechler sparked the first steroid investigation. Before the 1988 Michigan State game Schembechler looked across the field at the Spartans' massive lineman Tony Mandarich, famously called "The Incredible Bulk" on the cover of *Sports Illustrated*. Schembechler asked his strength coach, Mike Gittleson, "Why is Mandarich twice as big as our guys?"

Gittleson knew the answer: steroids. Schembechler called a friend of his at the FBI, Special Agent Greg Stejskal, who gave a speech to Schembechler's players every year about gambling and drugs. Stejskal started an FBI investigation called "Equine," (the steroids were made for horses), and caught Michigan State's "team chemist." When they found steroid use was far more common in baseball, they warned Major League Baseball's leaders about the epidemic under their noses. They promptly yawned.

This raises a question no one seems to ask anymore: Who is taking performance-enhancing drugs now, and what is it doing to them?

As kick-off approached, the atmosphere in the visitors' locker room at Spartan Stadium had a hissing intensity, like a fuse burning its way to the bomb.

Since the Brandon-Hoke era ended, the Wolverines had wisely refused to roust the Spartans with silly stunts like skywriting and stake planting. The Wolverines didn't need any extra gunpowder to get ready for this game, but the Spartans decided to give them some anyway.

During Michigan's allotted time to take the field for warm-ups, a few Wolverines, including Lavert Hill, Devin Bush Jr., and some strength coaches, walked down the tunnel to stretch out on the field. At about 9:50 a.m., the Spartans gathered at the other end of the field and spread out in a long line to conduct their ritual pregame march down the field, arms locked. They wore sweats and helmets, for some reason, while Dantonio walked right behind the line.

The Wolverines stretching on the field watched the Spartans slowly approach. When the Spartan line reached the Michigan players the Spartans didn't stop, resulting in a bit of jostling, and one Spartan snatching Lavert Hill's headphones off his head, then letting them go.

Devin Bush Jr. took exception.

"The mentality in South Florida is that football is life," he told me. "Football is respect, football is your pride, it makes you who you are. So when you're disrespected on the football field, you respond."

Devin Bush Jr. responded. As soon as the Spartans passed, he ran to midfield and started scraping the Spartan logo with his cleats. This went viral online hours before the noon kickoff, and traveled much faster than the footage of the Spartans marching past the Wolverines—which wasn't as photogenic, in any case.

"I feel I handled it in the best way possible," Bush Jr. told me. "Instead of throwing punches, I went after their symbol. No one was hurt—but I made my point."

When Michigan's strength coaches told Harbaugh what happened, he took no issue with Bush Jr.'s response. This scenario was what Harbaugh had warned them would happen in his speeches on Monday and Friday. And he had promised: if the Spartans took the low road, the Wolverines would beat them at their own game.

"Coach Harbaugh's got our back," Higdon told me. "That's everything—more powerful than any stunt they want to pull. That just amped us up for the game."

After fellow defender Michael Dwumfour had left the field before the incident, he saw it on a cell phone, then went up to Bush crying.

"'I'm sorry I wasn't out there!'" Bush recalled him saying. "He would have joined me. The coaches had my back. The whole program had my back. That's the kind of team we have now, way different this year. They know the type of person I am. They know I wasn't looking for trouble—but they also know I'm not going to back down if it finds me. And it found me."

"They really picked the absolute worst person to do that to," Bredeson told me after the game. "Of all the guys on the team, that is the *one* guy you don't mess with. Maybe some guys would've protected themselves and walked away. But Devin's not that kind of guy. He's never going to let that go. The locker room was already a pool of gas, ready to ignite, and Devin came in and lit that whole room up. His energy was at a new level and everyone fed off that."

Did Bush do the right thing?

"Oh absolutely he did," Bredeson said. "I'll back him up to the end of time. Everyone's behind him."

Because no one spoke to the team about the incident, and there were so few witnesses, word spread unevenly through the team. Not surprisingly Winovich quickly found the clip of Bush tearing up the logo on his phone and showed his teammates.

"We didn't even know what started it," he told me. "We thought he just went out and did it, but no one got mad at Devin. We trust him. No one asked, 'Why'd he do that? What an idiot!' Everyone was basically like, 'Fuck those guys.'

"I felt like Braveheart. 'Where are you going?' 'I'm

going to pick a fight.' 'Well, our boy just picked us a fight, so let's go out and finish it. We lose this game we're going to look like idiots. So we've got to go out there and win. Let's ride!'"

The far more soft-spoken tight end Zach Gentry heard about it when they were getting dressed. He was confident Bush would not have reacted without a catalyst.

"He's as tough as they come," Gentry told me, "but he's not stupid, and he's not a hot-head. I usually don't bite on that kind of stuff, but I was pretty pissed off, especially given the hate we already have for Michigan State and the hate they have for us. And that's what's great about this team: you mess with one of us, you mess with all of us. I haven't felt that around here in a long time. Once we heard what happened, we all knew: They're gonna get the whole crew.

"Cavalry's coming."

Exactly as Harbaugh had predicted, the Spartans' trash talk and dirty play started immediately.

Most of the Wolverines were content to ignore the trash talk, and even happier to shut it down.

"Just a lot of woofing and bullshit," Higdon told me.

"They are just terrible at trash talk," Winovich told me. "Not even original. If you found something about me on Instagram to make fun of, hey, I might even laugh. But I never once thought, 'Damn, you got me.'

"All they've got is: 'You guys fucking suck!' And they're saying that when you just stuffed 'em behind the line to finish a three-and out and they're walking off the field. Man, do your homework! Guess these guys aren't known for their research.

"I like messing with these guys. It motivates me. Sometimes I'd give a loud whisper to [MSU quarterback Brian] Lewerke. 'I'm commmming, Brian! Can you do me a favor and hold on to the ball for a couple more seconds?'"

On Michigan's second possession the Wolverines called a read option, and the Spartans blitzed. Patterson gave the ball to Higdon, who went one direction, then cut back. When the linebacker followed, "Bredeson is there and just takes him out. No contest. Then I hit the hole and meet the safety, blew him up, and got the first down.

"After that, they knew our O-line was dominating them, and I was going to be in their backfield all damn day. Then they shut up. Not too much to say when you're gasping for air. And they deserve it."

That drive consisted of four passes and ten runs, six by Higdon, to cover 84 yards and grind up 7:56 on the way to the end zone.

7–0 Michigan, five seconds into the second quarter.

At the end of the first half the Spartans' six possessions produced only four first downs, against three three-and-outs. On the other side of the ball, Michigan had amassed 170 yards, but still had only seven points to show for it. When the rain started coming down, the more paranoid Michigan fans—which is to say, most of them—had reason to fear another weird upset at the hands of their in-state foe.

"That ball was so slippery," Patterson told me, "even handing it off was tricky."

Early in the second half Higdon's backup, Chris Evans, fumbled the ball on Michigan's seven-yard line. The Spartans converted the gift into a 7–7 tie.

After the costly turnover, Winovich admitted, he was more nervous when Michigan's offense was on the field than the defense.

"But when the D got on the field," he told me, "I felt comfortable. I knew these guys can't do anything—*anything*—against us. We knew we were the better team. I just hoped the offense could hang on to the ball in the rain and put some points up."

After Michigan's offense stalled on its own 14-yard line, with the rain coming down and the home crowd getting louder, punter Will Hart boomed a 50-yarder.

Michigan State's Shakur Brown caught it at his own 36, then took off until Jordan Glasgow stripped the ball loose at the 46-yard line.

Joe Hewlett was running downfield as fast as he could when he saw the ball on the ground. He slid on the wet grass, gathered up the ball, and smothered it, just a few feet from Michigan's sideline. Fellow walk-on Jake McCurry jumped on top of Hewlett, with Noah Furbush close behind—exactly as they'd been coached.

"We had the ball surrounded," Hewlett told me. "There wasn't any way they were going to get that one."

When the official signaled Michigan had recovered the ball, Hewlett popped to his feet while his teammates jumped up and down, screaming, slapping, and hugging him.

"Pretty chaotic," Hewlett recalled. "After a big play it usually takes a minute for things to calm down on the sidelines. When the celebration settled down I found Jordan [Glasgow]. He made the play; I just finished it up for him. We sat down together, got some water and a breather, while everyone came up to say, 'Way to go.'

"It felt good to do that in a big game, on the road, and especially at State. I've never liked Michigan State— ever. It was pretty awesome."

The game rolled on, but Hewlett knew that was the biggest moment of his five-year career—and so did his dad, watching from the stands.

Michigan drove 24 yards down to State's 22-yard line, but failed to turn the fumble recovery into points when Shea Patterson fumbled the ball back to the Spartans.

After three more punts the Wolverines got the ball back at their own 21-yard line. With the score still tied 7–7, and only 2:24 left in the third quarter, Michigan's coaches, players, and fans still feared another painful loss, no matter how lopsided the play. That's when Shea Patterson dropped back, saw Peoples-Jones gaining a half step on his man along the right sideline, and threw a perfect pass just past the defender into Peoples-Jones's hands, allowing him to continue running full speed without a hitch for a 79-yard touchdown.

When he got to the end zone, Peoples-Jones indulged in a pose of the Paul Bunyan trophy—probably a first in the statue's 65-year history.

Michigan 14, Michigan State 7.

"I knew when he got the touchdown, it was done," said Winovich, whose logic was as straightforward as his math. "Because I knew there was no way they were going to score against us again."

After Lewerke threw three straight incomplete

passes the Wolverines embarked on a 13-play, 84-yard drive that gobbled up a full 6:41 on the clock, and ended with a Higdon touchdown for a 21–7 lead, with 10:21 left in the fourth quarter.

"State is the cheapest, dirtiest team we play," Devin Bush Jr. told me. "And this was the dirtiest game of the three I've played. But after that third touchdown, they didn't have too much to say."

Michigan's defense, which had given up only one first down in the entire second half, once again sent the Spartans packing after three plays, giving Michigan's offense the ball back on its own 25-yard line, with 9:00 left.

So this was the challenge, the same one Michigan's offense faced after going ahead in the Northwestern game: they didn't have to score. Their mission was to grind up the rest of the clock, which meant they had to avoid the sidelines, avoid incomplete passes (and therefore almost any passing at all), and all but tell the Spartans they were going to run on every single play—and still knock down enough yardage to keep the chains and the clock moving.

"For an offensive line, this is the ultimate test," Jon Jansen explained. "They know exactly what you're going to try to do: run the ball and kill the clock. And you know they know, but you're going to do it anyway because that's what you need to do, and you don't think they can stop you. So let's see who has what.

"You grind away, play after play. You move the chains and then you look up, and they have no more timeouts, and you don't need any more first downs. Victory formation. It's over—and there's not a damn thing you can do about it. That's an O-Lineman's dream."

The 2018 Wolverines sought to realize that dream against the Spartans.

Higdon six yards.

Higdon three yards.

Higdon three yards. First down.

Higdon one yard.

Higdon four yards.

Higdon five yards. First down.

Wilson three yards.

After seven plays, all no-nonsense runs, the Wolverines had only traveled from the 25-yard line to the 50. But they had cut the remaining 9:00 in half, down to 4:24.

"We just got first down after first down," Runyan said. "And they were the nation's top-ranked rush defense before the game. I thought we should've won that gave 35–0."

After a false start kept Michigan's O-line from finishing the job themselves, Devin Bush Jr. sacked backup quarterback Rocky Lombardi, and Michael Dwumfour did the same on the next play.

When Michigan got the ball back on its own 40-yard line, Higdon ran for five more, giving him 144 yards on 33 carries, and Ben Mason another five to give the Wolverines the last first down they'd need, and the game.

"That was one of the most physical games I've ever played in," Jon Runyan Jr. told me. "So much trash talking—and they're getting their asses kicked! It was not until Ben's first down they finally shut up. Guess they finally realized the game was over."

"With their whole student section staring at me," Patterson said, "I gave them the shhhhh signal."

And that was the last word.

"That was probably the best win I've ever had since I've been here," said Bush. "Big rival, plus the incident, and in their house. They started it. We finished it."

After the game ended the Wolverines retrieved Paul Bunyan and celebrated with him on the field for the first time, with a large group of fans cheering them on.

"Taking Paul out on the field—I liked it," said the normally reserved Furbush. "We were talking about taking the low road this time. I was all for it. Coach Dantonio once said 'Pride comes before the fall.' There you go. Felt real good to watch all their hopes and dreams burn. It turns out I *can* be a vengeful guy, so that was a lot of fun."

"The locker room—man, that was indescribable," Higdon said. "Crazier than Northwestern. Crazier than Wisconsin! Joyful, happy, celebratory—happy proud. Everyone jumping up and down—chanting, singing— one of those heartfelt victories. One of those moments you're really proud to be part of a team like this. Pure joy."

"I never saw Coach [Harbaugh] so happy," Winovich said. "He said this might be his greatest victory ever. He's won a few games, so that's a big statement."

"We've had some happy locker rooms," Patterson told me. "But this was something else. Coach Harbaugh was almost in tears after that game. He got choked up a little bit—not common for him. It's great to be a Michigan Wolverine."

"I don't think we stopped singing for 20 minutes," Bredeson said. "It took us a loooooong time to get to the showers, maybe an hour—twice as long as usual after a game. Coach didn't care. We were on our own schedule."

With the loss the Spartans fell to 4-3 overall, and 2-2 in the Big Ten—all but eliminating them from the East Division race with five games left.

For Furbush, there was a bigger takeaway. "From

our standpoint, having our team captain stand up for us, and our coach stand up for us," Harbaugh would defend them again in the postgame press conference, "that was a big deal. They didn't flinch, didn't back down. They stood their ground. Man, that's leadership. That's a team."

When Joe Hewlett finally walked up the tunnel toward the team buses, Rich Hewlett was waiting for him.

"I gave him a big hug," Joe said. "He was pretty fired up after that one."

Rich told his son, "That's one you're always going to remember," but it was a fair bet that Rich would never forget it, either.

"That game really was a fight," Joe told him. "All the trash talk, every play."

"That's what they do," Rich said. "That's what they *always* do. But that's why beating them feels so good."

The team took two buses home, with the offense starting the trip with Paul Bunyan, passing it from back to front with everyone taking photos with it. Halfway home, the buses pulled into a rest area so Higdon could give the trophy to Chase Winovich, who started the process all over again in the defense's bus. Michigan fans who recognized the buses honked their horns.

Borrowing a page from his UFC hero Conor

McGregor, Winovich could not resist tweeting the following: "I'd like to take this moment, TO APOLOGIZE FOR ABSOLUTELY NOTHING!"

It received 30,734 "likes."

In Ann Arbor Winovich joined his friends at a bar "with my hood up, trying to hide and stay low key, but it wasn't very effective. People were joyous."

The bars can be fun, but for the players they come with hidden dangers.

"The bars aren't worth the trouble," junior Tyler Cochran, son of Michigan All-American Brad, told me. "People figure out pretty quickly you're on the team, they've all got cell phones to record whatever happens, and a few frat guys might try to start a fight to prove how tough they are."

That's exactly what happened one night that fall at a popular college bar, when a fraternity member started mouthing off to one of Michigan's starting defenders. Nothing too unusual about that, but when the fraternity brother pushed it too far, a few sparks flew that could have grown into a brushfire.

Instead, a handful of Michigan football players seemed to materialize out of nowhere, like undercover agents called into action, and immediately mobilized. Two players bear-hugged the instigator and walked him out of the bar, depositing him outside, and telling him not to return.

Back in the bar a few more players formed a tight circle around the first player to keep the other fraternity brothers from kicking dust up, then they all left the bar calmly but quickly. Secret Service agents couldn't have handled it much better.

"It was all over in seconds," Bredeson told me. "Look, we don't practice this stuff, so it was amazing to see how fast we rallied. I felt good about that. We look out for each other when we're outside of the building. As much as everyone loves you, some guys want to make their name at your expense. The worst invention for student-athletes was the cell phone.

"Sometimes the bars can be a lot of fun. Do I think about how much fun we miss being football players? Sure, but I bet the other students think a lot more about being on the team."

The older players tend to celebrate at their homes surrounded by trusted friends instead of taking their chances on the unpredictable bar crowds. They often hang out with athletes from other sports, and date athletes. Their schedules are just as crazy.

The linemen also preferred playing noon games.

"You play at seven, and your whole day is shot," Bredeson told me. "We don't like lying around. We want to go hit someone! And we have no meetings on game days. If you don't know it by then, you're not going to know it. Coach [Harbaugh] lets us sleep in until noon, so we can 'cut the day in half.'

"So we love noon games. You're done by four, the sun is still up, your parents come over to your home and make a big meal for you. And it's fun. At 4:30, you've won your game, you've got a plateful of food in front of you, and you're watching big teams lose. That's great.

"That's what I live for: those few delicious hours after a nice win," Jon Runyan Jr. said. "Some of my best memories are just hanging out with my teammates and our parents at the house."

Runyan lived at the home the Glasgow family bought a few years ago called the Lumber Yard, along with Jared Wangler, tight ends Zach Gentry and Sean McKeon, quarterback Brandon Peters, and Glasgow himself, of course. Due to its location near Schembechler Hall it had become a drop-in home for other players.

On this particular night, the scene at the Lumber Yard was particularly festive. The Wolverines had beaten a ranked team on the road to end that 17-game losing streak that appeared endlessly on TV. Now they had the rest of the day to enjoy it with full plates of food and full houses, with big games to watch the rest of the night.

An eye-opener was playing out in West Lafayette, Indiana, where Purdue was making Ohio State look horrible.

"We just couldn't believe it," Runyan recalled. "The Purdue running back broke a few tackles, then busted out an a 40-yard run. We turned to each other in disbelief. '*Is this happening? Is this Ohio State?*'"

It was. Final score: 49–20. The Buckeyes had gotten smoked by the same team that had lost to Eastern Michigan.

After Winovich's group returned from the bars, the party continued at their home.

"We were all there," Winovich told me the next day, after his mandatory physical exam. "Shea and some football buddies, pumping the music, dancing, having a joyous time. Just carefree, for one night. Finally let myself breathe.

"It was the best day of my life. When I finally went to bed, I couldn't go to sleep. First time all day I had heard quiet, no noise. It was the weirdest thing.

"I was so happy and content with life, I didn't want to go to sleep. I didn't even care. With a bye week coming up, after I get home [today], I'm going to take the best nap of my life."

Higdon celebrated in an entirely different fashion, but with the same results. He had gained 144 yards, breaking 100 for the sixth game in a row—the nation's longest active streak. That gave him 831 for the season, just 169 shy of becoming Michigan's first 1,000-yard rusher in seven years. But Higdon, who had finished the previous season 6 yards shy after he injured his knee, knew how fragile that streak could be.

When he pulled into his parents' home in Sterling Heights, Kiyah was waiting.

"I walk in, she's sitting on the couch, watching more football, and walks up to me and screams 'DADDY!' and hugs my leg.

"How did Daddy do?"

She gave him two thumbs up.

PART IV

November

Chapter 30
"If Football Was Taken Away"
Grant Newsome

A handful of Wolverines had realistic NFL dreams, but Grant Newsome already knew his would never come true.

Grant's mother, Kim, graduated cum laude with a bachelor's degree from Princeton, where she met Grant's father, Leon. He had committed to play for Lou Holtz at Notre Dame before he decided to attend Princeton and play baseball. When he and his coaches couldn't balance practice and studies to his satisfaction, he soon switched back to football and became an All–Ivy League defensive end. He missed half his senior season due to injuries but still graduated on time, then joined the Secret Service, where he has worked for 26 years.

"That was my dream, too: Princeton baseball," said Grant, who grew up in McLean, Virginia, just outside D.C. In ninth grade he enrolled at Lawrenceville, an elite boarding school about 15 minutes from Princeton. He already felt burnt out on baseball, so he joined the junior varsity football team. Though he didn't start, he loved the game immediately—much to his father's chagrin. After a strong sophomore season on the varsity, Rutgers' head coach Kyle Flood invited him to visit.

"I really had no idea what to expect," Newsome said. "I had never talked to a college coach before."

Flood offered him a scholarship on the spot. Newsome was flattered, but the ride had just begun.

Schembechler liked to joke that if his sons went to see a movie in Columbus, East Lansing, and South Bend, then told the local paper where they'd been, they'd get ten scholarship offers that night—and that's about what happened with Newsome. The day after Virginia offered Old Dominion did the same. After Newsome performed well at Penn State's camp the next summer, 2013, then–head coach Bill O'Brien offered him a scholarship, too. Temple followed suit the next day, sight unseen.

"They hadn't even talked to me," Newsome recalls. "But that's how crazy that process can be."

It got crazier. After Newsome's junior year he had

34 offers, including Alabama, LSU, and most of the top 25 programs.

"Grant could have gone to any of the Ivies," Kim Newsome told me. "But he wanted the best of both worlds: football and academics."

She didn't know what big-time college football looked like until they visited Penn State's annual spring scrimmage, which attracted 72,000 fans—ten times what Princeton draws for its biggest games.

"I'd never seen a crowd so big," Kim said. "Fans are asking for his autograph. He's a recruit! This was a whole new world to me."

When Grant went home for Christmas his junior year, 2013, "the world looked a little different," he remembered. In the spring of 2014 Grant and his father revisited Penn State, where O'Brien had been replaced by James Franklin, who "had a way of making you feel like you were the most important person in the room," Grant recalled.

Next stop: Ann Arbor.

"I wasn't really thrilled about visiting Michigan," Grant confessed, but his parents urged him to go. When he did, "I said, 'Whoa! Where has this place been hiding?' I was kind of blown away."

On their visit Kim was impressed with Shari Acho, the co-director of the athletic department's Academic

Success Program, who told Grant, "It's great you're a big-time recruit. I would want nothing more for you than to have a 15-year NFL career. But let's have a Plan B. We have enough tools here to make sure you have a great career long after football is over."

There's a reason Michigan's coaches, academic advisors, and tutors remind the players that NFL stands for "Not For Long."

Harbaugh has taken Jerry Hanlon's observation, that you don't know what kind of team you really have for twenty years, and turned it into a phrase Michigan often uses in recruiting: "These next four years will determine your next forty. What program will best prepare you for the rest of your life?"

After Newsome's visit, he gave himself two weeks to decide.

"I loved the football aspect of Penn State, but everything else, I preferred Michigan. There was something indescribable about the culture that I just felt I could be comfortable there."

He was impressed by Michigan but still leaning toward Penn State. Kim vividly remembered them sitting in their family room, and Grant saying, "I don't know how I'm going to make this decision."

His mom asked a simple question: "If football was

taken away from you for some reason, what school would you want to attend?"

"No question," Grant said. "Michigan."

The Newsomes insisted Grant call Penn State before calling Michigan. "One of the toughest calls I ever had to make," Grant said.

Franklin took the call at his football camp, on speakerphone. After Newsome thanked Franklin for his interest, he told him he'd be attending Michigan. "Franklin couldn't have been more gracious. He told me he wouldn't pester me, but if I ever changed my mind to stay in touch. I thought that was class."

"I was confident Grant could handle the school-work," Leon said, "but I didn't know if he was cut out for football at that level. We figured if he didn't get into a single game, he'd still get a great education—and someone else would pay for it."

In the fall of Newsome's senior year in high school, 2014, they returned to Ann Arbor for his official visit. The Wolverines were already 5-5, the athletic director was gone, and Hoke needed a win to get a bowl bid and save his job. But Michigan lost to Maryland, 23–16, in front of a Big House half-filled with cold, wet, miserable fans—perhaps the lowest point Michigan football had seen in decades.

After the game the recruits visited in the Junge Champions Center with the coaches and their families. In the ladies' room Kim Newsome saw the coaches' wives sobbing at the mirror. When she told her husband and son, Grant recalled, "That was eye-opening. When you see these are people's wives and children who now have to read their husband's or father's or son's names getting trashed in the media, it shows just how brutal this business of college football can really be. Their lives get uprooted and they have to go somewhere else."

When Leon Newsome warned Grant not to pick a school based on the coach because they can always get fired or leave, Leon didn't expect to be proven right before Grant arrived in Ann Arbor.

Playing on Michigan's scout team throughout Harbaugh's first fall camp, Grant figured he'd be redshirted his freshman year. When the 2015 season started, he had already moved up to third string, and would be bumped to second after Logan Tillman was kicked off the team for videotaping himself and his girlfriend having sex. In Harbaugh's program, improper conduct is handled swiftly, and justice is blind to the players' value to the team.

"Logan's owned up to it," Newsome said. "A good guy who made a mistake."

Moving up to the second team meant Newsome now faced the first string in practice: Chris Wormley, Taco Charlton, Matthew Godin, and Ryan Glasgow.

"I'd just turned 18. I'd been playing the game for only four years, and just three at offensive line. And now I'm facing off with a first-round draft pick, a third-rounder, and two other guys who are still playing in the NFL today. If that's not trial by fire, I don't know what is. But this is Michigan football: adapt or die."

Newsome thrived. Midway into his freshman year Harbaugh called his parents to let them know he wanted to burn Newsome's red shirt and play him.

"You think about college football being this heartless machine," Kim said, "but that's not what it was for us. Harbaugh wasn't asking our permission outright, but he wanted our blessing to make sure we were okay with it. I thought that was so thoughtful—and really, unexpected."

Grant's parents knew before he did. At the hotel meeting before Michigan's eighth game, up at Minnesota, coach Tim Drevno asked, "Grant, are you ready?"

"I'll never forget it," Newsome said. "I wasn't even sure what he was asking. Ready for what, exactly? But when I nodded, he said, 'Good. You're going to be getting some reps tomorrow.'"

Newsome's parents also got a trial by fire when they

were introduced to the world of Twitter and sports talk radio.

"In his first game, and maybe on his first play," Leon recalled, "when Grant blocked down on the pass protection, the linebacker came free toward the quarterback. That was how the play was *supposed* to work, to lure the linebacker upfield, then throw the ball where the linebacker used to be. But they're ripping Grant for missing his man. Hey, know the game before you talk—and if you don't, bite your tongue.

"Now, you understand going in that social media is part of college football these days, and if you can't handle that, you shouldn't play—or be a parent of a player. But I can't say it doesn't bother me."

"I get that it's big-time college football and you'll get criticized by strangers," Kim said. "But for me the hardest part is how *savage* it can be, how deeply personal. It can be hard to shake when that's your son."

After Michigan's thrilling 29–26 victory over Minnesota, Newsome played the remaining five games that season and started the next year, 2016.

"My football career escalated very quickly," he told me. "It was another whirlwind, just like the recruitment process. I remember the build-up before that 2016 season. That team had a chance to be very, very special, and we all knew it, with the swagger you have when you know you're the baddest kid on the block."

That confidence looked justified when the fourth-ranked Wolverines waxed Penn State, 49–10—a team that would go on to win nine straight games and the conference title.

"We were thinking it would be a close game," Newsome said, "but we're the better football team. We know it. They know it. One thing that separates good teams from great teams is great teams give you no mercy, and we didn't. You go in, you punch 'em in the mouth, and you keep punching them until they're knocked out. That's what we did. That was the most fun I ever had on a football field."

It would also be the last game Newsome finished.

With his parents and two younger brothers in the stands for Michigan's game against 8th-ranked Wisconsin, Newsome knew he'd have a busy day battling T. J. Watt, who would become the Pittsburgh Steelers' first-round draft pick. After the Wolverines scored early in the second quarter to open a 7–0 lead, they were on the march again when they called "99 Truck," a toss play to De'Veon Smith toward the left side of the line—Newsome's side.

Newsome lined up, made his call, "TAR," or "tackle-around," and told the left guard, Ben Braden, and the tight end, Jake Butt, "If we get a '5 tech,' I'll be pulling." Which meant if a defender filled the gap between Newsome and Butt, Newsome would become the lead blocker running around the edge. If all went well Newsome would pull then look for the alley defender, the nine technique, who would appear in the gap between Jake Butt and the receiver, Jehu Chesson—all pretty standard stuff.

"But before the ball was snapped," Newsome recalled, "I got this premonition: If I don't cut my man (by driving his shoulder into his man's legs to take him off his feet), he's going to cut me. It was a very explicit, very specific, and very clear phrase in my head. I'd never had that before."

When Mason Cole snapped the ball Newsome went into action, pulling around Butt's block to lead the charge; Speight tossed the ball to Smith behind him; then Newsome looked to the alley for his next man: All–Big Ten cornerback Derrick Tindal.

"I see the guy I'm going to end up blocking, or try to block," Newsome recalled. "I see my guy start to rotate, as I start running upfield. I see our receiver, Jehu Chesson, block the man coming in front of me, and I remember thinking Jehu had been knocked too far back on the play, toward me. So I knew if I tried to cut Tindal, the hole we're trying to make would not be big enough for De'Veon to get through. It would close. So I'm thinking instead of cutting Tindal, I'll grab him and get him to the side, which will leave enough room for De'Veon to get downfield.

"That's the last thing I remember seeing on that play."

That's probably for the best, because what happened next ranks among the more gruesome football injuries. When Tindal saw that Newsome was staying on his feet instead of cutting him, Tindal went low, driving the full weight of his body straight into Newsome's right knee, with a force so great it shoved Newsome's knee backward until his thighbone and shin made a 60-degree angle—in the wrong direction.

Newsome crumpled to the ground, landing on his stomach. "But it was kind of weird: I didn't feel any pain. None at all—though maybe I just went into shock."

Unaware of the extent of Newsome's injury, Chesson said, "You gotta get up."

"I can't," Newsome said.

When head athletic trainer Dave Granito asked Newsome if he could roll over onto his back, he did—then heard a big "pop," the sound of his bones snapping back into their normal positions.

Newsome yelled, "I just tore my fucking ACL!"

When they performed the initial tests on the field Newsome's knee seemed relatively stable, but that was due to the massive swelling.

When Harbaugh came over Newsome said, "'I should've cut him.' And coach was like, 'Yeahhh, you probably should have.' It was funny at the time, because no one even imagined the severity."

Newsome thought he might have sprained it. Then he remembered his family was there and his mom was probably freaking out, so he walked off the field with help. From there the trainers took him in a Gator up the tunnel to the team training room, equipped with an X-ray machine, a fluoroscan C-Arm, and diagnostic ultrasound, where doctors can treat players with sutures, IVs, injections, and aspirations—basically a mini–emergency room. Dr. Asheesh Bedi, a Michigan Medical School graduate, tested Newsome's knee for ligament damage. It was so bad it seemed surprisingly good: with so much swelling the knee presented like an MCL sprain.

"I was already doing the math," Newsome said. "I'd be out for Rutgers the next week, but then we had a bye, Illinois, and Michigan State four weeks away. If I could get back for State, not so bad."

The doctors asked if he felt any numbness or tingling in his toes. Newsome replied, "Yeah, but that's probably normal, right?" The doctors looked at each other, then found that the pulse in his right foot was not as strong as the one in his left.

"We're taking you to the hospital. It's probably nothing, but we want to be safe."

When Newsome asked to take a shower first, the doctors said they could probably get in quickly and be back before the end of the game. After the EMTs loaded him on a stretcher, right as the team returned for halftime, his mother joined him in the ambulance while his father and brothers followed in their rental car.

The team doctors called ahead to ask the hospital staff to prepare to rule out any vascular issues, so they were able to run an X-ray and a series of tests in minutes.

Watching the second half in his hospital room, with the game tied 7–7, Newsome "was getting nervous, very nervous—about the outcome of the game!" With Michigan ahead 14–7, Wisconsin's final drive ended with a spectacular one-handed interception by Jourdan Lewis. When the Newsomes yelled, the nurses told them to keep it down.

But after a while Newsome "started getting that

sinking feeling, because no one is telling you what they think it is, and I picked up pretty quickly that they weren't about to say, 'Good news: everything's fine!'"

The tenor of the room changed dramatically when a vascular surgeon, Matt Corriere, ran several tests, then told Newsome his lower right leg was only getting about half the blood it needed.

"We need to put you into surgery," Dr. Corriere said.

"Am I going to have my leg coming out of surgery?" Newsome asked.

"We're going to try our best."

"I was shocked," Newsome recalled. "Never imagined anything like that."

Two minutes later, at almost 10 p.m., two nurses unlocked the wheels on his bed and rushed him to surgery. Dr. Corriere cut out Newsome's soleus, or calf muscle, because it was already 70–80 percent dead, then later removed two more pieces.

When Dr. Corriere examined Newsome's popliteal artery, which pumps blood into the lower leg, it looked like ground beef. After grafting a vein from Newsome's left leg to create a bypass, Dr. Corriere sewed up two long scars at about 5 a.m. to complete a seven-hour operation, about twice as long as expected.

"That was a long night, maybe the longest of my life," Leon Newsome confessed. "You're just sitting in the waiting room, watching the clock. But Dave Granito and Drevno and Harbaugh were there, and that helped. Finally the doctor came out and said they did everything they could, and thought his leg would be okay, but the next 24 to 48 hours would tell. It was hard to even think about the worst-case scenario."

But as soon as Newsome returned to his room he told the doctors he had no feeling in his leg. They decided to go back in to see if the arterial bypass was delivering blood to the leg as it should. Trying to do it a second time usually compromises the blood flow, which can result in amputation. To everyone's relief they found their first operation had held up, and the lack of feeling Newsome experienced was due to nerve damage, which would heal over time.

But they also discovered Newsome's knee joint was so damaged it could not support its own weight, and collapsed on itself, dislocating again. To make sure that didn't happen again—which could rupture the artery and result in amputation—they drilled two holes each into his tibia and his femur, then installed rods to create an external brace called a fixator to lock his knee in place so it could heal.

_____

After the crisis had passed, Dr. Corriere told Newsome if they had started the first surgery just 15 to 30 minutes later, the doctor would be forced to perform "a salvage operation," another phrase for amputation.

Yet Newsome still wasn't out of the woods. The next day his calf ballooned to the size of his thigh. Doctors worried the swelling would create "compartment syndrome" and cut off circulation. Newsome entered the hospital at 320 pounds, but just a day later the swelling and fluids pushed his weight to an astonishing 378. To relieve the pressure the surgeons made two six-inch long football-shaped divots in his calf, one of them recessed about an inch.

As bad as it was, David Granito was grateful Newsome received much faster attention than the average citizen would have, which could have cost him his leg.

"And then you consider the number of specialists involved," Granito told me, writing down seven on a dry-erase board, including cardiovascular, orthopedics, plastic surgery, and infectious diseases. With New England, Granito said, he would need to go through five different offices. At Michigan Granito already knew all seven in only his fourth month, "when I barely knew where the bathroom was."

Granito's team had two goals for Newsome: "One,

give him a healthy and normal life; and two, give him every chance to play if he wanted. We didn't tell him this but honestly, we thought it was a real long shot. If he had decided to quit on the spot, nobody would have blamed him."

Newsome's final stat line read as follows: torn MCL, PCL, and partial ACL; destroyed popliteal artery; fractured tibia; a tibial plateau fracture (instead of a round ball atop the bone, a crater); damage to three different leg nerves, the peroneal, tibial, and femoral, and the loss of most of his soleus, or calf muscle—all in a split second.

Given this laundry list of injuries, a normal man would probably count his blessings, give up the game, and focus on his studies. But Newsome, like so many football players, is not a normal man.

"There's just the sheer physicality of the sport, especially on the offensive line," Newsome explained. "Our job is to displace a man from a spot he does not want to leave. There's something so pure about that. As a player, it's enthralling. There are very few sports where your mission is to knock another man over— and I'm sorry, that's a satisfying sensation nothing else can really give you.

"Then there's the chess game. The game might not look complicated from the stands, but when you're playing offensive line you're constantly adjusting to the defense. It's a problem you have to solve on every play.

"And outside of the Xs and Os, there's the brotherhood, the unequaled feeling of relying on ten different people. That's not common in other sports. Football is one of the few team sports where one dominant player can't do it alone. Even the quarterback is only as good as his line. What else can give you all that?"

Knowing how Newsome felt, and how hard he was willing to work, "We didn't tell him we thought the odds of coming back were pretty slim," Granito recalled, "and we approached him like no one was thinking that. We weren't going to be the ones to tell him. We poured everything we could into him. No one cut any corners."

During this trying time the Newsomes met the "silent majority" of the fans, not the fringe that often dominates social media.

"There are a lot of wonderful, wonderful people in the Michigan fan base," Kim said. "The sad part is you don't get the full measure of that until your son is in the hospital. The letters came from everywhere, including from some who never went to Michigan. They weren't asking for anything; they just wanted to show their appreciation and support. And that's the beauty of it: you've got a group of people so united around something for decades, and they mobilize when you need them most."

They also received the full support of the Michigan football family. The parents of Matt Mitchell, the local kid who would come back for his fifth year in 2018 to make his debut in the Nebraska game, were sitting next to the Newsomes during that 2016 Wisconsin game. Before anyone knew the gravity of Newsome's injuries, the Mitchells delivered fancy Zingerman's bagels to the hospital. They were followed by coaches and staffers visiting almost every night, often with Grant's favorite milk shake.

"You don't forget those things," Leon said. "I think how the overall community—the hospital, the coaches, even strangers—came to take care of our family was really something."

"I have to say," Kim added, "the university could not have been more incredible. And Harbaugh was there all the time."

"*All* the time," Leon underscored. "And this is in the middle of his second season. He's busy. He's under pressure. This was far beyond making an appearance for a few nights. Harbaugh or an assistant were there *every* day and *every* night. After a while you realize it was not because they had to do it, but because they wanted to, and they really do care."

Next hurdle: Newsome had four classes but couldn't leave his hospital bed for a month.

"He only dropped one class," Kim said. "Part of that was Grant being who he is, but you have to give Michigan credit. I never thought such a big school could be so nimble to adapt. One class let him Skype in, another professor shifted the due dates on his papers, and these things made it possible. 'Okay, I can do school!' It was good that he could focus on something positive, instead of dwelling on what he'd lost."

The experience surely brought back Harbaugh's memories of Schembechler visiting him while he lay in his hospital bed after he broke his arm, tears in his eyes, asking Schembechler not to forget him. He knew what this felt like.

Harbaugh also harbored a bit of guilt. At Stanford he was one of the first coaches to require the linemen to wear braces for practices and games, which became the standard nationally. The linemen are just too susceptible to knee injuries, with guys diving at their knees and falling on them after the play.

"But the Niners are professionals," Harbaugh told me. "They asked to make braces for games optional because they felt they could play better, so we did, and it worked well. After my first season back at Michigan we did the same thing for 2016, giving them the option of wearing the braces for games. Well, just five games into that season, the Wisconsin linebacker comes in on a sweep play and takes out Grant's knee. Had he been wearing his brace he still would have been injured, but I have to believe the magnitude would not be as much.

"I will always carry that with me as a big mistake, one of the things I regret most in my coaching career."

After Newsome's injury all Michigan linemen were once again required to wear braces in practices and games.

After four weeks in the hospital Newsome started a painful rehabilitation program three hours a day, five or six days a week, just to bend his right leg, then relearn how to stand on two feet, then walk, then jog. A year and a half after his injury he graduated from Michigan in 2018 with "High Distinction" in American culture and a minor in African American studies.

When camp started that August the media reported Newsome might return that fall, but a week into the two-a-day workouts Newsome could see he might only be able to contribute as a backup halfway through the season—and was that worth the risk?

"I'd been grappling with that decision for a long time," Newsome said, "going back and forth between hope and caution. And then it hit me, about ten days into fall camp. I forget what drill it was, but all of a sudden the message came to me in no uncertain terms: 'I don't have it anymore.' At that moment I knew I was done. It was over."

"We all knew Grant was not likely to play football again," Granito said, "but it's amazing how close he came. We all felt he had the best possible outcome for anyone who's had that injury—athlete or not. Medically, that situation worked out really well. We achieved the first goal: the ability to lead a normal life, doing normal activities. But by August [of 2018], you could see that he still couldn't do this, he couldn't do that—not at the level you need to play—but you can't tell him that. It has to be his decision."

After almost two years of rehabilitation, entailing hundreds of workouts, Newsome couldn't kid himself: just three weeks before the 2018 season, he had to give it up.

"It was extremely disappointing," he said. "Any time you have something you love, and it's taken from you, it's going to affect you. But football ends for everyone at some point, and very few are able to leave this game on their own terms.

"I knew I was done, but I couldn't push the button on my phone to call my parents. This was going to be tough. Probably took me 15 minutes to call my dad. Calling my mom would be harder."

While Grant paced along the far grass practice field, still in his workout clothes, his dad's phone started ringing, and Grant started crying.

"I'm going to tell coach I'm going to retire," he told his father. "I'm done."

"Okay," Leon said. "But be sure. You worked this hard to get back to where you are, you need to make sure you won't have any regrets. Don't make a decision and say, 'What if?' down the road, because this is not the kind of thing you can take back."

"No," Grant said. "It's time. I know."

"If you can live with your decision, we will support you any way you want to go."

Newsome paced ten more minutes before screwing up his courage to call his mom. When he told her his decision, "I know she's crying because she goes silent, and takes 30 seconds before she answers."

Kim Newsome was crying, but not because he wasn't going to play football anymore. Truth be told, she was secretly relieved because she was "freaking out a bit" about how she would handle watching him play again after witnessing such a traumatic injury. No, she was crying because something her son had worked so hard to recapture was beyond his reach, and his dream had died.

After she gave him her blessings and said goodbye, Newsome took another 20 minutes to compose himself before climbing the stairs to Harbaugh's office.

"I knew it was the right decision," Newsome said. "Really, the only decision, but I hate quitting. I hate feeling like I failed. I had that horrible feeling of letting these people down.

"I knew it was the last time I'd walk across that field as a player. But then there was this great moment of peace."

Newsome knocked on Harbaugh's door, walked in, and saw Harbaugh talking with Matt Dudek and Sean Magee.

"Is now a good time?"

"Totally good!" the typically enthusiastic Harbaugh said.

Newsome sat down on a couch and got right to the point. "I just got off the phone with my parents, and I think I'm gonna hang 'em up."

"Oh, that's too bad," Harbaugh said. "Are you sure? Anything we can do?"

Newsome shook his head. "I'm good. It's time."

Harbaugh nodded. "We want you to stay in the program and keep your scholarship, and we'll do whatever we can do for you."

Newsome's mom worried about how Grant would react after spending so many hours with this group, then quitting cold turkey.

"I was not as worried about that," Leon told me. "He'd earned the respect of his teammates, and he was now ingrained in that culture. And I knew Coach Harbaugh would find a way to keep him involved."

Leon's assumption proved correct. They honored Grant's scholarship—not a small thing when it costs $67,160 for an out-of-state graduate student—then asked Grant how he wanted to contribute. Newsome decided to help break down video with the analysts, and assist the tight ends—close enough to his old position to be helpful, but not the same room as his previous line mates.

He had also started to serve as an informal advisor to Harbaugh himself.

"I've gone to Grant a half dozen times with a problem I wasn't sure how to solve, usually a personnel issue," Harbaugh told me. "I ask him, 'What do you think I should do?' And I'm telling you, he's spot-on every time. *Every time.* I do what he suggests, and it works."

Newsome had started his master's degree in public policy at Michigan's Ford School, with a 3.80 GPA.

"I grew up outside of D.C., so I've always had a passion for politics, and public policy in general," he said. "I'm fascinated by how change can be effected on a large scale, so this is a natural avenue for me.

"I went through a lot of adversity, but people go through adversity every day, and often much worse than mine. There are very, very few people who get through life not facing serious adversity. I thought I was a pretty hard worker before this, but this has instilled a level of hard work that I didn't know I had, another gear."

It also made him more grateful for his health, his family, and his opportunities—not to mention a mother who was wise enough to ask him four years earlier if his football career ended, where would he want to go to school?

Given everything, did Grant's parents think it was all worth it? What would they tell other parents whose sons wanted to play football?

"That was certainly the question I asked myself,

with all the reports on concussions and CTE," Kim admitted. "And part of me wished he'd never touched the field. But I only felt that way until I got to Michigan, and saw how hard he worked, and sacrificed, and wanted it. He was so excited when he got here, and thrilled when he started.

"I think if it's your child's passion and they're equipped to do it, then I think it is worth it. But a *lot* of it depends on who you're playing for. Like Leon said, you shouldn't pick a school just because of the coach, because they might not be there. Coach Hoke recruited Grant. But if you pick a bad coach, I wouldn't feel safe. I don't think Grant would feel safe. You have to know the coaches have good judgment, and care about you beyond football. Grant has been embraced by a coaching staff that cares about these men, beyond being football players. That's everything."

"Every day Grant wakes up and sees his leg, it will always be a reminder of his struggle," Leon said. "But he also has a degree from the University of Michigan, and next year he'll have a master's degree from the Ford School. He has something else, the steel to handle the next phase of his life, the next surprise—whatever it is."

That was the answer to the question my wife and I had asked ourselves after our three-year-old son,

Teddy, had such a great time running on the field at the Big House during the open practice: if he wanted to, would we let him play football? We weren't sure then, but we were now: Yes, provided he had good coaches in a good program, where the risks were minimized, and the benefits were greater than just winning games.

After all, why does a parent send their child to college? If it's more than an investment in job preparation, but to become a better person, the question of playing football answers itself.

"I believe to the bottom of my heart," Grant's father said, "that Grant will leave Michigan as well prepared to face the world as any young man could be."

That's what we wanted.

Chapter 31
Captain Comeback
1987–2014

The Chicago Bears used their first pick of the 1987 draft to select Jim Harbaugh the 26th player overall, and the fourth quarterback. It looked like Harbaugh had finally convinced the doubters, and his faith in himself—dating back at least to tenth grade, when he told his JV teammates he'd be playing in the NFL—had been vindicated.

Not quite. Chicago general manager Bill Tobin was big on Harbaugh but some teammates were not, notably quarterback Jim McMahon and backup Mike Tomczak.

"Every place Jim played they always had someone set up to beat him out," John Harbaugh told me. "Tomczak saw him as a threat, and McMahon wasn't too thrilled, either—though he bought us a round during training camp, so he can't be all bad."

Worse, neither head coach Mike Ditka and later Dave Wannstedt wanted him. Just to get on the field Harbaugh, the Big Ten MVP, had to volunteer for high-risk kickoff coverage—more proof of the NFL's fickle nature, and of Harbaugh's desire to play.

"There were GMs, scouts, coaches, and plenty of media that looked down on Jim early on," John Harbaugh told me. "He had to overcome that. But there were also people like Bill Tobin who believed in him, and Jim sure proved him right."

From grade school on most people didn't "get" Harbaugh, but crucially he always seemed to have one person who did: Mrs. Hiller in fifth grade, Rob Lillie at Tappan Junior High, Palo Alto basketball coach Clem Wiser, all the way to Schembechler and Tobin. John Harbaugh is convinced, however, that some of his brother's initial problems adjusting to the NFL were the result of his preparation.

"Michigan was the best and worst thing that happened to him," John said. "Bo was great for Jim, and he grew a lot at Michigan. But Michigan was playing an I-formation, play-action offense, which obviously worked for them, while Bill Walsh was winning Super Bowls throwing the ball around with his West Coast offense. When Jim got to the NFL he had to overcome all that, running the race from behind.

"Jim was also way underrated as an athlete. You see him in the NFL, scrambling to make a play—that's an athlete. His arm was stronger than he got credit for, too."

After McMahon went to the San Diego Chargers in 1989, Ditka started Tomczak eleven times and Harbaugh five. The team fell to 6-10, but Harbaugh set a team record with a 62 percent completion rate, earning him the starting job in 1990. After he had won ten of the Bears' first 14 games, Harbaugh's shoulder injury knocked him out of the last two games and the playoffs. He started all 16 games in 1991 and won eleven before losing in the first round of the playoffs.

No sooner had Harbaugh established himself as a bona fide NFL quarterback than the Bears dynasty fell apart. When the 1992 team finished 5-11, Ditka was fired. After the Bears went 7-9 the next year, with Harbaugh starting 15 games, Bill Tobin, now the GM of the Indianapolis Colts, picked up Harbaugh—once again over the objections of the head coach.

"In the summer of '95," Jack Harbaugh recalled, "we're in Indy, driving to lunch. Jim's in the backseat. He said, 'Get ready. I'm going to be cut in the next two days.'"

They had traded a first-round pick to get Craig Erickson, but Harbaugh was determined to battle for his job and stay on the roster.

"You don't see that anymore," tailback Zack Crockett told the *Indianapolis Star*. "To watch that in training camp, those two guys compete, it was unreal."

Erickson started the first two games, fell behind both times, and was replaced by Harbaugh, who led stirring comebacks, earning him the starting job. Trailing Dan Marino's Miami Dolphins 24–3 at halftime, Harbaugh's three touchdown passes led the Colts to a 27–24 overtime victory, and earned him the nickname "Captain Comeback." He kept it up against the defending Super Bowl champion 49ers and beat Marino again en route to a wild card berth. After taking only one week off for knee surgery, Harbaugh won two playoff games before losing to Pittsburgh when his Hail Mary to Aaron Bailey was ultimately ruled incomplete.

In Harbaugh's ninth season in the NFL he led the league with the fewest interceptions (five), a 100.7 passer rating, and three fourth-quarter comebacks. He earned his first trip to the Pro Bowl, and Comeback Player of the Year. No surprise he remembers 1995 as his favorite NFL season. He finished his career with brief stops in Baltimore, San Diego, Detroit, and Carolina.

In 2005 Harbaugh became only the third player the

Colts inducted into their "Ring of Honor." He is now one of 10 players whose names circle the field, alongside Eric Dickerson, Marshall Faulk, and Peyton Manning.

Not bad for a guy who told his parents he was about to get cut.

The year after Harbaugh retired in 2001 he applied to become Michigan's quarterback coach. When Lloyd Carr instead picked Scot Loeffler, with four years' experience, Harbaugh accepted Al Davis's offer to help Oakland's quarterbacks.

"Al Davis loved Jim," John Harbaugh said. "*Loved* him."

But Jim still had to put in typically crazy NFL coaching hours, which take their toll—something John could have told him. While Jim was playing in the NFL, John was paying his dues at Western Michigan, the University of Pittsburgh, Morehead State, the University of Cincinnati, Indiana, and finally the NFL with the Philadelphia Eagles (1998–2007), before becoming the Baltimore Ravens' head coach.

"In 2002 I was coaching in Philly," John told me, "and it's the middle of the season. My phone rings at 6 a.m., so it's 3 a.m. out in California. It's Jim."

"I've got a problem," Jim said. "I just woke up in my car in my driveway, and I can't remember if I was leaving the house to *go* to work or coming back to the house *from* work. What do I do?"

"Hm—there's no playbook for that," John said. "Go in the house, kiss your wife, and see how she reacts. If she says, 'Welcome home,' stay. But if she says, 'What are you doing here?' it's time to get back in your car and go to work."

When she welcomed Jim home, he stayed. What John didn't ask is why Jim was working so hard. He already knew: that's what it takes.

Still, it's more than a bit surprising that Jim, the 14-year NFL quarterback, wanted to do what John had been doing since graduation. Schembechler often lamented that so few of his 660 Michigan players pursued coaching, speculating that the long hours he and his staff worked probably scared them off. So it goes against type that the player who sought to follow Schembechler at Michigan wasn't a backup lineman, as you'd expect, but one of Michigan's greatest players at the sport's most glamorous position. To Harbaugh's credit, he never acted like it, paying his dues just like his brother.

In 2004 Jim Harbaugh applied to become head coach at Eastern Michigan University, just a few miles down Washtenaw Avenue from the University of Michigan. Although it was traditionally a graveyard of coaches,

Harbaugh was itching to get his start. Athletic director Dave Diles, however, wouldn't even give Harbaugh an interview, instead opting for Jeff Genyk, who would go 16-42. The next AD hired Ron English, who was even worse at 11-46.

Instead, Harbaugh left Oakland to accept the head coaching position at the University of San Diego—a I-AA Jesuit school that did not offer athletic scholarships but wanted to leverage football to attract more male students to a campus that was about two-thirds women. Harbaugh's first head coaching position paid $80,000 a year.

"Al told him, 'Jim it's USD, not USC,'" John recalled. "Al hated to lose him, but Jim wanted to be the head coach."

Al Davis was right about one thing: It wasn't USC. After splitting his first two games, Harbaugh's first USD team played Penn.

"They kick our butts, 61–18," Harbaugh told me. "You don't forget that. I was pissed at them for running up the score, but when I confronted Joe Magnoli, the Penn coach, he said, 'Recruit better or coach better.' And he was right. It's not their job to slow down. It's our job to *slow them down*. That's on us.

"It hurt. Losing always hurts. It *should* hurt! But that's why you wake up the next day, determined to make darn sure it never happens again. I always treat bad losses like bad dreams. Once you break down the tape and make a plan to fix it, you have to get that loss behind you."

After Harbaugh's first USD team finished a respectable 7-4, his 2005 squad soared to 11-1, winning the school's first league title since the program started in 1956. The next year they went 11-1 again and claimed their second league title.

Turns out the man could coach.

Between Harbaugh's third and fourth seasons at San Diego he met Sarah Feuerborn (pronounced Fearborn) in Las Vegas. The youngest of eleven children, Feuerborn grew up in Kansas City, earned her degree in education from the University of Missouri, then moved to Las Vegas, where she found she could make more money in real estate than teaching. Contrary to the rumor mill, when she met Harbaugh in 2006 she had no idea who he was, and was making much more in Las Vegas real estate than he was making in Division II football.

But they felt a connection, got married, and moved to Palo Alto in 2007, where Harbaugh took over 1-11 Stanford. Under Harbaugh the Cardinals won four, five, eight, and finally 12 games, including an Orange Bowl victory.

He repeated the trick with the San Francisco 49ers, taking over a team that had finished 6-10 in 2010. With Harbaugh at the helm the 49ers won an average of 12 games his first three seasons, including three straight trips to the NFC title game and an appearance in the 2012 Super Bowl in New Orleans. Because they happened to face John Harbaugh's Baltimore Ravens, the media renamed it the "Har-Bowl."

"I think we both handled it pretty well," John told me, "but we handled it differently. Jim's whole thing was to minimize the brother angle. 'It's all about football.' I figured I couldn't escape it anyway, so I embraced it. In the interview the Friday before the game, I said, 'There's no reason not to put your arms around it.'

"To be honest, on game day I think Jim was kind of being a jerk about it. During pregame warm-up I went over to talk to Jim, and he walked away. So I went over to talk to his kicker, a guy I knew from our time together in Philly. Jim comes back and says, 'Hey! What are you doing talking to him?'

"Hey, I gotta talk to someone out here, because you won't! Jim, how many cameras do you think are on us right now? You blow me off, it'll be everywhere."

Jim got the message, they chatted, and the cameramen got what they needed.

In a wild contest the Ravens took an early lead, the

power went out in the New Orleans' Superdome, then the 49ers launched a comeback that fell just one play short, with the older brother finally beating his younger brother.

What happened next is a story John loves to tell, and always gets a laugh.

"Now, I'd seen the scenes of all those great coaches who won the Super Bowl," John told me. "Joe Gibbs, Bill Parcells, Jimmy Johnson. They get their Gatorade bath, a ride on their players' shoulders. They look so happy. But after we won, I don't get that moment. No Gatorade bath, no shoulder rides. And I think it's because our players sensed that this is my brother, so it's different. They know I have to walk across the field and shake his hand, so it's not the time for all that.

"We've been battling since Jim was born, so I knew how emotional it was going to be to meet him at midfield. And I knew this was going to suck. This is going to be awful. I felt bad for him. I really did. But you gotta do it. I am his brother, and I know he felt the same way. So we go out there and I come up to shake his hand and give him the man-hug—but he gives me the lock-arm! I can't get any closer. And there's a picture of me wincing. What the heck?"

"There'll be no hug," Jim declared, jaw clenched.

"Whoa, okay!" John recalled thinking. "I was surprised, but not shocked."

John managed to get past Jim's hand to give him a hug anyway, and a quick, "Love you, Bro."

"But from that moment on," John said with a laugh, "I did *not* feel sorry for him! Jim probably wouldn't expect me to, either."

The David Letterman show invited John to appear four days later, on Thursday, February 7, 2013.

"I wasn't going to do it until the owner made me go, and I'm glad he did."

John traveled with his wife, Ingrid, and daughter Allison on the train from Baltimore to New York. When Letterman asked John if he'd talked with Jim since the game, he admitted, "I have not. We have not had a conversation since."

Did the Harbaugh parents show any favoritism growing up?

"I felt like Jim was the favorite pretty much our whole life. *Jim* felt that he was the favorite. But the truth is Joanie, our sister, she was truly the favorite."

"When will you talk to your brother?

"I'm hoping sometime soon."

Letterman asked if he was going to console his brother.

"There's no consolation," John said. "There's no way you console your brother. Anybody with a brother knows that. It doesn't work."

"Do you wake up thinking 'Thank God I beat him?' Or, 'Oh, I won, but too bad'?"

"You do wake up thinking 'Thank God I beat him.' You do, yes. [If I hadn't] it would have been a long life, you know."

On the train ride home John's phone buzzed with a familiar caller: his brother.

"Jim and I hadn't talked since the game," John told me. "I knew he still wasn't happy about the last two plays, and he was convinced there should've been a flag. But I think he saw the Letterman show and he wanted to get it behind us and move on."

When John picked up, Jim asked, "How're you doing? How's the family?"

"And then he gets right to his third thing," John recalled, "the reason he called."

"You know that last play was pass interference, or defensive holding at the least?"

"I know nothing of the sort," John replied. "Your guy Crabtree didn't know the route he was running, *twice*. He went the wrong way. You need to get 'em on the same page. That's on you. And how about [Baltimore quarterback Joe] Flacco gets hit five yards away from the play? And how about this: you smash into my punter and get no flag? If they called that, the game ends right then and there, and we take a knee. It's a Super Bowl, Jim. They're not pulling out their flags for some ticky-tack foul."

"That was pretty much the end of that conversation," John told me. "And we haven't talked about the game since."

Three years later, in April 2016, Jack and Jackie Harbaugh were still living in Milwaukee, watching the national championship basketball game between Villanova and North Carolina, when suddenly Jack felt as though he'd taken a punch right on the breastplate, something he'd never experienced before.

He turned to Jackie. "We need to go to the hospital."

At 4 a.m. a doctor in a white gown and a stethoscope over his shoulder woke Jack to tell him he had had a heart attack. John and Jim flew to Milwaukee the next day for support. A day later, during the quadruple bypass surgery, they found themselves sitting in the waiting area in the wee hours. Looking for something to do they found a chessboard. They hadn't played in years, but quickly got into it. After finishing a couple of games they started feeling guilty, so they relocated to their father's room to keep an eye on him through the night.

"You know, good sons and all," John told me. "We see Dad, and he looks like he's been through a fifteen-round title fight. He's beat up with all kinds of tubes going in and out of him."

In the dark room the brothers used a phone light to illuminate the board. Around three in the morning they started fighting over how many games each had won.

"I'm just coming to," Jack told me, "still hazy, eyes closed, and the first thing I'm cognizant of, I hear these two guys arguing about this or that and how long the longest winning streak was, and I look over and see a bright light over their chessboard and I think, 'Oh my God—I've died and gone to hell!'"

Jack's blanket had fallen off his feet, so he was trying to get their attention, but he was too weak to speak. In the middle of the brothers' argument Jim stopped to say, "I think dad's saying something."

"Yes! Yes I am!" Jack thought. "It's me! The guy with the heart attack!"

A few years later Jack told me, "I always thought hell might be completely dark, or intensely hot. But no: hell is this fight I've been hearing between these two for years and years, with numbing repetition, and it will never end! I'm shackled to this bed, and I'll have to hear these guys going at it for all eternity!

"Hell turned out to be worse than anything I'd imagined."

Whether it was in the backyard on Anderson Avenue, the Super Bowl in New Orleans, or their father's hospital room in Milwaukee, the boys' competition never stopped.

Chapter 32
"Hard to Beat the Cheaters"
Recruiting

Michigan's win over the Spartans, coupled with Ohio State's stunning loss to Purdue, nudged the Wolverines one crucial spot up to number five in both polls. More important, the first official College Football Playoff poll came out that week, starting Michigan at number five, too. Because third-ranked LSU (7-1) had to play undefeated, top-ranked Alabama the coming weekend, the Wolverines could sit back during their bye week and watch one of those two teams lose, knowing they would likely move up to the all-important fourth spot without tying their cleats.

The players were rewarded with a few welcome days off, but recruiting never rests. An old coaching maxim: Jimmys and Joes will beat Xs and Os every time, meaning great recruits will beat great coaches.

An oversimplification, surely—who doesn't love to see top talent get out-coached?—but if you recruit poorly, you'll never compete.

You can make a good case that Alabama head coach Nick Saban's success has depended more on recruiting than coaching. When he coached at Michigan State from 1995 to 1999, his recruiting classes were never in the top 10 of Tom Lemmings's lists, the only service that ranked recruiting classes at the time. In Saban's first four years in East Lansing his teams went a very unimpressive 25-22-1, never finishing higher than fifth in the eleven-team Big Ten, until his fifth season, a breakout year when the Spartans went 9-2. In East Lansing Mark Dantonio has done far better.

But Saban wisely took advantage of his one very good season and rode it to LSU, where recruiting is much easier. Three of his first four full recruiting classes at LSU finished in the top five—a far cry from his classes at MSU. Likewise, his five LSU teams had four good years on the field, from 8-5 to 10-3, and one great season, 2003, when the Tigers went 13-1 and won Saban's first national title.

When Saban accepted the Miami Dolphins' offer he discovered how effectively the NFL's draft system and salary caps prevent teams from leveraging large talent gaps. His 2005 Miami team went 9-7, and his 2006 team finished 6-10, last in the AFC East Division and four games behind the New England Patriots, one of the few franchises able to create lasting success.

Lesson learned, Saban took over Alabama's program the next year. Of his twelve Crimson Tide recruiting classes, *seven in a row ranked number one in the nation*—a staggering level of success that has fueled five national titles in 11 years.

What's the difference? Recruiting.

In fairness, the SEC schools have some inherent advantages over their Big Ten counterparts. Economic power has been leaking from the Rust Belt to the Sun Belt for decades, and with it, population and resources. The weather is better, and the South's sports culture is centered squarely on football, not diluted among basketball, hockey, and soccer, as it is in the North. The South supports 7-on-7 spring football leagues, virtually unheard-of in the North, and more substantial high school football programs that attract and develop better coaches.

Further, the Big Ten supports 28 varsity sports, with the average member funding 24 varsity teams. (Michigan and Ohio State field teams in all 28 Big Ten sports, plus a few outside the Big Ten.) The SEC sponsors only 21 sports, with the average SEC school fielding only 19, which allows SEC athletic directors to focus on football in a way Big Ten athletic directors cannot. Of the Big Ten's 14 schools, four favor basketball over football, while only one SEC school, Kentucky, would claim that. SEC teams also play only 8 league games, and notoriously soft non-conference schedules.

Finally, all but one of the Big Ten's 14 schools are members of the prestigious Association of American Universities, considered the top 62 research universities in North America. (Nebraska lost its membership, which it had been awarded in 1909, in 2011, partly because its teaching hospital is not on campus.) Of the SEC's 14 schools, only two qualified until Texas A&M and Missouri left the Big 12 for the SEC in 2012.

While the Big Ten's resources fund everything from more Olympic sports to research, the SEC makes no bones about focusing on football. The league's emphasis is manifest in its willingness to allow member schools to do things Big Ten schools cannot. This has included a practice called "over-signing," in which a coach will not just offer but sign more recruits to National Letters of Intent than he has scholarships to give, then run a quasi-tryout during August camp to eliminate the lesser players from contention.

In 2008, when reporter Ian Rapoport asked Saban how he planned to handle having more signed recruits than he had scholarships, Saban responded, in part,

"It's none of your business. Aiight? And don't give me this stuff about the fans' need to know, because they don't need to know. Don't even ask. Aiight?"

When Mississippi's Houston Nutt signed 37 prospects in 2009, when the NCAA allowed only 25 scholarships, even the SEC couldn't abide by it, passing a league rule limiting the number of signed recruits to 25. But that hasn't stopped Saban, who signed almost twice as many recruits in 2013 as he had scholarships, then winnowed the candidates through shortcomings in the classroom or the community, encouraging lesser recruits to delay their enrollment (a practice called "grayshirting"), or listing injured players as "medical redshirts," which don't count against the total. Many backups, seeing the writing on the wall, voluntarily opt to transfer for a better chance of starting, which helps solve Saban's problem. So long as Saban can get the number of scholarship players on the roster down to 85 before the season opener, he has not violated the NCAA or SEC rules.

Add it all up, and you get Nick Saban: mediocre at Michigan State, five-time national champion at Alabama.

Boiled down, the recruiting process is simple: Figure out which players you want, then try to get them. But both steps require a few dozen sub-tasks each. If you want to do it Michigan's way, the first step is the most important—and the most complicated.

During the 1985 season, Harbaugh's red-shirt junior year at Michigan, he completed his journey from the outskirts of college football, where he almost went unnoticed, to center stage by leading the Wolverines to a number two final ranking.

That same fall, five hours away in Indianapolis, a high school senior quarterback named Jeff George was basking in all the recruiting attention Harbaugh never received. George won the first Gatorade National Player of the Year award, and the Dial Award as the national high school athlete of the year, in any sport.

Dozens of coaches beat a trail to George's door, including Schembechler (who didn't name George in our book, but I will now). Thanks to the work of Harbaugh & Co. that season, Schembechler told me, "We thought we might have a shot at [George]. But when we got there, this kid was slumped in his chair, he didn't bother to get up to shake our hands, and he started barking at his mom to get him a pop or something—and she ran to the kitchen to get it for him! Boy, that wasn't the way *my* mom did it! It didn't take long for me to realize this boy might have been blessed with a golden arm, but he was also cursed with a nickel head."

After just thirty minutes Schembechler had seen enough, nodded to his assistant coach, thanked the family for their time, "then got the hell out of there."

Jeff George went to nearby Purdue for his freshman year, but when the coach who had recruited him, Leon Burtnett, resigned, George transferred to Illinois. He put up great numbers but tended to alienate his coaches and teammates wherever he went. After the Indianapolis Colts picked him first overall in the 1990 draft and gave him a record contract, his four Colts teams compiled a 21-43 record before Harbaugh arrived the next year. For the rest of his 13-year career, George would get traded, tick off his new coaches and teammates, then get traded again. He often put up good numbers, but never came close to a Super Bowl.

Schembechler liked to point out George never won a Big Ten title, either, unlike "every quarterback we've ever had here at Michigan. That long list includes Jimmy Harbaugh. Jim ended up being twice as good, in my book, as the Golden Arm—Harbaugh was the Big Ten MVP his senior year—and Jim's teammates *liked* him. Maybe Harbaugh didn't have half the arm of the Golden Boy, but he had twice the brains and ten times the heart. Give me those specs, any day."

Harbaugh would remember that lesson.

"If you want to make Michigan great, and make

yourself great, this is a great place to be," Harbaugh told me. "The ones you have to oversell what we have to offer, you know it's not going to work. If you don't get the appeal of this program, of a Michigan education, of the kind of camaraderie you get working with like-minded people—well, I don't know what to tell you. You'll probably be happier somewhere else—and maybe we will be too!"

Harbaugh also dislikes the specialization trend, preferring multisport athletes.

"We ask them, 'Why aren't you playing basketball or track or baseball?'" Harbaugh said. "'Oh, our basketball team is horrible.' Great, then you can start! Or, 'They're too good.' Great, then you can learn! Their attitude is, if they're not going pro at something, why do it? That's criminal."

Harbaugh cited some statistics off the top of his head: Of the first 32 players drafted by the NFL in 2018, 27 played at least two sports, and 23 played three.

"I think the lesson is pretty obvious: athletes want to play. Competitors want to compete. Those are the guys we want."

Jim's dad Jack added, "When I hear someone say, 'I'm concentrating on football,' an alarm goes off. That might not be the guy you want."

"Playing football for Michigan is a tremendous gift

you can give to yourself and your family," Jim told me. "Just picture the parents of all these players, boring the shit out of the neighbors, telling them, 'Our son's going to Michigan, he's playing for the football team, he's working harder than he ever has, and he might even get into the game.' Bet they say that a lot. Look at the parents of Navy SEALS, or West Pointers. Your kid's a Cadet at Army? That's a tremendous gift you can give your parents."

The man in charge of Michigan's recruiting operations is a roly-poly guy who stands 5-foot-5 and seven-eighths, by his own measure, a ball of energy with a thick, well-groomed beard. Put a black triangular hat on him and he could play a pirate's loyal, wisecracking sidekick.

Matt Dudek grew up in McKeesport, Pennsylvania, right outside of Pittsburgh, the son of an HVAC mechanic at McKeesport Hospital. Tom would work the night shift from 11 p.m. to 7 a.m., hang out at the union hall until 10 a.m., then sleep until 2 p.m., go assist the McKeesport High School football team, help with Matt's Little League practice that evening, then get a couple more hours sleep from 8 to 10 p.m. before doing it all again. Yet he still found time to put in AC units for his friends or fix an ice machine at his favorite bar.

"I saw this every day," Matt said. "And like him, I have a hard time saying no."

In sixth grade Matt volunteered to serve as the water boy for McKeesport, which made a historic run to the state title in 1994.

"This is Pittsburgh, a football hotbed," he told me. "It was like the Super Bowl. Getting off the bus after winning the title, the whole town had come out. You couldn't get off the bus! You could see what football did for these guys, and our town. I'll never, ever forget that moment."

In high school Dudek played baseball and center, guard, and defensive end on the football team.

"I loved baseball—*loved* it—but there's something special about football. So much more goes into it, at every level."

He summed up the sport's odd appeal in two lines: "In football you work so hard, for so few opportunities. It's the sport that best represents life."

That brief description effectively encapsulates the entire experience of just about every coach and player in this book. When I passed on Dudek's summation, they invariably said, "That's it!"

"Only football requires you to put in so much effort for that one pat on the back, or that one chance to prove yourself," Dudek continued. "Even in high school you play 30 baseball games, you can play basketball or golf any time. But football, you work all week for one game, and you might only get in a handful of plays—if you're lucky. Football teaches you how to prepare, how to battle, and how to keep going when you don't get what you want. Well, that's *life*, isn't it?"

After getting a bachelor's degree from Pitt, Dudek took a job in Phoenix with Maxim Crane Works, the world's largest crane company, as the assistant to the CEO. He traveled the world, made six figures, and woke up in a different city every day.

But before long he realized he wanted more from life. He returned to Pitt to become a teacher, and coached a baseball team of ten-year-olds, the Port Vue Bulldogs, to the league title. A chance encounter with Pitt football coach Dave Wannstedt and video director Chad Bogard resulted in an offer to film practices.

"But," Dudek protested, "I know nothing about filming."

"Keep the tackles in the picture, then zoom out and follow the ball."

"Done!"

Soon Dudek was getting coffee, making copies, picking up recruits at the airport, and giving them campus tours. Before Dudek started his teaching career Wannstedt hired him to be their recruiting coordinator—at $38,500 a year.

"With all the time I was putting in," Dudek recalled, "my wife, Lindsay, figured out I was making about 66 cents an hour. I wish I hadn't known that!"

The coaches could see Dudek had a knack for recruiting. One noted that, thanks to Dudek's unique background, which put him in contact with his dad's blue-collar colleagues, a diverse high school football team, and college-educated businessmen, "you can talk about sweat socks, the Pirates, and the stock market."

"And I love every second of it," Dudek told me.

After Wannstedt resigned in 2010, Greg Schiano hired Dudek for a similar role at Rutgers. Now 30, Dudek bought an air mattress and slept on his office floor every night for four months, while his wife, pregnant with twins, lived with their two-year-old back in Pittsburgh. She stayed there after Dudek took a job at Arizona with Rich Rodriguez in 2012. In the summer of 2017, while Dudek was sitting in a barber's chair in Tucson, Jim Harbaugh called his cell phone.

In the middle of the haircut, Dudek's apron still on,

he walked outside to hear Harbaugh's offer, and give him "a very quick and resounding yes. Nothing against Arizona, but this was Michigan. I didn't have to do a lot of thinking."

He did have to do a lot of work. Just six days into Dudek's new job Harbaugh put him in charge of the big barbeque at the Big House, one of the program's biggest recruiting events. Dudek was off and running.

Recruiting, Dudek explained, is a two-year cycle. Programs aren't allowed to contact prospects until September 1 of their junior year. Before that the prospects can contact the programs, and program employees can answer, but they can't prompt the prospects to call. The prospects can come to campus, but the school representatives can't go to their high schools and talk to them. Yes, it's that crazy.

Once the two-year clock starts Michigan's coaches, Dudek, and his staff follow a five-step process. First, they cast a wide net. Based on players they've seen, often while recruiting their older teammates, articles they've read, calls, emails, and texts they've received, and scouting services they subscribe to, Dudek collects some 4,900 names, and one or more coaches in the building will spend at least two minutes looking at every single one of them—a minimum of 160 hours of work.

Second, they boil that list down to the top 300 prospects, and create a ten-minute highlight tape of each player's best *and* worst plays, culled from at least six games. That process takes at least an hour per player, representing another 300 hours of work.

If they still like what they see, Dudek starts the third step: arranging for someone, usually a coach, to reach out to the player and his high school coach. If that goes well, they move on to the all-important fourth step: seeing the player's transcript.

"That eliminates a lot of the top 300," Dudek said. "From that step alone, there are probably 150 guys who just go away."

But they don't disappear. They go elsewhere, usually to top ten programs that have no qualms about taking players with poor grades, serious off-field infractions, or their hands out for illegal payments. (We can debate the merits of paying players but not the current rules, which clearly forbid it.)

Michigan's selectivity makes recruiting both harder and easier: Harder because it dramatically limits the number of players they can consider, and easier for the same reason: by bypassing those who lack strong grades, solid citizenship, or basic integrity, they reduce the number of players they need to spend time and effort recruiting.

"We're doing a better job figuring out who will fit here athletically, academically, and culturally," Dudek said. "All three have to work. A lot of guys simply can't make it here. Name another school that competes with the blue-bloods athletically—we're talking Ohio State, Alabama, Clemson—while competing with the blue-bloods academically: Stanford, Northwestern, Princeton. Most players we recruit are good enough to play for Alabama or Clemson, and smart enough to play for Ivy League schools. If you don't win in the classroom on Monday, you won't be here for many Saturdays."

Dudek usually finds gauging chemistry and character pretty straightforward, too.

"Honestly, I can tell in the first ten minutes if we're going to hit it off. If we do, he's one of my guys. But if he's a quieter guy, I let someone else take over. When it comes down to it, you really don't know what's going to tip the scales for them: a campus visit for a big game, following up to see how a big math test went, or talking to them about their parents. Everyone's different.

"But if your first conversation with a recruit is a series of one-word answers—'How were your classes today?' 'Okay'—you're probably not going to fit in here. Guys we like are enthusiastic, want to engage in conversation, and have something to say. We just signed Nolan Rumler. As soon as he sent his letter of intent in, he told us he went back to his workout and set some personal records. That's one of our guys."

In contrast, Dudek and company get leery when they see the recruits' parents' names in the press as often as the son's.

"You pay attention to that. What do the parents want? And when you see a player keeping three or four schools hanging, calling a press conference, and playing a game with baseball hats on a table—well, that guy is not our guy, either. You compare that to Ben Bredeson, who made his decision before his senior year—no hats, no drama. Karan Higdon, same thing. Those guys are what our recruits look like, and act like."

Once the recruiting process has gone through those first four steps, the fifth step, Dudek says, "is when recruiting really begins: the visits to campus, showing them what's best about the university, talking with the academic folks, the strength coaches, the trainers and the nutritionists, and answering all their questions.

"The next time you see them you know more about them and you target what they want to see—could be the business school or the strength staff or watching another practice. The whole time you're doing all that you're building a relationship, you're learning about them and their parents, and you keep the conversation going."

After all that Michigan offers scholarships to about 150 recruits to get the 25 "acceptances" they're allowed to sign in a given year. Michigan's six-to-one ratio is lower than most of Michigan's peers (although Harbaugh would like to end that by allowing recruits to sign whenever they like). The ratios vary by position, too. Michigan typically offers scholarships to 25 to 30 linemen to get five to sign, and six to eight quarterbacks for each one that comes to campus. (Michigan does not oversign.)

All in five easy steps.

In addition to filtering for academics, chemistry, and character, Michigan drops anyone who hints about getting paid. The rampant cheating among some of college football's highest-ranked programs is the worst-kept secret in college sports.

Years ago Schembechler taped a conversation with a high school coach asking for $5,000 for his player. Schembechler sent the tape to the NCAA, which promptly did nothing, which was exactly what Joe Paterno told Schembechler would happen.

There is little evidence that the NCAA does any more these days. For an earlier book I spent almost every Wednesday night of the 2012 season talking with Louisiana native turned Penn State star Mike Mauti, who had turned down money from several southern schools before accepting Penn State's offer of a scholarship, an education, and an opportunity—nothing more.

"I know for a fact there are players getting paid [at other schools]," Mauti said. "Guys I know are getting tens of thousands of dollars a year. They give you credit cards until they run out. There's a lot of money involved. One hundred thousand dollars? Over the course of five years? Easily. I was offered money. They don't come out and say they're going to give you this money, but their players know the way things work, and they tell you. It's a different culture out there."

Mauti and I shared the stories we'd heard about coaches channeling money through churches, a practice that few southern politicians or reporters would dare investigate; offering jobs to the parents in the city or county, not the school; giving recruits credit cards in someone else's name, or cases of casino chips to cash in; and two relatively new tricks, having a booster buy the family's home for far more than market value, and telling players to take their beat-up junkers into a Mercedes dealership, where they receive a high-end "loaner car" while they wait for a replacement part—which could take years, it turns out.

In this business you don't have to investigate the cheaters to find these stories. They wash up on your shore, unbidden. All the coaches, players, recruiting coordinators, and reporters know this stuff, without even trying. When Michigan's Lamar Woodley entered the Pittsburgh Steelers' locker room, still carrying his Nike bags and battered Velcro wallet from college, his new teammates laughed and asked why Michigan players didn't get Gucci bags, like they did?

After Mauti and I discussed these various schemes, he looked right at me and said, "Okay, I know what's going on. You know what's going on. How come the NCAA doesn't know what's going on?"

I didn't have a good answer, except the obvious: eleven NCAA executives make more than $450,000 a year, led by President Mark Emmert, who makes well over $2 million—all for running a non-profit driven by amateur athletes. They've got a good thing going. Why rock the boat? Worst-case scenario: they find a program that won a national title is guilty. Now what? Pulling down banners messes up the marketing plan.

"They have to *want* to go after the cheaters," Mauti said. "It's not the public's job to determine that—it's *theirs.* Otherwise, what's the NCAA for? What do they do?"

The media hasn't done much better. In fairness, reporters are hamstrung by journalistic ethics from publishing anything without sufficient proof, and that usually means eyewitnesses, on the record. As crime novelist Scott Turow once wrote about the law, "Hedged in by the formalities of the rules of evidence, our truth-finding system cuts off the corners on half of what is commonly known." So it is with journalism. There's a sizable gap between knowing something and proving it.

Nonetheless, while the NCAA and the announcers who shill for the top coaches on national television see no evil, the national reporters and columnists tend to take the flip side of that cop-out by claiming that the entire enterprise and everyone in it is corrupt, and "amateur athletics" and "student-athlete" are just cynical oxymorons.

But that is equally lazy and almost as dishonest. It not only ignores the coaches and players who are doing it honestly, at considerable sacrifice, but it also conveniently allows the reporters to avoid the uncomfortable business of actually investigating who's cheating and who isn't. They know if they do an honest job they will alienate the very coaches and players they need to interview for their articles, books, and radio and TV shows.

So they play along, invariably praising this team's or that team's new coach as "a great hire," and all backs get scratched. The show goes on.

As Harbaugh said to me, "Hard to beat the cheaters."

Where does that leave the coaches and players who aren't cheating? On the outside looking in, trying to do it the hard way, and getting no credit for it from the NCAA or the media. In this bizarre world where the guilty are praised and the innocent are punished, perhaps the biggest surprise is that some coaches still try to play by the rules anyway, and some players turn down illicit money to play for them. But how doubly delicious it is when an honest program actually beats the cheaters.

When I mentioned all this to Dudek, he shrugged. I was not telling him anything he didn't already know.

"You hear rumors," was all he said.

But he hears far more than that since Michigan and the programs that pay players occasionally battle for the same recruits, such as Rashan Gary. In this cynical age it's stunning that Michigan can win some of those recruiting wars, but generally only when the parents want something more lasting for their son than a handout.

When Michigan was recruiting against a school that

paid players a few years ago, Michigan's point man on the recruit, an assistant coach, returned from his trip dejected. He pulled down the recruit's magnet from the board and tossed it into the trash can.

"What happened?" a colleague asked.

"New car in his driveway," the assistant said. "We're not gonna get him."

It's also possible to "cheat legally." In 2015 the NCAA started allowing schools to pay student-athletes' "full cost of attendance," which includes travel, food, laundry, and other expenses not covered by scholarships, which pay for tuition, room, and board—a long-overdue reform, praised by all sides of the equation.

Before the rule passed, admissions departments had already been calculating the "full cost of attendance" to establish federal guidelines for all students. Michigan's admissions office reported that, for out-of-state students, the "full cost of attendance" averaged an additional $2,400 per term. After the NCAA rule passed, "because our school has integrity," Steve Connelly added, the figure remained the same.

Meanwhile, in the Southeast Conference, once the NCAA passed this provision Alabama determined that their "full cost of attendance" for out-of-state students suddenly came to $5,386—or 34 percent more than they'd claimed the year before.

"You can't tell me," Connelly said, "that all of a sudden it became 34 percent more expensive to drive to Tuscaloosa."

But Alabama's figure wasn't even the highest. Auburn claimed a bigger jump to $5,586, while Tennessee calculated an additional $5,666 per term, the highest in the nation. Why it costs 136 percent more to travel to Knoxville than Ann Arbor is a mystery, especially when Michigan has far more students traveling from both coasts.

"You can't tell me it's a coincidence that all three schools experienced a sudden spike in the actual cost of attendance," Connelly added. "You're giving these programs another advantage over our recruiters. Basically, those schools can give their players $3,000 more per semester than we do. Is it legal cheating? You tell me."

"Look," Dudek said, "we know there are people who don't operate on the same moral plane that not only Michigan expects, but Coach Harbaugh demands. So the last thing I'm doing is going down that rabbit hole—probably be the fastest way to get fired around here.

"The good news is we so rarely go so far down a path with a guy whose character we're not sure about that we get to a point where the kid or his family asks for a bag of money. I've never had anyone directly ask me for anything. If they're going to do that, they probably don't consider us very long."

In 2018, the recruiting cycle would peak the coming weekend at the Penn State game, when the corridors of Schembechler Hall would be teeming with 81 recruits in for visits, most of them A-list prospects Michigan would love to sign.

Once Harbaugh, Dudek, and their staffs determined who among the 81 players was mostly likely to fit in as Michigan Men, all they had to do was beat the cheaters.

Chapter 33
Turning the Tables

Penn State, November 3, 2018

When the NCAA's leaders introduced the 12th regular season game in 2007 they also added a mandatory bye week, which has created an ongoing debate over its costs, benefits, and how to handle it. But if you ask the players, there's no debate.

"You really do need to take a breather, for your body and your mind," Joe Hewlett told me. "We start at 6:00 in the morning, we lift, we get treatment, we go to class, we come back for more treatment or meetings, we practice for four hours, then more treatment, dinner, then study time. I don't care who you are: that's a grind."

I didn't hear one player say the bye week wasn't essential for study, rest, and recovery. But they agreed there was a fine line between getting rested and getting rusty. During 2017's bye week, for example, Harbaugh gave them just Monday and Wednesday off, with practice on Tuesday and Thursday through the following Friday—nine straight days. The Wolverines promptly got upset at home by Michigan State, 14-10, a loss that left Rashan Gary screaming and sobbing on the bench. The next week the Wolverines had to resort to overtime to shake unranked Indiana, then got trounced by second-ranked Penn State, 42–13—by far the worst loss of the Harbaugh era.

Harbaugh wisely decided to rethink their approach to the bye week in 2018, especially given the high intensity of the games surrounding it, by giving the players three straight days off, followed by three normal practice days, then Saturday and Sunday off, too. The idea was to return to work for Penn State rested and ready to go, but they wouldn't know if the new theory worked until that Saturday.

The bye week did offer a little time for reflection, something college football players can rarely indulge unless they suffer a career-ending injury like Newsome's, and have it forced upon them. Fifth-year senior Joe Hewlett used some of his time off to talk with his dad. A few days after the Michigan State game, in which Joe Hewlett had recovered a fumble, a fan sent Rich Hewlett an email reminding him that, after Rich had moved to defensive back, he had also recovered a fumble as a fifth-year senior on the road against Michigan State—almost certainly Michigan's only father-son combination to complete that trick.

"I think my dad was as excited as I was," Joe said.

Hewlett was taking stock. Michigan had four regular season games left and, at 7-1, had already qualified for a bowl game. Five games, provided he stayed healthy, and possibly one to three more. Because both Michigan State and Penn State had lost two league games, and Purdue had upset Ohio State, Michigan now had sole possession of first place in the East Division and the cleanest road to the Big Ten title game, and maybe the college football playoffs. If the Buckeyes somehow lost another game before Michigan visited Columbus in four weeks, they would be all but out of the race.

But no matter how the rest of the season worked out, all the seniors knew they only had two home games left, and most would be done playing football forever in January.

Rich Hewlett told his son, "You're going to feel sad when it ends, but also relieved."

"It's a lot," Joe said. "But not playing again, that's a

scary thought. I've done this my whole life. It will be very strange to be without it."

For most college graduates the real world is a rude awakening, filled with early morning alarms and regimented schedules five days a week. For college football players the "real world" demands considerably less time, effort, and discipline—and the older players know it.

"Thoughts of the end are slowly creeping in," Joe Hewlett said, "but I try to block them out, because they're outweighed by the opportunities we have ahead of us. We can accomplish a lot."

He hesitated to mention the most desired prize: not a Big Ten or even a national title, but a long-sought victory over Ohio State. But they were still too far away to say it out loud, especially with Penn State coming to town in a few days.

Ben Bredeson felt it, too—the tantalizing opportunities on the horizon, and the challenge right in front of them. "Penn State was the only team that truly beat us last year," he said. "As a team we struggled in that game, every aspect. So the Penn State game's gonna be a good one."

Despite losses by Michigan's opponents, the Wolverines' schedule still included five ranked teams, likely another one in a bowl game, and more if Michigan made it to the playoffs. (Northwestern would be ranked at season's end.) That meant at least half Michigan's opponents would be ranked, including three in a row during "The Revenge Tour." Before the season most prognosticators thought it would be a success if Michigan could win two of those three, but after whipping Wisconsin, 38–13, and beating rival Michigan State, 21–7, the Wolverines got greedy, and wanted all three.

Penn State entered the season ranked in the top ten, but slipped to 18th after painfully close losses to both Ohio State and Michigan State. Narrow victories over Indiana and Iowa nudged them back up to 14th, but the Wolverines didn't care.

"This game represents a great opportunity," Higdon said. "A *great* opportunity. This is my type of scene."

"Biggest game of the year," Higdon told me, then added, "so far. Especially with all the pressure on Coach Harbaugh and Michigan, and especially after last year. Penn State is a dominant team. And we haven't forgotten how proud their coach was of running that last play. We want to return the favor."

Higdon was referring to a certain play running endlessly in team meetings that week. In the final seconds of the Lions' 2017 beat-down they rubbed the Wolverines' noses in it by trying to score again with just two seconds left. The attempt failed, but the Wolverines remembered that, too.

"Man, Coach Brown played that back the whole week," Devin Bush Jr. said. "I can see that play in my head. I don't intend to see it again."

Neither did Brown, who said he hadn't slept well since that game, and woke up every morning thinking about it. It had been more than a year ago.

On an unseasonably warm, sunny afternoon, the Nittany Lions opened the 3:45 game with a 25-yard pass play—but that would be their longest play of the game. The Wolverine defenders responded immediately, sacking Penn State's quarterback twice, forcing them to punt. They kept it up all day, stopping Penn State behind the line of scrimmage six times, holding them to 111 yards total offense until their last-minute 75-yard scoring drive, and making them punt eight times.

The defense attacked, swarmed, and all but taunted the Lions to throw the ball. And when they did, Michigan swatted the ball away, or intercepted it—twice. The Wolverines didn't merely dominate the Lions, they embarrassed them—and they had fun doing it. No one on this defense was going to win the Heisman Trophy like Charles Woodson, the only defensive player to do so, and they might not win a national position award, either. But Michigan's 2018 defense had strong players at every position, playing in synchronicity with each other.

For the first time in many games the Wolverines were having a ball out there—at their opponents' expense—and it seemed contagious. When they sacked the quarterback or scored a touchdown, they imitated the celebrations their opponents had used on them the previous year. Even the stadium DJ was getting into the act, playing Wisconsin's trademark "Jump Around" against the Badgers, and Penn State's "Sweet Caroline" against the Nittany Lions.

"Whoever's doing the jumbotron is doing a great job of trolling everyone we play," Furbush said. "A lot of the guys went nuts when they played 'Sweet Caroline' when we were beating Penn State."

From 70 rows up you could tell these guys were dying to get back on the field and do it again, shutting down Penn State en route to a 42–7 thrashing. With Brandon Watson's pick-six near the end of the third quarter, Michigan's defense had tied Penn State's offense, 7–7.

"Another great win," Devin Bush Jr. said, "and pay back for last year. I didn't see anyone setting up for a two-point conversion at the end of this game."

By game nine, Michigan's defense had given the offense time to catch up, and it was working. In 2017 the Wolverines averaged only 11 points against Wisconsin, Michigan State, and Penn State—33 total. In 2018, they scored 101, more than three times more.

Higdon ran 20 times for 132 yards and a touchdown, marking his seventh straight game cracking 100 yards. His big game also gave him 963 yards for the season, just 37 from breaking the 1,000-yard mark. True, he finished a mere six yards short the previous year, but he was keeping his fear and paranoia at bay. He was confident.

Recounting the tipping point of his decision to come back for his senior year, Higdon refrained his high school coach's comment: "'You did it once, you can do it again.' But I'm doing it better this year."

The Wisconsin and Penn State games were both blowouts that ended long after dark, but unlike during the September games, the fans didn't leave early to beat the traffic, instead sticking around to cheer their favorite team, savoring the success just like the players. That month you could hear hundreds of fans and lettermen say the same thing: Michigan football was fun again.

"The crowd didn't leave," Furbush told me. "That's a good way to quantify it, what's happening around here. There's a particular kind of energy that we're vibin' on right now. Just seems like we're getting better every week, and everyone's into it."

Turned out revenge was a dish best served by the nation's top defense.

Some players went out to the bars, which were packed after a big win but still made room for their favorite gladiators. Shea Patterson, his family, and some friends filled a few tables in the back of the Brown Jug, a campus classic since 1936. When he took the chance to transfer to Michigan, not knowing if he'd be eligible, this was exactly what he'd been hoping for.

Zach Gentry had his aunt, uncle, and cousin in town for the game. They went out for a bite after the game, "but even just trying to get food after the game was a shit-show. I was tired and sore and wanted to go to bed. I went home and got some sleep—and that felt good."

Higdon went to his parents' home to see his daughter and a room full of relatives.

"Family comes over after the games, everyone's talking about certain plays from that day's game—always a great feeling," he told me.

When I asked him if he felt he was missing out on the carefree nightlife his teammates often enjoyed, he said, "Not at all. Some guys like to go out and drink and all that—but I've spent so much time with everyone, it's great to have some time to relax, and watch some football with my family. I wouldn't trade it."

On the eve of "the gauntlet," the Wolverines had a 5-1 record and a number 12 national ranking. A few weeks later they could count three straight wins over ranked Big Ten rivals, and woke up Monday morning to find themselves ranked fourth nationwide, the last spot for the College Football Playoffs. If the Wolverines beat Rutgers, Indiana, and Ohio State, they would be the East Division champs, with an invitation to the Big Ten title game. They were miles from where they found themselves after the Notre Dame game.

"Before the season started," Dan Dierdorf told me, "if you'd offered me two wins out of those three [Wisconsin, Michigan State, Penn State], I would have signed a legal document without talking to my lawyer first—in a heartbeat. And after the Notre Dame game, I might have signed for one win.

"When we're ahead of Penn State in the fourth quarter, 28–7, we went to a commercial break, and I turn to Jim [Brandstatter] and say, 'Is this really happening?' We'd just blown Wisconsin completely out of the stadium. Then we went up and pummeled Michigan State—I don't care what the final score said, that was a butt-kicking—then turn around and dismantle a very good Penn State team. That finished as impressive a run of big games as I've seen Michigan play. At that point, you look around and think, we can do it all—and you might be right."

Ohio State reporters told me Ed Warinner's offensive line would kick in around week six—and that's exactly what happened. Even Dierdorf was impressed.

"I don't think it's one of those dominant lines you can just get five yards for the asking," he said. "But if you ever want to see the value of good coaching, just look at the job Ed Warinner has done. He took the same group of guys that were having a hell of a time last year and turned them into a high-functioning unit.

"Are they all the way there? No, not yet. But they're clearly going in the right direction. It's been a joy to watch them progress."

Chapter 34
A Modest Proposal

Five decades ago Jack Harbaugh managed to run a winning high school football program with only two footballs, but such austerity is not a recommended way to succeed in the modern Big Ten.

Michigan equipment manager Gary Hazelitt works with two full-time assistants and 24 student managers, who must survive a rigorous tryout process. Yes, they have tryouts for volunteer equipment managers, and plenty don't make the cut. They need all those people to set up and take down equipment for drills, load and unload the truck for games, and organize and maintain thousands of pieces of equipment, tailored to the players' needs and preferences.

Hazelitt keeps 250 helmets in stock to custom-fit 140 players, using old-fashioned tape measures. Some programs use multiple helmets, "but Coach Harbaugh and I are both a little old school," Hazelitt explained, "and prefer one helmet." That has the added benefit of familiarity: players can quickly identify any problems.

Hazelitt and his staff change each face mask every two to three weeks, the hardware and most chin straps every week, and repaint them all every Friday night. The famed wings are not stickers but maize paint, painstakingly applied. Since Harbaugh returned, Hazelitt said, they have tried to match the current helmet's colors and decals to those from the Bo Era.

Every season they also supply the players and staff with 1,500 shoes, which come in different styles for lifting, training, practicing on grass, practicing on turf, playing games on grass or turf, and traveling. Likewise, they give out 2,000 pairs of gloves in five different styles, based on weather, position, and other factors.

Every season the program buys about 300 footballs, which the staff methodically breaks in with wax, buffing machines, "and good old-fashioned elbow grease," Hazelitt said. It takes a solid two weeks to break in a new football to a quarterback's liking, which is why the equipment staffers are constantly rubbing footballs while conducting practice. They whittle down the 300 new balls to the best 48 game balls, from which the quarterbacks and kickers choose 24 to start the season. Even the footballs compete for their positions; the managers cringe during games every time a ball misses the net and ends up in the hands of fans playing keep-away with the security guards, or worse, throwing it out on Stadium Boulevard. When they age the game balls are demoted to practice balls, then fodder for the Jugs machine, which fires them out to receivers during practice.

To clean all the socks, shorts, pants, shirts, jerseys, and sweatshirts the staff uses four 60-pound washers and four 80-pound driers to process 20 huge loads each day, including 300 bags of workout clothes, 140 jerseys, 140 pants, and some 600 towels.

For home games the equipment staff arrives six hours before kickoff to set up the locker room, the showers, and the sidelines, then tape every jersey tightly to the pads to give the opponents as little to grab as possible. For road games they pack a 53-foot semitruck Thursday morning, which drives all night to the next campus.

The packing list runs more than 50 items, most of which get their own trunk, from uniforms, rain jackets, parkas, sideline capes, and hundreds of towels to equipment for the videographers, trainers, strength staff, and even the cheerleaders' megaphones and flags. They also pack signs to signal plays, and directional signs for the visitors' locker room—which most players will use just once in their careers—to point people to the showers, training room, coaches' room, equipment area, meeting spaces, and the field.

"And of course," Hazelitt added, "we pack the portable GO BLUE sign to hang up over the exit door so the players can slap it on their way out."

They start putting everything back in the trunks during the third quarter so they can leave as soon as the players are showered and dressed. When they return they begin the process all over again, starting with laundry—which is a whole lot harder when they play on grass at Penn State, Michigan State, Purdue, or Northwestern, the last of the Big Ten's grass fields.

"Field turf is the best thing ever invented," Hazelitt said.

When each recruit finishes his tour of the facilities, Hazelitt and company fit the prospect in Michigan gear head to toe, including the player's preferred number. The prospects invariably put those pictures on the internet in about three seconds. If they decide to play for Michigan, they probably won't get their preferred number, but they will get a full set of perfectly fitting shoes, clothes, helmets and gloves, because Hazelitt keeps all the measurements from their recruiting visit on file.

"No other head coach appreciates the work done by the support staff the way coach [Harbaugh] does," Hazelitt said, "and he takes care of all of us."

They, in turn, take care of everyone else.

All the people working in Schembechler Hall and everything they work with—from food to footballs to defibrillators—cost money, and it adds up. The 2018 football team's operating budget came to $11.6 million— and that does not count the athletic department staff across the parking lot in Weidenbach Hall, nor the help the team gets from people on the Hill. It also does not count the $226 million renovation of the stadium, the $36 million to renovate Schembechler Hall again in 2018 (including $1.3 million for training equipment), or any other fixed costs, nor does it include personnel, academic support, medical care, athletic department career center services, and mental health and performance counseling, all of which the players receive without charge.

Divide that $11.6 million by 137 players, and it comes to $84,672 each, this year alone—and that's just your starting point.

The department's single biggest cost is tuition. Contrary to popular belief, the department does not get "free passes" for its scholarship athletes, but pays retail—no discounts—for every athlete. Fifty-seven of Michigan's 85 scholarship players are out-of-state, and most of them go three semesters per year. In 2018–19 the athletic department will spend $26.3 million for athletic scholarships—its biggest operating cost—with $6.4 million going to football scholarships, or $74,294 per scholarship player.

Put those two numbers together, and Michigan spends $159,966 per scholarship player per year—or a few bucks shy of $800,000 for their five years on campus. If you included all the expenses devoted to athletes excluded above, you could probably get to $1 million per five-year out-of-state player pretty quickly.

This brings us to the second-hottest topic in college sports, behind only concussions: pay the players, or not?

It's increasingly difficult to support the farce that is the NCAA, but we can't agree on how to fix it. We've seen proposals ranging from universities sponsoring professional minor league teams to ending big-time college sports altogether.

The most popular idea sits between those two extremes: give up the ruse and pay the players. After all, everyone seems to be making millions off the athletes, except the athletes. The most serious threat to big-time college athletics is not the endless scandals, which mainly affect only those who get caught, but the rampant greed, which affects everybody. As Michael Kinsley famously said, "The scandal isn't what's *illegal.* The scandal is what's *legal."*

With so many millions sloshing around the athletes, including multi-million dollar salaries for their coaches (and worse, insane million-dollar buy-outs for coaches who have failed miserably) it's no surprise the players are reaching their limit. From Northwestern's football players holding a vote to unionize, to Grambling's players refusing to play a game in protest, to the growing specter of players skipping bowl games, the players are starting to assert themselves.

But when pundits propose paying the players, they sound like eager Brits advocating for Brexit with little notion of how such a plan would actually work, and what the unintended byproducts might be. Even a modest $5,000 "salary" will cost more than its proponents imagine, since Title IX might require all scholarship athletes receive the same stipend, be they the All-American quarterback or the second-string coxswain on the women's crew team—and now you're cutting other sports.

Universities already have a difficult time controlling their athletic departments, and the pay-to-play plans won't make it any easier. They might turn the student-athletes into bona fide employees, which will open a Pandora's box of legal issues, and questions from the IRS. The pay-to-play proposals also assume the current record TV ratings, sweetheart corporate deals and sold-out stadiums will continue far into the future. But we've already seen plenty of signs that fans are also nearing their breaking point.

Despite the many good reasons to pay the players, I think there are better reasons not to—and a better way to fix the problem that paying the players is intended to fix.

What football and basketball players need is what baseball and hockey players have enjoyed for almost a century: a viable minor league, so players who don't want to be college students, and prefer to be paid in cash instead of scholarships, can do just that. This would reduce many of the problems that beset both sports, almost overnight.

Some say losing some of the NCAA's most exciting players to the new minor leagues would reduce the appeal of college football and basketball. But we don't watch college sports for perfection, but passion—which explains why college football and basketball are the only sports in the world that often draw more fans than the big leagues they feed.

We don't have to wonder if creating a separate minor

league system will work. We already know: Just check out college hockey. The players who would rather have a paycheck than a scholarship can jump straight to the minor leagues—and do. Because the players who opt for college are not forced to do so by the NHL, the graduation rates tend to be much higher in college hockey, and the scandals much fewer. College hockey fans love them all the more because they know the guys they're cheering for have *chosen* to be college hockey players. They're the real deal.

While the NBA has begun developing a bona fide minor league, the NFL continues to resist. But you could force the NFL in one step: bring back freshmen ineligibility. If you want to make it honest, that's how you do it. In fact, freshmen ineligibility was the rule from 1905, the year the NCAA was founded, until 1972, and for a simple reason: colleges believed their athletes should be students first, and that is how they proved it. Creating two paths to the pros will throw a bucket of cold water on the overheated facilities arms race, the soaring coaches' salaries, and the insane TV contracts, and restore a sense of proportion.

No, this solution will not create a perfect world. There will still be athletes who aren't bona fide college students. There will still be coaches and boosters happy to break the rules. And there will still be an outsized mania for the sport. The goal is not perfection, but sanity—to protect the integrity of the universities the players are representing, to preserve the passion the players and fans still feel for their favorite teams, and most important, to give young athletes real options to leverage their skills.

Most Michigan starters turned down money from other programs to attend the University of Michigan, usually because they thought it was their best chance to get a good education, with more security and a safer future than others offered. Given the many benefits they receive from the university, it seems likely most such players would continue to go to schools like Michigan, even if they had a minor league option.

The others could take the money and run—legally, this time.

Chapter 35
Business Trip

At Rutgers, November 10, 2018

After Alabama thrashed LSU, 29–0, the Tigers dropped to seventh in the second College Football Playoffs poll, leaving Michigan sitting pretty in fourth. Yes, Georgia and Oklahoma lurked right behind with identical 8-1 records, so Michigan could ill-afford to lose style points against a weak Rutgers team, but this was exactly the problem the Wolverines hoped to have with three weeks left in the regular season.

The Monday after the Penn State game Michigan's defensive players started sifting into the defense's meeting room after class. They wore hoodies, sweatpants, and satisfied grins. Furbush naturally got there first. Rashan Gary wore his glasses, as did Winovich, who had his famous long blond hair pulled back and tucked in—more Clark Kent than Superman. They sat in the cantilevered mini auditorium, which holds about 100 people, including assistant coaches, graduate assistants, and analysts. The seats are bigger than average, with thick folding desks, but do not recline.

At the front of the classroom Don Brown had created a grid with every opponent on the schedule, followed by 17 standards the defense tried to achieve each week: "No more than 17 points allowed," "No passes over 25 yards," and "No defensive penalties." Meet the standard, they get a big, maize block "M." Fall short, and they get a bright red "X." Against Notre Dame they posted 14 red Xs. Against Penn State, they earned 14 maize Ms.

"Lotta Happy Jacks in this room!" Brown bellowed, uncorking his boundless energy to get the meeting started.

Josh Mettellus raised his hand. "Coach, I got a question: you sleeping okay?"

Everyone laughed, knowing Mettellus was citing Brown's well-known line about not being able to sleep after last year's defensive debacle at Penn State.

He grinned. "Better, Josh—better!" Everyone laughed again.

After Notre Dame saddled the same defense with all those red Xs, the Monday meeting was a chore to be completed, an overdue trip to the dentist. Not on this day.

"42 to fucking 7," Brown said. "Let's make that clear! *42 to fucking 7!*"

Ticking through the 17 standards was a pleasure, with Brown stopping to savor a few of his favorite statistics. "Last three weeks, against three ranked teams, on third down conversions: 3 for 12; 0 for 13; 3 for 12. Hey! That shit's hard to do—and you did it! You did it!"

He stopped on another: "Third quarter shutout? Three of the last four weeks!"

After finishing all the boxes on the board he went through a few conference and national statistics, including these two: "In 26 of 35 categories, you are number one in the Big Ten. You are now the top-ranked defense in the nation—and we're not done! Last year our defense was ranked third in total defense in the country—and we just replaced ten of eleven starters, and we do it again?! *Come on!*"

"Now, time for my Happy Jack moment," he said, turning to the film, already set to the game's second and third plays. "72 City Overset. Second and ten on the fifty."

Brown clicked his handheld remote, which he worked back and forth like a skilled video gamer, so everyone could watch Winovich hunt down Penn State's star quarterback, Trace McSorley, and bring him to the ground with violence.

"Very nice," Brown said softly, as if describing a delicate cabernet sauvignon.

"Third down and sixteen," Brown announced, followed by silence, since video has no announcers, crowd noise, or bands. No sound, all business. On this play, Josh Uche got past his man, and enjoyed his turn taking McSorley down.

"Really well done, Josh," Brown said. "Love it."

Later in the film Brown remarked, "Now look at this: *two* guys in on the sack. Good shit! On third-and-eight, you end it with a sack, you take their heart away. Tear it out and show it to 'em! Good shit!"

Brown buzzed through the plays—all of them—always naming their defensive play, without notes: Matrix Cross, Stud Check Monster, and Viper Gun Over Double Below Hoss. When they finished reviewing every defensive play in a mere 10 minutes—thanks to Bromley and crew and Brown's time spent rehearsing—he concluded, "Now that's some pretty good film. PAYBACK'S A BITCH!"

They cheered again.

"Now, you're the best practice team in the country," he said, bringing his voice down. "Best I've ever seen—no bullshit. And that's a damn good thing, because the stakes have just gotten higher. You can start to think about all the things we want. They're getting closer. But *stub our toes*!?! And it's alllll gone, brother—all gone! So if you go out to practice today and think ol' D-Brown's a Happy Jack—brother, you got another thing coming!"

They laughed, but they got the message. The Penn State game was great, but it was gone—along with the gauntlet, and all the games prior. No more pats on the back this week. From that moment they would be focusing on Rutgers, with the coaches doing their best to build the Scarlet Knights up into a worthy foe.

"Let's sharpen it up for the stretch run! Defense on three! 1-2-3!"

"DEFENSE!"

Rutgers won the nation's first football game on November 6, 1869, beating Princeton 6–4. But since joining the Big Ten in 2014, the Scarlet Knights have been the worst team in the league, about to close their fifth season in the Big Ten with a total of 11 wins against 48 losses, making them a "bye week with benefits."

Harbaugh pulled Karan Higdon aside at practice to

let him know he would be getting limited playing time that week. There was no need to risk injuring their star tailback against Rutgers; Chris Evans and Tru Wilson needed more experience; and they also wanted to let Patterson pass more. Which is to say, they were looking ahead to a certain game in Columbus. That meant Higdon's streak of seven games with 100 yards or more would almost certainly end.

"I'm a team player," Higdon told me. "We're on a winning streak right now. We have bigger goals than my streak. So I was good with that, and if we get the W that's all that matters."

Nonetheless, according to Michael Persak's piece in the *Michigan Daily*, before the game Higdon let his friend Zach Gentry know he was a mere 37 yards from hitting his pre-season goal of 1,000 yards.

"We've got you," Gentry replied. "I'll be blocking for you."

True, anything could happen in college football— witness the infamous Appalachian State game. But that team was actually quite good, and probably would have beaten a few Big Ten teams that year. Rutgers simply stunk, having lost to every team on its schedule except Texas State.

No, the question was: could the Wolverines play the

worst team in the Big Ten and still stay sharp with the ultimate trap game coming up against Indiana, and the big finale against the Buckeyes? The jury was out when the Knights ran 21 yards for a first down, then stopped the Wolverines on fourth-and-one on Rutgers' 18. But after the Michigan defense notched another three-and-out, and Higdon capped an eight-play drive with a touchdown, the question seemed settled.

But on Rutgers' next play from scrimmage, Isaih Pacheco cut and dashed for an 80-yard touchdown, untouched, to tie the score at 7–7 with 0:26 left in the first quarter.

"That was just one of those things," Devin Bush Jr. told me. "Hey, they have scholarship athletes who get coached, too. Happened once. Won't happen again."

After that play, Rutgers's biggest run was 15 yards, while Michigan's offense settled down and rattled off 35 unanswered points to put the Knights away, 42–7.

Almost lost in the onslaught was Karan Higdon's drive for 1,000-yards. With Patterson completing 13 of 19 attempts in the first half alone, and seven other tailbacks—including Joe Hewlett, who ran the ball once for five yards, a career high after running twice in 2016 for minus-one—getting the ball 25 times, Higdon notched only 15 runs, just as Harbaugh had warned him.

Still, in Higdon's first ten carries he managed to get 35 yards, giving him 998 for the season—four more than the year before. With Michigan up 21–7 with 1:34 left in the first half, and the ball on Rutgers's 45, the Wolverines faced third-and-five. Patterson called the play, took the snap, and handed to Higdon, who plunged into the line for a mere two yards—three yards short of a first down—but exactly what Higdon needed to become Michigan's first player since 2011 to run for 1,000 yards.

No one celebrates a failed third down, but Higdon knew what he'd done, and so did his teammates, who talked to the media about it after the game. They also knew what that mark represented. Higdon had come back for his senior year, fully prepared for his best season, and suffered a relatively minor ding against Western. He'd run for a streak of seven 100-plus yard games—and this was his reward: a season so good, he needed only a failed two-yard run to get the mark.

His old coach was right: he did it once, he could do it again—and better this time.

Chapter 36
The Prodigal Son
2014–2017

After a 13-year Hall of Fame career playing right tackle for the St. Louis Cardinals, Dan Dierdorf enjoyed a 30-year run for ABC *Monday Night Football* and CBS. He stepped down after the 2013 season due to the rigors of travel but couldn't resist returning to his alma mater in 2014 to help his old friend Jim Brandstatter with the Michigan football broadcasts. He thought it would be fun—a nice, easy step down from his previous duties, on the way to a full retirement.

Little did he know.

Thinking like most observers that Michigan would bounce back that season from the 7–6 debacle in 2013, Dierdorf prepared himself to go easier on the college players.

"When you go to the NFL, you're an adult, a professional, you're paid, and you take on certain responsibilities," he told me. "You know the deal when you accept the check: screw up and you're fair game for the fans and the press. When I was covering NFL games, I can't say I worried too much about someone's feelings.

"But as soon as I took [the UM] job, I gave myself a talking to. 'They're kids! They're not old enough to drink, and don't deserve to be talked about the same way you'd talk about a professional.' Same goes for people on Twitter, with people pouncing on some kid who has a bad game, or just a bad play. If you can't understand they're just kids, subject to the ups and downs of adolescent life, then maybe you shouldn't have a Twitter account. When people lose sight of that it can get very ugly.

"So it's not my job to torch the Michigan players, no matter how bad they play. I knew I'd have to point out when they're not playing well, but with love."

But after watching the 2014 team, that balancing act looked harder than expected.

"You know, I didn't see this coming! I couldn't pretend it wasn't happening, and I felt bad about it. After a while, you don't want to beat the proverbial dead horse. But I have an obligation to the listeners, too. They're counting on us to tell them what's happening.

And what was happening wasn't very good. It wasn't fun to watch or describe."

Like just about everyone else attached to Michigan football, Dierdorf was hoping Hackett could land the "unicorn," Jim Harbaugh.

"Jim's record speaks for itself, wherever he's been, at every level," Dierdorf said. "Of course what I liked is that his teams were fundamentally sound, but that usually takes time to develop."

For the fan base, however, Harbaugh's return was not a time for rational thinking. If you had asked Michigan fans for their top three choices, they would say Jim Harbaugh, Jim Harbaugh—and probably Jim Harbaugh. If Harbaugh went to the Raiders, the Bears, or the Jets, he'd be received as a great coach with a promising future. But if he returned to Ann Arbor, it was clear he'd be greeted as a savior.

It turned out that was a gross underestimation. When Hackett landed Harbaugh, the response was something beyond euphoria. MGoBlog changed its banner to, "IT'S HAPPENING!"

Michigan fans felt emotionally validated that Harbaugh proved all the NFL experts wrong, and they put their money where their mouths were, quickly snapping up the thousands of season tickets that had gone unclaimed after the 2014 season, and just as important, plunking down big money for the 27 luxury suites that were up for renewal that year—a third of the total.

With the fans in a frenzy, Harbaugh worked furiously to put his program together, including his coaching staff, his first recruiting class, and even his family. One night Jim called his father in Milwaukee and said, "We're going over film, and I really need you here. No one knows this stuff like you do."

"Don't bullshit me," Jack replied. "You have kids who are 7, 5 and 3. You need a babysitter!"

Jim paused, then admitted, "That too. But can you come?"

They moved next door, where their grandchildren soon beat a path to their home.

Before Harbaugh and his crew coached a single game in Ann Arbor, he was already turning the established order upside down—and getting lots of attention for it, both positive and negative. Michigan fans loved his energy. He not only followed his father's lifelong advice to "Attack this day with an enthusiasm unknown to mankind," he repeated it often, establishing it as one of the Michigan mantras.

Harbaugh also attacked anyone attacking Michigan's program.

In Harbaugh's second month on the job, former Michigan commit Mike Weber's coach at Cass Tech accused Urban Meyer of making "false pretenses" to Weber to get him to flip to Ohio State. Harbaugh responded by tweeting his "Thought of the day—What a tangled web we weave when first we practice to deceive!—Sir Walter Scott."

The next year, when Ohio State athletic director Gene Smith said of Michigan's spring break practices at Florida's IMG Academy, "If we were jump starting our program, I'd probably try to do that too," Harbaugh fired back on Twitter, "Good to see Director Smith being relevant again after the tattoo fiasco [which resulted in coach Jim Tressell being fired]. Welcome back!"

Likewise, when Georgia head coach Kirby Smart wondered aloud if the IMG Academy practices might violate recruiting rules, Harbaugh tweeted, "If the Georgia coach is implying any intent on our part to break rules, he is barking up the wrong tree."

In 2017, after the Outback Bowl picked 8-4 Michigan over 9-3 Michigan State, which had beaten the Wolverines that year, Michigan State's Mark Dantonio said, "I'll just continue to concentrate on beating Michigan." Harbaugh responded with a tweet: "Saw Coach D comments on continuing to 'focus' on how 'he' can beat Michigan. Congrats on turning around a 3-9 team, plagued with off-field issues. Good for BIG to have him back."

Word got out: if you're going to come after Harbaugh's program, he's going to come after you. The days of Michigan committing silly pranks like stake planting, then apologizing, were over. Michigan fans loved it as much as Michigan's foes did not.

In 2015 Harbaugh embarked on a nationwide tour of "satellite football camps," to bring the coaches and the game to the players who couldn't afford to find them for a day or two, creating a convenient, cheap, and massive matchmaking service.

"We gave 58 satellite camps across the country," Harbaugh told me. "And we compared it to [Fielding] Yost's tour in the early 1900s. The idea was the same: to educate, to inform, and to inspire people to play this great game. We're under attack! So let's fight back. Well, we found football was much stronger than we thought. Thousands of kids, and their parents, wanted to be part of it. They were *enthusiastic*! Warmed the cockles of the heart."

Obviously, Harbaugh wanted to get the best players to play for Michigan and needed to build relationships with high school coaches across the country—just like admissions departments have been sending their representatives to high schools across the nation for decades to drum up interest and find the best students.

But the many critics of satellite camps whispered this as if they were discovering a dark secret. Harbaugh countered by inviting reporters and the NCAA to watch at every stop, and college coaches to participate. Of the 6,500 players who attended these camps, only six would go to Michigan. If that was the goal, it was a very inefficient means to achieve it.

"We saw a lot of kids who couldn't afford to go to a camp, and certainly not multiple camps," Harbaugh said. "We charged 'em 25 to 40 bucks to come to our camp. And they loved it! You're a kid seeing all those coaches at once, and you've never seen a college coach before! And you're doing the cutting-edge drills, running around the cones as fast as you can. It's *thrilling*. It's *inspiring*!

"When Sarah came to one of the camps, I asked her what she thought. And she says, 'I thought it was really cute.' And I say, 'Cute?!? We weren't aiming for *cute*!' And she says, 'Oh but it was cute, how you could just tell they were pouring everything they had into this, running around the cones. They were trying so hard to impress the coaches.'

"Okay," Harbaugh said. "You've touched upon the essence. We'll let 'cute' slide."

When Harbaugh set up camps in six cities from LA to DC the next summer, 2016, the coaches down south didn't take too kindly to it. The SEC had won eight of the previous ten national titles, and they had a virtual monopoly on their talent-rich states. They didn't need a carpetbagger from the North coming down to mess with a good thing—even if that meant limiting the options for the players themselves.

When Ole Miss head coach Hugh Freeze, who had replaced Houston Nutt, claimed conducting satellite camps would cut into his family time, Harbaugh told *Sports Illustrated,* "You've got a guy sitting in a big house, making $5 million a year, saying he does not want to sacrifice his time. That is not a kindred spirit to me. What most of these coaches are saying is they don't want to work harder."

Freeze responded by telling ESPN'S *Mike & Mike,* "I will never apologize for wanting to be a good father. I miss enough volleyball games. That is a priority for me."

When Tom Mars, the attorney representing former Ole Miss head coach Houston Nutt and quarterback Shea Patterson, exhumed Freeze's phone records, Ole Miss discovered Freeze had been using his work cell phone on recruiting trips to call escort services over several years, and released him on July 20, 2017. Apparently, Freeze's definition of "spending time with family" was broadly defined. (He is now the head coach at Jerry Falwell Jr.'s Liberty University.)

The SEC voted for an NCAA proposal to ban satellite camps, and the ACC joined in, which was no surprise. But it came as a shock to many coaches when their conference representatives at the Pac-12 and Big 12 voted for the ban, too, which seemed to run counter to their self-interest, not to mention the recruits'. Washington State's Mike Leach told Sirius XM College Sports he believed all Pac-12 teams but two were against the ban, but the conference voted for it anyway.

"I can't fathom how it's possible we voted to eliminate it," he said. "Whether it's smart, dumb, or in the middle, it's wrong. It's wrong. If we're even remotely close to what we say we are, that needs to be overturned immediately."

Tommy Tuberville had coached at Ole Miss, Auburn, and Texas Tech before taking the top post at Cincinnati. He told ESPN, "I just can't imagine, of all the rules in my 35 years of coaching college football, that this was even voted on, because it just doesn't make any sense for the players. Surely, we've got more sense than this."

At the time the NCAA allowed offseason satellite camps in every sport but football, but it was terrified of the SEC splitting off and taking the ACC and other Power Five conferences with it. So a version of the ban remained in place, and Harbaugh's goal of spreading the gospel was successfully squelched.

After rattling the establishment, Harbaugh turned around the Wolverines his first season, doubling the win total to 10-3 his first season, with a fiery sideline style reminiscent of Bo Schembechler. The next year, when the third-ranked Wolverines and number-two-ranked Ohio State played their second "Game of the Century" in 2016, it lived up to the hype.

Michigan led from the start but couldn't put the Buckeyes away due to an anemic fourth quarter, when its offense gained a mere five yards. This was exactly what Dierdorf was talking about: the O-line couldn't get a first down when it had to. In the second overtime, when the Buckeyes needed a first down to avoid losing, the refs ruled they had made it by a whisker. Photos of that spot have been broken down more minutely than the Zapruder film, and are even less conclusive. On the next play, Ohio State won the game.

Just a few minutes after Ohio State sealed the 30–27 victory and the Buckeye fans rushed the field, Harbaugh faced the press. Prompted by a reporter's question, he said he was "bitterly disappointed" in the officials, who had also given Harbaugh a penalty for throwing his clipboard behind him like a Frisbee. Harbaugh's quote echoed the famous line of his mentor, Bo Schembechler, after the Big Ten's athletic directors voted to send Ohio State to the Rose Bowl—back in 1973. In this rivalry, quotes have the half-life of uranium.

In the off-season the NCAA passed a measure quickly dubbed "The Harbaugh Rule." Instead of having to issue a warning, then two five-yard penalties before calling for a 15-yard unsportsmanlike penalty, the "Harbaugh Rule" allowed officials to skip all warnings and go straight to the 15-yard penalty whenever a coach steps on the field of play or "or otherwise demonstrates disagreement with an officiating decision."

NCAA officials hit Harbaugh where it hurt him most: his need to compete. Just a few games into the 2017 season fans and reporters noted Harbaugh's new sideline demeanor, free of rants, gestures, and stomping on the field. When I asked him about this, sitting at his parents' table, he explained simply, "They made a rule."

His father added, with a grin, "Jim changed his conduct out of respect for the Harbaugh Rule. If he didn't respect it, who would?"

Harbaugh had other reasons to shift his style, too. Unlike his 2016 squad, the 2017 Wolverines weren't loaded with senior leaders ready to play in the NFL. They were the youngest team in the country, replacing ten of eleven starters on defense, and breaking in a new quarterback—then another, and another. Harbaugh knew he needed more patience to bring along his young charges.

Harbaugh also largely retired from his famed Twitter wars, which had earned him two million followers—the most of any coach in America.

"It gets time consuming, and I just got tired of it," he told me. "Besides, I never started those fights. I was always the counter-puncher, like Sugar Ray Robinson," the middleweight champion of the 1950s. "Nobody's really saying anything bad about our program anymore, so there's no need."

Harbaugh's new style didn't bring better results—the 8-5 finish left the Wolverines unranked for the first time since the Hoke era, and the upward trajectory of Harbaugh's tenure interrupted—but perhaps it would have been worse if Harbaugh had applied his emotional approach to this far less experienced team. Regardless, none of that spared him a crescendo of criticism from fans and reporters alike. The national media crowed that Harbaugh was a bust, and for the first time a significant minority of the Michigan fans wondered aloud if that might be true.

Could Harbaugh recapture the promise of his first two seasons coaching in Ann Arbor? Would he do so by returning to his hotblooded coaching style, or sticking with his cooler approach?

The players got the answer before the public did when Harbaugh met with Higdon, Winovich, and other team leaders shortly after the Ohio State game to ask for their input—and act on it. He also impressed the players with his calmer demeanor.

"When I see coach sitting around the building these days," Bredeson told me, "he looks relaxed, just a lot more comfortable this year. He's opened himself up, and it seems like he's enjoying himself more."

If he is calmer these days, Harbaugh told me, it's because they have players who do the right things, and staffers who make life easier. "That makes me calmer!"

The fans saw that the "New Harbaugh" was back for another season during the Notre Dame game, which featured a few suspect calls that the old Harbaugh would have pounced on, but the new Harbaugh largely ignored, knowing a response could cost his team 15 yards.

It's rare to see a man in his fifties, and especially such a public personality in a volcanic occupation, change so much. But what fans wanted to know was this: would Harbaugh's cooler style produce better results?

Chapter 37
The Perfect Trap

Indiana, November 17, 2018

Indiana was much better than Rutgers, and had a habit of playing Michigan tough. In 2015 the Wolverines beat the Hoosiers 48–41 in triple overtime, in 2016 they won 20–10, and in 2017, they went to overtime again to win 27–20.

But because the Wolverines were also one game closer to everything they had been working for, it would take all their willpower not to look ahead to Ohio State, since beating the Buckeyes would likely be Michigan's biggest win of the young century. Adding to the distraction, this would be the last home game for

Michigan's seniors, and for those considering jumping to the NFL or transferring.

It was, in short, the perfectly engineered trap game.

Don Brown's defense would have something to say about that. Through ten games Michigan's defense had allowed a mere four touchdowns through the air, while scoring four touchdowns off pick-sixes. Opposing quarterbacks were as likely to throw a touchdown to one of their receivers as they were to one of Michigan's defenders.

They were on a nine-game roll, and Brown intended to keep them rolling. Shortly after they settled into the defensive meeting room the Monday after Rutgers, Brown got right to it, flashing slides with each point he was making.

"Let's knock this out," he said, his voice extra gravelly. "Couple interesting statistics for ya: We've allowed 99.4 yards passing per game in the Big Ten. Next closest in *any* conference is 127.2. That's a defense." And so it went with stats on quarterback pressure, coverage, total yards, and more. "Since the first half against Notre Dame we've defended against 113 possessions: 13 touchdowns, five field goals. 95 drives, nothing. 37 were three-and-out."

Despite routing Rutgers, Brown had his complaints.

"I didn't think we tackled great. We ran well—we weren't loafing—but we gotta get better on our angles."

After they broke down Indiana's tape, he turned to his players and said in his Boston accent, "I got up this morning, and looked at the man in the mirrah. And I thought, 'Holy fuck am I tired. Do I have 13 more days left in me?' Then I answered: 'Oh yeah. I got 13 more days left in me. Hell yeah!'

"Look, we're all tired. We're all busting our ass. But this is the opportunity of a lifetime. We've got all this right in front of us, everything we've wanted, everything we've worked for. And no one is gonna take it from us. We do the taking. We take the lunch money," he said, nodding at Winovich.

"We're gonna do it for 13 more days. That's what it takes."

For the seniors, the last home game also meant the last night at the Graduate Hotel.

"It's just weird," Joe Hewlett said. "We all know it's our last night, but everything goes by so quickly. One thing we've all known: these are the best times of our lives, so we want to enjoy it. Time spent together is time well spent, And winning helps!"

When John Wangler asked Jared if he was going to

try to get to an NFL training camp as a free agent, Jared didn't express the slightest interest.

"My graduate program ends in April," he explained, "when I get a master's in real estate development, from the School of Architecture and Design, which overlaps 75 percent with an MBA. I've got a 3.5 GPA right now. I know what I'm doing next, and it's not football. So it makes me focus all the more. I know this is it."

When the Wolverines returned to the locker room after warmups, a few checked their phones and were stunned to see the Buckeyes fighting for their lives against Maryland. They had to come from behind the entire game just to take the Terrapins into overtime, then stop a two-point conversation to avoid a season-crushing loss. On that final play Maryland's backup quarterback, Tyrrell Pigrome, making his first start, had a receiver wide open in the end zone—and threw wide.

While an Ohio State loss and Michigan victory would secure Michigan's first East Division title, Wangler and others said it would take away from the luster of the Game—and in any case, it had no impact on their primary goal: Beat the Bucks.

"But you see a game like that," Wangler said, "and

you know you have to be on full alert for an upset, especially against a team that always plays us tough."

There were still moments to savor. Before Wangler's last run out of the tunnel, "I was standing there for probably 30 seconds, taking it all in one last time. And then you run out there, and it was over and done so quickly. After I got to the other side of the field, I went, 'Wow, that was it. Last time, never again.' And that's how the whole thing goes: over before you know it."

On Michigan's opening ten-play drive, half of them Higdon runs, the Wolverines got it down to the Hoosiers' fourteen-yard line before running into an increasingly familiar problem: a weak red-zone offense. The stalled drive produced a 3–0 lead.

After Michael Dwumfour intercepted a pass at Michigan's 38-yard line, the offense again couldn't take advantage, leaving the field after three plays. A slow start was not the exception for Michigan's 2018 offense, but the rule. No surprise there.

What was surprising was the Hoosiers' ability to cut through Michigan's vaunted defense with slant routes and crossing patterns, which are difficult to stifle in man-to-man coverage, Brown's preferred approach. The Hoosiers had apparently seen the Northwestern tape, exploiting this weakness for plays of 35, 29, and

13 yards and a touchdown, a 7–3 lead, and a 17–15 lead at the half.

If this was a trap game, the trap had been set.

In the second half the Wolverines did what championship teams do: buckled down, eliminated mistakes, and played to their strengths. On Indiana's first four possessions, Don Brown adjusted his defense to smother the quick routes and send the Hoosiers back to the bench with no points.

Michigan's offense managed to put up 16 more points thanks to freshman kicker Jake Moody, who hit a school record six field goals in his first start. Michigan 31, Indiana 20. The Wolverines were far from dominant, but good enough to escape the trap and allow the seniors to enjoy their final plays in the Big House.

"It wasn't until we got the ball back at the end that we got sentimental," Hewlett said. "Seeing guys on the sidelines giving hugs. It probably looked the same as two weeks earlier (against Penn State) but it didn't feel the same. This wasn't just winning a game. This was completing a mission. Only we know what kind of journey it's been. It wasn't pretty when we got here. It was miserable. But we all stuck it out, and now we're 10-1, with a chance at everything we want next week."

Michigan's tenth straight victory sealed the longest

streak since 2006, and before that, 1997; a perfect 8-0 home record; and Michigan's first share of the East Division title since the divisions were created in 2012.

The seniors ran to the student section to sing "The Victors" one last time, then enjoyed an additional bonus: the staff let their families on the field to congratulate their sons one last time, and take a few final photos. Wangler sought out Chris Partridge, who had convinced him to turn down Indiana's scholarship offer and pay his own way for his last year. When Wangler told him how much he appreciated him, Partridge asked, "Aren't you glad you didn't go to Indiana?"

"Oh yeah," Wangler said. "No regrets!"

Dierdorf had a bigger takeaway. "On Senior Day, ten fathers who had played at Michigan walked under the banner for their sons—the sign of a healthy program. I can't imagine anything that would have made Bo more proud."

In the locker room Harbaugh led his team in "The Victors," but without the exuberance of the celebrations after Northwestern, Wisconsin, Michigan State, or Penn State. It was more business than pleasure, because they already had something else on their minds. When they finished Harbaugh said, "It's Ohio State week, so that was a playoff win. We know what's at stake.'"

Harbaugh didn't have to explain.

Chapter 38
Collapse in Columbus

At Ohio State, November 24, 2018

After 155 weightlifting sessions running one to two hours, 112 practices that lasted two to four hours—totaling more than 500 hours of sweat—countless film sessions, a few hundred team meals together, one loss, and ten straight wins—it was finally here: Ohio State. The Wolverines had arrived with all their dreams intact.

Whether the Buckeyes could still get into the playoff after being blown out by Purdue was still a question. But despite that loss and a narrow escape in Maryland, the Buckeyes were also 10-1, with a share of the division crown, the Big Ten title game, and their ninth Big Ten title this century all theirs if they simply beat Michigan, as they'd done in 16 of the previous 18 years.

All the chips were in.

Don Brown started his defensive meeting that Monday with a pile of good stats, but with the Buckeyes up next nobody was in the mood to celebrate. On the board they noticed 13 red Xs against only four maize Ms. Indiana had drawn some blood.

"Let me just say this to you," Brown said, "we looked at what Indiana was doing to us at halftime, and we fixed it—and that's a credit to you guys. But we haven't played against an up-tempo offense in a while, and we might see it again this weekend, so that's a great thing, *a lucky break,* that we saw it against Indiana. Let's *use* that and get ready and get better.

"This one here is fun. This one here is personal. Last of the Revenger Tour!"

Brown started the Ohio State scouting video, and they went to work.

For Michigan's fifth-year seniors it took all five years to get to the Horseshoe with this much momentum. Their freshman year they dragged their 5-6 record to Columbus for Hoke's last game—a death march. They had a shot at a Big Ten title their second season, 2015, but got blown out at the Big House, 42–13. They had a better chance their third season, 2016, but they had just lost to Iowa two weeks earlier to take some of the luster off. And the previous season, 2017, they already had lost three Big Ten games before Ohio State, when they blew a 14–0 second quarter lead.

To be ranked fourth in the country and a 4.5-point favorite against Ohio State—in Columbus, no less—was a heady feeling for them. Another new sensation: they were *convinced* they were going to win—and it seemed like most Ohio State fans agreed. The Buckeyes hadn't looked like their usual dominant selves against a host of middling Big Ten teams, including Minnesota, Purdue, Nebraska, Michigan State, and Maryland. You had to wonder if something was amiss in Columbus, especially when their injured captain, Nick Bosa, not only quit the team mid-season but left campus.

One thing all Wolverines believed: this game meant a lot more to Michigan than it did to Ohio State. You got the feeling the rest would be gravy.

For an Ohio native like Noah Furbush, Ohio State was the whole meal. When informed that the seniors had gone 28–4 at home over the past four years (with all four losses to Michigan State and Ohio State), Furbush was only moderately impressed. When told his team had already won a share of the East Division title for the first time in the division's seven-year history, he said, "Co-champs? Huh. I doubt you're going to see that on a banner around here."

What he wanted was what his teammates wanted, and maybe a little more.

"This game is different than all the rest. I don't care if we lose eleven games so long as we win this one. Growing up an hour from Columbus, every time I go home, I get the same narrative, even at church. After the service they say, 'I'll root for you as hard as I can, I love you, but I can't root for That Team Up North.' And every time I hear that I think, 'I appreciate that, but if you're not rooting for *all* these guys with me, guys I love and work with and became brothers with over these years—then you're not with me.' And I think about giving it back to them."

Instead, Furbush just smiled and kept his own counsel, knowing full well the only message that matters would be the one delivered on the field that coming Saturday.

"Everything's on the line," he said. "*Everything*. Like Cortez said, 'Burn the ships.' So let's burn 'em."

Adding the twelfth game and a bye week pushed almost all season-ending rivalry games to Thanksgiving Saturday. While that denies many students the chance to see their team in the year's biggest game, it does provide the players a lighter schedule when they need it most, with most professors surrendering to their out-of-state students' travel plans and holding classes on Monday, occasionally Tuesday, but almost never on Wednesday.

There is also the practical matter of practicing during Thanksgiving week, which costs most players Thanksgiving at home. Some are lucky enough to have their parents drive to campus to make a home-cooked Thanksgiving dinner, and the rest are lucky enough to know someone whose parents are cooking.

"We've become really good friends with Ben's roommates," Deb Bredeson said. "The moms all cooked a big dinner at their house."

They actually did one better. After the players left Ben Bredeson's house for the team buses Friday afternoon, the mothers gave the place a thorough cleaning— no small feat in a house filled with football players—then festooned the inside with Christmas decorations, while the fathers strung old-fashioned Christmas lights on the outside. They even stocked the fridge with food, including Thanksgiving leftovers, and plenty of cold beer.

Whatever happened Saturday, the parents felt good knowing their sons would have a nice surprise waiting for them when they returned.

Despite owning two indoor practice facilities, the team would practice outside for a simple reason: The Horseshoe has no roof, and the young winter's first big snow had already left fresh mounds on the Schembechler statue's hat, shoulders, and hands. No one ever dares whisk the snow off, as a show of respect—exactly as he'd want it.

As Schembechler was fond of saying, "If you're going to *play* in the North Atlantic [some of the world's roughest seas], you have to *practice* in the North Atlantic!"

On defense, because Michigan had allowed just 123 yards passing per game, leading the nation by almost 20 yards, the plan was to stick to the plan: send Michigan's killer D-linemen after Ohio State's Dwayne Haskins, and force him to run—not his strength.

"Everybody's in," Winovich told me. "Everybody's ready."

At 6:00 a.m. on Saturday, November 24, two commercial buses hummed in the dark, empty parking lot of Ann Arbor's Briarwood shopping mall. Cars slowly rolled up to let passengers out, who quietly boarded the buses, as if part of a secret rendezvous. The players' parents filled every seat on both buses, wearing jerseys with their sons' numbers and names, packing enough snacks to keep everyone happy for the drive to Columbus—normally three hours, but on this day, four. They were buoyant, stunning the smattering of Ohio State fans at a fast-food joint along the way.

More Michigan football parents traveled by themselves—though some thought twice. In 2016 the Bredesons drove to Columbus to see Ben play as a freshman. After Michigan lost in overtime the abuse became so nasty they felt compelled to surround their 12-year-old son Max in a tight triangle of mom, dad, and son Jack for safety.

"We wore our Michigan stuff, but that shouldn't be a problem," Deb said. "It isn't anywhere else. The yelled everything at us, nonstop. A woman my age with pom poms shoves them in my face and yells, 'Yoooooooouuu lost!'"

Michigan fans can tell you stories of full beer cans thrown at their heads, grandmothers yelling the "C-word" at their girlfriends, and local police looking on, unmoved. After years of this Michigan president Mary Sue Coleman felt compelled to send U of M police officers to protect Michigan players, parents, and fans. I always assumed the worst Ohio State fans only cranked it up for Michigan, until I traveled around the league to research *Fourth and Long* and discovered they are the most disliked fans in the Big Ten—the only one fan base other fans consistently despise.

But it must be said that if 10 percent of Ohio State fans behave as if they were raised by wolves, the other 90 percent spend their time apologizing for the 10 percent. I have had nothing but positive experiences with Ohio State fans, though Michigan fans tell me I've been lucky.

Despite their vows, the Bredesons returned to Columbus in 2018. It would almost certainly be their son's last game in the Horseshoe, and family ties are hard to break.

Before every home game, Deb Bredeson found her son walking into the stadium and gave him a hug and a kiss. Before every road game, including this one, she texted him a kiss emoji, and Ben, the 330-pound junior captain, texted her back a hug.

With that, Deb Bredeson had done all she could do.

Some thought it would be a battle, others a Michigan blowout, but no one predicted what happened next.

While Michigan's offense had to settle for field goals, the Buckeyes employed the same attack that Northwestern and Indiana had used—slant routes and crossing patterns—to build a daunting 21–6 lead with 3:18 left in the first half.

The Wolverines, accustomed to staying cool under pressure, countered with a 79-yard drive to cut the lead to 21–13—close enough to take to the locker room and regroup. Then, a gift: the Buckeyes fumbled the following kickoff on the nine-yard line, Patterson hit a wide-open Chris Evans, and suddenly the score was 21–19.

After Michigan attempted an ill-advised two-point conversion and failed, the Buckeyes got the ball on their 25-yard line with only 41 seconds left. Three Michigan penalties and one 33-yard pass later the Buckeyes were down to Michigan's three-yard line. On second-and-goal from the two, Haskins ran the option to the right side and tossed the ball to Tate Martell, who looked like he had plenty of space to score.

But Noah Furbush, who had returned to beat the Buckeyes, stepped up to throw everything he had to stop Martell cold with technical perfection and five years of rage. The Buckeyes had to settle for a field goal and a 24–19 halftime lead.

"You think about a guy making a play at a tough moment in the game," Jansen said. "You just backed us down 70 yards in less than a minute, but I'm not going to give you this last yard. I refuse. I'm going to fight you for every inch. That defines Noah Furbush as a player, as a leader on this team, and the man that he is."

Furbush's four-point save seemed like the kind of play that might be remembered for a long time. Since 1970, four points would have changed the outcome of 15 Michigan–Ohio State games—almost a third.

The Wolverines were right there, but Winovich had a bad feeling.

"Indiana set the template to beat our defense," Winovich told me, just as Brown had warned them. "But the Buckeyes took it farther, because they have better athletes than Indiana. Ohio State came in knowing the crossing routes would be a severe problem for us, and they went up-tempo more than any team we faced. Makes things far more confusing and harder to adjust to for a defense."

Winovich could pinpoint the moment he knew they were in trouble.

"I got a tackle for loss and did the cross-armed signal: 'You're not going there!' But they got back to the line of scrimmage so fast, ready to run their next play, it was almost like I hadn't made a play at all. No time to celebrate!"

"It wasn't like we didn't adjust. A big misconception was that we just ran [man-to-man coverage] the whole game. But when we switched to one kind of zone, then another, then another, they were ready for all of that, too, and they were just faster than us. At halftime it was close, but you already got the feeling we were in trouble. Those guys had us figured out. They knew us. That thought was prevalent throughout the game. At no time did I feel like we had momentum."

The Wolverines still trailed by only eight points midway through the third quarter when Zach Gentry dropped a first-down pass at mid-field. On the following punt the Buckeyes blocked it and ran it back for a touchdown. 34–19.

Three plays later Patterson threw an interception that the Buckeyes quickly converted to another touchdown for a 41–19 lead, en route to a 62–39 thrashing— the most any opponent had ever scored in regulation in 140 years of Michigan football.

After the stunning loss Michigan's locker room wasn't just quiet, but eerie.

"A lot of guys were just zoned out, looking into space," Higdon said. "It was not just that we lost, but *how* we lost. No one saw us getting blown out—not the way we've been playing. It kinda took your breath away."

"There are a couple things about the way we play D," Dierdorf told me. "If you're going to play man coverage [instead of zone] as much as we do—and I don't care if you have Charles Woodson back there—you're asking for trouble if you can't generate pressure on the quarterback. It's nearly impossible to cover a crossing pattern when the quarterback doesn't have to hurry his throw. It's a simple equation: crossing patterns plus no pressure equals big problems."

Dierdorf believed Michigan's plan still could have worked, "so long as you have a counter, and it's called a pass rush. But if the pressure is not there, it all goes up in smoke. And we got zero—and I mean *zero*—pressure on Haskins. I don't recall him even getting knocked down. Forget Haskins' passing, their running back, and defense. In my mind, Ohio State's offensive line won that game."

Haskins himself confirmed Dierdorf's first point at the press conference. When he watched Michigan's man-to-man coverage on film that week, "I was licking my chops. That's a quarterback's dream."

Combine Michigan's man-to-man coverage with a feckless pass rush and a few injuries and you get seven offensive touchdowns—triple Michigan's average.

"We had opportunities," Jansen said. "But that was a faceplant."

If Ohio State looked nothing like the team that lost to Purdue, Michigan didn't resemble the squad that ran the gauntlet, either. Simply put, Michigan picked a bad day to play its worst game of the season, and Ohio State picked a great day to play its best.

After the game the Michigan parents gathered by the wrought-iron fence outside the visitors' locker room. When their sons walked out, they found their parents, gave them a hug over the chest-high rail, and muttered a few words of somber disappointment. Their mothers and fathers nodded and whispered consolation and support, but nothing cleared up their sons' teary eyes.

Jared Wangler was tight-jawed, red-eyed, and soft-spoken. There wasn't a lot to say. After Jared told his dad how shocked he was, while constantly running his hand through his still-wet hair, his father pulled him in and said, "Hey, sometimes it's not your day. But Jared, I'm proud of you, and what you've fought through to put yourself in position to play and contribute. You've been a great teammate, a leader on a team that's accomplished an awful lot, and you earned the respect of the players and the coaches. As a dad, I couldn't be prouder."

When Ben Bredeson finally emerged from the visitors' locker room, it was like the Notre Dame game—but worse.

"There wasn't even a hug this time," Deb said. "He was just holding in the tears, as he was walking to the bus. Fans don't understand what sacrifices these kids make for this. For Ben, his whole life has literally been for *this*. Even in high school he didn't get to have a normal experience. Everything was about getting ready for this—tons of work, good nutrition, no blemishes on his record, good grades, get mentally strong. Then you play a big game that means so much, that you've been waiting for all year, and it doesn't happen. As a parent it crushes you to see your son have so much heartache. Unless you've been a parent of a kid who lives and breathes competition, you can't know how much it hurts him to lose."

John Wangler and Rich Hewlett already knew how painful it was to lose to the Buckeyes. Wangler had won four of five, while Hewlett's teams had won two of five—but the wins never erased the losses, even decades later.

After they talked with their sons, John Wangler and Rich Hewlett walked off together around the Horseshoe toward the parents' buses. Despite their heroics in that very building decades ago, no one approached them. The two didn't seem to notice, or care. They didn't see themselves as former players, but as fathers.

"I've been poor, I've made some money, and I couldn't care less," John Wangler told me. "Your legacy is your kids, and who you've helped over your lifetime."

Being recognized is not why they did what they did all those years ago—and it wasn't why their sons just did what they did an hour ago, either.

On the bus ride home Wangler assessed Jared's tenure on the team, which they now knew would not include a win over the Buckeyes, a Big Ten title game, or a playoff game, just one more bowl game.

"I'm sure he'd have liked more playing time and more touches," John said, "but he did more than most people probably expected. And to switch from defense to fullback your last year, and to play a solid role and have some success at a new position, that showed something.

"But in the end the stats don't mean much. It's not the tackles or the touchdown. It's your effort and your ability to meet a challenge, head on. It's an experience like no other that prepares you for anything. Trust me, Rich and I know this. When you get together ten years from now, twenty years from now, thirty years from now, that's what they'll be talking about: the shared experience.

"The fans will come and go. They'll love you when you win and forget about you when you're gone. It's the relationships that you keep—relationships that go deeper than any others. They last forever."

After the team buses dropped everyone off at Schembechler Hall about nine o'clock, Bredeson and his roommates walked in the cold and dark to their home, where they received their first pleasant surprise of the day.

"We'd put a timer on the lights we'd strung up on their house before we left for the game," Deb Bredeson said. "That way they could see their place lit up all the way from the end of the street—the only house with lights on over Thanksgiving weekend."

When they opened the door they were met with a surprisingly clean home, decorated for Christmas, and a refrigerator fully stocked with food and cold beer. Their parents were still an hour from Ann Arbor, but their cell phones soon started buzzing.

"I thought this was going to be the worst day of my life," Bredeson texted his mom, "but you guys made it so much better."

Even the ultra-confident Harbaugh was brought low by the loss to the Buckeyes.

"The bus ride back from Columbus wasn't too much different than that station wagon ride after I lost my first Punt, Pass, and Kick competition in Des Moines," Harbaugh told me a few months later, then demonstrated by standing up, pressing the side of his face against the wall, and gazing hopelessly off into space. "Just staring out the window for three very long hours. Felt about the same, too."

Back at the Harbaughs' home, Sarah said, "After a loss Jim closes down, silently beating himself up for losing. I try not to sleep next to him after a loss because his sleep is often interrupted. He'll wake up and yell something that went wrong, or he'll yell a play, like he's still coaching. You can tell his subconscious is just replaying the whole thing. It must be awful."

Perspective is not a great attribute of college football fans generally, and perhaps of Michigan's in particular. A century of success will do that. If you told Michigan fans after the Notre Dame game, when so many were convinced the team was imploding, that the Wolverines would win ten straight games, they'd be ecstatic. If you added that Michigan would score 39 points against

Ohio State, they'd be thrilled—and probably assume Michigan had blown out the Buckeyes.

There was no spinning the fact that Harbaugh had yet to beat the Buckeyes or win a Big Ten title, but the three previous coaches had failed to win a crown for a decade. This was not a hole that Harbaugh had dug, but the shovel was in his hands now.

Considered objectively, that shovel was in very good hands. In the eleven years before Harbaugh returned Michigan managed to win ten games exactly twice. Harbaugh had won ten games in three of his first four seasons—the first Michigan coach to do that since Fielding Yost. And he was building it to last, on and off the field. The only questions remaining were how long would it take him to finish the job, and how long would the fans wait?

Just as Harbaugh had done after the Ohio State game the year before, as soon as he got home he started writing down what they could do better next year.

He already had some ideas.

PART V

Postseason

Chapter 39
Hard Choices

December 2018

Days later the Ohio State game was still ringing in the players' ears, and impossible to avoid outside their heads, too.

Because they would not be preparing for the Big Ten title game, they had a week off between the Ohio State game and bowl practice. What might be a welcome respite, especially with term papers and final exams looming, was anything but. Everyone in Schembechler Hall would have preferred another week of work for a Big Ten title game than more time to dwell on the blowout in Columbus.

In the Commons nutritionist Abigail O'Connor had

turned the four big screens from ESPN to reruns of *Tom and Jerry* cartoons to avoid any mention of the game just past, and the Big Ten title game coming up.

But O'Connor couldn't shield them from classrooms, dormitories, restaurants, bars, and social media. For Zach Gentry, who dropped the pass against Ohio State, followed by the blocked punt and interception which cost Michigan 14 points, the comments on Twitter became so toxic that he canceled his account.

But he still couldn't avoid the critics, even on campus. Standing at the bar one night he listened to a student he'd never met before go on about how "Gentry played the worst game of the year!" and "How do you drop that many passes?" Gentry couldn't resist putting out his hand and saying, "Well, I'm Zach Gentry."

The conversation ended with the young man's jaw dropping in Gentry's wake.

Seven days after Michigan's historic loss, Northwestern gave Ohio State a scare in the Big Ten title game before going down, 45–24. A solid victory, but not good enough to overcome the 12-1 Buckeyes' loss to Purdue. For the second year in a row the Big Ten failed to send a team to the national playoffs.

That came as a crashing disappointment to the people in Schembechler Hall. They wanted their archrival to get a playoff bid because that would likely send the Wolverines to play Washington in the Rose Bowl, just like old times.

Instead, on Sunday night, December 2, the Wolverines watched ESPN's bowl selection show, and hoped for the best.

What used to be a great honor 50 years ago, when there were only 10 bowl games for 20 top teams, is now just another game on the schedule for just about every program that can still field a team. Contrary to popular belief most bowl teams lose piles of money on these expensive trips, partly because the bowls require them to buy tickets no one wants.

But that hasn't stopped the sponsors from promoting every silly bowl game you can imagine, and a few you couldn't have, like the Cheribundi Boca Raton Bowl and the Bad Boy Mowers Gasparilla Bowl. Why go to all this trouble, when so many players and fans could do without most of these bowls? Here's a hint: Of the 40 bowl games, 32 of them—fully 80 percent—would be broadcast by ESPN.

When ESPN announced the Peach Bowl in Atlanta had picked the Michigan Wolverines to play Florida, it was good news—on paper. The 7th-ranked Wolverines had qualified for one of the prestigious "Super Six

New Year's Day Bowls." But the Peach Bowl would be played on December 29, and lacked the status of the Fiesta Bowl, where the Wolverines hoped to play after Ohio State got the Rose Bowl.

The Lions Club of Atlanta started the Peach Bowl in 1968 as a fund-raiser, but due to lackluster attendance the Atlanta Chamber of Commerce took it over a few years later. Of the bowl's 100 teams, only seven have come from the Big Ten, all average, and five of them lost. The Peach Bowl rose through the ranks until it was elevated to New Year's Six status in 2014, thanks to Chick-Fil-A's sponsorship.

Another problem: Michigan would face Florida for the third time in the last four years—the same number of times Michigan had played Wisconsin. Michigan beat Florida in 2015 and 2017, and twice before that, with no losses. Michigan fans were already tired of playing Florida, and felt they had nothing to gain.

Michigan's coaches and players tried to stay motivated. At the team meeting Harbaugh told them they could win eleven games, something only nine of Michigan's 140 teams had ever achieved.

"We could go down as one of the better teams in Michigan football history," he said. "That's saying something."

In their heart of hearts, the players still felt a Peach

Bowl invitation against Florida was a consolation prize, but Florida wouldn't be a pushover. The Gators' first-year coach, Dan Mullen, was a rising star. A win over a marquee team like Michigan would prove he had the Gators going in the right direction.

Two days after the Ohio State game Rashan Gary announced he would enter the NFL draft. No surprise, since he was projected to be a top ten pick, which could mean $20 million or more. After the Peach Bowl selected Michigan, Gary decided to skip the game to avoid a career-threatening injury—the kind that teammate Jake Butt suffered in the Orange Bowl two years earlier, which cost him millions. Gary would soon be joined by Devin Bush Jr., who was still nursing a nagging hip injury, and Karan Higdon—meaning that three of Michigan's most important players, and two of its four captains, would not be making the trip.

Players at other schools had been skipping bowl games for years, but this was the first time it had happened at Michigan. Some fans on social media blasted the players, calling them traitors and worse. But if the players' decisions were selfish, they were selfish for all the right reasons: trying to protect a career they'd sacrificed so much to build, and in the case of Gary's mom and Higdon's daughter, looking out for others.

"So, I had to make this decision," Higdon told me. "And I had to think about my future, and my daughter. I'm responsible. What do you do?

"I talked to my teammates, mainly the O-Line, in the locker room before I talked to anyone else, out of respect. I love those guys. It was casual, really just showing them my thought process, and I think I got the overall support of each and every guy. They were cool. After I talked with my teammates, I had a tough conversation with Coach Harbaugh. He wasn't happy, but he didn't try to stop me."

When I asked Harbaugh about the players' decisions to skip the bowl game, he said, "I love Devin. I love Karan. I love Rashan. I love all those guys.

"I told them they should play, but they took advice from other guys. I think they'll regret it one day—but I want nothing but the best for them.

"I just. . . ." He squeezed his eyes shut, tilted his head back, and put his hands behind his head, straining to compose his thoughts. After a few moments, he leaned forward and said, "On the last day of the 1941 baseball season, Ted Williams was hitting .39955. If he didn't play in the doubleheader, he knew they would have rounded that up to .400—the first guy to bat .400 in eleven years, and there haven't been any since. He could have sat out, no problem. But he played both games, he hit six for eight, and he finished at .406. I admire that. I'll just leave that there.

"But those guys are still part of my family. Always will be."

What seemed irreconcilable—the shared desire to stick together, to compete, and yes, to beat the Gators, versus the players' risk of ruining a career over a largely meaningless bowl game—ultimately wasn't: the players loved the team, and the team loved them back. It wasn't fun, but they were still family.

Their teammates would have loved to see them suit up one more time, but they seemed to understand and defended them publicly. Grant Newsome, whose career-ending leg injury two years earlier had turned him into a graduate assistant coach, felt compelled to tweet about fans who criticized the athletes for protecting their futures.

"As if they wouldn't walk out of their office tomorrow," he wrote, "if they were guaranteed millions to do so."

In our conversation, Newsome added, "Jake Butt and I could tell you just how quickly it can all be taken from you," something Higdon got a taste of with his knee injury against Western.

Before the team flew to Atlanta the coaches were busy making sure all their recruits remained committed through the December 19 "early signing day," when almost all of their recruits would send in their National Letter of Intent.

On Saturday, December 8, Sherrone Moore and his wife were driving down I-94 to join Matt Dudek, Jim Harbaugh, some other coaches, and a few recruits at Ruth's Chris Steakhouse, when Moore looked at his watch, which receives texts. Five-star recruit Daxton Hill's name "flies up, and it's a long message. I'm like, 'Whoa whoa whoa!'"

When Moore pulled off the highway he read Hill's message: "Sorry Coach to hit you with this over a text message, but I think I'm going to decommit. I think I'm going to go to Alabama."

"I was just in complete shock," Moore told me. "My wife was too. This has to be a joke. I'm texting Daxton, I'm texting his parents, and there's no response. Not good. When we walk into the restaurant with a table full of recruits, I'm in the worst state I could be in, and I have to look brave."

But Moore proved to be a poor actor.

"Sherrone came in with the most somber face I've ever seen," Dudek told me. "And he's the guy who lights up the office, so we knew there was something wrong."

Moore whispered the bad news to Harbaugh and Dudek. While the others talked with recruits, they huddled, trying to think of a plan—but what could they really do?

Near the end of the meal Hill finally called Moore, talking in a slow, measured manner, as he if were a hostage forced to read a script.

"Come to find out," Moore told me, "the parents wanted what we had to offer, but at the end of the day they wanted whatever Daxton wanted. They thought he wanted Michigan, but now he wants Alabama."

Later that night Moore talked to Daxton and his parents and asked point-blank: What happened? Did we mess up? They could only say Daxton had a change of heart, and his parents were very apologetic.

"Daxton, I want you to come here," Moore finally said, "but if you really feel in your heart that Alabama is the best place for you, I'll give you all our blessings. Just know that if you change your mind, we'll be here."

Moore felt his message hit home with the parents. "It showed that we really cared. Lot of times in these situations coaches go the negative route."

"Most of the time," Dudek corrected him.

"When they do," Moore added, "that actually confirms their decision to flip."

When Hill tweeted his decision it attracted plenty of attention nationwide, but the next day Hill sent Moore a text: "I don't want to talk about it right now but need to talk about something. It's on my chest, and you're the only person I can talk to about it."

The next day Moore was in the Glick Indoor Fieldhouse when Hill called, as promised, and got right to it.

"Coach, I made a mistake. I apologize. I'm so sorry. I do not want to decommit. This is my home. I don't know what I was thinking. I want to come to Michigan."

Moore, an even-keeled man, was on the verge of tears. He asked Hill, "Can I tell Coach Harbaugh, and everybody else?"

When Hill said sure, Moore sprinted upstairs to share the good news. But how should Hill handle the switch back? If he announced it, he would generate even more attention—the last thing he wanted. Michigan's staff and the Hills decided to "let sleeping dogs lie," Dudek recalled. "We've already taken the knock. No reason to put the wolves on Daxton and make it worse."

They kept Hill's flip-back a secret, leaving him to announce his final decision on signing day. In the meantime someone at Michigan talked to Hill every day, and Harbaugh and Chris Partridge flew to his home the day before signing day and stayed as long as they could. They were taking nothing for granted.

When Hill faxed his paperwork in, Moore, Harbaugh, and Dudek were as excited as they were relieved. Their top recruit had been secured. The future was a little brighter.

Chapter 40
What Really Matters

Dearborn, Michigan, December 20, 2018

On Thursday, December 20, a few weeks after the Ohio State game, Harbaugh gave a speech at the Michigan chapter of the National Football Foundation's banquet for the All-State team in Dearborn, home of the Ford Motor Company.

Although the bowl games were already under way, and the Peach Bowl was just nine days off, Harbaugh never mentioned the Wolverines in his 30-minute speech. He also didn't mention his own career, which is hard to avoid with his résumé. His entire speech focused on the high school players being honored that night, and the inherent value of the sport they had gathered to celebrate. None of that had been affected by anything that had happened during Michigan's season, good or bad.

Harbaugh's message was the opposite: playing in the Big Ten or the NFL does not enhance the value of the game one iota. In fact, he argued, the heart and soul of the game was best expressed by the high school players in front of him.

"Thanks for having me," he said, exuding an ease he rarely emitted in press conferences. "I don't get invited to be a guest speaker very often, because I'm not a real good talker. But I've written a few things down, and mainly tonight it's about the award winners: you guys.

"I was never an All-Stater. Always wanted to be an All-State football player, an All-State basketball player. Wasn't good enough to be an All-State baseball player. So that's a signature moment, to be an All-State player. I know you're going to put that on your wall. Your parents are going to bore the heck out of your neighbors telling them you're an All-Stater and how well you're doing in school."

Harbaugh then asked for all those who had played football at any level to stand up.

"Amazing. Amazing. This is fantastic. The greatest game ever invented, I think, because there's *structure*. There's *discipline*. You don't play football without developing your toughness and your courage. So many great lessons are learned through the game of football.

"I want to tell you the greatest lessons I learned through football. The most significant moment of my life happened in 1973, my first year in tackle football. My dad's coaching for Michigan, and I'm playing for the Ann Arbor Junior Packers."

The first two days they practiced without equipment, he said, but before the third day they were issued their uniforms and equipment. Harbaugh took his home and laid it out on his floor like a stickman—a routine he kept up for the rest of his football playing days, in front of his locker. Then he put it all on, strapped the chinstrap just so, looked in the mirror, and said, "Jim Harbaugh. *Football player.*"

The crowd laughed.

The next day at practice they ran the Oklahoma Drill, with one runner dashing through a narrow chute, and a tackler trying to stop him. Harbaugh found himself seventh in the tackling line, counting off whom in the other line he'd be facing. When he got to seven, he saw Ralph, the biggest kid on the field.

"Oh, dear Lord," he recalled thinking. "I know I haven't been the best kid, but I haven't been *that* bad." His prayer of facing someone else when he re-counted to seven was not answered. Still Ralph.

In the fall of 1973 Harbaugh was just a few months shy of his tenth birthday and weighed about 87 pounds. "Not a frail lad," he said. But Ralph weighed about 130 pounds, with a five o'clock shadow.

"I had two eyebrows. He had one. So I decided right then and there: I'm really good at basketball. I'm one heck of a baseball player. I'm okay at hockey. But who needs this football? I'm just going to quit."

Then he remembered two weeks earlier his father had bought brother John and him cleats at Moe's Sports Shop for $14 each, on the condition that they had to play the entire season—and the threat that if he saw them walking up Anderson Street before practice was over, they'd have hell to pay. There was no getting out of this.

When Jim's turn came he stood in the chute and faced Ralph. The whistle blew.

"There was foam coming out of Ralph's mouth, and he was snorting like a bull. But I took that first step, got my second foot in the ground, and unloaded on him. Everything I had."

Harbaugh felt Ralph's knee driving up through his sternum, lifting him off the ground—but Harbaugh held on for dear life. The next thing he knew Ralph was pulling him like a plow through the ground. Harbaugh had closed his eyes, so he wasn't sure how long it took, or how Ralph went down—but he did.

"That's a tackle. *That is a tackle!*"

His eyes still closed, he scanned his body to make sure nothing was broken.

"I'm good! Then I opened my eyes, and it hit me: everything's dark. I'm blind. *I'm blind!* Am I dead? So this is where it ends. I was just staring into blackness when all of a sudden I saw a circle of light—and then I realized: I'm not blind. I'm looking out the earhole of my helmet!"

Harbaugh straightened his helmet, jumped to his feet, then ran back to the line of players who received him as a liberator. "You tackled Ralph!"

"I felt great about myself, and fell completely in love with the game of football that day, that moment—and for the rest of my life. The one thing I've learned from football is that if you just give it everything you've got you will feel good about what you've accomplished, no matter what level you rise to."

He then made the point his brother and father had before the 2018 season started.

"I've never heard any guy who played football say, 'I wish I hadn't played.' I know you've all learned lessons from football. You got instruction from it. You got discipline from it. You got the thrill of it. You got happiness from it."

Playing football was its own reward. Harbaugh then

explained the incredible odds of the game giving you anything more.

"I've got a couple numbers for you here," he said, then listed the following statistics:

There are 1,086,627 football players in America, at all levels.

310,465 of them are high school seniors.

70,147 play for an NCAA team, at any level.

20,042 are freshmen.

So only 6.5 percent of high school players will make a college team, at any level.

Of those 20,042 freshmen, 15,588, or three-quarters, make it to their senior year.

6,500 college players get scouted by the NFL.

350 college players get invited to the NFL combine.

256 players get drafted by the NFL each year.

300 rookies make a team each year, including practice squads.

So the percentage of the 20,042 college freshmen who make it to the NFL is 1.6 percent.

Of those, only half will play long enough to get a second contract.

In 2018, the NFL's minimum salary is $480,000. After income tax, that's $288,000.

So, Harbaugh said, if you're lucky enough to be among the 6.5 percernt of high school players to play college football, and then lucky enough to be among the 1.5 percent of college freshman players to make it to the NFL, you'll be lucky to get three years out of it. At the minimum salary, you'll make $864,000—minus your agent's fee and your cars, your down payment, your mortgage—so that will not be nearly enough to live on for the rest of your life. Thus, even if you manage to get into the top 3-tenthousandths of all high school players, you won't make enough to live on for a decade.

"Which makes education the best guarantee you have for success," Harbaugh said. "There is no salary cap at Goldman Sachs."

If you're playing football for the money, you've made a fool's bet. You play for the experience, and the relationships.

But to maximize that experience, Harbaugh had some advice. Listen to your coaches. Respect your teammates. Do a little more than everyone else—on the field, in the weight room, and in the classroom. A little more goes a long way.

For the parents, he had a list of ten commandments that were just as simple, but probably followed less often, including:

Be positive, and be realistic.

"The good Lord gave us all certain abilities. Accept your son as he is. Know your son's limitations and encourage him to make the best contribution that he can.

"Insist that your son study and earn good grades. If you put academics first, your son will be more successful.

"Sever the umbilical cord. It's a tough world out there. Let him begin preparing for it. Let the coaches push your son. Let the coaches make him tougher mentally by challenging him."

And finally, "You had a chance to be young. Let your son do his thing. Don't force football or any sport down his throat."

In that speech was everything Harbaugh was trying to do with the Michigan football program: not create NFL players, though Michigan did that as well as anyone, but create a "factory of good men," as Jon Jansen said, adults who are hardworking, honest, tough, team players, with the education to make a difference in the world.

Harbaugh was paraphrasing what Jerry Hanlon had told him back in 1986: we won't know what kind of team you have until you come back twenty years from now.

In Harbaugh's mind even the historic blowout by

the Buckeyes, hard as it was to swallow, hadn't diminished the value of the sport in the slightest. Football's
ultimate benefit wasn't winning a Big Ten title. It was
tackling Ralph.

"Been a pleasure being here," Harbaugh said, "and
thank you very much for having me."

Chapter 41
Consolations

January 2019

The Peach Bowl might have been a consolation prize, but it still provided the seventh-ranked Wolverines a chance against the 10th-ranked Florida Gators to end the season on a positive note.

On Michigan's first play, Shea Patterson ran for 21 yards to Florida's 47-yard line. Two plays later freshman Christian Turner, running in place of Karan Higdon, ran to the right side, got to the edge, and bolted down the sideline for a touchdown. His teammates jumped off the bench and onto the field to cheer him down the sidelines. The Wolverines had woken up.

But a review revealed Turner had grazed the out-of-bounds line just eight yards into his 46-yard dash, putting the ball at the Florida 38-yard line, with one yard to go for the first down. When Ben Mason's two plunges failed to get that yard, Michigan gave the ball back to Florida with no points to show for it.

The rest of the half the two teams exchanged the lead before going to the locker room with Michigan trailing just 13–10. But, like the Ohio State game, midway through the third quarter, a costly Michigan turnover—this time an interception at the Florida goal line—opened the gates for the Gators.

They proceeded to score 28 points that half, taking advantage of Michigan's missing defenders, while holding Michigan to a mere five points. That left the Wolverines to ponder another embarrassing loss, 41–15, and a #14 ranking, the same place they started the season. Was nothing gained?

Before the national title game on January 7, 2019, between Clemson and Alabama, three Alabama players were sent home for violating team rules, while three Clemson football players tested positive for a banned performance-enhancing drug called Ostarine, which functions like an anabolic steroid.

When someone asked Clemson head coach Dabo Swinney if it was possible the players ingested Ostarine in a Clemson-issued supplement or were exposed to it in some other way, Swinney replied, "Oh yeah, I mean, there's a chance that it could come from anything. They're going to test everything and look at everything. And that's the problem. As you really look at this stuff, it could be a contaminant that came from anything, something that was cleared and not a problem, and all of a sudden, it becomes something."

It was not clear who, if anyone, believed a word Swinney said—including Swinney. Despite Swinney's promise, Clemson's athletic director later announced the school would not be testing any Clemson players for anything. But the exchange gave us at least a partial answer to the question posed earlier: Who is taking performance-enhancing drugs now?

The NCAA reported 1,110 athletes are tested per year at NCAA championships, and "fewer than 10-percent on average test positive for the NCAA's PED category." Of course, that is a potentially whopping number, especially when the athletes know in advance they could be tested at the championships.

But no one seemed to care. The trophy was Clemson's.

By late January Michigan's players had gained a little perspective on their season, and could consider the good with the bad. It didn't hurt that the All–Big Ten teams brought plenty of good news for the Wolverines.

On defense, the news couldn't have been much better. All eleven Michigan defensive starters were named to one of the All–Big Ten teams, which include first, second, and third teams, plus honorable mention, with one set voted on by the media, and another by the coaches. Devin Bush Jr. was the break-out star, winning both linebacker of the year and Big Ten defensive player of the year, and later, All-American. He was joined on the coaches' first team by Chase Winovich, Rashan Gary, Lavert Hill, and David Long.

If you wanted to make a case for Don Brown's coaching methods, you could stop right there. Even with two bad losses Brown's defense still ranked first in the nation.

The All–Big Ten offense held more surprises, and more promise. Here again, all eleven Michigan starters made one team or another—a dramatic improvement over the previous year, when only three Michigan offensive players made any team.

Karan Higdon earned first team honors, as expected, but all five of Ed Warinner's linemen made one team or another, versus just one, Ben Bredeson, in 2017.

"I was in the backyard cooking chicken on the grill," Bredeson told me, "when I got the text from coach

Warinner, who sent us a graphic of the All–Big Ten team. Eleven guys! Pretty cool. I sent it to my parents. But I was not surprised. There's an expectation at a place like this where a lot of guys will stand out—and we're meeting that expectation."

That same night Jon Runyan Jr. was lounging on his couch watching TV—a rare extravagance—when he got Warinner's text. Because Runyan didn't know the Big Ten was announcing awards that day, and Warinner's text appeared a bit blurry, he went online to learn he had been named to the All–Big Ten first team. Quite a leap for a guy who hadn't played left tackle since high school and was beaten repeatedly in his first start against Notre Dame.

When he forwarded the text to his parents his father replied, "Congratulations!" followed quickly by, "Repeat it next year."

"Me and my dad are not too into the individual awards," Runyan Jr. said. "We'd much rather get a win at Ohio State than first team All–Big Ten. But it's kind of insane my name and his name will be up on the same list for once. And I'm coming back next year, so I could do it twice. My dad played 14 years in the NFL, but he never did that."

There was something else Jon Jr. wanted that his dad didn't have: a degree.

"My dad left a semester early, so he didn't graduate. He only has like 12 credits left to finish, and it didn't really matter with what he's done. But I know it's something he wishes he'd finished, a point of pride. So he told me when he dropped me off here: 'You're going to get your degree.'"

As of this writing, Jon Runyan Jr. is within a semester of his bachelor's degree.

Assessing the entire year, the players also considered what the media almost never does: the conduct of the players in class, and on campus.

Michigan's 137 football players pursued 31 different fields of study—and only 6 in general studies, about 10 percent of the total when the *Ann Arbor News* investigation came out. 71 of them finished the 2018 fall term with GPAs higher than 3.0, with two hitting a perfect 4.0, and 64 had cumulative GPAs over 3.0. For the fall of 2018, 47 players were named to the Academic All–Big Ten team, one shy of the school record set the year before, and second only to Northwestern. The list included Devin Bush Jr., Noah Furbush, Rashan Gary, Joe Hewlett, and Jared Wangler.

Grant Newsome would have easily qualified with his 3.8 in the Ford School, but the Big Ten no longer considered him a member of the team. His teammates surely did.

And once again, in the four-year APR rankings, Michigan finished ahead of Stanford.

What people consider even less is the comportment of the players on campus, and in the community.

"We spend maybe five percent of our lives at the stadium, if that," Bredeson told me. "We don't live there. We live *here.* We go to class, and we go out when we can. But you didn't hear any negative stories—no guys screwing up, everyone's working hard, everyone's going to school, and everyone's doing the right things. We'll get a beer, but no one's being an idiot."

It all sounds simple enough, but how many other football teams could say the same—or fraternities, for that matter? Since Harbaugh had arrived in 2015 Michigan fraternities had been closed for fights, sexual assault, hazing, and in one memorable case, destroying a northern Michigan ski lodge to the tune of $430,000.

"You don't hear any of those things about the football team," Bredeson said, "because they're not happening. Everyone's got a cell phone. If we screwed up, somebody would record it, and you'd know about it that night. And if one guy screws up, the whole team gets blamed—kind of like one big offensive line. But there's nothing. I'm as proud of that as I am of anything. This is a very good bunch of dudes."

The Ohio State loss would continue to sting, they said, for the rest of their lives—especially for those who wouldn't be coming back. But Bredeson and Runyan also had enough judgment to recognize the 2018 season had been a great success.

"I thought we had a hell of a year!" Bredeson said. "It was nothing like last year. [The O-Line] played our worst game of the year against Notre Dame, then we got better, and we still had a chance at the end. We lost to two ranked teams in hostile environments, but we had a lot of big wins over good teams, we got on a roll, and we beat a ranked Michigan State team on the road. This was fun!"

"We beat three ranked teams in a row in the middle of the season," Runyan said. "A ten-win season, with our schedule, most programs would kill for that."

The 2018 Wolverines were one of only five teams to enjoy a ten-game winning streak that season, along with Clemson, Alabama, Notre Dame, and the University of Central Florida. The program was far beyond where it stood four years earlier, when Harbaugh took over, and significantly better than it was just one year earlier, when pundits said the Harbaugh experiment was failing.

Michigan would lose some key players the next season, mainly on defense, but Levert Hill decided to stay, and every offseason Don Brown seemed to reload, not rebuild, with the likes of five-star Daxton Hill. On offense eight starters would be returning, including Patterson—with Dylan McCaffrey and Joe Milton on his heels—the receiving corps, and four of the five offensive linemen.

"The O-Line got up to about an 8.5 out of 10 this year," Warinner told me. "But we have another click left—I'm sure of it—and more talent coming in."

That last click might be what allows the O-line to get that final first down to ice a game, when your opponents know you're running, and you get ten yards anyway.

In the off-season, Harbaugh replaced offensive coordinator Pep Hamilton—who would soon be coaching the XFL's Washington, DC, franchise—with Josh Gattis, a thirty-four-year-old rising star, fresh from a stint as Alabama's co-offensive coordinator. Harbaugh promised to "hand the keys" of the offense to Gattis, who runs the kind of no-huddle, up-tempo offense Ohio State used against Michigan. For the second year in a row, Harbaugh showed he was willing to make dramatic changes if they increased his team's chance of success.

For all these reasons Michigan was favored in every game going into the 2019 season, and ESPN was picking the Wolverines to make the playoffs.

Wolverines take losing hard and losing to Ohio State the hardest. But after a few days of watching *Tom and Jerry* cartoons in the Commons, they could recognize Harbaugh had the team going in the right direction.

And if not Harbaugh, who?

When the NFL regular season ended it could only mean one thing in Ann Arbor: time for rumors of Harbaugh going to the NFL—an inescapable condition of the Harbaugh era, one that opposing coaches used shamelessly to persuade Michigan's recruits the head coach would be gone before they got there. 'Tis the season—and likely would be every year Harbaugh coached at Michigan, any NFL team needed a coach, and any reckless reporter wanted a few more Twitter followers.

"I don't know Jim as well as others," Dierdorf told me, "but I'm a very vocal defender. When he says he wants to stay here, I'm one of those guys who actually believes him. For one thing, I just can't see him pulling a bait-and-switch on his recruits.

"Another thing the experts don't take into account is that he has his life pretty much in order here. There's a lot of intangible stuff that he can't get anywhere else. Every week he does a podcast with his dad, and he loves that." One reason: Harbaugh wants his children to have a record of his relationship with his father.

"Don't take for granted that every morning he drops off his daughter at the same school he attended, then he goes to an office building with a statue of his old coach outside. You can't get that in the NFL, either. There might be a few NFL jobs that you could argue are as good as this—but only a few."

This brought Dierdorf to a larger point.

"Everyone thinks college football is here," he put his right hand out, "and the NFL is here," putting his left hand higher. "Well, I've seen plenty of both, and I'm here to tell you, it just isn't so.

"You look round—and I have, and Jim has—and you see it just doesn't get much better than this."

Epilogue
Was It Worth It?

Winter 2019

On Friday, March 15, 2019, Michigan hosted three dozen NFL scouts, general managers, and staffers to watch Michigan's 16 NFL prospects perform a series of drills on Pro Day.

Two weeks earlier at the NFL Combine in Indianapolis, Rashan Gary had put on a show, demonstrating a combination of power, speed, and agility that earned him "freak" status, with some experts saying he could be drafted as high as second. On Pro Day he showed the Combine had been no fluke.

Minutes after his last test that day he told me, "I'm

in a good place," and couldn't repress a slight grin at the understatement. "It's all good."

When I asked if he had any regrets, he paused.

"My only regret was that I couldn't win a Big Ten championship, and a NCAA championship. But I think these guys will," he said, pointing his thumb toward the hallway where the current players walked by.

What was harder, football or school?

"School. School. School. Man, when I write a text, I got to read it four times before I send it to make sure I got it right. Multiply that times a term paper."

But when I asked him what he was most proud of, that answer came just as easily.

"I was All–Big Ten Academic two years in a row. That's a testament to a lot of hard work to battle through dyslexia. The people here push excellence— they weren't interested in any excuses—and excellence is what's expected of you."

When Gary finished the winter term a few weeks after he was drafted, he was close enough to finish his degree in the offseason.

After unconfirmed stories swirled about his right shoulder needing surgery and his score on the Wonderlic, the NFL's IQ test, rumored to be 9 out of 25 (with no consideration for Gary's dyslexia, apparently, even if true) Gary's stock seemed to be tumbling. But on Thursday, April 26, the Green Bay Packers used their first pick to select him 12th overall. The celebration in his hotel room, surrounded by family and friends, was cathartic. His long journey to security seemed to be complete.

In January 2019, I asked Karan Higdon to recall his best and worst days as a Michigan football player.

"That's easy," he said. "My best day was waking up after I made my decision to come back for this season and knowing I was going to work with the best guys I've ever met."

Higdon had been named a captain, gained 1,178 yards, and made first team All–Big Ten—up from third team as a junior—while earning his bachelor's degree and leading his team to a ten-game winning streak. His old coach was right: if you did it once, you can do it again—and do it better.

"My worst day? The day I made my decision not to play in the bowl game. It was one of the toughest decisions I ever had to make in my life," Higdon told me. "If not *the* toughest.

"But ultimately, a Peach Bowl, a Rose Bowl, a Big Ten championship game, and a playoff game—those are all valued differently. The NCAA values them differently, too—and that's how fans look at it. So, are you willing to risk your career for a game that not even the NCAA values? Or would you rather risk it for something that everyone values more? If you got hurt in the Peach Bowl, that's not the same as getting hurt in the playoffs, or a Big Ten title game."

Higdon knew he had his critics, and wanted to address them.

"Instead of people focusing on athletes skipping bowl games, what about the athletes who skip the whole season by leaving early—they're missing *all* the games. Do they say they abandoned their teammates? What about the guys who take a game or two off in the middle? Aren't all games important?

"Maybe people should worry about guys who leave without getting their degrees, not guys who leave without getting a bowl ring. I came back and got my degree, but you never hear about that, do you? They lose sight of what's truly best for the player."

That was Higdon's job, and his decision, but no one could question that he was mature enough to make it.

To the surprise of Higdon himself, he went undrafted, but was quickly picked up as a free agent by the Houston Texans who needed a tailback. Once again, Higdon would have to make it the hard way, and prove his doubters wrong.

Chase Winovich was approaching the NFL draft as an underdog, but after running an eye-opening 4.59 40-yard dash at the Combine and finishing in the top four at his position in three other key measures, his stock had risen, thought to be on the cusp of the first round.

"Everyone's underestimated me my whole life," he said. "End of the day, I'm showing up. I'm going to be in shape, ready to go, and give it everything."

When he looked back at switching from linebacker to tight end to defensive end, and all the workouts and practices and classes, then coming back for a fifth year for more of everything, was it all worth it?

He thought for a moment, then said, "Yes. Entirely."

Then why the pause?

"Because I'm thinking of a quote from Teddy Roosevelt, 'The Man in the Arena,' and it's great."

He recited a few lines. "It's not the critic who counts; not the man who points out where the strong man stumbles . . . The credit belongs to the man who is actually in the arena, whose face is marred by dust and sweat and blood . . . If he fails, he fails while daring greatly."

I added the rest: "So that his place will never be with

those cold and timid souls who know neither victory or defeat."

"It's so true," Winovich said. "Maybe it's a loser's quote, like some people were tweeting at me when I posted it after the Ohio State game. Well, fuck 'em.

"At the end of the day, even if the season wasn't perfect, we invested in this. We didn't just show up on game day. We battled the last four or five years, every day, to get there. In my opinion, the three losses don't discredit the effort going in. Good or bad, it's ours forever."

On the second day of the draft, the six-time Super Bowl champion New England Patriots used their third pick to select Winovich. His disappointment at not being picked higher was quickly overshadowed by his excitement over who picked him.

"The Patriots are a great organization, and really know how to get the most out of their players. Can't wait to be a part of that. No regrets at all."

After Jared Wangler and Joe Hewlett returned from the Peach Bowl, they started their last semester. Brian Cleary, a former backup quarterback at Michigan who rose as high as second string for the 2013 spring game ("Good dude," Wangler said) had since enrolled at the

Michigan Medical School and formed an IM basketball team, the Inspiratory Reserves, a medical pun. Because they were short on athletes, Cleary asked his old teammates to join them.

"Hew and I were free agents," Wangler cracked, "so he picked us up on waivers."

On a Monday night at Michigan's Intramural Building, built in 1923 with steel beams supporting a tall ceiling, brick walls, and hardwood floors, all four courts were filled with IM basketball players wearing maize and blue pullovers. Even with three former Division I football players on the Inspiratory Reserves, they weren't very good, trailing a not terribly athletic fraternity by 21 points with 2:03 remaining.

This mattered, because when a team trailed by 20 or more with 2:00 or less left, the mercy rule kicked in, and the game would end. With only three seconds to spare Wangler made a steal and threw a pass to a teammate, who made a layup to cut the lead to 19 points, with exactly 2:00 left. They had avoided the humiliation of being mercied.

With the loss the Inspiratory Reserves' record stood at 2-1—good enough to make the playoffs the following week. Wangler and Hewlett packed up their gym bags and walked toward the door.

In the lobby, purely by chance, they ran into Noah

Furbush, who had come down to work out among the other students on the "civilian" equipment.

"Hey, Furbs!" Wangler shouted.

Furbush turned, he smiled, man-hugged, and spent a few minutes catching up.

"You lost weight, man!" Furbush said to Wangler, lightly punching his gut.

"Dude, I'm down 21 pounds," Wangler said, "from 246 to 225. That's what happens. You lost some too!"

"Twenty pounds," Furbush said.

Even Hewlett, the leanest of them, had lost 13 pounds, from 200 to 187.

"Your joints feel better," Wangler explained, "you move around better, and you're not thinking about eating all the time, so you eat less, sometimes just two meals a day."

After five years working 40-hour weeks in the weight room, the classroom, the film and meeting rooms, the practice field, the academic center, the labs, and the stadiums of the Big Ten, they were no longer student-athletes, just students.

The time dividend was dizzying. They barely knew what to do with the free hours they suddenly had—but they all spent some time contemplating what they'd just done.

"Looking back now," Wangler said, "I appreciate

every second of it. I know that I'll be more prepared than almost anyone when I begin my career as a working man."

Wangler had also gained some perspective on the season.

"Look, the Ohio State game was very disappointing, especially for the seniors. But after you get through a couple weeks of getting upset and mourning over it, you realize we did something very special. We were 8-1 in the Big Ten. We had two losses, both to top-six teams on the road. We blew out some very good teams and beat some very good teams on the road. We're proud of where this season went.

"We left the program a lot better than we found it."

The program could say the same about them.

When I asked Deb Bredeson, Ben's mom, if all the work and sacrifices were worth it, she laughed.

"I ask him that all the time! 'Are you absolutely sure this is worth it?' You've got to know in your heart the sacrifices you're making are worth it. He certainly thinks so.

"As a mom, do you worry? Of course. But the experiences! He's been to Europe twice. He's playing top-notch football for a first-class coaching staff, and he's earning a good degree from a great school. He's learning to lead and handle pressure at a level most 50-year-olds never see—even when he loses. Where else can you get all that?"

On a Sunday in mid-February Harbaugh called a team meeting—rare, for that time of year. When Bredeson first saw the text even he was annoyed to see one of their few off-days interrupted by football. But when they settled in the team room they soon discovered the subject was not workouts, spring ball, or schoolwork, but their third overseas trip: South Africa.

As soon as Bredeson walked out of the meeting he called his mom. "He talked and talked, and I couldn't get him off the phone!" Deb said. "As a captain, he gets to work with operations to plan the activities. So he got to go to Paris, Rome, and now South Africa, three places most Americans will never see, staying at the finest hotels, eating at the finest restaurants, going to the Vatican and seeing Normandy.

"That's their mental health trip. That's the reward they get for all the work they do. People can bash the trips, they can bash the coaches, they can bash the players, but they don't realize what those kids go through every day. And the bonds they have will last forever. Like Ben said, 'These will be the guys who stand up in my wedding, my best friends for life.'"

Harbaugh noticed Bredeson took his duties as lone

returning captain seriously, even planning the trip to South Africa.

"It's a long trip, 20 hours, not as simple as getting to Europe," Harbaugh told me. "So we said, 'If you don't want to go, great, you don't have to go. Then we don't have a guy on the trip whining and ruining it for everyone else. And it's $8–10,000 a player, so we'll save some money.'

"But Ben got all the guys together and said, 'We're all going.' And they are. And that was that.

"I thought that was very interesting. Interesting—but not surprising."

I caught up with Devin Bush Jr. when he came back to town for Pro Day. He had his picture taken that morning in the infamous scratchy wool "M" sweater, for his All-American photo, which would be on the wall with 130 others that fall. The unwritten code, going back more than a century, is that unless you're Desmond Howard or Denard Robinson, you don't smile for this photo—but Bush couldn't help it.

"I smiled a bunch. I know you're not supposed to, but I had to. It's a very, very accomplished feeling. I did it."

Like Gary, Bush had raised a lot of eyebrows at the Combine, performing so well that many scouts pushed him as high as 15. Pretty good for a guy everyone said was too short at 5-10 to play linebacker in the NFL.

When I asked him the low point of his time at Michigan, he said, "Ohio State, this year. Definitely the worst. No contest."

And the best?

"The locker room, and the relationships," he said, in a bit of a surprise for someone who had achieved so much. "I loved coming here every day."

When I pointed out that, of all the schools he had considered, he had picked the one with the worst weather, the hardest academics, and the least money—zero—he laughed.

"When everyone goes left," he said, "I always go right."

As he had promised his father, driving in the car one day, he had been named to the Big Ten–All Academic two years in a row.

Which was harder, school or football?

"To be honest, both had their moments, but both were kind of easy, the way I prepared for them. School threw me off one time, this last fall, because I was so focused on winning, I just fell behind in my classes. You can't do that here. But I caught up after Ohio State."

Like Gary, Bush took a full slate of classes winter term and plans to finish his degree in the offseason.

"If I can do this, I can do anything," he said. "Consider the weight of a degree from the University of Michigan with my name on it. You can do a lot with that, after football's over."

I mentioned former Michigan defensive lineman Mike Martin, who got his degree at Michigan, played four years in the NFL, and earned his MBA while still playing in the league. Bush nodded, unsurprised.

"My point," he said.

At the draft the Pittsburgh Steelers wanted Bush so badly they traded their 20th pick for the 10th pick to get him—16 spots before Atlanta had picked his dad with the 26th selection back in 1993.

Junior had finally surpassed Senior.

A couple of months after the season it was clear Grant Newsome had made a surprisingly smooth transition from a sophomore starting offensive lineman to a coach, analyst, and graduate student. While the NFL, which once seemed so close, was now forever out of reach, the possibilities—in academia, politics, business, or even coaching—seemed boundless.

"Everything about Grant is just A-plus-plus," Harbaugh told me. "Nothing I love more than to sit down with him and savor my intellectual disadvantage!"

Harbaugh was already fielding calls on Newsome's

behalf from career recruiters, including someone at Goldman Sachs who wanted to talk with Newsome after seeing him on TV. Newsome had to postpone one of our conversations to prepare for that interview. He got the offer—then turned it down.

"I believe President Obama's office is talking to him about an internship, too," Harbaugh said, "and they'd be wise to give it to him. I don't know how you could do any better."

Meeting with Newsome in early 2019, in the middle of his two-year master's program, I asked him: Was it all worth it? Would you do it all again?

"I get that question a lot," Grant Newsome told me. "If I knew then what I knew now . . . I'd wear knee braces against Wisconsin!

"Michigan football has given me so much more than I can ever give back—and not just the games and accolades. The support, the teaching, the experience. The alumni network. And especially the guys you get to know, on a level I don't think other students could even understand.

"So if you ask me, would I do it all again—*all* of it? My answer is simple: Absolutely. In a heartbeat. Sign me up. I don't regret a second."

What was particularly interesting about Newsome's answer is how he defined the question. In another program, the "it" is simple: football. If that's how you define "it," the answers are just as simple: No, sacrificing this much for football is not worth it if you blow out your knee and end your career, or simply lose to Ohio State. But if you define "it" more broadly, the answer changes, too.

It was all worth it for Newsome because he sought more than football—just like his mother had advised him.

After the Peach Bowl the Wolverines scattered across the country for a few days. Some went down to Florida, some back to their homes, and a few to their workout camps to get ready for the NFL Combine.

Noah Furbush spent some time in Fort Lauderdale with his family, then headed to Pensacola to undergo three days of testing in the hopes of achieving his next big dream: Marine pilot.

"The first day, for all the tests, you get there at 4 a.m., and you don't eat until 7 p.m.," he told me. "If I hadn't played football, that would've been a grind."

They would also check his blood pressure and administer an EKG, a blood test, an eye, ear, and throat exam, X-rays, a musculoskeletal exam, and "pretty much any test you can imagine, they do."

The purpose was simple: they wanted to find a handful of perfect humans before they spent more than $10 million on each one to become a Marine pilot.

Furbush knew the three-day screening would be rigorous, but if there was one candidate who wasn't concerned about being in shape, it was probably him. That's not to say he was relaxed.

"I'd been thinking about this for years. I was sick a week before the Peach Bowl with a sinus infection and respiratory problems. I was just trying to get better before the exam, because it's not something you can push back."

He was also worried about his eyesight since he was the only member of his family who didn't wear glasses.

"My eyes were not as good as they wanted, at 20-25, but within the range they accept, which is 20-35. So I was happy to squeak by."

Having passed the gauntlet of tests on Day One, on Day Two he underwent a rigorous dental exam and a handful of measurements, including height, reach, and other specifications, designed to determine if he could function effectively in a small cockpit. Unlike his NFL-bound teammates, at 6-4 Furbush was worried he was too tall, but he received some good advice when the gunnery sergeant pulled him aside and said, "Furbush, listen: there's a difference between sitting *up*, and sitting up," he said, falling into a deep slouch. With that tip, Furbush passed the height exam, too.

After surviving the first two days, Furbush and 12 other candidates—including a woman who was in danger of being too short, and a former track star at the Citadel whose heartbeat barely registered on their machines— went to the Naval Aerospace Medical Institution to review their medical history. For Furbush, that included X-rays on his right knee, his left shoulder, and his left wrist, which he had injured playing football and basketball in high school.

He was most concerned about his shoulder, which he'd injured in a high school football game. He'd already had his torn labrum surgically repaired his first year at Michigan. When that checked out Furbush felt he had passed the worst, but they wanted a better picture of his wrist with a CT scan. Because it would take a few days to analyze the results, Furbush returned to Ann Arbor to finish his master's degree and wait for the results of his last test.

"I was worried. Very worried."

He kept playing over in his head the original injury, which occurred in basketball practice his junior year of high school when he jumped, got his foot tangled up in someone's jersey, and extended his wrist to cushion his fall to the floor. Thinking he had just sprained it, he ignored it for six months. But during summer football camp the pain wouldn't go away, so he got it checked out. When a doctor told him he had broken it and offered to give him surgery immediately or after his senior year of football, Furbush predictably picked the latter, playing the entire season with a big fiberglass club on his hand. When the season ended the doctor screwed the two pieces of bone together. The next year Michigan team doctor Bruce Miller fixed Furbush's left labrum, which cost Furbush his freshman season.

Could that injury, now a few years old, kill his dream?

A week after Furbush returned to Ann Arbor he had just sat down for the first day of his Space Systems Engineering class, investigating high-altitude balloons, when his cell phone buzzed. He recognized the area code: Pensacola.

"Fuck yeah I took the call."

He walked to an empty stairwell. The military doctor on the phone told him the two pieces of his wrist bone had never healed properly, creating a fibrous union, not rigid bone.

"Unfortunately," she said, "that is disqualifying."

"She told me she had consulted with her superiors and other people in her department, and they all agreed. You could tell she definitely did not want to tell me the news."

She said he could get it operated on again, hoping for a better outcome, but she wasn't recommending it.

Sitting on the cold, concrete stairs, getting heartbreaking news just six weeks after losing the most important game of his career, "I'm getting emotional. Very. Crying? Absolutely. Talk about a rough fucking month."

Still, she had given him enough hope to follow up with Dr. Miller and Dave Granito, who put him in touch with another specialist, but the odds still weren't very good for a better outcome. He then talked with his recruiter, "a guy who had gone to bat for me a million times."

He told Furbush that they're looking for "the perfect person. They want Superman, who's got good grades, doesn't smoke weed, has a history of playing sports and being a leader but somehow never got hurt. That guy doesn't exist."

Furbush shakes his head at the military's decision.

"For five years I've been smashing the biggest, toughest people in the world with my wrist, and for some reason she thinks I can't move the joystick in a cockpit around. Very frustrating.

"It's been a real shit sandwich of a winter. When I

got that news, that was really tough for me. For the past five years I've busted my balls to be a leader on the football team, to do the best I can, to be an aerospace engineer, so when I get done with this, I could be a pilot in the military and maybe one day an astronaut. But with a ten-minute phone call—snap—it's gone. And now I'll probably never do that."

Instead of giving up, Furbush decided, "I at least want to serve in the military and get as close as I can to being a pilot than miss out entirely on it. If I had a billion dollars, I would do what Elon Musk is doing, and build my own rocket to live my dream.

"I will probably join the Marines in a ground Military Occupational Specialty (MOS), which is another term for 'job.' I'm interested in becoming an intelligence officer, but which MOS I get won't be decided until after I complete Basic School. I couldn't give a shit how much money I make."

When I asked him for his high and low points, he said, "Ohhh, boy. It's hard to put my finger on a high point, because I've got a lot of good memories. The low point—that's easy. The Ohio State game this year. Five years straight, never beat 'em, and never will. That will always hurt."

After so much sacrifice led to two crushing disappointments in two months, was it worth it?

"That's a billion-dollar question right there," he said, mulling it over.

"I played football in high school, and I was good at it, because it gave me an outlet for my aggression. I kept playing in college, not because I wanted to get to the NFL, but because I wanted to play in the Game—and I wanted to beat the Buckeyes.

"That game was why I came back. It was my Super Bowl. I was just so sick to my stomach after that game. Really, a feeling I still haven't shaken. Took the wind out of my sails. To end my time here and not beat Ohio State, that's really frustrating.

"So why play those five years, if we never beat Ohio State? Because of all the people you're going to meet, and all the experiences you're going to have. Maybe in the military you can get the kind of bonds we have here, but I don't know if they could be any closer.

"I've done some shit that no one else could do at this age. I've worked with NASA on their human mission to Mars. I've had the Palace of Versailles to myself and saw a marriage proposal in the Hall of Mirrors. And I've played in the Game.

"The best part of it all is that I got to take my family along the road with me. They never missed a game in five years. I think that's pretty special.

"And it gave me an important lesson I'll take with me my entire life: it's not always enough to do your very best."

This is exactly what you'd expect to hear from a man who does not traffic in moral victories. For Furbush, the Ohio State game and the Marine test were heartbreaking losses, plain and simple, with no silver linings.

But he has gained something in the bargain: if he's not a Michigan Man, who is? If that has value, then Furbush has earned all benefits in full.

Furbush might not realize it yet but battling for five years to beat the Buckeyes and become a Marine pilot, then losing out on both, has all but inoculated him against failure. If five losses to Ohio State and rejection by the Marine pilot program couldn't crush him, then what could?

You'd be a fool to bet against Noah Furbush, but only if you knew his story. Not the one we watched unfold in the stadium and on TV, but the one he's lived everywhere else, during the other 8,700 hours.

That is ultimately the secret to all the players who put in 60-plus-hour weeks lifting weights, going to class, meeting, practicing, watching film, and studying, even if the NCAA only counts a fraction of those hours. They know their stories are too complicated to squeeze into a sound bite, a program bio, or a player profile.

Plenty of Michigan fans can tell you how John Wangler came back from his knee injury to lead the Wolverines to Schembechler's first Rose Bowl victory. But only he and Rich Hewlett can describe their intense battle for quarterback, and how it made them not enemies but best friends.

Our memories of one game, or one season, are harmless, so long as we celebrate the truly admirable and not just that day's winners—who too often are the least admirable people in the sport. The coaches who pay players, ignore bogus classes, and provide performance enhancing drugs are too often the ones who win the banners.

Does anyone care?

To be fair, it wasn't much different in Schembechler's day. He knew Barry Switzer was paying players when Oklahoma beat Michigan 14–6 in the 1976 Orange Bowl to win the national title. He knew Michigan State's players were taking steroids when he started the FBI investigation into banned substances. He knew others were doing that and more when he coached, and he also knew the NCAA wasn't going to do anything about any of it. Yet, as competitive as Schembechler surely was, he didn't stoop to his opponents' level just to beat them.

So how do you beat the cheaters? That hard question turns out to have an easy answer: you don't cheat. You start building from there until you defeat them on the field, off the field, and everywhere else. Few experiences in life are sweeter than beating the cheaters without cheating, but the one certain way to lose is by cheating yourself.

A few days after Schembechler died on Friday, November 17, 2006, they held a service for him at Michigan Stadium on a frigid Tuesday afternoon—a workday. Some 20,000 people showed up, and although the speeches lasted two hours in the bitter cold, they stayed. They weren't sitting there to honor Schembechler's national titles. He never won any. They were honoring his values, which had outlived his victories.

At Michigan, that's how you get a building named after you, with a statue in front.

In a sport awash in corruption it's notable that the Harbaughs see football as a means to build character. They are working to save the game *because* of the values it teaches.

They're not blind to the cheating going on across the country. They know who's doing what, and how. But that's why they're determined to do it the right way and spread the gospel. They remain convinced that once you boil away all the dirt that too often covers the game, football's values are as sterling as ever.

If the rest of the nation hasn't caught on, Jim Harbaugh's players have.

Despite the sacrifices the coaches, staffers, players, and parents make; despite the grief they get when they lose, and the accolades the cheaters get when they win; despite all that, doing it the right way still matters to them.

For all their accomplishments, that was the most important.

Acknowledgments

Few people are busier than the players, coaches, and staff members of a major college football program during their long season. But whenever I asked for five minutes here or even a couple hours there, just about everyone at Michigan said yes, every time.

That began with Jim Harbaugh himself, who permitted his players and staff to speak with me. He fit in quick conversations throughout the season and a long interview when it was over. All these favors were essential to this book.

Jim's dad, Jack Harbaugh, met with me many times from the pre-season to the post-season. He and his wife, Jackie, told me stories about their extraordinary children that no one else could.

With Jack beside him, John Harbaugh, coach of

the Baltimore Ravens, spoke with me for almost three hours, telling stories from their childhood to the Super Bowl, and beyond. Sarah Harbaugh invited me into their home, and shared stories behind the scenes that surprised even a seasoned journalist. Sarah's brother, John Feuerborn, who is also one of her husband's best friends, told of his adventures with his brother-in-law.

The Harbaugh family certainly doesn't need more publicity, and they have good reason to be wary of the media, but they told their stories from World War II to the present. While their good cheer and humor have no direct bearing on the book, it made my work much more enjoyable. I looked forward to talking with all of them.

I'm grateful to these players for giving me their time and trust: Ben Bredeson, Devin Bush Jr., Michael Cessa, Tyler Cochran, Ryan Glasgow, Joe Hewlett, Karan Higdon, Dan Jokisch Jr., Matt Mitchell, Grant Newsome, Shea Patterson, Jared Wangler, and Chase Winovich.

Many parents of players were equally generous, including Deb Bredeson, Rich Hewlett, Kim and Leon Newsome, Sean and Karen Patterson, Loretta and Jon Runyan, Sr., John Wangler, and Michael and Angela Wilson. Special thanks to Lorraine Wangler, who sacrificed her seat on the parents' bus so I could talk to her husband and other parents on the road to and from the Ohio State game.

Extended interviews with coaches provided insights no one else could have. I'm especially grateful to Don Brown, who let me watch meetings with his defensive-team staff; Chris Partridge; Ed Warinner; Mike Zordich; and Ben Herbert. Seeing how much these coaches care about their players as human beings helped sustain my faith in college football.

A small army of unseen staffers are essential to a great program's success. At Michigan, these staffers showed me how that works: analysts Brandon Blaney, Devin Bush Sr., Jordan Kovacs, and Ron Prince; videographers Phil Bromley and Kevin Undeen; the athletic department's Director of Academic Services Stephen Connelly; resident legend Jon Falk; athletic trainers David Granito and Phil Johnson; equipment manager Gary Hazelitt; football operations director Sean Magee; Jim Harbaugh's executive assistant, DeAnna McDaniel; nutritionist Abigail O'Connor; and gatekeepers Michelle Guidry-Pan, Kelly King, Dave Pishe, and Jim Plocki.

Dave Ablauf, associate athletic director for public and media relations, and his assistant, Chad Shepard, could have charged me rent for use of their office. If they hadn't provided their help and expertise with coaches, players, staffers, parents and me almost daily, this book wouldn't exist.

Athletic Director Warde Manuel and his assistant, Doug Gnodtke, were open, honest and fair throughout. Their transparency speaks well of Michigan's athletic department and the university itself.

A cadre of longtime Ann Arborites helped me understand Jim Harbaugh's early years, including Dan Chace, "Tiger" Ray Howland, Derek Lee, Ken Magee, Niel Rishoi, Al Smith, Brian Weisman, and Tappan Junior High School teacher Rob Lillie. Dr. Jeffrey Kutcher lent his expertise to the section on safety. Thanks also go to Ricardo Cannon, Karan Higdon's former coach and mentor, who provided hard-to-find information and fact-checks on short notice.

I'll remember the tailgate hospitality of Dick Caldarazzo, the Wanglers, and a host of others in the Crisler Arena parking lot, where I conducted a lot more research than I should admit. Conversations with Dan Dierdorf and Jim Brandstatter after every home game and in a long session in Atlanta provided observations that could only have come from these two. Other lettermen I relied on included John "The Flame" Arbeznik; Doug James; and especially Jon Jansen, who met with me almost every week to give his insider's take on the team and the players and his larger thoughts about what Michigan football means.

Before I started to work on this project, I had to answer a few key questions: After four books about Michigan and college football, was there anything more to say? If so, did I have the energy? I decided that if I focused not on the games but the people behind the masks and the scenes, I could write one more, and withstand one more eight-month sprint to the deadline.

The last question: Would a good publisher agree?

Here I had a lot more help.

At the creative agency William Morris Endeavor, Jay Mandel and his assistants, Lauren Shonkoff and Sian-Ashleigh Edwards, helped make a successful pitch to HarperCollins-William Morrow, where Vice President and Executive Editor Peter Hubbard directed the project with both supreme skill and understanding. He is simply the best, and proved it again on our second book together. Associate Editor Nick Amphlett wore too many hats to count; literary lawyer Victor Hendrickson; publicist Maria Silva; and Andrea Molitor, who runs Morrow's production editorial department. Molitor and her staff could have killed me for the many changes I requested, yet let me live.

For help with photos I'm grateful to the families

of Ben Bredeson, Noah Furbush, Joe Hewlett, Grant Newsome, Shea Patterson and Jared Wangler; to Roger Hart and Nicole Kinnunen at Michigan Photography; Eric Upchurch; Suzie Baker; and the renowned photographer David Turnley, whose considerable generosity was a lifesiver at the last minute.

Smart readers told me what was working and what wasn't: Thomas Lebien, who expertly read several drafts; Evan Caminker, former dean of Michigan Law; Jim Carty; Vince Duffy, news director of Michigan Radio; Bruce Madej; Dr. Steve Papadopoulos; James Tobin; and Ira Weintraub. My weekly meetings with Tobin helped keep me on-track and as sane as possible.

My wife, Christie, contributed at every stage of the project, including research, editing, photo selection, and setting up an 18-state book tour. She did all this while keeping our home and family humming, often in my absence, taking trips with three-year-old Teddy to far-off places so I could toil uninterrupted in the "writer's cave." But on most days she was home, an oasis after a long day staring at a screen.

Whenever Jack Harbaugh talks about his career as a football coach, which involved more than a dozen moves across the country, he always uses the plural "we," as in "when we took the job at Michigan." Now

I know why. It would have been impossible to do what he did without Jackie, and Jack knows that better than anyone. Now I do too: *we* finished this book.

As for you, Teddy, I have good news: Daddy's book is done. Let's go play.

HARPER (LUXE)

THE NEW LUXURY IN READING

We hope you enjoyed reading
our new, comfortable print size and found it
an experience you would like to repeat.

Well – you're in luck!

HarperLuxe offers the finest in fiction and
nonfiction books in this same larger print size and
paperback format. Light and easy to read, HarperLuxe
paperbacks are for book lovers who want to see
what they are reading without the strain.

For a full listing of titles and
new releases to come, please visit our website:

www.HarperLuxe.com

HARPER (LUXE)